Bullying

■ ■ ■

Bullying

■ ■ ■

A practical guide to coping for schools

Third Edition

Edited by

MICHELE ELLIOTT

Pearson
Education

PEARSON EDUCATION LIMITED

Head Office:
Edinburgh Gate
Harlow CM20 2JE
Tel: +44 (0)1279 623623
Fax: +44 (0)1279 431059

London Office:
128 Long Acre
London WC2E 9AN
Tel: +44 (0)20 7447 2000
Fax: +44 (0)20 7240 5771
Website: www.educationminds.com

Third edition published in Great Britain in 2002

ISBN 0 273 65923 5

First Edition 1992 © Longman Group UK Limited

Second Edition 1997 © Pearson Professional Limited

British Library Cataloguing in Publication Data
A CIP catalogue record for this book can be obtained from the British Library

10 9 8 7 6 5 4 3 2 1

Typeset by Pantek Arts Ltd, Maidstone, Kent
Printed and bound in Great Britain

The Publishers' policy is to use paper manufactured from sustainable forests.

About the editor

■ ■ ■

Michele Elliott is the Director of the children's charity Kidscape which deals with the prevention of bullying and child abuse. She is a teacher, psychologist and the author of 23 books, many of which deal with bullying. She has chaired World Health Organisation and Home Office Working Groups on the prevention of child abuse and is a Winston Churchill Fellow.

About the contributors

■ ■ ■

Valerie Besag is one of the UK's leading experts on bullying. She is an experienced teacher, having taught in primary and secondary schools. In addition, she is a chartered, consultant, educational psychologist. Val's current work encompasses training and publications for teachers and others working with young people. A recent Churchill Fellowship allowed her to seek out the best peer support work worldwide relating to bullying, gender issues, depression and suicide. Val's doctorate work was on girls' bullying.

Kevin Brown is a freelance trainer and educational consultant, providing regular consultation to most of the 32 Scottish EAs' lead officers for raising achievement and out-of-school-hours learning (OSHL). He is at the forefront of work on relationship issues in Scottish schools and has undertaken extensive work on anti-bullying and non-attendance with teachers, parents, children and multi-agency staff. He is the author of books and video packs on bullying, a book on child sexual abuse, the Scottish Executive Education Department-funded CD-ROM on *Dealing with Disruption* and its double CDi pack *Co-ordinating Staff Development*, as well as the Prince's Trust CD-ROM *Raising the Standard* on OSHL. He is Director of the Scottish Study Support Network and Scottish Development Officer for Education Extra.

Linda Frost was the head teacher of a primary school in North London, where she taught for 13 years. She has had articles published on child safety and was a member of the Home Office Working Group on The Prevention of Child Abuse.

Francis Gobey, building on 12 years' education work with young people's theatre companies such as Neti-Neti and Theatre Centre, has written books on bullying, grief, self-esteem and using drama in PSHE. He is performance arts tutor with Art Shape, Gloucestershire, and youth participation officer with Gloucester City Council, for which he is writing a schools' training pack on young people's rights. He is married, with four young children.

Carolyn Hamilton is Director of the Children's Legal Centre, a national charity which promotes the rights of children. It operates a national legal advice line, produces *Childright* and carries out research, policy and campaigning work. She is also a Senior Lecturer in the Department of Law at the University of Essex. She is the author of *Family Law amid Religion* and *Family Law in Europe* as well as numerous articles in the field of child law, family law, children's rights and evidence law. She was recently commissioned to write one of the study papers, 'Children's Rights and Humanitarian Law', for the UN Study on the Impact of Armed Conflict on Children, headed by Graca Machel.

Hereward Harrison is the Director of Policy, Research and Development at ChildLine UK. He is a trained social worker and psychotherapist with 30 years' experience in the helping professions. He has specialised in clinical work, the supervision of mental health professionals and teaching. Before joining ChildLine he was Principal Social Worker (Teaching) at Guy's Hospital, where he specialised in paediatric social work and child abuse.

Eve Halbert is a teacher, lecturer and therapist who worked in many difficult areas of Manchester for 17 years. Whilst working in a Child Guidance Centre, she initiated support groups for adults and children who had suffered from mental, physical and sexual abuse. She also trained teachers, social workers, foster carers and others who worked with children in mental health strategies and child protection issues. Her chapter is part of her work to find solutions for working with disruptive and aggressive pupils and their families. The core of the work, which evolved from going into schools and working in partnership, is making schools sanctuaries where mental health, self-esteem and positive attitudes are paramount. The strategies outlined worked especially well to change the disruptive behaviour of the one in five children estimated to be suffering from a mental illness.

Eric Jones spent eight years in motor insurance before training as a teacher at Westhill College, Birmingham University, in the 1960s. He has spent his entire career in the inner city of London at schools in Brixton, Tooting and Camberwell, only returning to Birmingham to gain an honours degree in Education in the 1970s. He was the deputy head of a London school until he took supposed early retirement. Unable to stay away from education, he is now working in a secondary school in charge of drama production. He produced and directed the first production to go into the new Globe theatre, using children from his secondary school. He has also written books for the Boys' Brigade. He can be contacted at ericjones@dramaed.freeserve.co.uk

Dr L.F. Lowenstein is Chief Examiner in Advanced Educational Psychology, College of Preceptors, London. He is also a Visiting Professor at the University of Khartoum, Sudan, and was formerly a chief educational psychologist in Hampshire. Dr Lowenstein pioneered research on bullying in the UK in the early 1970s. He is the author of numerous books and hundreds of articles, and is Director of Allington Psychological Service. He is a behavioural expert for the National Police Faculty.

Pauline Maskell is a teacher, consultant, trainer, counsellor and author. She organises peer mentoring groups and trains people to start their own peer mentoring schemes. She has carried out extensive research into the benefits of peer support in a variety of situations and educational environments. She has published training materials for peer support and health education.

Andrew Mellor is in the unusual position of being a teacher with 25 years' experience who is also a researcher and developer. In 1988–89 he conducted the first substantial research on bullying in Scotland. As the Scottish Anti-Bullying Development Officer from 1993 to 1995 he played a major role in highlighting the seriousness of bullying in schools. In April 1999 he left his post as Principal Teacher of Guidance at Dalry School in Galloway to become Manager of the Anti-Bullying Network, which is a Scottish Executive-funded initiative based at the University of Edinburgh.

Astrid Mona O'Moore is a graduate of Trinity College, Dublin. She then qualified as a Child and Educational Psychologist with the University of Nottingham. Her Ph.D., in the area of Special Needs Education, was with the University of Edinburgh's Psychology Department. She is founder and Co-ordinator of the Anti-Bullying Research and Resource Centre at Trinity College, Dublin. She is the Head of the Education Department at Trinity College Dublin.

John Pearce is a qualified doctor and has worked in the field of child and adolescent psychiatry at the Maudsley Hospital, Guy's Hospital and the University of Leicester. He is Professor Emeritus of Child and Adolescent Psychiatry at the University of Nottingham. He is working at Thorneywood Clinic and Adolescent Mental Health Services, Nottingham. His research interests include emotional disorders in children. He has written several practical guides for parents (including *Fighting, Teasing and Bullying)* and has appeared on radio and TV speaking on child care issues.

David Smith is the Principal Educational Psychologist with Durham County Council. He trained as a primary teacher and then went on to undertake an MEd in Educational Psychology, subsequently working mostly in the north of England. David's interest in bullying dates from the early 1980s when, with Peter Stephenson, he undertook a number of studies on the subject in Cleveland schools. Since then he has contributed to various seminars and undertaken in-service work for individual schools, as well as organised courses for head teachers and senior management.

Wendy Stainton Rogers graduated in psychology in 1967 and then spent three years teaching science in secondary schools. After a period working in market research and supply teaching she was appointed by the Open University as a lecturer, first in Psychology and subsequently in Health and Social Welfare. She is providing training for the Children Act 1989 and related legislation, having completed the production of a distance learning course on child abuse and neglect. She edited *Child Abuse and Neglect: Facing the Challenge* and has written and lectured extensively in the areas of child protection and children's rights.

Contents

■　■　■

Introduction

■ ■ ■

In the second edition of this book I invited readers to contact me if they had suggestions for a third edition. Contact me they did, with all kinds of ideas, suggestions and corrections. So in this third edition you will find new chapters on peer mentoring, classroom activities, school non-attendance, teachers holding the key to change, children in care and the long-term effects of bullying, as well as revised and updated chapters on practical ways for teachers and staff to deal with bullying on the coal face.

Many teachers rang and wrote to say how bullying had affected their lives and how they were determined that the children in their care would not suffer the same way they had. 'I became a teacher in spite of the bullying that I endured at school. I guess I wanted to prove to myself that they couldn't defeat me. I still despise the bullies who made my life a misery, but they've had horrible lives so what goes round comes round.' This from a 35-year-old teacher, now married with two children.

Have things changed since I first started writing about bullying in 1984? Yes, and for the better. Schools have recognised the problem of bullying much more than they did 20 years ago and the vast majority of teachers want to stamp it out. You rarely hear someone say that 'bullying is just part of growing up' or that teachers shouldn't get involved (unless you happen to have a diehard on your staff who persists in telling everyone their views on the world – I suspect these people were the classroom bullies of their day).

The law has changed so that schools must have an anti-bullying policy. There are growing pockets of good practice and more and more great schools where children and young people feel safe from bullying. The ideas in this book come from that good practice.

I expect that those who read this book are already convinced that bullying is wrong, harmful and unnecessary. Do me a favour – do us all a favour – and pass the book on, after you've read it, to those few remaining dinosaurs who think that bullying is OK.

Having been a teacher myself and having a husband who has taught for nearly 30 years, I have an idea of some of the stresses and strains teachers are under these days. I hope this book makes your lives, and those of the children you teach, that little bit easier and you have my heartfelt gratitude for the job you do.

Thanks,

Michele Elliott

PS If you have any ideas for the fourth edition, please let me know.

1

■ ■ ■

Bullies and victims

MICHELE ELLIOTT

- ► Bullying affects the lives of thousands of children and young people
- ► What is bullying? Signs and symptoms
- ► Girl vs boy type bullying
- ► Bystanders
- ► Chronic bullies and victims
- ► ZAP courses and citizenship

Nine-year-old Mark was walking home from school when a gang of bullies set upon him. His arm was broken, his money stolen and his books destroyed. His self-confidence was also destroyed. He became withdrawn, hated to go to school and eventually had counselling to help him through the trauma. He knew the boys who attacked him, but refused to tell who they were. He was frightened of what they would do if he told.

Fourteen-year-old Sarah was cornered on the playground by a gang of ten boys and girls. She was stripped to the waist and had to beg on her knees to get her clothes back. She was pushed, punched and had her hair pulled. 'Tell and you'll get worse', was the parting shot from one of the girls. Sarah didn't tell until they did it again and took photographs. When her mother confronted the school, she was told it was only 'horseplay'. Sarah, who attempted suicide after the latest incident, was transferred to another school in which she is thriving.

In a similar case, 13-year-old Theresa was held down by a gang of nine girls, physically assaulted and then stripped in front of a group of boys. Her distraught father rang the Kidscape helpline because the school advised him that he should not go to the police. He was also advised that the gang of girls would be leaving the school within weeks so the school were not taking any further action, having given the girls detention.

Twelve-year-old Simon was bullied over two years by three boys at his boarding school. He was beaten, locked out of his room, shoved outdoors in his underwear on a freezing January night and constantly subjected to taunts about his weight. Simon ran away from the school and had a nervous breakdown.

Debbie was sent to Coventry (excluded) by her former friends. Liz was the ringleader – she became jealous of how well Debbie was doing in school. Liz exerted enough power over the other girls so that they all refused to sit with Debbie, wrote nasty things on the chalk board about her, turned their backs on her if she approached them and made her life miserable. Debbie's work deteriorated, she found excuses not to go to school and became withdrawn. Whenever her mother asked what was happening, Debbie said nothing.

The extent of bullying

Isolated cases of bullying or just the tip of the iceberg? Most studies show that bullying takes place in every type of school. Teachers and staff may do their best to eradicate it, but every school has to face the problem at some time.

The first UK nationwide survey of bullying was conducted by Kidscape from 1984 to 1986 with 4,000 children aged 5 to 16. The survey revealed that 68% of the children had been bullied at least once; 38% had been bullied at least twice or had experienced a particularly bad incident; 0.5% of the students felt it had affected their lives to the point that they had tried suicide, had run away, had refused to go to school or had been chronically ill (Elliott and Kilpatrick, 2002). Subsequent studies have found very similar results. A Department of Education-funded project at Sheffield University found that 27% of the pupils who took part in the project in junior and middle schools in Sheffield were bullied – 10% indicated that they were bullied once a week (Whitney and Smith, 1993). Researchers at Exeter University questioned 5,500 children aged 13 and found that 26% of boys and 34% of girls had been afraid of bullies sometimes, often or very often (Balding, 1996).

In 2001, ChildLine, the national telephone helpline for children, received nearly 20,000 calls from children and young people who were worried about bullying (see Chapter 19). Kidscape receives calls from more than 16,000 parents each year who say their children are being bullied. Bullying affects not only the child but also the entire family.

Bullying is not only a UK problem – it happens throughout the world. Dan Olweus, the world-renowned expert, has been researching the problem of bullying in Norway since 1973. He has estimated that 1 in 7 students in Norwegian schools has been involved in bully/victim problems (Olweus, 1993). Similar findings in other European countries and in Canada and the USA indicate that if adults are willing to listen and investigate, children will tell them that bullying is one of the major problems children face during their school years.

What is it?

Bullying takes many forms. It can be physical, like a child being pushed, beaten or thumped with knuckles. It can involve a weapon and threats. One seven-year-old boy had a knife pulled on him in the playground. Bullying can also be verbal and emotional, racial or sexual. A 13-year-old girl was told she was dirty and ugly by one group of girls. She used to wash two or three times a day to try to win their approval, which was never forthcoming. An Asian boy was taunted with racist remarks and eventually played truant rather than face his tormentors. An 11-year-old girl found herself the victim of continuous sexist remarks because she was beginning to develop physically – she tried to tape her breasts so the comments would stop. A 14-year-old boy was taunted constantly by being called 'gay'.

Girls and boys

Cases assembled by Kidscape since 1984 used to indicate that boys were more likely to be physical in bullying, while girls tended to be cruel verbally. Research by Dan Olweus (Olweus, 1993) indicated that girls were more often exposed to harassment such as slandering, spreading of rumours and exclusion from the group rather than physical attacks. Olweus said it must be emphasised that these gender differences were general and that in some schools girls were also exposed to physical bullying, while some boys verbally attacked one another. Recently the calls to Kidscape have begun to show a worrying trend including cases in the UK in which girls have violently and aggressively attacked other girls, as happened to Sarah and Theresa mentioned at the beginning of this chapter. There was one widely reported death caused by young teenage girl bullies beating up a 13-year-old girl who was trying her best to stop a fight. It cost her her life. The incidents of girls being violent does seem to be increasing and is a trend that must be viewed with concern.

A prevailing attitude about bullying is that 'boys will be boys' and that being aggressive and bullying is to be expected. There have been efforts to change this attitude, but in the meantime it appears that some girls have decided to be more 'laddish' than the lads. There may be several reasons for this disturbing development:

- lack of responsible parenting;
- increase in violent female role-models in the media;
- trendy approaches to dealing with bullying which seek not to apportion blame or give consequences to bullying actions;
- girls who think being aggressive gives them status;
- girls confusing being assertive with being aggressive.

It is significant that the research at Sheffield University mentioned above suggests that girls are just as likely to use violence when bullying, but more likely to be ashamed to admit it than boys. If this attitude continues there may be hope that the increase in girl violence may slow down. However, most teachers feel that this unfortunate tendency is here to stay.

Bystander attitude

If a child is bullied, peer pressure sometimes makes it difficult for the victim to rally support from other children. As one girl told me: 'I don't like it that Gill is bullied, but I can't do anything about it or they will turn on me, too.' This 'bystander attitude' also hurts the children who feel they can't help the victim. In several schools teachers report that children who witnessed bullying were badly affected by what they saw. Some of them felt anger, rage and helplessness. Several had nightmares and were worried that they might be the next victims. Most felt guilty that they did not stop the bully, but really did not know how to help the victim.

We know from our work with schools that one of the most effective ways to cut down on bullying is to work with the bystanders and those who are on the periphery of bullying groups. The power that the bully has is because those around him or her do nothing or even encourage the bullying behaviour because it causes excitement. When we remove the bystanders and the periphery group, the bully is isolated and then may be motivated to change his or her behaviour.

Meeting with these students individually and removing them from the equation is a vital first step in stopping the bullying. It may be that they are told they cannot play with, eat with or be around the bully – this depends upon your school's way of dealing with such problems. In a sense you are bringing them back into your code of conduct and telling them that you want them to be a positive part of the group. You are offering them better choices than the one they've made. It is important then to praise them for good behaviour. Of course this takes valuable time, but it does pay dividends. Without this peer support, the bully may try to ensnare other children, so it is wise to keep an eye out. What we have found is that the bully is more willing to change his or her behaviour when the kudos and fun of bullying is curtailed because there is no audience or applause.

The telltale signs

A child may indicate by signs or behaviour that he or she is being bullied. Sometimes this is the only clue adults have about what is happening because of the code of silence so often maintained about bullying.

Children or young people may:

- be frightened of walking to or from school;
- be unwilling to go to school and make continual excuses to avoid going;
- beg to be driven to school;
- change their route to school every day;
- begin doing poorly in their schoolwork;
- regularly have clothes or books or schoolwork torn or destroyed;
- come home starving (because dinner money was taken);

- become withdrawn;
- start stammering;
- start hitting other children (as a reaction to being bullied by those children or others);
- stop eating or become obsessively clean (as a reaction to being called 'fatty' or 'dirty');
- develop stomach and headaches due to stress;
- attempt suicide;
- cry themselves to sleep;
- begin wetting the bed;
- have nightmares and call out things like 'leave me alone';
- have unexplained bruises, scratches, cuts;
- have their possessions go 'missing';
- ask for money or begin stealing money (to pay the bully);
- continually 'lose' their pocket money;
- refuse to say what's wrong;
- give improbable excuses to explain any of the above.

If a child is displaying some of these symptoms, bullying is a likely cause, though obviously not the only possibility.

Chronic bullies

In the Kidscape studies we found many reasons why children bully and that much of the bullying behaviour was occasional, not chronic. Some children were spoilt brats – over-indulged by doting parents who felt their child could do no wrong. This kind of bully was completely selfish and hit out if anyone got in his way. Other children who were bullying were victims of some sort of abuse or neglect. They had been made to feel inadequate, stupid and humiliated. Some children who were bullies also seemed to be popular with other children. Upon closer examination it was evident that they were 'popular' because children hung around them to avoid becoming a victim themselves or because they thought the bully had status. Whatever the various reasons for bullying behaviour, only a small number of children become chronic bullies and these are the ones who cause the most problems.

What also emerged from our work is that chronic bullies are unlikely to respond to methods such as the no-blame approach which attempts to instil empathy for victims in the bully. Chronic bullies are quite skilful at manipulation and may appear to have sympathy for the victim because that is what they know the teacher wants to hear. The bully uses his manipulation skills to pull the wool over the adult's eyes and then ensures that the victim never tells again. The method seems to work because the bullying is driven underground.

What teachers say does work is isolating the power of the bully and then helping him or her to make better choices to become part of the school community instead of a troublemaker. The problem is that this takes time that teachers do not have and so the decision to exclude the bully may have to be made. Then the bully becomes someone else's problem and most probably grows up to join the ranks of big bullies who bully their children, spouses and workmates.

Children who are abused at home and go on to become chronic bullies are to be pitied. Children who are nurtured and loved can cope with being vulnerable and dependent, and with making mistakes or not doing everything properly. This is a normal part of growing up. Abused children are punished or humiliated for things they cannot help, like accidently wetting the bed, not being hungry when adults decide it is time to eat, spilling a drink, falling over and getting hurt or putting on a jumper back to front.

The adults expect impossible things from the child and make it clear that being dependent and vulnerable is not acceptable. Being strong and humiliating others is the acceptable way to behave. Indeed, this is the only way to behave if the child is to survive. The child comes to deny and hate this vulnerable self. It is linked with weakness and being weak is associated with pain. When this child perceives that another child is weak in any way, he or she attacks. But the sad fact is that this child is really attacking himself – it is self-hatred that makes some bullies.

Bullies need help, but usually reject any attempt to help them. Realistic, firm guidelines and rules may help them to control their reactions and lashing-out behaviour. Also trying to help them achieve some success can make a difference.

One boy was nurtured by a teacher who helped him to learn skills in woodworking. He began to produce beautiful boxes which the teacher made sure were prominently displayed and admired. The boy found a part of himself that he could like and stopped bullying others. Unfortunately, the 'success' that most bullies achieve is by being a bully and other children need help to cope with the problem.

John Pearce gives an excellent background and suggestions about how children become bullies and how to help them in Chapter 7.

Victims

Many children are one-off victims of bullying. They just happen to be in the wrong place at the wrong time. They become victims of bullying because, unfortunately, the bully chooses them to torment. If no one stops the bully, these victims start to think that they are to blame. The reality is that the bully needs a victim. Kidscape has found that often these children get along quite well in one school, but are victimised continually at another. This may be because of the particular mix of children at the schools, but more likely it is because the policy of one school has evolved towards bullying while the other school takes firm action against it.

A small minority of children seem to be perpetual victims. They are bullied no matter where they go and it even carries on into adult life. Several people have contacted Kidscape to say that they were bullied at school from an early age. Subsequently they have been bullied all their lives – at work, in marriage and in all relationships. They have developed a victim mentality and are unable to stand up for themselves.

In one study Kidscape found that some of the children who were chronic victims were intelligent, sensitive and creative, but they were also lacking in humour. They had good relationships with their parents and families, but were inclined to be intense and very serious. The everyday 'give and take' of life was not easy for them. A small group of the chronic victims seemed to almost seek out being bullied. These children were often victims of some other kinds of abuse and actually had much in common with the chronic bullies. Some had been both victim and bully.

Children first need to know that there are some situations which might be impossible to deal with – a gang of bullies attacking one child or a bully with a weapon. Since the child's safety is the primary concern, advise that money or anything else is not worth getting badly hurt over. Sometimes it is better to give the bully what he or she asks for and get away and tell an adult.

Some adults feel it is best to just give as good as you get. If a child reports being bullied, the response is 'hit back or you will continue to be bullied'. While this tactic can work, it places the often smaller, weaker victim in an impossible situation. And bullies are most likely to choose this kind of victim. In Chapter 6, Andrew Mellor gives some effective suggestions for dealing with the victims of bullying.

Suggestions for dealing with bullying

The children who always seem to be bullied need as much help as possible. The first thing to do is to examine the child's behaviour to find out if he or she is acting and feeling like a victim. Perhaps the child needs to learn to walk in a more confident manner or learn to express feelings of anger and become more self-assertive.

One family helped their son by practising walking, which also increased his self-confidence. They first had the child walk like he was frightened, head down and shoulders hunched. They then discussed how it felt inside. 'Scared', replied the child. They then had him practise walking with head held high, taking long strides and looking straight ahead. Asked about what it felt like, the boy said 'strong'.

It was a simple way to begin to help him understand how the bully might be looking at him. It is best to repeat this kind of exercise over weeks and involve other family members or friends, giving the child lots of praise. It should not be done if it creates tension or if it becomes a form of bullying, which would only make the child feel worse.

ZAP

Kidscape recently began working with children and young people who have been bullied. They come to our one-day course called ZAP and learn ways to feel better about themselves and how to become more self-assertive. During the day they meet others who have experienced bullying and learn techniques and strategies that help them stop thinking of themselves as victims. One boy said that he went back to school and pretended that the bullying did not bother him and eventually the acting turned into reality. Another child said how good it was to meet other children who had been through similar experiences and that she didn't feel she was the only one any more. Many of the children are keeping in contact with each other. The parents also meet during that day and we help them to find ways to reduce the bullying and the stress on their children and their families.

Several teachers have now asked us to run these courses in their schools and we will be monitoring the progress and seeking funding to continue. Contact Kidscape if you think someone you teach might be interested in attending a ZAP course or look on our website for details – www.kidscape.org.uk

Coping

If a child is tied up in knots by a difficult situation such as bullying, help them get the anger out and express those feelings. Drawing, keeping a diary and using plasticine are three good ways to do this. For example, it is therapeutic to make a plasticine model of the bully, even for older students, and act out inner frustrations. This can lead to more open discussion and help you to develop strategies with the child about how to cope and what to do.

Coping might include getting other children to help, if possible, as in the school situation mentioned below. One little girl practised saying 'no' in front of the mirror for a month, learned to walk in a more assertive way and her mother arranged for another child to walk with her to school. When the bully approached, the girl looked her right in the eye, said 'leave me alone' very loudly and firmly and walked away. The bully started to follow and the girl and her friend turned around and shouted 'get away from us'. The bully left.

One mother was more direct. She went to school, sought out the groups which had been terrorising her daughter and told them: 'I don't care if you don't like my daughter – that's your right. But heaven help you if I find that you go near her or talk to her or even look at her. Is that clear?' She fixed them with such a stare that they nodded meekly. The mum made it her business to be around for a week after that.

The girls turned to a new victim – one without an assertive mother, no doubt! Although some people would not agree with this mother's approach, in this case it did solve the problem. Her daughter told me that she was at first embarrassed but then really proud that her mum cared enough to try to protect her.

When a child has been part of a group that turns and starts to bully him or her, it is particularly difficult. Sometimes it is one of those temporary phases where one or another of the group is in or out of favour. Other times it becomes a real vendetta, usually led by one of the old gang. When this happens, the only choice may be to find a new group – often very difficult – or to try to stop the victimisation and get back into the group.

One mum successfully helped her son to break the cycle by inviting two of the boys and their families around for a barbecue. It broke the group's desire to bully this boy. It also eventually led to a parents' group which worked on the general problem of bullying in the neighbourhood. Part of their strategy was to say to their children that it was all right to tell if they were being bullied – that is not telling tales.

But if children tell, adults must be prepared to try to help, as these parents did. Bullying then becomes unacceptable behaviour within the community and the children feel comfortable supporting one another.

Teachers of younger children might suggest that parents invite over one or two children in the bullying group, who are not ringleaders. By ensuring that there is a lot to do and that they all have a good time, it becomes much more difficult for the children to want to bully the victim. Gradually increase the size of the group so that the 'victim's' home becomes a focal point and somewhere that the children want to go. This is extra work, but it is usually worth it. Better to spend energy creating a positive situation than trying to pick up the pieces of a bullied child. See Chapter 4 about younger children.

Older students might try activities outside the school to make new friends or take up some new activity in school such as music or art or sport of some kind. Exercise can also help as it allows the student to get out frustrations and unwind and may lead them to develop a new skill as well. The local authority should be able to help in finding what is available near you.

Co-operation

Teachers have a major role to play in the prevention of bullying. Kidscape suggests that lessons on co-operation and how to prevent bullying should be part of the normal school curriculum. All of the Kidscape programmes, which range from age 3 to age 16, include lessons about the problem of bullying and how to develop strategies. The students role-play situations, discuss the issues and decide how to best tackle the problem. Again, peer pressure is a formidable force and should be used. See Chapter 11 for information about anti-bullying practices in schools.

A slightly more controversial approach which Kidscape initiated in some schools is the bully court – we call them councils, the students call them courts. These can be set up easily, but only in the right school context where a policy has been established and there is solid backing from parents and teachers. The courts are a way of getting children constructively involved in citizenship and in taking responsibility for one another (see Chapter 15). In fact, good citizenship is the basis for prevention of bullying – when students learn to work together, help one another and form a cohesive group, bullying all but disappears. It is vital that the students get involved in solving problems and coming up with ideas so that they feel responsible for their behaviour and the wellbeing of those around them. The most successful anti-bullying policies we have seen come from schools that involve the children in decision-making.

One example is a secondary school that had several classes of problem students – you know, the kind of class that every teacher dreads. One teacher, having inherited the 'class from hell' as a double lesson, told the students on the first day that this was going to be the year they lost that reputation. She immediately gave them 20 minutes to begin to find solutions. She observed their feeble efforts to figure out what to do – 'like a headless octopus' was her description. But she did not intervene. At the end of the session, she said they would have a 15 or 20-minute session the next day and they needed to come back with ideas. The other teachers thought she had lost her mind, but she stuck it out. After a few weeks, the students had laid down ground rules, worked out a method of discussion and were starting to be more civilised, according to other staff members. To cut a long story short, the students eventually became a coherent group and all credit was due to the teacher who had the courage and stamina to teach them good citizenship. Credit, too, to the head teacher who supported her.

Of course, the problem of bullying is best addressed by a joint approach of parents, teachers, playground supervisors and children. The prevention of bullying then becomes a priority. In the Kidscape programmes, bullying is one of the most important lessons dealt with because it is one that concerns everyone. The students usually respond to this lesson so well that some schools report that bullying is reduced to a minimum, although no one claims that it has stopped altogether.

Cowardly

Bullying was reduced or stopped because the children learned that bullying was cowardly, that they could not be bystanders and that everyone had a responsibility to stop this kind of behaviour. The bully was quite often left without victims to bully and sometimes became a positive member of the group.

Summary

Bullying will never go away completely, but by condemning bullying behaviour and acting to stop it, we can prevent thousands of children suffering. After all, we used to shove children up chimneys and stuff them down mines. Today, that would seem totally unacceptable. Perhaps in time the idea of bullying will seem equally unacceptable. The good news is that now the vast majority of schools recognise that bullying is a problem and that most teachers want to see it stamped out. As one teacher commented: 'It's a lot easier to teach kids who aren't worrying about what's going to happen to them at the break. It's good to see the former bullies (some used to frighten me) feeling better about themselves. Maybe they are finally learning a bit of math!'

References

Balding, J. (1996) 'Bully Off: Young People Who Fear Going to School', Schools Health Education Unit, Exeter University.

Elliott, M. and Kilpatrick, J. (2002) *How to Stop Bullying: A Kidscape Training Guide*. Kidscape.

Olweus, D. (1993) *Bullying at School: What we know and what we can do*. Blackwell.

Whitney, I. and Smith, P. (1993) 'A survey of the nature and extent of bullying in junior/middle and secondary schools', *Press Educational Research*, Vol 35, No 1, Spring.

2

■ ■ ■

Why some schools don't have bullies

PETER STEPHENSON AND DAVID SMITH

▶ Head teachers in the low bullying schools attach more importance to managing and preventing bullying

▶ Cross-age grouping seems to encourage a more caring, less competitive ethos among children

▶ Action needs to communicate unambiguous disapproval of bullying behaviour

▶ Suggestions for creating the 'perfect school for bullies'

▶ Suggestions for creating a 'bully-free' school

Introduction

We define bullying in our work as an interaction in which a more dominant individual or group intentionally causes distress to a less dominant individual or group. This definition makes explicit the unequal nature of the interaction which is a key feature of bullying. The bully is the more dominant individual and the victim lacks the power, strength or will to resist. Bullying is, essentially, the abuse of power.

It is helpful, in practice, to classify bullying behaviour as either verbal or physical and as either direct or indirect. Examples of direct verbal bullying might be name-calling or verbal abuse, whereas an example of direct physical bullying might be a physical attack. Indirect verbal bullying might take the form of spreading rumours or belittling victims in their absence. Indirect physical bullying might include defacing or hiding possessions or exclusion from the group. In effect bullying may take a wide variety of forms – see Table 2.1.

It is the intention behind the act as well as the act itself which is important. A mere 'look' or 'gesture' or a refusal to reply becomes bullying if the behaviour

Table 2.1 Types of bullying

	Verbal	Physical
Direct	Name-calling Verbal abuse	Physical attack
Indirect	Spreading rumours Belittling victims in their absence	Hiding or defacing possessions Exclusion from the group

is intended to and does, in fact, cause distress. Parodying a person's speech or behaviour is not bullying if the intention is to please rather than to cause distress to the other person. Similarly, verbally or physically attacking another is not bullying if, for example, the intention is to defend property or territory rather than to cause distress.

When individuals or groups perceive themselves as being bullied these perceptions should be taken seriously and investigated appropriately. However, for bullying to have actually taken place there would, according to our definition, have to be an intention on the behalf of the perpetrator and behaviour intended to hurt.

One final observation. Most research has included within the definition of bullying that it involves *repeated* acts of aggression. It is assumed that the repetition of the behaviour is a crucial aspect of the definition of bullying. Bullying has even been defined in the High Court as, among other things, conduct that persists over time (Bradford-Smart v West Sussex County Council, November 2000). We would like to query this. Child abuse does not have to be repeated to be classified as 'child abuse'. Why should it be so in the case of bullying? If only a single incident of bullying takes place, it is still important to take action to stop it. There is evidence that children themselves do not consider that the behaviour needs to be repeated in order to be considered as bullying (La Fontaine, 1991; Madsen, 1996).

The Cleveland research

In research undertaken by the authors in the 1980s, teachers of final year primary school children in 26 schools were asked to provide information on all the children in their classes. They collected information on over 1,000 children in the 26 schools. The schools were chosen so that they provided a representative sample of catchment areas.

The teachers reported bullying to be a common occurrence. About a quarter of the children were involved as either bullies or victims. Bullying was reported to persist. In about 80% of cases it was said to have been going on for a year or longer. There was no evidence that it sorted itself out. The problem was reported to be more common among boys than girls. The boys were reported to use mainly direct physical or a combination of direct verbal and physical techniques, whereas the girls were reported to use mainly verbal and indirect forms of bullying. All these findings have been replicated in other studies (Smith, 1999).

We did not feel that there was just a group of bullies and a group of victims. The situation was more complex than we had anticipated. We found five distinct groups involved.

About 10% of the children in the sample were reported to be bullies and the majority of these were described as being active, dominant children. They were not rated as being insecure or unpopular with other children. They appeared to be children who enjoyed exercising power over others. A number of them might well be successful in their chosen careers when they left school.

We did find that a small number of these children – 18% of the 112 bullies – had different characteristics. They were rated as being insecure, as lacking self-confidence, as being unpopular and as being behind in schoolwork, and were more often reported to have difficulties at home. These children appeared to be more like the traditional stereotype of the bully who is said to compensate for feelings of inadequacy by bullying. We called these children 'anxious bullies', borrowing the term from the Scandinavian researcher, Dan Olweus (1978).

About 7% of the children in the sample were reported to be victims. The majority of these children were said to be passive individuals who lacked physical prowess, had low self-confidence and were unpopular with other children. They were very much children who would have difficulty in coping with being bullied.

We again found that a small number of these children – 17% of the 73 victims – had different characteristics. These children were said to actively provoke the bullying to which they were subjected. Whereas the main group of victims seldom told their teachers that they were being bullied, the group of 'provocative victims' (a term again borrowed from Dan Olweus) frequently told their teachers.

Finally, there was a group of children who both were bullied and themselves bullied other children. There was a surprisingly high number of

Figure 2.1 Children involved in bullying of the 1,000 surveyed

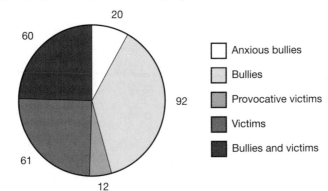

these children – 6% of the total sample. These children, who we refer to as 'bully/victims', were rated as being the least popular with other children of all the groups identified and appeared to have some of the characteristics of both anxious bullies and provocative victims.

The psychological wellbeing of the anxious bullies, provocative victims and bully/victims is of particular concern. Other studies confirm that provocative victims are a particularly vulnerable group of children (Smith *et al.*, 1993). Figure 2.1 shows how many of the 1,000 children fell into the particular categories.

School factors

We identified a variety of factors that might contribute to bullying. The problem was reported to be very much more common in some schools than in others. In three of the 26 schools, 30% or more of the children were said to be involved, while in another school over 50% of the year group was said to be involved.

It may be significant that two of the three schools in which there was said to be no bullying at all were unusually small schools, both of which employed cross-age grouping of pupils. A teacher at one of these schools expressed the view that cross-age grouping encouraged a more caring, less competitive ethos among children and that this discouraged the emergence of bullying. If children of the same age are grouped together, issues of dominance are perhaps more likely to arise.

Generally speaking, bullying was reported to be more frequent in schools located in more socially deprived areas. There also tended to be rather more bullying in the larger schools with larger classes, though this finding was not statistically significant. A difficulty here was that some schools in the more deprived areas were also smaller schools with smaller classes so that it was difficult to disentangle the operation of the two factors.

Research by others also found that bullying was more common in disadvantaged schools but there were no significant correlations between the incidence of bullying and either school or class size (Whitney and Smith, 1993).

In our study there were exceptions to the general rule that there was more bullying in schools in more deprived areas. In some schools there was more bullying than expected and in other schools there was less than expected. In fact, one school located in one of the most socially deprived areas and which also had large classes had one of the lowest levels of bullying. When this was investigated further, enquiries suggested that there was, in fact, very little bullying at the school which had an exceptionally caring ethos.

We also looked in more detail at the six schools with the lowest and the six schools with the highest levels of bullying. A difference that emerged was that the head teachers in the low bullying schools tended to express more articulate, considered views on bullying and attached more importance to managing and preventing its occurrence (see Table 2.2).

Table 2.2 School factors

	More bullying	Less bullying
Class size	Large	Small
School size	Large	Small
Deprivation	High	Low
Ethos	Competitive and uncaring	Caring, less competitive
Class organisation	Age groups	Cross-age
Head teacher attitude and views	Lack of awareness and give low priority to it	Awareness of bullying issues and give higher priority to resolving them

How to encourage bullying

Thus the evidence suggests that the incidence of bullying does vary from school to school and this suggests that while social, family and personality factors are probably important, the effect of the school upon the level of bullying must be examined. Bullying is a highly complex behaviour, difficult to define and often near impossible to witness. We have no doubt that the factors contributing to bullying are equally complex and difficult to identify.

In looking at which aspects of school life might contribute to bullying we decided first to imagine that we wished to create a school which prided itself upon its bullies and which fostered the bully ethos. Imagine, for instance, that a management consultant has been asked to design a school to meet these requirements. Perhaps his report might contain some of the following suggestions.

Management consultant's report

1. The school should have many areas which are difficult for staff to supervise. These areas should include the entry and exit points to the school, playgrounds as well as toilet and washing areas.
2. The children should be placed in these areas at times of least supervision. This should include break times and lunch times, as well as at the beginning and end of the school day. However, on wet days the school should arrange for all children to remain inside the school building, perhaps restricting them to classroom areas with again little or no supervision.
3. The school should ensure that if some supervision is provided at lunch time it is by untrained and underpaid staff. These supervisors will then have little authority and should enjoy only minimal respect from teachers and pupils alike.

4. The school day should be arranged so that the whole age range of the school arrives at, and leaves, at the same time. Similarly, the whole age range could be thrown together on three occasions each day. There should be no designated places of respite for children and the majority of the areas where the children congregate should be dominated by fast and furious games (apart, of course, from the area behind the bicycle shed). No constructive activities should be encouraged and few, if any, seats should be made available.

5. The school should establish a firm rule that any child seeking to leave these areas by entering the school or leaving the school premises should be penalised.

6. Wherever possible arrangements should be made by the school which contribute to large numbers of children having to move around the school in different directions at the same time. Thus the timetable could be designed so that virtually the whole school has to move from one lesson to the next simultaneously, several times a day. Children should be asked to travel different distances between lessons but to get there in the same length of time. All children should use the same corridors.

7. The school should be designed so that the corridors used at changeover times are narrow. Perhaps lockers could be placed down one wall of the corridor, thereby increasing congestion as children try to get things in and out of the lockers. In addition, we recommend swing doors at the end of each corridor which can be pushed in either direction.

8. Again we envisage little supervision being provided at these times. Staff would either be preparing for the next lesson or moving themselves hurriedly to the next classroom.

9. We would suggest that classrooms should be designed with little or no thought as to how they might affect children's behaviour. There will usually be only one door into and out of the classroom. Many classrooms should be sited on the first or second floors and have windows facing out but not inwards. The only means of supervision from outside of the classroom should be via a small window in the door. This should encourage children who are left unsupervised in the class to feel that they are unlikely to be observed.

10. We should ensure that materials and equipment are in short supply so that children have to share. The majority of resources should be allocated to children with the fewest educational problems. This should indicate to the pupils the priorities of the school.

11. Teachers should be encouraged to arrive late to lessons whenever possible. This could be facilitated in a number of ways. The staffroom should be sited a long distance from the majority of classrooms, perhaps in the separate administration block. Ideally the school should be organised on a split site, with those involved in drawing up the timetable taking little or no account of distances teachers need to travel from one lesson to the next. Staff meetings could be organised before school with an agenda which is bound to

17

overrun. Teaching arrangements could be made or altered without regard to where the materials required for the lesson might be kept.

12. The school should be organised so that there is little or no liaison between subject departments and the pastoral system. Subject departments should view their remit as solely concerning academic issues, with no formal arrangement for linking with the objectives of the pastoral system.

13. There should be no agreed, clear and consistent way of recording incidents. Whether, and how, a bullying incident is reported or recorded should be a matter for the individual teacher to decide. When incidents are recorded they should not include details of the actions taken and outcomes. Teachers should not be told who to pass such records to.

14. Teachers should feel free to adopt patterns of behaviour for themselves that they would not accept from pupils and should see no link between the ways in which they behave and the ways in which children behave. They should feel free to employ bullying tactics in controlling children.

15. There should be a lack of rewards available for teachers to use in school, which combined with many of the factors already mentioned should encourage teachers to use threats and sarcasm as their main means of control.

16. There should be a lack of any clear and agreed policy on the use of sanctions. Similar pupil behaviour should lead to wide variations in teacher responses from one teacher to the next. This should confuse pupils as to what is and what is not acceptable and appropriate behaviour.

17. We recommend that whenever bullying does occur in the school this should be viewed as part of the 'normal growing-up process' and as 'helping children to learn how to stand on their own two feet' and 'giving them backbone'. Children who are victims of bullying should be viewed as 'asking for it' and/or as 'inadequate'.

18. The school should encourage the view that high academic achievement rather than relative achievement or effort is valued. This should ensure that for many children school life has little to offer and that they feel inadequate. We should ensure that lessons are not differentiated sufficiently to meet the needs of children.

19. We should ensure that curriculum space is filled as far as possible by academic subjects, with little or no time for pastoral issues, and that these are dealt with in an insular rather than in a cross-curriculum fashion.

20. Finally, we must at all costs avoid developing anything that vaguely resembles a whole-school policy on bullying.

If the school agrees to follow these recommendations in full we have little doubt that an ethos will be created in which bullying behaviour will flourish.

Yours sincerely,

Keith (Flashman) W.

How to discourage bullying

We have described above action that might be taken to encourage bullying. The description given is not dissimilar to the way some schools are organised at the present time. We will now stand these recommendations on their head. How would we organise schools to discourage bullying?

School ethos

Our first recommendation is that action should be taken that contributes to the development of a school ethos that encourages 'non-bullying' behaviour and views bullying as unacceptable. Whatever is done in response to bullying should have the goal of bringing about a situation in which a non-bullying ethos is created – one in which relationships are based on mutual respect, trust, caring and consideration for others rather than on power and strength. If an ethos is created which promotes these qualities, bullying will be marginalised – children will not even consider the option of engaging in bullying.

It is often assumed that bullying is an inevitable fact of life – it is just one of those things. In fact, as indicated by our research, bullying is very much more common in some schools than in others and this does not just reflect the catchment areas of the schools. Schools are able to make a difference.

In present-day society generally, strength tends to be admired and weakness despised. Whatever the difficulties, we are all expected to be able to cope. If we are having a rough time, we are expected to keep quiet about it and just put up with it. Children are told to 'take it like a man'. This thinking needs to be challenged. Children subjected to bullying are the very children least able to cope with it. Both victims and other children should be encouraged to report bullying. Reporting incidents of bullying should be viewed as taking responsible action rather than as 'telling tales'.

It is likely that, on at least some occasions, part of the motivation for bullying is to impress other children – to impress bystanders. If an appropriate ethos is established, children will not actively join in the bullying or even encourage it by smiling or laughing but will take steps to stop the bullying and will report it to a teacher.

There is some evidence that bystanders are more likely to help victims of aggression if they know what to do and have been given training on what to do. The implication here is that children should be given training in helping skills and be given the opportunity to practise them.

All schools are now obliged by law to have a written anti-bullying policy. We suggest that this policy should underwrite the non-bullying school ethos. If staff and children are engaged in the development of the policy, they are more likely to actively support it. The policy is of little value if staff and children are not committed to it. There is research evidence that anti-bullying policies are effective only if they are kept 'active' (Eslea and Smith, 1998).

The policy should stress the need to prevent and not just manage bullying. It is not enough to reprimand the bully and to offer support to the victim. As well as dealing with the immediate situation, it is necessary to ask why the bullying has taken place and to take appropriate measures.

Supervision and monitoring

Staff need to be aware of signs that may indicate that a child is being bullied and need to be alert to the possibility of bullying taking place. Signs that may indicate a child is being bullied include:

- cuts, bruises, aches and pains which are not adequately explained;
- clothes or possessions being damaged or lost;
- the child starts going to or returning from school at an earlier or later time or starts using a different route;
- the child starts refusing to go outside at break times or refuses to stay at school for school dinners;
- the child requests to change classes, options or school;
- reluctance or refusal to attend school, for example by feigning illness;
- any unexplained and sudden change in the child's behaviour.

There should be adequate supervision arrangements, particularly at times and in places where bullying is likely to take place. Spot checks might be carried out in places where bullying is likely to occur. In this context, ensuring that children are not regularly unattended in classrooms and cutting down the number of children moving around the school at any one time, for example by staggering the school day, are steps that might be taken. If pupil surveys of bullying are carried out on a regular basis, this not only provides a check on the occurrence of bullying, it helps maintain awareness of bullying as a problem.

There also needs to be an adequate system for recording incidents of bullying which ensures that there is good communication between staff, and that no divisions exist between the academic and pastoral departments. In all cases reports of bullying should be taken seriously, enquiries should be made and the outcome fed back to those involved. The effectiveness of action taken to stop the bullying should also be monitored and fed back to those involved. Unless such steps are taken, bullying will be seen to be condoned.

Playgrounds and school buildings

Playgrounds tend to be a focus for bullying. Their design should encourage a diversity of constructive, creative play. In reality they are often barren wastelands, and ways of redesigning and zoning physical space need to be explored. Bullying is likely to flourish in unstructured, unsupervised situations given over to boisterous play. Playground rules and procedures should be developed.

It is often assumed that the physical appearance of the school buildings is unimportant. There is in fact evidence that there is a relationship between standards of behaviour in schools and how well cared for the school buildings are, e.g. whether they are free from graffiti and rubbish. Surveys have been carried out in which children have been asked what they like and dislike about school. The responses suggest that children have difficulty in coping with features of school life such as smelly, unhygienic toilets which offer limited privacy, and noisy, crowded dinner halls.

The status and role of the lunchtime supervisor in managing behaviour and facilitating play should also be acknowledged and appropriate training offered. A number of INSET (In Service Training for teachers) packages for training lunchtime supervisors are now available.

Teaching and classroom management skills

The relationship between teachers and children should be characterised by mutual respect and trust so that the children feel able to tell teachers if they are being bullied or if they witness bullying.

Teachers should be aware that children sometimes model their behaviour on the behaviour of adults they admire. They should, therefore, be careful to avoid engaging in bullying themselves. Emphasis should be placed on praising good behaviour rather than on the use of sanctions and there should be positive expectations of pupil behaviour. Teachers should make every effort to arrive on time and be well prepared, and senior management should make punctuality a priority.

Overcoming bullying is not easy. Teachers require time, patience and skills to deal with children involved in bullying and their parents. In this context adequate support should be made available to teachers, especially those new to the profession.

Children should be encouraged to participate in the management of the class and the school. There is evidence that this leads to improved pupil behaviour and is, in part, the rationale behind approaches such as Kidscape and Teenscape (a programme devised by Kidscape to teach personal safety, including how to deal with bullying, to teenagers).

Curriculum matters

Our research found that most of the children involved in bullying were underachieving, particularly the anxious bullies. It is important that an appropriate curriculum appropriately delivered is offered to those children involved in bullying. Non-academic as well as academic achievement and co-operative as well as competitive learning should be valued.

In addition, discussion of bullying should be incorporated in both the academic and PSHE (personal, social and health education) curriculum. Techniques such as social and friendship skills training should also be incorporated in the PSHE curriculum.

Help for bullies and victims

We suggest it is necessary to take action which communicates unambiguous disapproval of bullying. We stress that disapproval should be aimed at the behaviour of the child and not at the child itself. At the same time, action should be taken which encourages the development of caring, responsible behaviour on the part of the bully, for example through peer tutoring. The aim is to channel the dominance of the bully into more productive and fruitful activities. There is some evidence that counselling-based approaches which focus on solving the problem rather than on apportioning blame have some success (Pikas, 1989; Duncan, 1996).

As regards victims, and to some extent all children involved in bullying, steps should be taken to improve their self-confidence, self-esteem and social skills. There is evidence that assertiveness training, victim support groups and peer counselling approaches help empower these children (Arora, 1991; Smith and Sharp, 1994; DfEE, 2000).

Bystanders, as well as the children immediately involved in bullying, should be offered advice and support. Immediately after a bullying incident all those involved or who have witnessed it should be debriefed.

Some questions for schools

1. Is bullying seen as a problem by staff in your school? Do they recognise that it occurs? Do they think anything should be done about it?
2. Do the physical characteristics of the school contribute to bullying? If so, how could they be altered?
3. How and by whom are rules determined in your school? How are rules communicated? Are they applied consistently by members of staff?
4. Is there an efficient communication system between different parts of the school organisation?
5. Are topics such as bullying looked at in PSHE or tackled in a cross-curricular fashion?
6. Are incidents of bullying and how they are dealt with recorded, discussed and evaluated by staff?
7. Are there agreed procedures for dealing with bullying? Are they followed?
8. Does the school inform parents of bullying incidents? How is this done?
9. Are children encouraged to 'tell' if they have been bullied or have witnessed bullying?
10. If the school has a whole-school policy on discipline, is bullying mentioned specifically?

The role of parents, the local community and other agencies

Parents should be kept informed if their child is involved in bullying and should be encouraged to work with the school to overcome the problem. Parents should also be made aware of the complaints procedure.

Traditionally schools and parents have tended to be wary of each other and have tended to blame each other for behaviour difficulties presented by children. It is now much more widely accepted that schools should aim at establishing a genuine partnership with parents. This partnership should include school governors, the local community, the Local Education Authority (LEA) support services and other agencies. Bullying is too large a problem for schools to be able to deal with on their own.

Summary

Many schools do now acknowledge that bullying exists and are making efforts to deal with it. However, in other schools recognition and ownership of the problems still remain an issue. Some schools minimise the serious impact that bullying has upon the lives of a significant proportion of pupils.

For those schools that are not sure what action to take, we conclude with a set of guidelines they may find of value.

Guidelines

1. Ensure that any action taken in response to bullying contributes to the development of a school ethos that encourages non-bullying behaviour and that views bullying as unacceptable.
2. Ensure that the school anti-bullying policy underwrites this ethos and stresses the need to prevent, not just manage, bullying.
3. Ensure that all staff are actively committed to and apply consistently the anti-bullying policy and the ethos that underlies it.
4. Ensure that steps are taken to publicise the policy to children and parents and enlist their support.
5. Seek to bring about the situation in which children actively discourage bullying and view reporting incidents of bullying as being responsible rather than as 'telling tales'.
6. Ensure that there are confidential reporting arrangements in place.
7. Ensure that staff are alert to the possibility of bullying taking place.
8. Ensure that there are adequate supervision arrangements, particularly at times and in places where bullying is likely to take place.
9. If there are narrow corridors or inaccessible corners, ensure that special supervision arrangements are made.
10. Operate a system of spot checks.
11. Cut down the number of children moving around the school at any one time.

12. Ensure that children are not regularly left unattended in classrooms.
13. Ensure that there is an adequate system for monitoring and recording incidents of bullying.
14. Ensure that there is good communication between staff in monitoring and managing bullying problems.
15. Carry out pupil surveys to monitor the occurrence of bullying.
16. Ensure that the design of playgrounds and the use made of them encourages a diversity of constructive, creative play.
17. Ensure that the status and role of lunchtime supervisors in managing behaviour and facilitating play are acknowledged and appropriate training offered.
18. Ensure that the playground and school buildings are well cared for and free from graffiti and rubbish.
19. Ensure that the relationship between school staff and children is characterised by mutual respect and trust so that children feel able to tell school staff if they are bullied.
20. Ensure that school staff model non-bullying behaviour – ensure that methods of teaching and/or control do not endorse bullying tactics.
21. Ensure that there is emphasis on praising good behaviour rather than on the use of sanctions and that there are positive expectations of pupil behaviour.
22. Ensure that teachers arrive on time for lessons and are well prepared.
23. Ensure that the curriculum encourages non-academic as well as academic achievement and co-operative as well as competitive learning.
24. Ensure that discussion of bullying is incorporated in both the academic and PSHE and citizenship curriculum.
25. Encourage children to participate in the management of classes and the school.
26. Ensure that techniques such as social and friendship skills training are incorporated in the PSHE curriculum.
27. Ensure that adequate support is made available to school staff, especially those new to the school, in handling bullying problems.
28. If children or parents report bullying, the report should be listened to, taken seriously and appropriate enquiries made.
29. The outcomes of enquiries should be made known to those involved.
30. The effectiveness of action taken to stop bullying should be monitored and discussed with those involved.
31. Ensure that action is taken which communicates unambiguous disapproval of bullying to bullies and that additional action is taken which encourages caring, responsible behaviour.
32. Take steps to improve the self-confidence, self-esteem and social skills of victims and, to a lesser extent, the others involved in bullying.
33. Ensure that bystanders as well as the children immediately involved are offered support and help.
34. In all cases, inform the parents of those children involved and seek their involvement and co-operation in resolving the bullying.

35. Ensure that there are procedures for dealing with parental complaints about bullying.
36. Enlist the co-operation of parents and the local community in dealing with school bullying problems.
37. Make effective use of LEA support services in tackling bullying.
38. Enlist the support and advice of school governors in dealing with bullying.

References

Arora, C. M. J. (1991) 'The use of victim support groups', in P. K. Smith and D. Thompson (eds), *Practical Approaches to Bullying*. London: David Fulton Publishers.

DfEE (2000) *Bullying. Don't Suffer in Silence*.

Duncan, A. (1996) 'The shared concern method for resolving group bullying in schools', *Educational Psychology in Practice*, Vol 12, No 2, July.

Eslea, M. and Smith, P. K. (1998) 'The long-term effectiveness of anti-bullying work in primary schools', *Educational Research*, 40, 203–18.

La Fontaine, J. (1991) *Bullying: The Child's View*. London: Calouste Gulbenkian Foundation.

Madsen, K. C. (1996) 'Differing perceptions of bullying and their practical implications', *Educational and Child Psychology*, Vol 13, No 2.

Olweus, D. (1978) *Aggression in Schools: Bullies and Whipping Boys*. Washington DC: Hemisphere.

Pikas, A. (1989) 'The common concern method for the treatment of mobbing', in E. Roland and E. Munthe (eds), *Bullying – An International Perspective*. London: David Fulton Publishers.

Smith, P. K. and Sharp, S. (1994) *School Bullying – Insights and Perspectives*. London: Routledge.

Smith, P. K., Bower, L., Binney, V. and Carde, H. (1993) 'Relationships of children involved in bully/victim problems at school', in S. Duck (ed), *Learning About Relationships*. Sage.

Smith, P. K. *et al.* (1999) *The Nature of School Bullying*. London: Routledge.

Whitney, I. and Smith, P. K. (1993) 'A survey of the nature and extent of bully/victim problems in junior/middle and secondary schools', *Education Research*, Vol 35, No 1, pp 3–25.

3

■ ■ ■

Practical considerations in dealing with bullying behaviour in secondary school

ERIC JONES

▶ Preparing the ground for an anti-bullying school

▶ Beware the joke that isn't funny, the game not everyone is playing

▶ What to do when bullying happens – it will happen!

▶ Teachers between experts and 'isms'

There is a joke which occasionally does the rounds and which our profession finds amusing, even if it is a little cruel towards those who work with people in a social setting. The story is of a social worker, teacher or priest (suit yourself) who comes across the bruised and battered victim of a mugging, stoops to look at the damage and exclaims, 'My goodness, I bet the person who did this has got some problems …'!

As professionals in teaching, we are as concerned as anyone with the underlying causes and reasons for the behaviour of the bully. We are interested in prevention and this chapter will outline some of the strategies which have already proved useful in preventing outbreaks of bullying behaviour. But, in addition, we are technicians, operatives in the school situation, and as such find ourselves having to act when a bullying incident has occurred, responding to both victim and culprit. We have to sanction and control. Strategies for operating in this situation, at the 'chalk face', are our concern.

The context

The context in which this piece was originally written is an inner-city comprehensive school. Nearly 50% of the mixed-race population come from single-parent homes. The school is surrounded by poor housing, unemployment is high, and there is considerable disenchantment on the part of many pupils and parents. The 'establishment' includes teachers. The law and the police are not looked upon with great favour.

The advantages of an education are not always acknowledged. Less than academically successful parents do not tend to breed wildly enthusiastic scholars. Parents who cannot read at all pose a particular problem. Well over half the yearly intake arrive with a reading age two or more years behind their chronological age. Attracting teachers to fill vacancies takes up a distorted proportion of the working week, and providing extra help for the seriously disadvantaged, academically or socially, is a logistical nightmare.

Many of the parents and children have been bullied already, by the society in which they find themselves, the demands made of them and the restrictions placed upon them, all of which some find extraordinarily difficult to handle. A lot of bullying goes on – by officials enforcing regulations, by the comfortably-off towards the hard-up, by those in employment towards those who seek to work, by the literate towards those who find it hard to learn, and by whites who were born in Britain towards young blacks and Asians who were also born in Britain, and vice versa.

Nevertheless there is success. Many achieve commendable results in GCSEs. Some achieve outstanding success. Nearly every pupil gains some graded results in some subjects. The results do not always please the media or the education statisticians (or target-setters) but teachers are exhausted and pleased when an entire year group can go out on work experience and when the entire fifth year population leaves school with comprehensive records of their achievements. And when boys and girls in their first year pull up their reading age by well over a year in the first few months it is at enormous cost, deserving no little acclaim.

There is also success in dealing with the problem of bullying. Outlining the context was necessary in order to see how some of these anti-bullying strategies might be appropriate and useful. Looking at one's own education environment is essential.

N.B. Since this author originally wrote this piece he has moved on, semi-retired, teaching at a 'middle-class' private boys' school south of London. Everyone can read well. Nearly 100% gain five or more A*–C grades at GCSE and parents are motivated and supportive. There is still some bullying and the same strategies are effective.

Defining the bully/victim

We shall almost certainly fall short of a universally acceptable definition, but here goes. The bully is someone who is responsible for premeditated, continuous, malicious and belittling tyranny. The victim is on the receiving end, repeatedly, defencelessly and typically without a champion.

Is everything that gets labelled 'bullying' really that, or is it that because the victim says it is? Teachers should and do try to deal with all the problems, but these are not all bullying, as defined above. The worry is that quite often teachers, parents and pupils talk about bullying when they ought to be talking about something else – rather like all headaches, to some people, come to be called migraines. That is not to say that there aren't any migraines, or that headaches are not serious in themselves. Everything needs to be dealt with for what it is.

None of us likes children who mock and giggle, pointing fingers at others for their idiosyncrasies, but they are not 'career' bullies who pick out a weaker victim and repeatedly use strategies to make them feel small; they are children growing up and doing what children do, rather cruelly, but predictably. We seek to teach them better attitudes and we try to solve the problems that they cause.

Nobody likes children who steal money or sweets from others, but beware of giving them the notoriety of being called bullies. They are thieves. We seek to teach them better social behaviour and the law. Bullies tend to extort money from a weaker victim or victims, systematically and repeatedly. This may be prompted by greed (and is still theft) but primarily it is an act of power.

Teachers get remarkably fed up with children who scrap and fight with one another. But they are not bullies because they fight and the one who wins is most certainly not a bully because he/she wins. The mindless and degrading violence of the strong against the weak may be bullying, but fighting, by definition, is not.

Here, there is a risk of offending people if it is said that some of the so-called bullying is part of growing up and learning to cope. It does not excuse the bully, but some of the behaviour of both the victim and the bully is predictable and may even be unavoidable. As children move into their own circles and grow out of full-time adult supervision they make the most dreadful mistakes in the way they treat each other. Perhaps it should be called the development of peer structures. They learn from it and before the rot of megalomania or dire timidity sets in teachers should seek to direct the lessons they learn from it. Responsible adults must teach and guide. They must not allow unbridled nastiness and exploitation, but must allow children to grow and to learn from real situations how to handle life itself. Both the strong and the weak must be monitored.

Some children thrive on attention from older pupils. It can be healthy, but sometimes it is not. Young leaders can be a power of great good. The very best of prefectorial systems and uniformed youth organisations can vouch for this. Strong youngsters can also be a cancer in a young society. We often find that young victims, perhaps because they have no better example or model, and maybe even crave some attention, go back for more and are treated unmercifully, abused and exploited. It is a fact, however, that not all such peer structures and relationships are bad per se.

Finally, within the meaning of our definition above we ought also to include now, in the twenty-first century, the e-mail and text-messaging bullies. Posting insults and lies on the internet and electronically rubbishing your victim for all the world to read is a particularly insidious form of bullying, almost impossible for the victim to reverse. It stands alongside all the traditional methods and is equally 'criminal'.

Prevention

Having said all that, and having to keep all that in mind, here are some strategies that have worked.

Prepare the ground

Teachers must talk to youngsters about the possibilities of being bullied as they arrive at secondary school, even before they arrive. On Induction Day (a day in the summer term when primary school children can come and spend a day at their new school), don't brush the subject aside. Bring it up even if it does not arise naturally (as well it might) among the questions. During the first week in the new school talk about it alongside where the toilets are, dinner queues or what happens if you are late. Let children know that sometimes there are bullies abroad and that we do not tolerate them. Above all, do not try to pretend that there used to be bullies and now there aren't.

Drama and tutorial work

If there is active tutorial work (and if not, why not?), use it to discuss the topic. Mention it in assemblies. Use the perfect safety of drama lessons or a dramatic piece in an assembly (created and composed by the youngsters themselves, of course) to enact how to rebuff the bully attempt or how to say 'no' to the thief, or how to 'go and tell'. Laugh at it, but be sure to prompt sensible discussion about what happens to the bully as well as the victim. Children can be very cruel towards the 'nasties' and perhaps they must face the ideas of forgiveness and responsibility to each other.

Don't kid the parents

It is essential that teachers do not give the impression that, somehow, one school has cracked it and that 'here in this school, bullies are a thing of the past'. Mention the well-known fact among adults that some children in every generation are nasty to others. Then teachers are free to inform parents about attitudes of the school towards such pupils and their victims, methods of responding and so on. Make sure there is a school policy on bullying, print it, make it available.

Create a contract

It may be proper to tell pupils the school rules but it is even more important that they create their own, a contract, to refer to in their own group. This is a mutually agreed set of guidelines about what we, in class 7T or 1W, regard as good and bad, acceptable and unacceptable. Everyone signs it, including the teacher, and it stays on the tutor group notice board. Of course, it includes many things, maybe about the room, property, etc. In fact it takes a while to generate in detail but it ought to include the way we treat others and what the school thinks of those who exploit and abuse others (see Chapter 25).

Be around

Hopefully it is not too obvious to suggest that bullying might be avoided in some of its manifestations if the opportunities are not there for it to flourish. Teachers ought to be on time for lessons and in corridors and 'doing their proper duties' if they don't want to spend a lot of time later sorting out what happened when the bullies stalked the quiet corners of the playground. Beware the evolution of no-go areas. 'My god!' says one teacher, 'I would never go round the back of there. You'd never come out alive!' That might be funny in the staff room of a 1950s schoolboy story but it is not good enough in the present climate.

Getting to know you

'The State of the Nation Address'! For a new group, thrown together as a form, why not celebrate everyone's individuality quite early on? It can be a process which takes weeks, a few minutes at a time when available, but it is always rewarding. From a simple, safe questionnaire the tutor finds out about pupils' interests, homework practices, modes of travel, hobbies, favourite TV, music, etc., and after sifting through all this information makes his State of the Nation Address. It is all fairly lighthearted, but all true. 'Nearly all of "us" watch *EastEnders* but nobody likes *Ground Force*! Only three come to school on foot and Jeremy has to take two buses and a train! Over 60% of us do homework as soon as we get home, but nearly everyone admits to leaving some of it for late on Sunday evenings.'

Having done this exercise and allowing a few weeks to get to know each other, it is possible to go on to Stage II. Everyone in the group writes a positive comment about everyone else, a simple statement acknowledging their particular skills or sense of humour. It can be an affectionate phrase – 'He's a really good mate to have around' is OK – and we will be surprised just how honest and sensitive even 14+-year-old boys can be when asked to do this. The teacher collates and rewrites this without revealing named sources and eventually gives every tutee, an A4 piece which outlines what their peers have said about them – and it is all positive.

We have found such an exercise has a dramatic effect on everyone's self-esteem and attitudes to others in the group with whom they spend most of the day.

Testing

Some quick tests might help to take the wind out of an assailant's sails. Try these ideas to stop him (usually a 'him') in his tracks when he starts to make excuses for his behaviour.

- Beware the joke that isn't funny. 'It was only a joke' is a phrase we all might have heard at some time muttered by the naughty child or hardened bully. The acid test is whether everyone was laughing. If they were not, then either it was not a joke or it was in very poor taste and quite obviously directed against somebody. Tripping up, taking property, hitting, pushing into a corner are all very poor jokes indeed. If one person was not party to the humour of it but was rather the victim of it, then it wasn't a joke. Don't accept it as such.

- Beware the game that not everyone was playing. 'We were only playing.' There it is again, and a very poor excuse it is for leaving somebody bruised and crying. The furious ball game is poor cover for knocking people over if the game was just that – a cover. If the person who gets knocked about was not playing and, **curiously,** appears to be the same victim as yesterday, then it was not a game! We do not accept that it was. Incidentally, the reverse of this is the bully who declares that he was playing but in fact was joining in someone else's game unwanted and uninvited. Get the facts and put it to him that he was not playing, he was invading their game.

- Beware the non-accidental accident. We have heard this one too, have we not? 'It was an accident.' The victim ends up in a heap at the bottom of the stairs or in a corridor, or with a torn bag and belongings scattered everywhere, but 'it was an accident'. This, too, has a foolproof test. If you did something accidentally to someone then you should stay behind and do what people normally do when they accidentally do such things … help! If you did not pick up the victim, apologise, assist, collect the belongings, take her to the nurse, etc., then it doesn't count as an accident and we do not accept it as such.

- 'I found it' is just one more cry from the bully who is in possession of someone else's property. If bullies and thieves knew how many times we have heard the 'I found it' excuse and how stupid it sounds they would not use it, but they still do because they think it is acceptable. It is not. As teachers we will never convince the culprit that practically every person we ever speak to in similar circumstances uses the same excuse, but we can ask the simple question, 'Why did you keep it?'

- 'I was only borrowing.' That is a poor excuse for taking money from someone. Always ask the question, instantly, of the bully, 'Right then, what's his name? Where does he live? What class is he in? When's his birthday?' Anything, to prove that the bully knows nothing of the victim and that he had no way, and thus no intention, of returning the cash. Besides, we do not, in our society, go around borrowing money from each other, certainly not from strangers and from weak anonymous little strangers. It is unacceptable, and if you do it, it very soon crosses the threshold from 'borrowing' to mugging. (I love telling such borrowers that I can't wait for them to grow up and become bank managers, because I'm going to come and borrow money from them and they won't even ask my name and address!)

- The discussion with the alleged culprit might include the question, 'Do you accept that we have a problem?' The chances are he will say, 'Yes.' The allegations and the culprit's own written account, looked at calmly, will reveal that there is something to sort out. The discussion can go on to show that the 'accused' was in control of what happened. The victim had no choice as to the outcome. What happened, happened *to* him. The alleged bully must face the fact that he could have handled it differently. He could have behaved differently and could have avoided being accused. He is responsible for the current situation which is 'the problem'. We can say, 'You are responsible, and if you are a bully – so be it. We will deal with you. If you are not, then learn from this occurrence. Handle it differently next time and remember, all this is on record.'

- Do not allow the use of the words *only* or *just* when listening to or reading an account from somebody accused of bullying behaviour. It is a cop-out, their own devaluation of the magnitude of the incident. If you don't believe that, just try to explain your last motorcar accident without using these words. Boys and girls must be encouraged to say, 'I hit him', or 'I took the money', not 'I *only* hit him a bit', or 'I *just* took a few pence.' In a written account, cross out these **two** words.

Attitudes and responses

What happens, and what pupils, parents and teachers *do* in the event of an incident, are the dynamics of these situations.

Children ought never to succumb to the 'stay quiet or else' threat, whether spoken or implied. 'We did not say anything because it would have been worse the next day' is, frankly, crazy. Of course it is difficult for the victim, but the alternative is worse, far worse. It means that a deliberate decision has been taken to allow the bully to go on bullying as long as he likes. We must help children to 'tell' and respond in such a way that they trust us. 'Telling' should become the norm.

'Telling' is crucial. Not tomorrow, not when you get home, not a month later when it has become intolerable, but *now*. Of course, the advice about telling is fraught with danger. Some victims believe that the reward for telling is to be able to dictate the punishment – 'Is he going to be expelled, Miss?' Also, most teachers are frantically busy most of the time, so we must qualify the 'tell now' instruction.

The best way is to have covered the dynamics of 'telling' during the discussions when children arrive, as already mentioned. Remember, too, that one push does not make a bullying; one hit does not make a beating. Teachers want to know what is going on, but a brief record and a quick warning ought to be enough in the event of a single incident. Then, stay alert. The victim must be prepared to write it down, with help if need be, perhaps even overnight, and then let us deal with it.

Also, just because the child tells us immediately ought not to mean – indeed cannot mean – that there will be instant retribution. 'If it is revenge you want, you've come to the wrong place' is best said in the early days, well before incidents take place. On the strength of a reported incident no teacher can drop everything and abandon a class, rushing off to mete out instant and severe punishment to the accused. The trouble with *not* doing that is that the victim invariably goes home and says, 'Miss So-and-so did nothing' and up comes mum, breathing fire. Not everything that is important, even urgent, is a crisis. A fire is a crisis. Bullying is important.

If one confronts the bully in a mood of crisis it will be a lost cause. 'Why did you hit so-and-so?' will almost certainly be rebuffed by, 'I didn't', or, worse, 'Who said I did?', to which you have no useful answer. The discussion is doomed. Bide your time. Similarly, if the victim is in distress then the available teacher should deal with the distress or the injury. Deal with the bullying later. Don't rush in like a bull into the precarious china shop of negotiations with the bully and the victim.

Ideally the best solution is to sit the child down and get a written report of the incident. That can be hours later, even days later, but of course the sooner the better. The problem is then taken on board, not in an air of crisis, but calmly. The written report is on record, the teacher can show the accused and warn him off. He can see the account. He ought even to write his own (but before he sees the victim's). If the bullying accusation has no foundation he has nothing to fear – it will die a natural death and never be mentioned again. If it is the start of a 'career', then the facts and the warning are on record. If it is the most recent in a line of career incidents, then of course you have a problem. So has the bully.

There is another form of written account that really does work. For the victim who is troubled by a sequence of annoying but relatively minor 'attacks', get him/her to keep a diary. For five or ten school days the pupil should not respond or over-react to these incidents but 'record' each one: day, date, time, place, culprit. In the experience of more than one school the diary, when shown to those accused, has a startling effect. The 'chapter and verse' detail usually astounds them. They are not being told off or shouted at, they are simply being told that all their unacceptable behaviour is being monitored and is on record. In 99% of cases they apologise, say they had no idea that the victim was having such a regularly rotten time and agree to lay off. Of course, this also comes with a warning that that's precisely what you expect of them.

Bullies like nothing worse than realising that you know what is going on and that the record is on file. They can see it if they wish. So can their family. Call their bluff. Go public. Tell the assembly what has been going on and what you have done about it. Mention no names, just make it perfectly clear that you will not tolerate it, and why.

Sometimes that works in reverse. It is possible to announce in an assembly, 'I want to see, after this assembly, the people responsible for such-and-such an incident (but of course I won't mention your names here!).' After the assembly up they come, never knowing that you didn't actually know who was going to appear. It is a tricky card to play.

Here's one for mums and dads. Please, do not keep the child victim at home 'until it is sorted out'. First, because we cannot sort out a one-sided account on the strength of the story your child has told you and which will, sure as eggs, not be the same story that we get from the accused. And second, because we should not lift a finger to sort out a one-sided affair. The accusations will be flying in all directions on the strength of a distraught phone call (the victim telling his mum on a mobile before he even mentions it to a teacher) while little Johnnie – who actually might have made it up to get out of Games – will be sitting at home watching the lunch-time edition of another Australian soap. The teacher is lonely, stuck in the middle, bursting blood vessels and accusing people with no real evidence, mum is fuming at 'that dreadful school', and the alleged culprit is indignant, while Johnnie is dipping his hand into his second packet of crisps. Mum has to bring him in, or send him in, and contribute to the solution.

The parents of the accused ought also to be invited. Again, not in an air of crisis, but calmly. Say to the parents, 'There is something you ought to know, if possible today. Can you come and pick him up from school? I'll keep him until you get here.' Or, 'We have a problem and I'd like you to be here, perhaps to help sort it out. Your son could be excluded, but first can you come and see me straight away, like tomorrow morning?' Put the onus on parents to come and have some control over their child's destiny. Children are their parents' responsibility, not, in the end, ours.

It is not wrong to confront bully and victim. The idea that victims insist we punish the nasties but want to be a million miles away when we confront the bullies with the story is nonsense. We cannot say to the bully, 'I've been told that you bullied someone. I believe it and I'm going to punish you. Oh, and by the way I cannot tell you who it is who accused you.' If the bully can see that the victim will repeat the accusations in your office, he has lost the best weapon he has – the silent victim. Very often the victim is amazed to see how cowed and cowardly the big guy really is. It is also a very useful fact that, quite often, the families of victims and accused will, in school, accept the problem quite amicably when put face to face.

In the event of a bruise or injury, why not photograph it? The quickest way is to give a child money to go to a photo booth on the way home (along with a brief letter or a following phone call home to explain what's going on). The accused and his parents are invariably confounded by the evidence of a swollen eye. Dad will be aghast at the fact that his son 'did that', even while the son is pleading accident, joke or game.

It is a good idea to use a simply designed 'incident slip' as a universal way of recording incidents in school. It needs a space for name, date, form, teacher, the incident and the action taken. Of course there will always be copies of letters, interviews and pupils' accounts, but the incident slip, if it is not too big, concentrates the mind of the reporting teacher beautifully. Half an A4 sheet, cut lengthways, is almost perfect. If the school decides to use one colour to report 'good things' and another for 'bad news', so much the better. Some pupil files take on a certain hue when one thumbs through them.

Use the rules and use the law. Record the punishment and the reasons for it. Show them what you are putting on file and make them pay with whatever time it cost you to sort it out.

Of course, exclusion may be the sanction decided upon. In that case, yet again, be sure to report reasons and everyone's account. Play it by the book and insist upon a proper interview with parents before re-admission. Our concern is to build a relationship between aggressor, family and school, not just to hand out punishment. We are not in the eye-for-an-eye business. The victim should not see the outcome as some kind of victory over the culprit. All concerned should try to achieve an outcome in which the victim feels he has been supported, need fear no more, and in which the bully and his family feel the school has dealt with the situation compassionately, if strictly, for the benefit of all. The culprit is welcomed back, having 'served his time'. Such outcomes are rarely perfect, but are achievable and should be the objective.

As far as the law is concerned we should not fear to teach or remind bullies about common law. The laws concerning assault, threatening behaviour, actual bodily harm and theft apply to them as to every other citizen. Advise victims' families to go to law and offer to co-operate if they do. If, however, they ask the school to deal with it, as invariably they do, make two things clear to all concerned. One, to the victim and family, that having asked the school to deal with it, they let the school get on with it. Two, to the accused and family, that they should co-operate with the authority of the school because the victim's family have asked it to handle things instead of going to the police.

Finally, as a general rule, we should never teach children to criticise and hate. Some pupils are always swearing at and vilifying other children (these days it is called *bad-mouthing!*). Then they run off home yelling 'bully' when they get a smack in the mouth for some of the really nasty things they have said. Even if the potential bully is a natural and well-known nasty piece of work, it really is rather provocative for another child to point that out to him. 'My mum says I'm to keep away from you because you're a rotten bully' is hardly going to gain any child the school peace prize.

The best way to make friends is to be friendly.

A word about the locals

A lady arrived at school one morning with her daughter, a pupil, and said that her daughter had been attacked on the bus on the way home from school last night. She knew which school the attacker went to and the name of the girl, so she thought that perhaps the school would like to get in touch and …

No, not really. If the lady's daughter was the victim of a crime in a public place then she ought to have gone to the police. The school has no more authority over girls from other schools committing crimes on buses than anyone else. If your daughter was mugged in August, would you wait until September, the new term, to tell the school? I hope not.

This is a very touchy area, but local people, shopkeepers, residents and parents of other children will insist on referring to pupils as 'our children'. With respect they are not; they are their parents' children. Teachers must control what goes on in school, but they are not and cannot possibly be responsible for what goes on outside. They can advise, of course. They can even help. They should not, however, take **over** the role of parent or police.

It is very sad that a mother can come into school and say that her son has been mugged on the street and that they have not been to the police. They have come to ask the teacher what they should do. Perhaps one should be flattered, but the sadness is overwhelming especially when one hears, 'the school did nothing about it'. When the writer's own son was attacked on a bus after school, we ploughed an instant furrow between home and the local police station before he'd even finished telling the story.

Once the pupil leaves the premises, even truanting, the parents must take their share of responsibility. Even the security manager of a large London store has been known to telephone, telling the school the name of a shoplifting culprit and asking if someone can come and fetch him. He says, 'Well, we don't want a lot of fuss or the police involved. We thought the school could sort it out.' Frankly, the school cannot. Apart from usually being short of teachers, how could the school, even with a full complement of staff, release teachers to go on a collecting mission? Are we then expected to punish the child in school, for what he or she (allegedly) did criminally outside it? For all we know, shoplifting could be the family business and the shop manager would be highly critical if the same child returned.

Such an example is not one of bullying but it highlights the fact that so many people believe that teachers ought to sort out everything. There are other agencies, not least parents, who are responsible for the children too and must play their part.

Does it all work?

If the school says that these **approaches** and strategies have proved useful in dealing with aggressive children, it does tend to prove that the problem most certainly exists. If the school says that these ideas solve the problem and that there is no bullying, no one will believe the school. We all know there is a problem.

The truth is of course that schools are ongoing, living communities. One does not solve anything once and for all. Immunising the girls against rubella one year, no matter how well organised or pure the vaccine, does not solve the problem for ever. Each new intake of pupils has to learn how to behave, as 11-, 13-, 15-year-olds. But it should be possible to create an atmosphere, an ethos, in school in which maltreatment of one's peers is not acceptable and is openly discussed – an atmosphere in which incidents are reported, recorded and dealt with; a policy understood and followed.

The example given of the writer's son was 'solved' by the police warning off the aggressor within a couple of hours. However, the culprit then tried to make matters worse by making sure his friends gave my son a hard time *at school*. That was the school's problem and ours and it lasted just a day or two. We wrote, put the facts, named names and were delighted with the outcome. The boys were seen and warned and it all blew over pretty quickly. Maybe it would not have if we had stayed quiet for fear of reprisal.

Perhaps this is a good moment to refer to the model shown in Figure 3.1. It may not be perfect but it does try to show that early discussion of the possibility of bullying *could* lead directly to no incidents occurring. At the other extreme a bully might return again and again to his unacceptable behaviour provoking incidents.

In the inner city there are youngsters suffering from startling disadvantages. Those with stunted growth, bad burns scars, harelips as well as non-English speaking refugees, all are quite likely to become victims of the strong, mindless bully, alongside the feeble and the bookworm. The suggestion is, however, that the policy, the discussion and the firmness in handling the potential and the actuality of bullying help to create an atmosphere in which youngsters do not get away with it. The rub is, of course, that the atmosphere is perceived differently by pupils and teachers. The predictable

Figure 3.1: Dealing with bullying – actions and outcomes

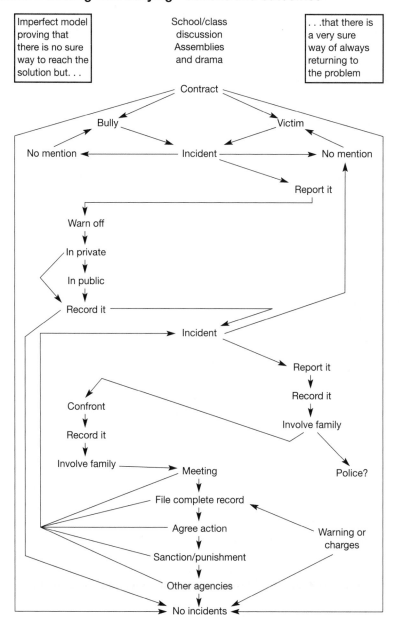

delusion of the deputy head is that she or he thinks that they see the truth of what is going on in the playground.

Will the teachers ever see it all? Whatever the answer they must continue to keep proper records of a proven, minor incident, then forgive and promote the relationships involved. Children might then learn to be very wary of what the outcome of a major incident would be. It is foolish to ignore minor incidents as trivial. Teachers must then follow their own advice and hope that there are no ongoing or major incidents happening about which they know nothing. They have got to make it worthwhile for children to bring the teachers in, so that they can solve what is possible, report and refer elsewhere what isn't and never fear to admit that children are sometimes nasty to each other.

Professional concerns

I began this chapter by putting the teaching situation into an inner-city context. We conclude by putting the teacher and the bully into a teaching perspective. The teacher's professional concern is with the bully and his victim, as pupils. It cannot however, with the best will in the world, be the total preoccupation. If what follows appears to be off the subject, I make no apology. The wonder is not that teachers deal quite successfully with some bullying but that they have time to handle any of it at all.

Thirty years ago teaching might have been considered a fairly straightforward professional task. One prepared, one taught, one marked books and reported on achievement. Pupils were prepared for public examinations, all sat down in June and the papers were sent off. There were sports days, concerts, speech days and prizegivings. There were detentions and the notorious punishment book. These words do not hanker after those days, with all their faults, but so much has happened to the teaching world that many teachers and observers of education are now left breathless at what is expected of the profession. So often, too, demands have been made without the resources being made available to fulfil them. The overall task has burgeoned to extremes.

Once, each of us in the profession was a teacher. Now, even taking into account the differences that an elevated post may make, it is difficult to tell whether we are teacher, friend, public enemy, social worker, doctor, accountant, personnel manager, counsellor, judge, jury, police officer, lawyer, Father Christmas or Florence Nightingale. Additions to the task load and to the curriculum during recent years have left some fine teachers punch-drunk.

Think about it. The public examination system begins now in mid-April, involving all years 11,12 and 13, and goes on for two months. Much of the marking and individual testing is now done on site by teachers who are unable to teach mainstream classes and who thus occupy specialist rooms to the detriment of younger pupils for much of that time. Endless moderating meetings are demanded by the boards, taking teachers away from the 'chalk face' time and time again.

The whole concept of negotiating and consulting (with pupils, among ourselves, with the authority and parents) occupies thousands of hours of meetings. What that does to the general atmosphere of schools and learning can only be guessed at. Having 'supply' or 'cover' teachers, sometimes several times a day, no matter if the system pays for it or not, is not good for pupils, discipline or continuity of courses. Readers who are teachers will know that.

The number of subjects somehow expected to 'appear' on the timetable for teachers to pass on to the next generation has nearly doubled. Some of them are, without doubt, the political flavour of the month: Business Studies, Commerce, Accountancy, Catering, Leisure Pursuits, Computing, Careers – these are some of the more obvious ones. Consider also boys' subjects for girls and vice versa (adding to the load of both), Consumer Awareness, Industry Links, Work Experience, Aids, Sex Education, Travel and Tourism, Sexism, Child Abuse, Racism, Alcoholism, Drug Abuse, Health Education, Nutrition, Child Care, Equal Opportunities, Community Service, the Third World, the Elderly, Media Studies – Oh! and Bullying. Add to all that the constraints placed upon teachers and heads by new legislation, the additional considerations required by pupil and parent power and the time taken up by records of achievement, continuous assessment, local budget management (with heads of average secondary schools managing some £2 million a year) and we get some idea of why pupils in the street don't always know who the six wives of Henry VIII were! I wonder if the amount of government interference in education increases in perfect ratio to the number of 'isms' ex-teachers now advising the government can think of.

Some secondary school teachers are still teaching 400+ different children a week. A 60–70 hour week is not uncommon, much of it spent in exasperating negotiations, meetings and continual justification of one's actions. The mental exhaustion has to be experienced to be understood.

A lot of discussion has taken place in recent times about methods of teaching, particularly whether we have children in rows facing the teacher! Teachers, as always, have been caught in the middle of 'experts' vying with each other for sound-bite headlines about what's best for our children in our schools and what teachers should be told to do today, tomorrow or the day after. One wonders if the gradual abolition of 'battery-taught' children in rows with narrow discipline and curriculum methods – unsatisfactory though that was in many ways – might just have left little room for free-range bullies.

Summary

That is the background against which the teacher operates. The bottom line is that everyone has the right to go home happy at the end of the day (and with the same number of teeth and amount of property they arrived with!), be they pupils or teachers and whether it be a normal school day or at the end of a difficult interview. The teacher's onerous task is to see that, as far as possible, it always happens. Even the culprit and his family have the right to go home feeling they have been fairly treated. Which nearly brings us back to our opening 'joke'.

The task is always to open up the field for discussion and put it on the agenda of the school, building relationships in an open and learning atmosphere in which bullying is unacceptable. There are so many pressing and important things for the teacher to do for the benefit of all pupils.

The task must be to anticipate, prepare, prevent and deal with bullying if it arises and when it is reported, and to take whatever time it needs to put the situation right. Teachers continue to strive to do just that.

4

■ ■ ■

A primary school approach

LINDA FROST

- ▶ Identifying potential situations and observing behaviour
- ▶ Structure of the peer group
- ▶ Protecting the child who tells
- ▶ Empowering children
- ▶ Involving parents

The problem with bullying, as with education itself, is that almost everyone has had a personal bad experience or has an anecdote they can quote about someone who has.

Being the emotive subject it is, involved parties hardly ever view bullying with detachment. Opinions are entrenched and polarised from the outset, because it appears to be a clean-cut issue – X child bullied Y. What are you going to do about it?

Initial reaction

My initial response to a bullying incident in school is to talk it through individually with the children who are involved. This is often exasperating for the victim and seldom seen as helpful to the bully either, as a bully rarely sees him/herself as being in the wrong, and the ensuing reports seldom combine to form a coherent picture of the incident. What it does serve to achieve, though, is a framework in which disagreements are aired and both sides at least have the opportunity to express an opinion and feel that someone is listening to them and that their viewpoint matters.

In the course of these discussions, two words are frequently overused by the bully. They are 'just' and 'only' – 'I was just playing with her' and 'I only tapped his ear with my foot'.

It is helpful to tell the children that these two words are not allowed in any explanation. They invariably serve only to justify and lessen the offence in the eyes of the perpetrator.

It can also help to keep these time-consuming processes to a minimum if questions are short, sharp and unambiguous. 'What did you do wrong?' leaves little room for needless argument and requires one of two specific answers: either 'nothing' or an admission of some understanding of how an action or attitude contributed to this negative situation. A 'nothing' answer might be accepted after explanation at face value or amended to one accepting some degree of responsibility for the outcome. 'If I asked your opponent what you did wrong, what would he say?' is also a useful way of encouraging a child to see a different point of view.

In the school situation, talk is the most powerful weapon in the armoury. We talk to children, we talk to parents, we talk to colleagues. I often wonder if a compulsory dose of laryngitis wouldn't work wonders in fulfilling the other aspects covered by the head teacher's job description!

It is also helpful if children answer these specific questions. Often 'What did you do wrong?' gets the response, 'He was rude to me this morning and ...' and this followed by an immense dissertation on the shortcomings of the other protagonist. Whilst giving an indication of the degree of resentment of the one child towards the other, it again avoids the issue and needs redirecting towards identifying the specific incidents or attitudes which could be changed to ameliorate the situation.

Talking is the first line of defence because it takes the heat out of the situation, allows a forum for views to be expressed, and shows to the other children that the matter is viewed seriously and that adults will listen. This is a most important aspect if children are to have the confidence to trust us and seek our help if they are bullied.

Defining the problem

Before you can hope to deal with bullying, you need to define it. I wouldn't attempt to provide a formal definition of bullying, but in my school I have found that bullying:

- varies from situation to situation and from child to child;
- depends on status in the peer group;
- varies with the degree of personal stress involved;
- can be not only physical but verbal;
- can be conveyed purely by body language;
- can include isolating the victim by influencing the rest of the peer group;
- can be as subtle as a curl of the lip or a cut of the eye;
- can be as obvious as a bloody nose or a kick in the groin.

The following illustrate a number of situations which I would consider involve at least some degree of bullying:

- following someone or menacing stares;
- mother-cussing, which is when children make derogatory remarks about each other's mother, often implying prostitution, obesity, or being racist in

undertone. This can even be stylised down to saying 'M' and seen as an enormous provocation by some children. I have yet to discover how to sanction appropriately a child who says 'M' to another;

- swearing, bearing malice and 'getting even';
- rubbishing other children's work;
- wilful destruction of someone else's work or property;
- stealing – valued possessions, packed lunches, etc.;
- intimidation and extortion;
- physical violence;
- mental cruelty.

Mental cruelty seems to have a very damaging effect. For example, which is worse, a bully saying, 'Your mum's new baby is going to be deformed just like you' or the bully giving the victim a punch in the eye? Both bring immediate misery, but the effects of the former may still cause anxiety when the bruise from the latter has faded.

Survey

Recently, I did a survey with our new Year 3 intake two weeks after they had started in the junior department. Only 5% felt that they had never been bullied. Over half felt they had been bullied in their first two weeks. However, on further examination, it seemed that the timescale was confused. Once children had identified someone as a bully, the impression and memory remained very strong, even if not reinforced by future experience. Having experienced bullying, the perpetrator then remained a person to be feared, and further interaction involving that person was always viewed at best negatively, or sometimes fearfully, hence the bullying persisted in the victim's mind.

I also asked children, in confidence, to identify children they believed to be very bad bullies. Four or five names appeared continuously and this was mirrored in responses from children throughout the school.

There were factors which many of these bully figures shared. Often they were the youngest sibling in the family. Each of them felt they were bullied, not bullies, and constantly unfairly picked upon. Most of the parents of these children were unwilling to believe their child's bullying behaviour. Girl bullies often resorted to mental cruelty, whereas boy bullies were more often more physical. This may seem a sexist generalisation, but this was our experience, at least in the past. However, we have noticed a slight increase in girls using violence – a worrying development we hope does not continue.

Sages

One of the interesting factors to emerge from the survey was that there were a small group of children who claimed they had never been bullied. These were not bullies but children whose demeanour, behaviour and attitude exempted them from this kind of interaction. I nicknamed this group the 'sages'. They were usually intelligent, non-contentious, seen by other children as fair and generally held in high esteem by their peer group.

Outsiders

Another group I called the 'outsiders'. These shared some characteristics with the sages, but were principally children who 'didn't need anyone', and to a great extent they remained uninvolved in the group dynamics. These children tended to go their own way and had little effect on their peers, either positive or negative.

Victims

Yet another group appeared after discussion with the 'sages'. These were the 'victims'. Often they were children of low prestige in the group. They were often seen as misfits, either for reasons of appearance, lack of friends or other trivial reasons. The basic problem was one of body language. These children almost seemed to invite bullying by compliance rather than aggression, or by being thoroughly irritating. They had low self-esteem and didn't tell if they were victimised. Often they would cry or stamp their feet but would not follow this up by asking for support. They therefore offered all the excitement of an anguished victim with no fear of repercussions. I asked one child who was identified as a victim why she didn't ask for help. She responded, 'Bullied? I don't get bullied. It was much worse at my last school. It's better here.'

While trying to sort out the various problems of the victims, I found that many of the children who behaved in a way that invited bullying seemed to have parents who had suffered bullying themselves in their school days. In fact, the behaviour and body language of the children were remarkably similar to that of their parents. In some cases the behaviour was a form of attention seeking – one child persistently stood in the playground goalmouth, where he was continually jostled and hit with the football. For these children, any attention is better than none. It also reinforces their self-image of being a victim.

Bullies

The last groups to emerge were the bullies. Often it was physically impossible to pick them out – they weren't necessarily the biggest or strongest. They had no clearly defined ranking in the peer group order. Some were respected but feared, some had physical or other skills which were admired. One group were outcasts who managed to keep friends only by offering treats and were socially isolated. Often, like their victims, they suffered from very low self-esteem, but had channelled their weakness offensively rather than accepting their fate compliantly. They saw an aggressive role as one necessary for survival and had built upon it to reinforce their prestige.

Secret bullies

Another group the children identified as bullies was a surprise to me. The behaviour they showed to adults was totally at variance with that they showed to their peers. They gave the impression of being class leaders – the most popular child in the class. In effect, their dominance was accepted and the response of the other pupils was to appease or 'keep on the right side of them'. Such children came to expect that others would carry their coats and books or share their belongings to remain in favour.

A thorough knowledge of the dynamics of the group involved, especially from the children's viewpoint, can therefore be highly enlightening and can help when planning positive strategies.

Supervision and observation

Bullying flourishes where supervision is minimal. Travelling to school, leaving, lunch-breaks, playtimes, moving between classes and 'playing out' after school and at weekends affords the bully the best opportunities.

Identifying areas in which bullying thrives is helpful when considering positioning supervisors at lunch or playtime. I asked the meals supervisors to mark the location of any act of bullying with an X on the map of the school for a period of one week (see Figure 4.1). The outcome was predictable but reinforced the need for supervisors to be strategically placed. (You can ask the children to do the same – they may show up places adults did not even consider.)

I then took a video camera around to these areas during a lunch break. Surprise, surprise! Smiling children walked in gentle fashion to the stairs without the customary pushing and jumping and the huddled groups behind the play apparatus and out of sight in the toilet entrance melted away as soon as the camera approached. A case for CCTV?

Figure 4.1 The school playground – X marks the bullying spot

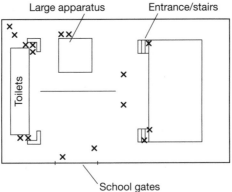

Merely observing a child's interaction in one of these situations, when he is unaware of being watched, can clearly show the number of negative contacts a bully can make in a very short period. If the parents can be persuaded to come into the school without the child knowing and look at their child at play for half an hour from some vantage point, they are often totally amazed at their child's behaviour and more willing to co-operate to improve it.

In a 45-minute lunch break, one father witnessed his son instigate five separate incidents involving taunting, tripping, barging and threatening with no provocation. By the end of the break, the father was groaning with embarrassment and far more willing to support the school in a behaviour modification programme for his son.

Parental support

Parental support is crucial if a child's behaviour is to be changed. Sometimes a child feels his parents will be more impressed if he can 'stand up for himself'. Sometimes parents have different views of their child's 'macho' behaviour, particularly when it is one parent only who bears the lion's share of the responsibility for 'picking up the pieces'. In some cases, this parent can be enlisted to persuade the other partner into a frank discussion with the child over a changed set of values to make life more tolerable and less stressful for all concerned.

Living up to a tough image to impress people who matter can be just as precarious and stressful as waiting for the next round of bullying to start.

Anti-bullying policy

It helps if a school has a clear anti-bullying policy from the outset. Although an anti-bullying policy is required by law, some school policies are too ambivalent. Ideally, parents and children should sign an agreed behaviour contract on admission. This should accurately reflect the social aims and ethos of the school and delineate the range of sanctions that will be enforced for non-compliance. This contract should be drawn up in consultation with all the involved parties: teachers, parents, children and governors. The Local Education Authority should have helpful guidance, if you are lucky.

Your anti-bullying approach could be explained in a letter home to parents as follows:

Dear Parents,
I should like your help with a matter that concerns us all.
Just recently there have been children involved in isolated incidents of violent behaviour. These concern very few pupils, but are carried over out of school at hometime and are causing great anxiety to the victims and to younger children and their parents.

Our school has a very good reputation in the area. It is one of the most controlled, and the majority of pupils can be relied upon to act in a responsible manner. I am very concerned that the behaviour of a few should not reflect on everyone else, and that a few irresponsible people should not be allowed to get away with intimidating and frightening others.

We spend an enormous amount of time in school sorting out children's problems. We allow 'time out' for children to calm down and avoid incidents, and encourage them to talk about and share problems.

Please ask your child not to 'give as good as s/he gets'. This only exacerbates the problem and every child involved in a row always sees him/herself as the victim, not the offender.

We hope you will help in the following ways:

- *Please let us know if your child has been bullied or threatened, or hurt by another child.*
- *If your child is one who punches first and thinks later, please have a serious talk with him/her.*

I view this as such a serious problem that I intend in future to suspend children who have borne grudges and taken revenge days later, or ganged up with others to pick on one child, or indulge in violent, unprovoked behaviour.

I do hope that you will do all you can to support us in stamping out this undesirable trend towards violence. It is in everyone's interest that such antisocial behaviour should be dealt with most severely.

Yours sincerely,

The reaction I received from parents to such a letter was that the majority were reassured and pleased; a small minority implied this was an unfair device to suspend their child.

Right to be safe

Each class should participate in drawing up an acceptable code of behaviour which emphasises the 'dos' rather than the 'don'ts'. I think the message should be quite simple: children have a right to feel safe and protected in school. Children who recognise they are about to violate this right should be allowed 'time out' to cool down and ask for help to resolve the difficulty. All adults have an obligation to support this principle and all children should be encouraged to share in the responsibility for the safety and wellbeing of each other. Children who do not make use of the appropriate channels, and who are consistently guilty of premeditated attacks or violent revenge over long-held grudges, should be suspended.

However, these extreme measures should not be used in isolation. It is vital to build up an ongoing picture of the child's behaviour patterns, keeping close contact with the parents to try to establish reasons for the problems, and seeking ways of moderating their negative effects. Of course, rewarding good behaviour is part of this.

Children may turn to bullying when weighed down by inherited anger or highly stressed by some external social factor. Identifying with a trusted adult may be all that is needed. If the parents are willing to co-operate at an early stage, a two-way diary, stressing the child's positive achievements at home and school, may be adequate to raise self-esteem and counter feelings of persecution which start the spiral of negative behaviour.

Incidents log

Negative incidents should be separately logged, indicating the date, time, place and name of the adult filing the report (see Figure 4.2). It helps if these forms are colour-coded for easy access (e.g. behaviour reports, orange, and parent interviews, bright blue). These reports help to establish any pattern (e.g. playground behaviour significantly worse after a weekend) and also chart whether a child's misbehaviour varies according to the approach, status or attitude of the person dealing with the incident. Teachers should contribute to behaviour reports, as should all staff concerned with caring for children in school: secretary, support staff, meals supervisors and schoolkeeper – all see a different facet of a child's behaviour. The wider the consensus, the less easy it becomes to blame 'a simple clash of personalities' for the child's problem.

Figure 4.2 An example of an incident log

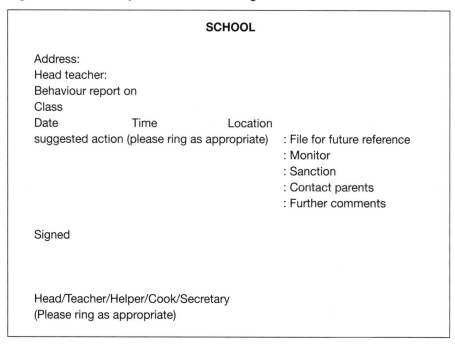

SCHOOL

Address:
Head teacher:
Behaviour report on
Class
Date   Time   Location
suggested action (please ring as appropriate)   : File for future reference
                                                 : Monitor
                                                 : Sanction
                                                 : Contact parents
                                                 : Further comments

Signed

Head/Teacher/Helper/Cook/Secretary
(Please ring as appropriate)

Telling

Children should be strongly encouraged to think of 'telling' as positive behaviour, not as 'sneaking'. In this way, the bully cannot be sure of maintaining a conspiracy of silence and it becomes more difficult for him or her to single out a victim without interference from others. However, one of the difficulties which can result from 'telling' is retaliation.

When an adult intervenes to protect a victim, unless the sanction is very powerful it will be effective only for as long as the situation continues to be closely monitored. As soon as the bully sees his opportunity, he will be tempted to seek revenge. The victim is then in an even more vulnerable position and dependent on remaining in proximity to the protecting adult for safety. The victim has therefore sacrificed freedom of movement for what might be temporary sanctuary, unless we ensure that the whole school is safe for all children.

The alternative is to create very clear rules for an institution and if you wish, support them with draconian sanctions, but what is the benefit if all you are achieving is removing the problem from your patch to someone else's?

'Miss, if I kick him will you suspend me?'
'Yes!'
'But what about if I leave him alone in school but get him when he's
walking down the street on Sunday afternoon?'

So we need to ensure that at least in the school the victim is safe and the bully may have to have his or her freedom restricted. It may not solve the long-term problem but it will provide much-needed limits for the bully and relative safety for the victim.

Problems

The first problem is that we have to realise that our sphere of influence is limited to the school environs and the bully's interpretation of our actions may well be that we are the ones who are the biggest bullies of all. In other words, it's a dog-eat-dog world, so keep biting even if you're being bitten because only the biggest dog survives in the end.

The second problem is one of the expectation. If children see bullying as endemic, rather like the common cold – you suffer a bout of it but there's no known cure so you put up with it and hope it goes away soon – then we never find out how serious and widespread the bullying problem is.

The third problem is one of apathy. Bullying becomes a cheap spectator sport – the 'cheer it on and be glad it's not you' mentality.

Often the instigator is the brighter child who stays out of trouble him/herself but winds up someone with a short temper and then stands back to enjoy the show. Sometimes this kind of intelligence can be turned round to work positively to protect the more vulnerable class members by ensuring that the instigator becomes a mentor instead.

Solutions

I believe that the solution to all these problems and the most effective sanction must be peer group pressure. Children should be empowered, with the support of adults, to be made accountable for their actions and responsible for each other's safety. It utilises the key groups I have already identified – sages, bullies, victims and outsiders – in a forum such as a school council or what the children may call a 'bully court'.

If each child is given this forum to identify and debate antisocial behaviour towards himself or his peers, then every child assumes the role of protector. The identifying force ceases to be only the victim. It becomes everyone.

In a bully court situation (see Chapter 1), the sages assume the role of advocate and improve their perceived status still further. The bullies see the balance of power shifting away from them and their opportunities for retaliation diminished. The outsiders are drawn in as impartial observers. The victim becomes the focus of everyone's concern.

In a situation where children are regularly given the opportunity to discuss issues and change practice, they feel empowered and respond more readily to the need for social responsibility in a wider context.

Given this forum from a young age, they feel part of the justice system, not just passive recipients. Developing skills for citizenship must start at the earliest possible age. Then the ethos of a child's right to be heard when he has a problem or feels strongly about an issue will be firmly established within the school philosophy.

Summary

We must look at the problem of bullying dispassionately and deal with it in partnership with parents using this raft of measures to encourage children to be confident and feel supported as they grow into responsible, empowered citizens. Current government emphasis on teaching good citizenship skills reflects the growing concern over violence and antisocial behaviour in our schools. You can overcome the problem by employing practical strategies, such as bully courts, a whole-school anti-bullying policy, two-way involvement with parents, the acceptance of telling and sharing problems, and encouraging children to have a sense of communal responsibility. The insidious power of the school bully can then be undermined eventually and a more responsible, positive set of social values can be established as the norm for all children.

Only by instituting a clear anti-bullying policy and ongoing dialogue with parents will we develop in our children a belief that telling is right and that we share a communal responsibility for one another.

5

■ ■ ■

Bullying and the under fives

MICHELE ELLIOTT

- ▶ Reports of bullying among the under fives has increased
- ▶ Practical suggestions for helping this age group
- ▶ Activities for young children

'Bullying is part of human nature, something children must learn to cope with if they are to survive the rough-and-tumble of everyday life.' This can be a hard line to swallow for those who work with tender four- and five-year-olds. Little ones may find the playground jungle a sinister place at first, so it is often thought that any distress shown by young children is just natural. In fact, some nursery nurses don't think that bullying affects their charges. One nursery nurse said, 'It was only children playing – it wasn't bullying.' She was dealing with a parent's concern that her child was being consistently punched and pushed by another child. It turned out that the punching child was lashing out not only at school but also at home and just about everywhere else. She was only four, but she knew she was hurting others; she attacked them only when there was no one looking. Yes, she had problems, but she *was* a bully.

The mother of the bullied child also recognised that her child had problems. Sam was having difficulty outside the nursery school, as well. His mother said that she took him to the toy library, where he was pushed over. 'I hadn't even taken off his coat, but it's always like this. Other kids pick on him the whole time. Taking his toys, pulling his hair. Even when I'm there, I can't protect him every second.' Sam is only three and yet he is already a victim of bullying.

It seems surprising that bullying should be an issue for young children, but at Kidscape we have had a 40% increase in the number of cases involving children aged five and under. The actual numbers are still low compared with reported cases of older children, but it is a worrying trend.

A father rang to say that his five-year-old daughter had been threatened on the playground by a boy wielding a knife! When he complained that the other child had been readmitted to the school after a brief suspension, he was told that the boy 'had family problems'. He was also five years old. Of course, this was quite serious and might not be considered bullying. However, it turned out he had been bullying children since the age of three.

The mother of a four-year-old boy was in great distress after her son came home covered with mud and sporting a black eye. He had been set upon by a group of five-year-olds and told that he had better not tell or they would beat him up again the next day. Fortunately, the nursery school in this case took immediate action and the bullying was nipped in the bud.

If children as young as three or four might become victims and bullies, what can nursery nurses and reception teachers do? Is it best to make a big fuss or to leave children to sort it out? More and more nursery school teachers feel that bullying should be taken seriously and stopped from the earliest age. One teacher commented that the behaviour of children in her nursery school had definitely changed over the past 15 years. 'Children are more likely now to lash out at each other and to act out violence on the playground than they were in the past. I am alarmed that some children deliberately bully others and cannot seem to understand the concept of kindness. If we don't stop them bullying now I think we are laying the foundations for short-term misery and later adult aggression. After all, versions of the playground heavies and their victims are re-enacted in sitting rooms and boardrooms daily.'

It is common sense that tackling bullying issues with young children should eliminate a lot of problems for them as they grow up – both for victims and for bullies.

Who bullies?

Probably all young children bully once in a while – brothers and sisters, if no one else. Also young children may be so intent on getting what they want that they just bowl over anyone in their way. The child doesn't even realise that she or he is harming someone. Or a young child may go along with the crowd and say or do hurtful things without thinking through what they are doing.

While all children need to learn to get along with others, concern about young bullies should be focused more on the child who deliberately sets out to cause distress to another child or who is a danger to other young children, such as the child who brought the knife to school mentioned above. These are the children who have problems and may share the characteristics outlined in Chapter 1 of this book.

Who are the victims?

The under fives who become victims of bullying are described by their teachers as sensitive, gentle children. They are often not used to conflict, so when bullies come at them they don't know what to do. They frequently ask why someone would want to bully them – they've done nothing to deserve it and they haven't been treated this way before. The sad fact is that, from the bully's viewpoint, they make excellent targets because they are nice and won't fight back. They might even cry, a bonus for the bully. If you could point out one 'fault' of these victims, it would be that they are too nice! In a nursery or play-group which doesn't tolerate bullying, they have no problems.

There are, however, some children who seem to get bullied everywhere – at school, parties, activities, the local playground, the toy library – you name it and they are bullied. These are the children who seem almost to thrive on the negative attention they get when they are bullied. It is as if the bullying confirms their opinions of themselves that they are worthless and deserve what is happening to them. There may be problems in the lives of these children or they may have been bullied right from the day when they started nursery school and never recovered their confidence.

Practical suggestions

Bullies depend for their success on a code of silence. It is based on, of all things, honour ('It's wrong to tell tales') or on fear ('Don't tell anyone or I'll thump you'). Either way, it prevents children from telling when they have been bullied or have seen someone being bullied.

To crack the code of silence, those who work with the under fives may try to:

- become 'telling' schools. The nursery nurses and teachers make it clear that bullying is unacceptable. Children have an obligation to *tell* if they are bullied or see bullying take place;
- ensure that the adults do something when they are told. Children must be able to rely on a sympathetic and helpful response if they do tell. In this way they learn that speaking out will make things better; keeping quiet will make things worse;
- constantly monitor the trouble spots, like the playground. If lack of staff is a problem (where isn't it?), enlist parent helpers;
- use stories, activities, art, etc. to reinforce the anti-bullying messages (see box on pages 56–7 for ideas);
- put up a photograph of each child and write something good about the child under the photo. Try just a few words, like A Good Friend or Helps Others or Kind Person or Good to Pets. Change the words once a week and ask children to help think of good things about each other;
- give stickers or rewards of some sort each day to a child who has been nice (sometimes it is difficult to 'catch' a problem child being nice, but it is worth the effort to reinforce good behaviour). Children will vie to be good if they get recognition. Make sure that every child gets recognised;
- organise a 'Kindness Week' and have the children draw posters. Give prizes for the best posters and ribbons or certificates for children being kind to others. Involve parents, if possible.

Set up student helpers

The idea of using students to help others is as old as teaching itself. I used this method years ago when I had a classroom of 34 five-year-old children and a few older children were making it their business to bully the younger ones. These ideas work better if there is a nursery attached to a primary school so there is a pool of older children available. Try to:

- assign an older 'helper' to act as an adviser, protector and mentor to each new child. Usually older or bigger children pick on younger or smaller ones *who are alone*. This eliminated that problem and the older children took pride in helping 'their' charges;
- set up student 'counsellors' who are chosen anonymously by the children and teachers as 'other children you would most likely seek out to talk to about a problem'. This is particularly good for children who don't have close friends. It may help to foster friendships. The 'counsellors' talk to the bullied children and go with them to tell the teachers, so it is still the responsibility of the adult to sort out the problems. Children sometimes find it easier to talk initially to other children than to adults.

Help the bully

Sometimes it is possible to help a bully by recognising that she or he, too, is a victim; perhaps unloved or mistreated at home, or covering for a feeling of personal inadequacy by dominating others. In these cases, treating the underlying cause may also eradicate the bullying. For example, a child doing badly is encouraged to work hard and excel at something – drawing, gymnastics, plasticine modelling, skipping, putting together puzzles, racing – and may in the process gain enough approval to stop bullying. The younger the child, the better chance we have of changing their behaviour. Reforming older chronic bullies is not easy. (Significantly, when schools organise meetings to discuss the problem of bullying, it is usually the parent of the victim who turns up.)

When working with a young child who is bullying, try to:

- remain calm;
- find out the facts;
- talk to the child to find out if she or he is upset or has been bullied and is lashing out as a reaction;
- find out if the child realises that she or he is bullying and hurting someone else – sometimes young children don't know how their actions affect others;
- talk with the parents of the victim, if possible, to set things right and to avoid the bullying carrying on;
- set up a behaviour chart using stars or stickers – give a reward for every five or ten stars but make sure that the time between the good behaviour and the reward is not too great, especially for very young children. For example, some children may need hourly help to behave while others can go for a whole day.

If the parents of a bully ask for advice from teachers, suggest that they try:

- working with you to figure out the best way to help their child;
- talking to their child and explaining that, whatever problems there may be, bullying is not the way to solve them;
- working out a 'behaviour plan' and reward good behaviour;
- arranging a daily or weekly report from the school to them and vice versa;
- setting up a star chart on the refrigerator and giving a star for each good report from school, followed by some sort of reward after so many stars;
- seeking counselling or professional help if the child does not respond after a reasonable time. The child may have problems which need to be sorted out before he or she can stop bullying.

Help the victims

Some bullies, especially young ones who receive help, can be sorted out. Often, however, we have to work around bullies by teaching children how to cope with threats and how to avoid attracting them in the first place. Some children seem more prone to bullying than others. This may result from factors beyond their control: the colour of their skin, for example, or some striking physical feature – being above or below average height – that sets them apart from the others. Or it may be that, if they are repeatedly bullied, children start acting like victims. If this happens, children can be helped, both at school and at home. Try helping them to:

- walk tall and straight, in a confident way, rather than hunched over, looking scared and uncertain;
- practise looking in the mirror and saying 'No' or 'Leave me alone' in a clear voice, looking into their own eyes as they say it. A firm rebuff will often deter a bully who is looking for signs of weakness;
- role-play, something that has been used with great success with young children both in schools and at home. Act out the threatening situation and practise responding calmly but firmly. This type of imaginative play can also help defuse some of the anger that builds up inside children who are persistently bullied;
- ignore the bullying, pretend not to be upset – turn and walk away quickly and tell a grown-up;
- use humour. It is more difficult to bully a child who refuses to take the bullying seriously. This is especially useful with verbal bullying;
- stay with groups of children, if possible;
- respond to taunts saying the same thing over and over. This is called the broken record approach. For example, to a taunt such as 'You've got glasses', tell the child to respond with 'Thank you' and just keep saying it over and over – 'Thank you, thank you.' It is a silly response and it becomes boring for the bully after awhile.

In order for children to feel confident using some of these ideas, practise with them and see if they can come up with others. Obviously the ability of the child to try these things depends upon their age and maturity. Adult supervision and intervention with young children is vital.

Nursery teachers can also try to give children confidence by:

- assuring them that the bullying is not their fault;
- telling the child that you like him or her (bullied children feel unlovable);
- helping them to stop any bad habits which might be contributing to their being bullied (such as picking their nose or wiping disgusting things on their sleeves or grabbing toys from other children).

If a child continues to be bullied, it may be that counselling would help. Like the bully, the chronic victim and his or her family may need some professional guidance to prevent the child from becoming a life-long victim.

Summary

The one thing that emerges time and time again in all surveys is that bullying is one of the most difficult social problems children have to deal with – and it's probably been made harder by the outmoded notion that everyone should grin and bear it and that the best way to deal with any problem is a stiff upper lip. But this tacit approval of bullying is one inheritance we needn't pass on to the next generation ... they need not suffer in silence.

ANTI-BULLYING ACTIVITIES FOR YOUNG CHILDREN

Rip-rip

Give each child a large cut-out figure of a child, on A3 paper (or smaller if you can't manage the larger paper). Explain that the 'child' is a whole, happy person who is going to school one morning feeling good. But during the day other children make comments or do things which make the child feel bad. Ask the children to make a little rip in their cut-out figure every time they think the figure is hurt by something in the story you are going to read out.

Rip-rip story

I can't wait to get to school. I know it's going to be fun. Oh, look, here come some other kids.

'Hello, my name is Jane. What's yours?'

What are they saying to me? They said I was ugly and they wouldn't speak to me.   **(Rip-rip)**

Here come some other children. Maybe they'll be friendlier. What are they doing? Oh, they're looking away and pretending not to hear the mean children calling me names. I wish they would do something. I feel so lonely.   **(Rip-rip)**

I guess I'll just play by myself today.   **(Rip-rip)**

On the playground some of the children wait until no one is looking and then they trip me over. One of them says not to tell or I'll be in trouble. I don't tell.   **(Rip-rip)**

No one will sit by me at lunch. The mean children have told them not to talk to me or eat with me.   **(Rip-rip)**

When my mummy comes to collect me, she asks me if school was fun today. What should I tell her?

You can make up your own story or add or subtract from this one. The children's figures will be in shreds by now. Discuss with them how it feels to be picked on like this and how they could have helped the cut-out child. Make a list of their suggestions and post it up in the class. Remind them how comments and actions can affect people and encourage them to make kind comments to each other.

That's my potato!

Give each child a potato and ask them to look at it carefully to see things like green marks, spots, its shape, 'eyes', etc. Try to ensure that the potatoes are not completely uniform. They should give their potato a name and make up a story about it:

- What does it do for fun?
- What kinds of food it likes and dislikes.
- How old it is.
- Does it have brothers and sisters?
- And so on.

Have the children tell their Potato Story to each other in small groups or to you, if you have enough time and not too many children. Then put all the potatoes in a bag, jumble them and put them on a table for the children to come and find their potato. (If the children are likely to disagree, you will have to put a dot or some mark to avoid arguments.)

Explain that it is the small differences that make people individual but they are still all people, just as the potatoes may each be different but they are all still potatoes. Once you take the time to look at someone and really get to know them, you can see that person is not the same as everyone else and that differences are no reason to bully anyone. After all, just because their potato may have three 'eyes' and someone else's potato may have six 'eyes', does that mean that their potato should be singled out for bad treatment?

Drawings

Ask the children to draw a picture of a playground where everyone is happy and no one is being bullied. Then ask for a picture of a playground where children are being bullied. Use the pictures to have a discussion about bullying.

6

■ ■ ■

Helping victims

ANDREW MELLOR

- ▶ Bullying is complex and has no single simple solution
- ▶ Research shows that it is widespread, but there are significant variations between schools
- ▶ To help victims effectively it is necessary to create a school ethos in which bullying is unacceptable
- ▶ Head teachers have a legal duty to do all in their power to protect children from bullying, but the law, as it operates at present, leaves victims who seek redress facing a battle which could cause as much psychological damage as the original bullying
- ▶ Young people who have been bullied have a right to be fully involved in any discussion about what coping strategy should be applied. They may also have an important role to play in the development of anti-bullying policies in schools

Bullying cannot be cured just by treating the victims. They are not suffering from a disease but are involved in complex social situations, each of which is unique and requires individual action. Parents, teachers, friends and bystanders all play a part in the confrontation between bully and victim so they must also be included in any coping strategy.

Lone parents or teachers have little chance of successfully helping victims unless a school has a clear, well-developed, anti-bullying policy. Some do not, despite the publicity given to this issue in the past few years. In such cases the first step must be to create a climate of concern: teachers and head teachers must understand the feeling of helplessness experienced by victims.

> I think I felt that I was the only person that had ever been bullied and if I told anybody they would think I was stupid and a wimp.

11-year-old girl

Victims need to be reassured that they are not alone and that it could happen to anyone; all it takes is to be in the wrong place at the wrong time. Such an assertion may contradict the popular wisdom of the playground:

I would say that bullying usually happens to people who are different (e.g. colour, religion or some disability). People who are shy or have a weak character are usually the ones who are bullied.

15-year-old girl

If victims believe this they may feel, however erroneously, that they are to blame for what has happened. The endless repetition of the bully's taunts can cause such distress that rational thought becomes impossible. Victims believe that they are being bullied because they are fat, bespectacled, shy or just different and that no one, least of all an adult, can help. It only takes one bad experience to confirm this belief:

When a friend told the teacher I was being bullied he said I was old enough to deal with it myself.

14-year-old girl

Lest we be too censorious of this girl's teacher it is well to remember that, until the 1990s, virtually no guidance was available to schools on how to deal with bullying. Official recognition of the problem had been limited. The Pack Report on Truancy and Indiscipline in Scottish Schools (1977) merely listed bullying as a form of indiscipline, without further comment. In 1989 the Elton Report on discipline in schools in England and Wales devoted three paragraphs to the subject. While three English paragraphs may be better than one or two Scottish words, this was not much progress in 12 years.

Elton recommended that head teachers and staff should:

- be alert to signs of racial harassment and bullying;
- deal firmly with all such behaviour;
- take action on clear rules which are backed by appropriate sanctions and systems to protect and support victims.

All perfectly valid points, but teachers may have difficulty in implementing these recommendations because victims and others are afraid to talk. The section on bullying concluded with a unique and vacuous recommendation that 'pupils should tell staff about serious cases of bullying and racial harassment of which they are aware'. The other recommendations in the report were aimed at adults such as teachers, parents and educational administrators. It is difficult to believe that any children would read this weighty tome, so it seems that this recommendation was included without much thought as to how it was to be implemented.

A firm and clear discipline policy will never succeed in tackling bullying unless strategies are adopted which encourage victims to seek adult help. The taboo against telling that exists in British society ensures that children will go through agonies before seeking help. It is not only the threat of physical retaliation that deters them but also the endlessly repeated playground taunts:

Tell-tale tit, your mammy cannae knit.
Your daddy cannae go to bed without a dummy-tit.

Scottish playground rhyme

School must create an atmosphere in which telling is always encouraged and teachers must create situations in which it is possible. But this still leaves the victim with the responsibility of judging whether an incident should be reported or shrugged off. Would the complaint be treated seriously and wisely?

I honestly don't know if I would tell someone if I was being bullied. I would feel I was being silly about the whole thing. I'd be too frightened in case I'd be laughed at.

15-year-old girl

Most older children will have learned through experience to assess the gravity of bullying and identify those incidents which are likely to be taken seriously – and which are the best adults to approach. However, younger children do not have this experience to draw on. Anything that is happening to them at the time is serious, and for all they know, permanent. Teachers of such children run the risk of being overwhelmed by trivia so it is perhaps understandable that they may on occasion seem less than welcoming.

Inspiration from Scandinavia

Fortunately, help and guidance on dealing with victims started to become available in the late 1980s, in the form of a number of books and the creation of specialised agencies such as Kidscape and ChildLine. This awakening of interest was largely a result of the European Teachers' Seminar on Bullying in Schools held in Stavanger, Norway in 1987. Many of the delegates, inspired or influenced by the Scandinavian example, later became involved in promoting research into anti-bullying strategies in their own countries.

When the Norwegians began to be concerned about bullying in the early 1970s they did not have a word of their own to describe the phenomenon so they borrowed the English word 'mobbing' from the work of renowned researcher Konrad Lorenz. Throughout the 1970s and 1980s there was extensive research and a government-funded campaign against bullying. This was in marked contrast to the situation in the UK where there was a paucity of large-scale research and only limited expressions of concern.

A sign of some official recognition came when I was awarded a grant by the Scottish Office Education Department to investigate bullying in ten Scottish secondary schools. The 942 pupils who completed questionnaires in February and March 1989 represented a cross-section of the Scottish secondary school population stretching from the inner city to the agricultural periphery of the country. The project set out to do two main things – to identify variations in the incidence of bullying and to investigate and describe successful coping strategies. The children's responses provided the assurance that being a victim of school bullying is a common experience. However, their candid comments also revealed the anguish of victims and how adults often underestimate the scale of the problem.

How many victims?

Half of the 942 pupils said that they had been bullied at least once or twice during their school careers; 44% admitted they had bullied someone else. Less than a third said that they had never been involved either as bully or victim. These figures seem all the more remarkable when it is realised that a narrow definition was borrowed from Norwegian researchers – 'Bullying is long-standing violence, mental or physical, conducted by an individual or a group against an individual who is not able to defend himself or herself in that actual situation.' One-off incidents and fights between equals were specifically excluded.

Many of the victims wrote about what had happened to them years before, but some revealed a current torment:

I am scared stiff all the time and my schoolwork is being affected. I am also scared to go out. I want to stand up to the girl who is bullying me because she is making my life a misery, but I can't.

14-year-old girl

The pupils were asked how often they had been bullied since Christmas. This was chosen as an occasion which all could remember well and provided an accurate measure of their experiences over the previous six to ten weeks. Six per cent of the children said that they had been bullied 'sometimes or more often' in this short time, which was identical to the proportion of victims found in the very large Norwegian government-sponsored survey carried out by Dan Olweus in 1983.

We must be cautious in making general assumptions from these findings because of the small size of the sample, but interesting trends were noticed which may be of use to teachers, parents and others who are trying to help victims.

Although boys and girls were equally likely to be victims during their school career as a whole, there were fewer girls than boys among recent victims. As children grow up they appear to be less likely to become victims, presumably developing protective or avoidance strategies of their own. But older girls seem to do this better than older boys, who sometimes feel that they have no one to turn to:

I have been picked on. People think I am nothing and say anything they want to me. Every day I feel rejected. It's not that people use violence much, but I feel as if I am treated as a dustbin. I do want to come forward about this but as I am leaving in a few months I don't see any reason to do so. Nor have I the courage.

16-year-old boy

Although the proportion of 15–16-year-old boys who were victims of bullying was relatively small (4%), their sense of alienation and failure could be severe:

Sometimes you feel like dying because you can't face up to it.

15-year-old boy

Twelve per cent of 15–16-year-old boys claimed that they had recently bullied others. For them there seems to be less shame in admitting to being a bully than in being a victim. Virtually all the girls who commented thought that the answer to bullying lay in the adoption of a collective remedy:

People who are being bullied feel as if they are alone in that problem and most people, if not everybody, are against them. They need to be shown that they are not alone and unless they tell somebody, nothing can be done.

15-year-old girl

Boys tended to suggest that victims should stand up for themselves. Quite a few said that they had taken up weightlifting or the martial arts, but with varying success:

I get bullied quite a lot. I try not to let it happen but I just can't find the courage to fight back. I do press-ups and weights to give me more muscle so I can fight back and have a chance of winning. I don't like fighting anyway. I think it's a mug's game.

15-year-old boy

Society expects its young men to be aggressive but, paradoxically, punishes those who fight and alienates those who reject violence. No wonder adolescents are sometimes mixed up. Sue Askew and Carol Ross have described the social pressures which force many boys to choose what is for them an inappropriate method of defence:

Toughness and aggression are approved of in boys – the argument goes as follows: boys are encouraged to be tough and stick up for themselves. This is not usually meant as an open encouragement for them to be violent, but more of a message that violence is all right if not taken to extremes ... and can, in many circumstances, be a way of improving social status with other boys.

from *Boys Don't Cry* (1988)

An older boy who is not aggressive and who is bullied by others may lose so much status that life becomes unbearable. Seeking help could be perceived as a further sign of weakness. Perhaps as a result of this only 38% of male victims had told someone else that they were being bullied, in contrast to 61% of girl victims. Given the success of older girls in avoiding bullying and their readiness to seek help, it is clear that schools must develop a telling ethos. Nobody, of whatever age or whatever sex, must ever feel that there is any shame in speaking openly about fears or concerns.

There are many potential benefits in store if this ideal can be achieved. Children may talk about other problems they are experiencing at school or at home; most will be fairly minor but others could be of the utmost gravity. Encouraging children to talk about being bullied by other children will make it easier for them to talk about being victimised or abused by adults. But this will only happen if schools are successful in creating an atmosphere of openness – and that will be difficult unless there is a national climate of concern about bullying and aggression.

Just flavour of the month?

Between 1990 and 1995 a national climate of concern seemed to have grown. Central government funded a number of research and development activities. In England and Wales, the DfEE/Sheffield University anti-bullying project provided the focus for this activity. North of the border, the Scottish Office sponsored the production and distribution of training and support packs for teachers and advice leaflets for pupils, parents and school boards. It also funded my appointment as the Scottish Anti-bullying Development Officer, with the remit of providing support to schools and local authorities which were developing their own policies.

However, this flurry of activity ended in the mid-1990s, which might appear to make the senior education official who opined to me that bullying was 'just flavour of the month' seem prophetic. On the contrary, I believe that real progress was made and continues to be made – training materials and advice are available to local authorities, schools and concerned individuals; we know a lot more than we did about the complexities of the relationship problems which can underlie a seemingly 'simple' case of bullying; a number of strategies have been evaluated and continue to be developed; and, most importantly, there is now a much greater chance of the victims of bullying having their pleas heard and their predicament acknowledged.

A duty to protect

Pupils have the right to be educated in an atmosphere which is free from fear. Head teachers and others responsible for running schools have a duty to do all that they reasonably can to protect pupils in their charge from intimidation, assault or harassment. This right and this duty are enshrined within documents such as the UN Convention on the Rights of the Child, the Children (Scotland) Act 1995 and the European Convention on Human Rights.

It should also be remembered that schools are subject to the law of the land. Assault, harassment and intimidation are offences, whatever the age of the perpetrator or victim. Despite this, teachers are often reluctant to refer incidents to the police. Sometimes there may be good reasons for not involving the police, but at other times it seems that an assault against a child is treated less seriously than if the victim were an adult.

A number of recent developments have helped to define more clearly the duty of teachers in relation to bullying. For example, a recent agreement between Scottish teachers and their employers said that a teacher's duties include *promoting and safeguarding the health, welfare and safety of pupils*. The UN Convention on the Rights of the Child has been endorsed by the Scottish Executive. Article 19 states that children should be protected from *all* forms of physical or mental violence, injury or abuse. Bullying is one of the most common forms of abuse. The fact that it is perpetrated by children rather than adults does not necessarily reduce the harm that can be caused.

In England and Wales, schools are *required* to take measures to deal with bullying. The School Standards and Framework Act 1998 states: 'The head teacher shall determine measures (which may include the making of rules and provision for enforcing them) to be taken with a view to:

(a) promoting, among pupils, self-discipline and proper regard for authority;

(b) encouraging good behaviour and respect for others on the part of pupils and, in particular, preventing all forms of bullying among pupils.'

This Act does not apply in Scotland but the advice issued in Scotland by government ministers and school inspectors can reasonably be interpreted as placing an at least equal onus on schools to tackle bullying effectively.

Can the law protect victims?

The Human Rights Act allows people to claim their rights under the European Convention on Human Rights. Although the Act does not contain any specific mention of the right of a child to be protected from bullying, it may be that its existence will make it more likely that authority and school policies and practices will be challenged in the courts. The threat of litigation looms ever larger in the minds of school managers.

In recent years a number of victims or their parents have taken legal action against schools, alleging that they have not done enough to protect them from bullying. The Anti-Bullying Network has published an information sheet on its website (www.antibullying.net) which discusses the pros and cons of involving a solicitor. The possible advantages are that:

- victims and their families sometimes feel that their concerns are not being treated seriously. Involving a solicitor can change this;
- a solicitor can provide support to individuals who may feel powerless against school authorities;
- a court decision in favour of a victim could help that person to come to terms with their experiences by ruling that the school did not act properly;
- the court may order that damages be paid as compensation for the harm suffered;
- a high-profile court case can help to clarify the duty of schools to protect victims. This could make it less likely that others will suffer in the future.

Possible disadvantages of taking legal action include that:

- it can be very stressful. If the case is defended, an emotionally fragile victim may be subjected to lengthy cross-examination;
- any resolution will be severely delayed. Papers have to be prepared and witnesses who are willing to testify must be found. Meanwhile, victims and their families will not be able to put the events behind them and get on with the rest of their lives. Deborah Scott took Lothian Regional Council to court over bullying which occurred in 1988 and 1989. It was ten years before the case was heard;

- the outcome is uncertain. Deborah Scott lost;
- enormous expense can be involved, especially if the claimant does not receive legal aid. Becky Walker lost her case and was ordered to pay Derby County Council's costs, which were estimated at £30,000. The judge in that case revealed that even if she had won she would have been awarded only £1,250;
- once a head teacher knows that there is a possibility of legal action it will become more difficult for him or her to admit that mistakes may have been made and that a new approach is needed.

The law certainly has a place in defining what protection should be given to actual and potential victims of bullying. It also provides a means of redress when things go wrong. However, as it operates at the moment, the legal system is slow, expensive and cumbersome. The onus is on the victim to prove fault. Local authorities and their insurers fight every case vigorously for fear of conceding expensive precedents. Victims with limited emotional and financial resources face an unequal battle which has the potential to cause them as much harm as the original bullying.

An anti-bullying policy for schools

Many schools have now developed anti-bullying policies and, considering the amount of help and advice which is available, there is no excuse for those which have not. Bullying happens in every school in the country, although research suggests that some have more than others.

There were very significant differences in the level of bullying in the ten schools studied in my 1989 survey. The number of recent victims varied from 2–15%. Attempts to explain this in terms of social class, family background, deprivation or privilege were not very convincing, but it was clear that some schools were far more successful in containing the problem than others. Three schools had less than 3% of recent victims, but they were very different – one was in a rural area, the other two were in inner-city areas of multiple deprivation. These schools had little in common, other than that pupils and teachers seemed to treat each other with concern and respect.

Observing schools which are tackling bullying effectively leads me to believe that whatever the moral, religious or disciplinary standards of a school, there are three prerequisites for the creation of a successful anti-bullying policy.

- *Honesty* – teachers and parents must be prepared to acknowledge that a problem might exist. There is no difficulty about this in Norwegian schools, but they do not have a parents' charter which obliges schools to compete for the available pupils. Head teachers have a right to expect support from parents and the community when they admit that a problem exists and take positive steps to address it.

- *Openness* – the creation of an open atmosphere is a major challenge to schools. It can be done but has consequences which go beyond making it easier for victims of bullying to speak out: children will talk about other problems, at home or elsewhere; they will be more likely to challenge school rules which they perceive to be unfair; and they will make more complaints against teachers.
- *Involvement* – if parents, teachers and pupils are involved in formulating an anti-bullying policy, they will have a vested interest in making sure it succeeds.

Just how these ideals are to be achieved will vary from school to school. To be effective, any policy must recognise the history and traditions of the school; it must build on existing strengths and repair recognised weaknesses. Table 6.1 shows the process by which this could be achieved.

Table 6.1 Developing a school policy against bullying

Stage	Groups involved
1 Recognition	Teachers and parents
2 Investigation	Teachers and pupils, possibly with outside help
3 Consultation	Teachers, parents, pupils, ancillary staff
4 Implementation	As above
5 Evaluation and modification	Teachers using existing consultation procedures

Stage 1 – Recognition

In some cases school boards, which were established in Scotland in 1989, have helped this process. Elected parent and teacher members have the power to require head teachers to make reports on matters of concern. In the past, individual parents who complained about bullying felt isolated. They were often told that their children's problems were exceptional incidents or that there was nothing that the school could do. Now there is a forum in which the issue can be discussed, although whether or not this happens depends upon the personal interests of the handful of parents and teachers who are elected to the boards. It also depends upon the ability of members to persuade head teachers to treat the matter seriously. A head teacher who was determined to sweep things under the carpet could easily concoct a report showing that there was little or no bullying.

Those schools which have no board, or where the business of the board becomes bogged down in minutiae, will have to rely on groups of forceful parents, or possibly concerned teachers, to initiate change. Whoever performs this function will have the task of trying to create an atmosphere of common concern about bullying. There must be clear agreement that aggressive behaviour will not be tolerated and that all concerned – pupils, parents, teachers and ancillary staff – will work together to eliminate it.

It is possible that the schools which have already developed policies are those where head teachers and staff are most progressive and receptive to the notion that education is about more than just academic endeavour. If this is true, campaigners for change in the remaining schools will have a particularly difficult task. A very powerful argument they can use is that schools in all parts of the UK are now officially encouraged to develop anti-bullying policies. Schools which fail to do this, or which do it in a token way, risk censure by school inspectors. More importantly they give out the message that individuals and minorities do not matter.

Stage 2 – Investigation

Teachers are in the best position to carry out this process. Guidance teachers or those responsible for pastoral care have the opportunity to carry out surveys as part of a programme of social education. In other schools it could be teachers of Religious Education, Social Subjects or English who do the work. This process also allows teachers who would not normally see the reduction of bullying as being part of their role to become involved. For example, teachers with mathematical or computing skills can undertake the analysis of questionnaire surveys. The result of the surveys will allow an assessment of the size of the problem and should also indicate any aspect which needs special attention, such as particular age groups or places where bullying is common. Sometimes, such a survey will reveal other, related problems which require policies to be examined and modified on matters such as child protection, anti-racism or equal opportunities.

Stage 3 – Consultation

A successful strategy to defeat bullying needs the co-operation of teachers, parents, pupils and anyone else involved with a school. Human nature is such that this will be more easily achieved if all these groups are involved in the development process. Schools with a consensus style of management will be best able to do this. Authoritarian head teachers may feel threatened by this suggestion. Thus the degree of involvement will vary widely. In Norway, special meetings about bullying are held, to which parents, pupils and teachers are invited. Pupils sit with their parents rather than as a group and all are invited to contribute to this discussion. A video is usually shown first to create the right climate and the parents may be given the result of a school survey on bullying.

An alternative to an open meeting specifically about bullying is to raise the topic at a meeting of the school board or parent–teacher association. The disadvantage of this is that it could exclude children from the discussion. No policy against bullying can be successful without their active co-operation.

Lest the idea of pupils having a say in the formulation of school rules is considered too revolutionary, let us recall what the Pack Committee said as long ago as 1977:

... we think that there could be some advantage in rules being the product of joint consultation between head teacher, staff, parents (e.g. parent–teacher association) and pupils (e.g. internal school council).

An increasing number of Scottish schools have school councils. It is difficult to know how many of those that do exist are functioning well. The Elton Report suggested that school councils are a way of encouraging the active participation of pupils in shaping and reviewing the school's behaviour policy in order to foster a sense of collective commitment to it. But Elton also discouraged the creation of token councils.

If it becomes clear to pupils that staff are taking no notice of their views, the council is likely to become a liability rather than an asset.

R. F. Mackenzie introduced councils to Scottish state education in the 1960s with limited success.

This experiment in self-government could hardly be called successful. The council have had considerable success in recovering stolen money and property ... but in other ways the council have been less successful. I had hoped that by now they would be arranging their own meetings, preparing the agenda, discussing quietly, and carrying out their own decisions, but it doesn't work like that so far.

State School, 1970

To see how a long-standing school council operates, the author made a visit to Kilquhanity School at the invitation of the Principal, John Aitkenhead. With his wife Morag, he founded the school in 1940 and ran it for more than 50 years. He died in 1998. Although inspired by A. S. Neill's Summerhill, Kilquhanity soon developed a distinctive character of its own. Unlike Summerhill, lessons were compulsory, and so was the weekly council meeting. Staff and pupils were summoned to the purpose-built circular building at 1.55pm every Thursday. By 2pm everyone was in place and the meeting began on time.

This particular meeting turned out to be especially interesting. It was chaired, extremely ably and efficiently, by a teenage girl. The secretary was also a pupil. No one spoke until invited to do so by the chair. Like all committees there was some routine business to begin with, but this was dealt with promptly and calmly. The agenda seemed to be dominated by domestic arrangements – broken plates, noisy dormitories and the like. But the pupils were allowed to raise any matter that was concerning them.

On this occasion an 11-year-old boy complained that some older boys had been teasing him. Two admitted it and said they were sorry, but with little conviction. There seemed a danger that the matter would be glossed over, but some of the other children (mostly older girls) described how the boys constantly teased the younger one about his hair and clothes.

Even though the staff had to wait their turn to speak, they were able to play a very significant part, pointing out that it is not good enough just to apologise without meaning it. Morag Aitkenhead became angry at some of the older boys who seemed to think that a fuss was being made about nothing.

We must recognise that it took a lot of bravery for ... to say that he was being teased and no one should ridicule him for this. This is one of the most central things to this school – everyone must feel this is a good place for them and that they are happy in it.

What was a comparatively minor case of bullying was dealt with at some length. John Aitkenhead asked the bullying children to consider why they had behaved as they had. Other pupils expressed dissatisfaction with their explanations. Eventually the boys were prompted to make a more sincere apology and a promise to stop the teasing. Although outnumbered by pupils, the teachers had been able to show their dislike of aggressive behaviour, but it was a pupil who eventually suggested that bullying could become a regular agenda item, just like laundry and breakages.

It is doubtful whether such a forum could operate in the same way in a state school. Kilquhanity had only about 60 pupils and the council, as it operated in the 1990s before the school closed, was the end result of 50 years of research and development. One could not help being impressed by the way that even young and less articulate children were able to express their viewpoint and play a part in decision-making.

The next point that was raised showed that the meetings did not always go smoothly. Some older pupils challenged John Aitkenhead to explain a decision he had made with regard to a member of staff. John declined to do so because:

Adult decisions are not always well understood by kids. This is a matter concerning professional ethics – I don't mind being asked but I don't think I should answer.

In the ensuing discussion the pupils accused John of being a dictator and of pretending that the school was a democracy when it was not. Morag explained that she saw the school as being like a family and sometimes parents had to take tough decisions which they could not explain but which were, nevertheless, in their children's best interests. John conceded that the school was not a true democracy but was a good training for democracy.

The children had been able to express their dissent in a forceful way and they had been courteously listened to. But they had explored, and reached, the limits of the power of the school's council. Consulting pupils does not mean that teachers have to lose all their authority. Giving pupils a voice does not destroy a school's hierarchy, but it does make it more accountable.

Even if a school does not have a pupils' council it is surely necessary to have some mechanism for consultation. The sheer size of most secondary schools means that it is not practicable to have a council composed of all pupils and teachers. An alternative is to have an elected body, with each year group choosing one or two representatives. But this has the disadvantage that the representatives may become distanced from their electorate, especially if their efforts seem to produce little effect. Schools which totally reject the idea of pupil councils could utilise the guidance or year group system to measure opinion – teachers holding discussions within tutor groups and reporting back to management. Under this system pupils would have no direct voice and would not be responsible for the agenda, so it would be fairly easy to introduce such a system and might be more acceptable in a school with a traditional, authoritarian ethos.

Stages 4 and 5 – Implementation, evaluation and modification

These stages, together with the previous one, form an inter-linked and continuing process. Whatever policy a school adopts, regular consultation must take place. Without this there is a danger that the bullying policy will become just another booklet filed away until the next visit from the school inspectors.

It is likely that a school will discover various bullying flashpoints during the consultation process. Perhaps it is common on school buses or in the playground. Maybe it happens at certain times of the day, for example during the morning interval. Playgrounds are often unsupervised and victims may have literally nowhere to hide. Sometimes bullying involves only a small group of children while others are vulnerable only at particular times, perhaps during a family crisis or after transfer from another school. Sometimes it is found to be happening in classrooms, which is a challenging fact for teachers to accept.

In all these cases supervision arrangements will have to be carefully reviewed. It is not enough to tell children that they will be safe if they spend their break and lunch times in sight of the staffroom windows. This merely adds to the victim's sense of isolation and may increase their attractiveness as a target for the bullies. Supervision must be carried out by an adult who has been trained to spot signs of bullying and to provide appropriate support for victims.

Of course, children cannot be supervised all the time – to do so would restrict their freedom to develop as individuals – but they can be protected in situations where bullying is known to be common. Pupils themselves can help to provide this protection but they will need the assurance that any sanctions to be imposed are sufficiently strong to deter retribution against a helpful bystander.

Counselling and support should be provided for victims who have been seriously affected by their experiences. This could come from a guidance teacher, educational psychologist or simply a trained adult with whom the pupil can identify. But children will seek such assistance only if bullying has been raised as a topic during normal classwork. This can happen in Social Education, English, Drama or RE, it does not really matter where, providing it is dealt with seriously and it is unequivocally condemned. Of course, support for victims will not serve much purpose unless the people doing any bullying are helped to modify their behaviour in some way. Indeed, if support for a victim is the only remedy on offer it can send out the unintended but hurtful message that he or she is at fault because he or she is the one who has to change. This is the lie that bullies tell their victims. It is a lie they believe, and this belief can have serious long-term consequences.

Since 1990 a number of new anti-bullying strategies have been developed and introduced. These include the shared concern method, the no-blame approach and various types of peer support or counselling. All of these have their merits and can be made to work within the framework of an agreed whole-school anti-bullying policy. But none of them will work effectively over a long period unless they are subjected to regular evaluation and modification.

Giving victims a voice

Victims of bullying should always be involved in any discussions about possible remedies. We should encourage children to *talk* rather than *tell* when they are being bullied as a sign that this will be a two-way process in which their opinions and their fears will be fully respected. Children who are being bullied often say that the main reason they have not told an adult is that they fear that the adult, however well meaning, will do something to make the bullying worse. As a minimum, children should always be told about any action which is being taken on their behalf. It is much better, however, if time is taken to discuss and agree any proposed action with them.

Children who have experienced bullying will have opinions about their school's policy on bullying as well as about how their own particular experiences were handled. They could have a key role in helping to improve anti-bullying strategies – if they are encouraged to speak out and if schools set up mechanisms designed to facilitate this.

The UN Convention on the Rights of the Child states that a child 'who is capable of forming his or her own views [has] the right to express those views freely in all matters affecting the child, the views of the child being given due weight in accordance with the age and maturity of the child'.

The Standards in Scotland's Schools etc. (Scotland) Act 2000 charges head teachers with a specific duty to consult pupils: 'The development plan shall include an account of the ways in which, and extent to which, the head teacher of the school will consult the pupils in attendance at the school; and seek to involve them when decisions require to be made concerning the everyday running of the school.'

The full implications of this requirement to consult pupils are as yet unclear, but in the light of this Act, it would be very difficult to defend a head teacher who wrote a school policy on bullying without a meaningful input from pupils, especially those who have first-hand experience to inform their views.

A cause for concern

If helping the victims of bullying is so difficult, if it requires schools to make a fundamental re-evaluation of policy, why bother? Such thoughts probably explain why bullying has been largely ignored for so long. That, and the fact that it was difficult for teachers to provide a non-violent role-model for pupils when the normal method of punishment for serious offences was the cane or the tawse. But now that shadow is lifted there is the opportunity for teachers to work with parents and pupils to minimise bullying.

Summary

We are now moving into a phase where the initial media attention given to bullying is waning and schools are faced with the task of consolidating the gains that have been made, while maintaining the search for better solutions. Teachers can now benefit from a wealth of literature about bullying. Some of this material, such as the DFES pack for schools, has been revised as a result of recent research or because of development work in schools. Teachers can also draw on the expertise of organisations such as Kidscape, ChildLine and the Anti-Bullying Network. But if the motivation to continue to strive to reduce the incidence of bullying is to be maintained – at a point when we have made inroads into the problem but what remains can appear intractable – we must remind ourselves constantly what can happen to victims. A few are driven to the edge of despair and beyond. The great majority suffer less obvious, but nonetheless serious, consequences.

Children who are bullied are unable to concentrate on their schoolwork. A few are physically hurt, many are psychologically damaged. The lesson that they learn may toughen them up but it may equally well make them believe that adults just don't care about children. If that is not sufficient reason for doing something about school bullying, then consider this poignant plea from a 12-year-old girl:

> *People just go against me in everything I say and laugh at me. In science I said something and everyone laughed except my best friend Linda who helps me out when they make a fool of me. They call me K9 Keenan. That hurts me very much. I get very upset. I tried to tell my Mum but she told me to tell a teacher – but I just can't. Please help me.*

The Anti-Bullying Network

The Anti-Bullying Network at the University of Edinburgh is freely open to all and provides a range of services including an InfoLine (see 'Help Organisations' on page 317), a website which is packed with free information and which includes a 'Bully Box' where messages can be posted (see 'Help organisations'), newsletters, information sheets and conferences.

Scottish schools – a note

Scottish education is entirely the responsibility of the Scottish Parliament and the Scottish Executive, which were established in 1999. Although Scottish schools have many similarities to those in England and Wales, there are important differences. Children transfer from primary to secondary schools a year later, at the age of 12. Most schools are run by local councils under the overall direction of the Scottish Executive Education Department. In 1989 school boards were introduced. They have some similarities to boards of governors in England and Wales but with fewer responsibilities. A system of promoted posts in guidance was introduced in 1974. This means that all secondary schools have a number of teachers responsible for the pastoral care of pupils and experienced in interviewing and counselling.

References

Askew, S. and Ross, C. (1988) *Boys Don't Cry*. Open University Press.

Clay, D. (2001) *Secondary School Councils Toolkit*. School Councils UK.

Cowie, H. and Wallace, P. (2000) *Peer Support in Action – From Bystanding to Standing By*. London: Sage.

Department of Education and Science (1989) *Discipline in Schools – Report of the Elton Committee*. HMSO.

Department for Education and Skills (2000) *Bullying – Don't Suffer in Silence – an anti-bullying pack for schools*. HMSO.

Johnstone, M., Munn, P. and Edwards, L. (1992) *Action Against Bullying: A Support Pack for Schools*. Scottish Council for Research in Education.

Mackenzie, R. F. (1970) *State School*. Penguin.

Mellor, A. (1990) *Bullying in Scottish Secondary Schools*. Scottish Council for Research in Education.

Mellor, A. (1997) *Bullying at School – Advice for Families*. Scottish Council for Research in Education.

Mellor, A. (1995) *Which Way Now? A Progress Report on Action against Bullying in Scottish Schools*. Scottish Council for Research in Education.

Mellor, A., Phillips, P., Walker, S. and Munn, P. (1998) *Promoting Personal Safety – and Child Protection in the Curriculum*. The Scottish Office (available on request from the Anti-Bullying Network, 0131 651 6100).

Olweus, D. (1993) *What We Know and What We Can Do*. Oxford: Blackwell.

O'Moore, A. M. (1988) *Bullying in Schools – Report on European Teachers' Seminar*. Council for Cultural Co-operation, Strasbourg.

Rigby, K. (1996) *Bullying in Schools and What to Do About It*. London: Jessica Kingsley.

Roland, E. and Munthe, E. (eds) (1989) *Bullying – an International Perspective*. David Fulton Publishers.

Scottish Council For Research in Education (1993) *Supporting Schools Against Bullying*. SCRE.

Scottish Education Department (1977) *Truancy and Indiscipline in Schools in Scotland – the Pack Report*. SED.

Smith, P. K. *et al.* (1999) *The Nature of School Bullying – A Cross-National Perspective*. London: Routledge.

7

■ ■ ■

What can be done about the bully?

JOHN PEARCE

▶ Explanations of different kinds of bullying – aggressive, anxious, passive
▶ Various factors that encourage children to be aggressive and to bully
▶ Supervising and channelling aggression
▶ Avoiding the promotion of aggression
▶ Making amends for the distress that has been caused is an effective measure

Introduction

Aggression comes in many different forms and bullying is one of them. Our attitude to bullying is important because it sets the standard for the general level of aggression that is deemed to be acceptable. So when we say to the victim of bullying, 'You will have to get used to it – bullying is just part of everyday life,' we make a statement accepting that degree of aggression and violence. Many of the issues that relate to bullies also apply to vandalism, hooliganism and other forms of violence and aggression in society. Until we are prepared to deal with bullying wherever it occurs, there seems little chance that other forms of aggressive and destructive behaviour will reduce in frequency.

Definitions of bullying vary, but there are three essential elements that are always present:

● deliberate use of aggression;
● unequal power relationship between the bully and victim;
● causing of physical pain and/or emotional distress.

The aggression of the bully can take many different forms, ranging from teasing at the mild end of physical violence or emotional abuse at its most extreme. The overlap between bullying and teasing is an important one to recognise because teasing is usually considered to be quite acceptable. But if the teasing involves intimidation and results in distress, it clearly falls within the definition of bullying.

It is the intentional use of aggression that on the one hand makes bullying so appalling and yet on the other hand means that the aggression can, at least potentially, be controlled. In the same way that bullying is started on purpose, it can also be stopped deliberately – if the bully so wishes. It is this element of control over the aggressive behaviour that makes it possible to be optimistic about being able to reduce the frequency and severity of bullying.

In order to deal effectively with the bully it is helpful to have some background information about the frequency, methods and outcome of bullying and aggressive behaviour. This chapter will consider these aspects first and then go on to look at what makes a bully and what can be done about the bully.

How often does bullying occur?

The research on bullying has produced results that show a wide range in how often it occurs. Much of this variability is due to differences in the way bullying is defined and how the data is collected. Some researchers, such as Olweus (1987) in Scandinavia, have used a definition that requires bullying to be repeated, which therefore excludes the single episode, no matter how severe. For many years Professor Dan Olweus at the University of Bergen has been a leader in the research on bullying within schools. He has mainly used questionnaires completed by pupils to identify bullying behaviour. The use of peer report has much to recommend it because the children are directly involved and they can give first-hand information. There is no evidence that children give false answers.

Using reports from children, teachers and parents, Olweus (1989) found that about 11% of primary school children experienced significant bullying. By secondary school age the number of victims had been reduced by half. On the other hand, the number of children identified as bullies stayed fairly constant at around 7% at both primary and secondary age. An overall figure of 15% of Scandinavian children involved in bullying as victims or bullies is rather lower than some of the UK findings. For example, Elliott (2001) found that almost 40% of children had experienced bullying and Stephenson and Smith (1988) noted that bullying in some primary schools was found to involve up to 50% of children, but some children – usually in much smaller schools – reported no bullying at all.

Bullying is carried out in many different ways. When it occurs in groups, it has been referred to as 'mobbing' (Pikas, 1975). But more usually bullying occurs with a single victim being the target. Bullying can be either direct or indirect. Direct bullying consists of physical aggression, hurtful words or unpleasant faces and gestures. Boys engage in direct bullying about four times more frequently than girls. Indirect bullying involves ignoring, isolating or denying wishes and is used more frequently by girls (Olweus, 1993).

An important subgroup are both bullies and also the victims of other bullies. In a nationwide survey of school children in Norway, Olweus (1989) found that about 20% of the bullies fell into this category. These children who bully and who are themselves bullied are generally regarded as more disturbed than the typical bully. We will refer to them again later.

Looking at the problem of more generalised aggression, up to 30% of children aged 8–12 years were found to be significantly aggressive (Pfeffer *et al.*, 1987) and in the classic study of children of a similar age on the Isle of Wight, 1% were observed to show seriously aggressive behaviour (Rutter *et al.*, 1970). It is reasonable to conclude that at any one time at least 1 in 7 schoolchildren are either bullies or victims, but during a whole-school career an even larger number of children will have been affected by bullying. The finding that the frequency of bullying reduces by half in secondary school does not mean that children stop bullying as they grow older; in fact it seems that the number of bullies remains much the same, but the victims are fewer and the episodes of bullying are less frequent (Olweus, 1989).

Does bullying matter?

If bullying is so common, why should anyone bother about it? What is the evidence that it is harmful? Could there be a connection between the level of aggression we accept in our children and later acts of violence, such as football hooliganism and domestic violence? The answer is almost certainly 'yes', but so many different factors have an influence that it is difficult to disentangle them.

There is good evidence that aggressive behaviour in children over eight years old has a strong tendency to continue. In the important 30-year follow-up sociologist Lee Robins (1978) found that children with aggressive and antisocial behaviour were likely to continue to behave in this way, with more than one in four still showing significant aggression control problems. Very similar findings have been reported in a 22-year follow-up by Eron *et al.* (1987) and a review of 16 shorter longitudinal studies of aggressive children followed up over various periods from 2–18 years also concluded that about one in four grow up into aggressive adults (Olweus, 1984).

The following adult problems have been shown to be significantly associated with aggressive behaviour during childhood, especially for older children:

- aggressive behaviour;
- criminal convictions;
- alcohol abuse;
- child care problems;
- employment problems;
- marital breakdown;
- psychiatric disorder.

The very poor outlook for some 25% of aggressive children seems to be similar for males and females. However, it is probably not a direct relationship and is more likely to be due to an accumulation of negative life experiences. Although the prognosis for aggression in childhood is gloomy, it is important to remember that a significant number of aggressive children manage to gain some control over their antisocial behaviour and do reasonably well.

What happens to children who bully is less well researched than the fate of children with generalised aggressive behaviour. However, in a 12-year follow-up of 12-year-old bullies, Olweus (1989) has shown that they were twice as likely to have a criminal conviction by the age of 24 than the general population. And multiple offending was four times more frequent in the bullies.

Unfortunately even less is known about the long-term effects of bullying on the victims. The short-term distress is obvious enough, but what happens later on is less clear. There are reports from adults who have been subjected to physical abuse as children that there are serious long-term effects (Abramson *et al.*, 1987), but it is not clear how much of this is due to the direct experience of violence and how much due to a more general neglect of their emotional needs.

Olweus (1978) suggests that victims – he calls them 'whipping boys' – tend to be unpopular, generally anxious and to have low self-esteem. How many of the victim's characteristics were there before the bullying and how many are caused by it is unclear, but a three-year follow-up showed that there was little change in the victims and they remained as unpopular as ever. The social isolation and anxiety of victims is bound to have an adverse effect on the development of self-image and self-esteem which have been shown to be so important in protecting children from negative life experiences (Rutter, 1987).

Being bullied is a potentially damaging experience for the victim and there may be long-term consequences for vulnerable children. There is some evidence that merely observing another child being bullied can be emotionally damaging (Olweus, 1978). The outlook for the bully is particularly poor, with a significant number continuing to behave aggressively, causing a heavy cost to society in terms of finance, emotional distress and physical damage over many years.

The typical bully

It is helpful to make a distinction between three main types of bully because each one requires a rather different approach in the way they are managed.

The aggressive bully

Most bullies are in this group. They are generally aggressive and are prepared to direct their aggression against teachers, parents and other adults as well as other children and they see little wrong in their aggression and bullying. Aggressive bullies are often involved in other antisocial behaviour and they are *not* anxious, insecure or friendless. The following characteristics are typical of the aggressive bully:

- aggressive to any person, no matter what position of authority;
- poor impulse control;
- violence seen as positive quality;
- wishing to dominate;
- physically and emotionally strong;
- insensitive to the feelings of others;
- good self-esteem.

The anxious bully

About 20% of bullies fall into this category. They are generally more disturbed than any of the other types of bully or victim and they share many of the characteristics of the victim at the same time as being a bully, such as:

- anxious *and* aggressive;
- low self-esteem;
- insecure and friendless;
- pick on 'unsuitable' victims (e.g. more powerful than they are);
- provoke attacks by other bullies;
- emotionally unstable.

The passive bully

The majority of bullying involves more people than just the bully and the victim. The bullies often gather a small group around them and then select a single victim who is isolated from any protective relationships. The bully's followers get involved partly to protect themselves and partly to have the status of belonging to the group. These bullying gangs sometimes operate in a rather similar way to the Mafia and engage in extortion and protection rackets. The followers become involved in bullying in a passive way and have the following characteristics:

- easily dominated;
- passive and easily led;
- not particularly aggressive;
- have empathy for the feelings of others;
- feel guilty after bullying.

How bullies are made

So far we have looked at how frequent and how serious bullying is. Having identified the three main types of bullying we now need to consider the various factors that encourage children to be aggressive and to bully. This in turn will help us to know what to do about this destructive form of behaviour. It is now clear that there is a wide range of different factors that interact with each other to produce aggression in children. In order to simplify the very complex issues, the main causative factors will be grouped under three headings: those that arise within the child, those in the family and those that come from society and the outside world.

The child's contribution

Being male seems to predispose to aggressive behaviour, but is this innate or due to cultural expectations? A detailed review by Maccoby and Jacklin (1974) concluded that both human and animal males show more aggression than females. Another study that looked at children from six separate cultures found that the sex differences persisted across cultures (Whiting and Edwards, 1973). It is reasonable to assume that constitutional factors (i.e. 'how you are made') play an important part in aggressive behaviour.

The male sex 'Y' chromosome may play a direct part in the development of aggression or may work indirectly through the production of the hormone testosterone. These effects are brought about through the complex interactions of many different factors rather than by a single cause. David Shaffer *et al*. (1980) examined the various constitutional influences and noted the following research findings:

- Individuals with an extra Y chromosome tend to show increased aggression.
- Criminal males are more likely to have additional Y chromosomal material.
- XYY individuals are more likely to have abnormal brain function as measured by the electro-encephalograph (EEG).
- Some studies show that exposure to high levels of female hormones is associated with a decrease in aggression in children.
- Some studies show an increase of aggression associated with high levels of testosterone in both boys and men.
- Other studies don't show this, but none shows that testosterone decreases aggression.
- Certain parts of the brain, particularly the hypothalamus and the midbrain, can cause or inhibit aggression, although this may depend on previous experience of aggression and the social context.

It is well recognised that boys are more overactive than girls and this increased activity is, in turn, linked to the later development of aggression and antisocial behaviour (Richman *et al*., 1982).

A child's temperament has been shown to have an influence on behaviour. Important research in America by Thomas and Chess (1977) reported on nine temperamental characteristics that were noted shortly after birth and then followed up into later childhood. The following characteristics were found to be associated with an increased frequency of difficult behaviour, including aggression, tempers and irritability:

- irregular, unpredictable eating and sleeping habits;
- strong, mostly negative moods;
- a slowness to adapt to new situations.

Very similar findings were reported by Graham *et al.* (1973) in the UK. Using the above characteristics, they identified a temperamental adversity index that was able to predict those children who were likely to have problems a year later. A high score gave a threefold increase in the risk of difficult or aggressive behaviour at home and an eightfold risk of problems at school. Children who show the above characteristics from birth onwards are often said to have the 'Difficult Child Syndrome'. Such children are reported to push, hit and fight more in nursery school (Billman and McDevitt, 1980).

The influence of the family

Family influences are frequently blamed for children's bad behaviour, but as we noted above, there is plenty of evidence to suspect factors outside the control of the family. So what part does the family play? A review of the research on aggressive and antisocial behaviour in children by Wolff (1985) concluded that the following family factors were associated with childhood aggression:

- absence of the father;
- loss of a parent through divorce rather than through death;
- a depressed mother;
- an irritable parent;
- marital discord;
- socio-economic disadvantage;
- large family size.

Some of these factors could cause childhood aggression, but they could also be the result of having an aggressive child. For example, having an aggressive and difficult child would be enough to make any parent irritable, but on the other hand it is easy to see how an irritable and hostile parent could make a child feel aggressive. What usually happens is that a vicious circle develops between the child and the parent, each making the other more aggressive. Patterson (1982) has described aggressive behaviours in children and parents which lead on to a predictable sequence of events called 'the coercive system' as follows.

1 Aggressive children make it difficult for their parents to use the more subtle forms of management of deviant behaviour and to encourage good behaviour.
2 The aggressive child may produce an aggressive response from the parent, which then serves as a model or example for the child to follow. Or the parent may give in 'for a quiet life', in which case the child will learn that it pays to be aggressive.
3 The level of aggression in the family rises and anarchy follows, leading to a further breakdown of caring and helping behaviours in family interactions.
4 As a result, the parents tend to become miserable and irritable. They lose their confidence and self-esteem and their children have similar feelings of frustration.

5   Family members disengage from each other, the parents become disunited and the control of aggressive behaviour breaks down, resulting in still further violence.

Olweus (1984) has suggested that there are family factors that predispose children to become bullies. In particular, the style of relationships and attitude to aggression seem to be most important, as outlined below:

1   a negative emotional attitude from the primary caretaker, characterised by lack of warmth and lack of involvement;
2   a tolerant or even permissive attitude to aggression, with no clear limits for aggressive behaviour;
3   a power assertion approach to child rearing, where physical punishment and violent emotional outbursts are the usual control methods.

The links between the characteristics of the individual child, the family and the social setting in which the aggressive behaviour occurs are increasingly seen as important (Goldstein and Keller, 1987). Therefore what happens in the home and at school must always be taken into account when trying to work out why a child is aggressive.

Outside influences

The children who are eventually excluded from school share some of the characteristics of bullies in that they are usually boys who are physically and verbally aggressive (Nicol *et al.*, 1985). But they also have some of the characteristics of the victim in that they are likely to have been rejected by the other children and to have had a poor school attendance. Excluded girls are just as aggressive as the boys and the majority seem to fall into the category of the 'anxious bully', adding to the evidence that this is a more disturbed group. Unfortunately, once excluded, very few of these aggressive children return to normal schooling (Galloway *et al.*, 1982).

The school itself may influence the development of aggressive behaviour (Besag, 1995). Several studies show that even if school-intake factors are controlled for, there remain consistent findings that bullying and aggression occur more frequently in schools with:

● low staff morale;
● high teacher turnover;
● unclear standards of behaviour;
● inconsistent methods of discipline;
● poor organisation;
● inadequate supervision;
● lack of awareness of children as individuals.

Large schools, large classes and the type of punishment were not directly linked with aggressive behaviour in children.

Influence of TV and films

There is increasing evidence that watching aggressive acts in real life or on TV lowers the threshold for aggressive acts in children and that this effect is more marked in children who already tend to react aggressively (Friedrich and Stein, 1973). A review by Henningham *et al.* (1982) concluded that the introduction of TV to the United States has led to an increase in crime rates. Similar findings have been reported in the Lebanon where the effect of real-life and film aggression as well as cartoons on children attending a primary school was studied by Day and Ghandour (1984). They found that:

- boys showed more aggression than girls;
- filmed violence increases aggression in boys but not girls;
- real-life violence increases aggression in both boys and girls;
- Lebanese boys are more aggressive in their play than American boys;
- the effect of aggression in cartoons was as powerful as human aggression on film.

There is evidence that some children are more vulnerable to the effects of TV than others. The 1982 US Public Health Report on the effects of TV concluded that:

- children with low ability and restricted social life watch more TV;
- heavy viewing was associated with high anxiety, maladjustment, insecurity and a feeling of being rejected (i.e. the anxious bully);
- heavy viewing and aggression were strongly linked in younger children;
- bright children tended to fall behind with their work.

In spite of all the accumulated evidence, the adverse effects of TV remain difficult to quantify because there are so many variables. However, there is general agreement that certain children are particularly susceptible to becoming more aggressive as a result of watching violence in films, even if this is in cartoon form.

What can be done about the bully?

It may seem that a lot of background has been covered before considering how to deal with the bully. However, unless there is a very good understanding of the underlying issues it will be difficult to manage aggression successfully. This section will look only at the strategies for dealing with the individual bully rather than more general approaches such as the bully courts and non-aggression contracts between the school, the parents and the pupil. The more general approaches that schools can use to deal with bullying are dealt with in other chapters.

There are some principles of aggression management that need to be identified before starting to deal with the bully:

- Bullying in any form is unacceptable.
- Early intervention is important.
- Individuals must take responsibility for their own actions.
- Parents must take responsibility for their children.
- Failure to deal with the bully will only encourage further aggression.

Prevention of bullying is obviously the first goal to aim for, but if this fails, the motivation for the aggression needs to be considered before taking action against the bully. At the same time, the victim will need protection and help to become more assertive and less of a target for bullying (see Chapter 11). Finally the bully must always be expected to make reparation for any damage and distress that he/she has caused.

Prevention of bullying

Most of the preventative actions against bullying should be started at home before a child even enters school. Parents have the important task of preparing their children to fit into the social world outside the family. By the time children start school they should have been taught to have some control over their aggressive impulses and to appreciate that other people have needs too. Children vary a great deal in how easily they learn to be socially competent, but however slow they may be, the process is the same. Parents can help to socialise their children in the following ways:

- setting an example of good relationships;
- having good aggression control themselves;
- making it clear that violent aggression is unacceptable;
- stopping any show of unacceptable aggression immediately;
- identifying and naming the effects of aggression;
- describing how the victim of aggression feels;
- teaching caring and empathic relationships.

Unfortunately there has been a tendency to assume that any repression of aggression is bad and that children should be allowed or even encouraged to show their feelings openly. In fact most young children are only too ready to let everyone know how they feel! Children can best learn self-control by being given external control first, which is then internalised to become incorporated as part of themselves. As children grow older, the amount of external control and supervision they need decreases, but if it is phased out too quickly or not provided in the first place, the result is likely to be an uncontrolled and disobedient child. The balance between external and internal control is a delicate one that has to be continuously readjusted to the needs of each child at each stage of development – a process that is more an art than a science.

Children who are constitutionally predisposed to aggressive behaviour as a result of their genetic, hormonal or temperamental make-up will require special attention to prevent the development of aggression and bullying.

However, the approach is no different than that for ordinary children. There is no magic solution or missing extra ingredient that is necessary. In practice all that these difficult children require is 'super parenting' – in other words, the best possible child care, which would include:

- teaching responsibility for self and others;
- teaching respect for self and others;
- teaching caring and gentleness;
- teaching appropriate assertiveness and aggression;
- providing firm, clear and consistent standards of behaviour;
- maintaining a predictable, regular routine for everyday life;
- channelling all show of aggression by distraction and early intervention;
- supervising situations where aggression is likely;
- avoiding exposure to violence in the home, at school or on video/film/TV;
- never allowing unacceptable aggression to produce beneficial results for children – it must always have a 'cost' that has to be paid in reparation.

Note that the first four items on the list involve teaching. This is an important point that underlines the necessity for active prevention of bullying. It is no good expecting children to naturally grow out of their aggression without adult intervention – the active training of children is significant in the prevention of unacceptable aggression.

Teaching responsibility for self and others

There is only one way of learning responsibility and that is by being given it. But if children are given too much responsibility before they are ready, this can lead to excessive anxiety or even failure to cope. The responsibility has to be increased gradually, step by step, and adjusted to the individual child's special requirements. This can only be done with a good understanding of the unique needs of each child and with continuing supervision. The supervision is necessary to identify any problems early on and to protect children from failure, which in the context of taking responsibility can be particularly damaging or even dangerous.

These points may be obvious, but the implications are frequently missed. To teach a child responsibility not only demands a detailed knowledge of that particular child but also takes time. This is made even more difficult when children have to be dealt with as a group or where the adults have other commitments or priorities. However, if concerned adults do manage to take time out to consider the needs of an individual child and to provide one-to-one attention when required, the payoff for all concerned is great.

Teaching respect

Self-respect and respect for others are intimately bound up together. They complement each other, the one being the mirror image of the other. So a child who lacks self-respect cannot be expected to have respect for others. It is not difficult to find children who have little self-respect – in other words, a poor self-image. Children who feel bad about themselves will not only find plea-sure in behaving badly but will also have minimal respect for themselves or for others – unless they too are also bad in some way. Teaching respect can, therefore, be achieved by improving children's self-image and by showing them respect. The setting of a good example by adults is one of the best ways of teaching children about these highly complex issues that are extremely dif-ficult to explain in words. Just saying 'Do it this way' is not sufficient – most children also need an example to follow.

Teaching caring and gentleness

Some children seem to be naturally caring, but most are not and have to be taught patiently. As we have already highlighted, an adult's good example is one of the best ways of helping children to learn how to be caring – children who feel cared for will also care for others. In addition to this, it is usually necessary to specifically teach children how to be kind and gentle. This may mean taking a child by the hand and demonstrating in minute detail exactly what is required, in much the same way that a child might be taught to write a word – 'This is how you do it. Now you do it.'

Teaching appropriate aggression

There is nothing wrong with aggression that is properly directed and ade-quately regulated. For example, many sports require the use of controlled aggression which can serve as a good learning experience for practising the management of anger and aggression. Some of the martial arts are particu-larly good at aggression control. There are very clear rules about how and when aggression can be used and very close supervision is given to make sure that the strict code of conduct is followed.

Children also learn about aggression control through play, both in imagina-tion and in play-fighting games with other children. Once again, close supervision, and if necessary active intervention, is required if the level of aggression gets out of hand. It is not unusual for children to play very aggres-sive imaginary games with bombs, blood and bodies everywhere and it is easy to be perplexed by how such seemingly innocent children can be so aggressive. Imaginary play and rough-and-tumble games are a helpful way for children to learn how to gain control over strong emotions. However, excessively aggressive play of any kind should be actively discouraged and the energy directed more constructively. This limited setting for aggressive display in the safe situation of play and imagination is by far the best way of teaching children about aggression control.

Setting rules and routines for everyday life

To some extent the display of unacceptable aggression or bullying can be seen as a failure of discipline – where the child has either not learned the rules of reasonable behaviour or has deliberately broken them. It is worth remembering that the word 'discipline' comes from the Latin *disciplina*, meaning to teach. The importance of teaching the management of aggressive impulses has already been stressed and clear, consistent discipline is a necessary precondition if children are to have a chance of learning right from wrong.

It obviously helps if there is consistency between the standards set at home and those set at school, but this is not essential because children are quite good at knowing what is acceptable behaviour in different situations. For example, children soon learn to behave very differently with those teachers who are strict compared with other teachers who are easygoing in the standards of acceptable behaviour that they set.

Rules usually need to be repeated over and over until they become an automatic part of everyday life. This is the advantage of making aggression control so much part of the regular daily routine that bullying would be unthinkable in the same way as it would be to go to bed with shoes on or to eat sitting on the table! The incorporation of rules of social relationships into the routines of daily life is a very effective way of achieving required standards of discipline. Once this has been achieved it will only occasionally be necessary to repeat the rules or to have to use discipline, and bullying will be much less likely to occur.

Supervising and channelling aggression

The crucial importance of closely supervising children to prevent bullying has already been stressed. The necessary level of supervision that each child requires will vary, but it is not difficult to tell whether or not the level has been judged correctly – if bullying occurs it can be reasonably assumed that there is insufficient supervision. Although this may sound an impractical and superficial approach, most bullying takes place when normal supervision is at its lowest. Good supervision is not only very effective, it allows any bullying to be dealt with immediately before too much damage is done.

One of the advantages of channelling aggression into sports, as suggested above, is that sporting activities usually have a high level of supervision. The rules of behaviour in all sports are clear and have to be applied consistently under close supervision. Sport and competitive games have the potential to provide an excellent basis for channelling and managing aggression.

Avoiding the promotion of aggression

All the hard work outlined above may be to little effect if at the same time bullying and other unacceptably aggressive behaviour is being encouraged either by example or by being rewarded. The adverse effect on vulnerable children of observing violence and aggression either in reality or in fiction is now so well established (see page 82) that it would be incongruous to allow children to be exposed to this and then to complain that they are aggressive bullies.

If aggressive behaviour is seen to bring rewards, it is, of course, likely to continue. The reward of bullying may be something that is less obvious than the immediate excitement of having power over another person, such as achieving high status within a group or gaining a perverse personal satisfaction by passing on to someone else the aggression received from another bully. All possible rewards that could be had from bullying must be considered and avoided as far as possible.

Most of us would find the above programme for the prevention of aggression difficult to keep to and some less adequate parents could not be expected to follow it through at all. In such cases extra help from relatives or other family supporters, playground leaders or teachers will be needed. This additional help can be very effective and can make all the difference to a child.

Dealing with the bully caught in the act

Bullies who are caught in the act can be very difficult to deal with because they will easily turn their aggression onto whoever tries to intervene, often with very little concern for who it is. Here are some guidelines to take into consideration when planning to stop bullying at the time that it is happening.

- It is usually best to remove the victim from the scene as quickly as possible rather than challenge the bully. This resolves the problem without the risk of escalating the violence.
- Telling a bully that he or she will be dealt with later without specifying how or when can be very effective. The bully is likely to worry about what may happen and they will have a chance to reflect on what they have done wrong.
- There is no point in being aggressive with a bully. Aggression only breeds more aggression, so the problem will probably become worse.
- Any physical intervention will almost certainly lead to someone getting hurt, unless the bully is very young. If the bully is a teenager, some form of damage is predictable. Very rarely it may be necessary to get physically involved to protect a victim, in which case it is best to obtain as much additional help as possible.

After the bullying

Every time bullying takes place it marks a failure, a failure that could potentially have been prevented. There are several different aspects to the failure which affect the bully, the victim and the observers:

- The bully has failed to learn that bullying is unacceptable.
- There has been a failure to teach the bully aggression control.
- The victim has failed to be assertive enough and failed to be protected.
- There has been a failure in adult supervision.

The above points highlight the fact that responsibility for a bullying episode should not be focused on the bully alone. Parents, teachers, other adults and the victims all have a part to play, so that just focusing on the bully is unlikely to be effective on its own.

All the issues highlighted in the section on the prevention of bullying need to be reviewed following an episode of bullying, as well as a further consideration of the factors that predispose to bullying. Have all the points been thought through? Has everything been done to change those aspects that can be altered to make bullying less likely? Probably not!

Although it should be made clear to bullies that they are responsible for their actions, it is important that the adults responsible for the supervision and teaching of aggression control should also take some responsibility. The parents and teachers must therefore co-operate to improve the supervision and training to try to prevent a repetition of the bullying. Adults are good at making excuses and it is important not to be thrown by these. Preconceived ideas need to be challenged and excuses such as 'I can't do anything about it – I have tried everything' or 'It is nothing to do with me – you deal with it' should not be accepted.

The fact that adults are taking bullying seriously can have a powerful effect on children, especially if they see adults coming together and acting in unity against the bully. Action also needs to be seen to be taken to protect the victim. The serious discussion of a bullying episode (involving everyone concerned) is an important step to take whether at home or at school. The bully court is a helpful and structured way of doing this, but may not suit all situations (see Chapter 1). The seriousness with which adults take the bullying can be enhanced by exaggerating the formality of the occasion and of the discussion, even if it occurs within the informality of a family home.

The three different types of bullies may require rather different management, although the basic principles are the same and have already been covered.

The aggressive bully

The approach outlined above is particularly relevant to the aggressive bully. The more aggression the bully shows, the more applicable it is. A very aggressive child will require special management and extremely close supervision if the aggression is to be brought under control. It may help to ask for outside help at an early stage and to be prepared to put a great deal of effort into getting things right – and, most important of all, to stick at it. As a rough guide, if every intervention is being carried through correctly it should be possible to achieve an improvement in six weeks and a satisfactory state of affairs in six months. However, it must be recognised that other children also have needs and there are natural constraints to what can be done within the context of everyday life.

The anxious bully

This small but important group of bullies needs special consideration over and above the general management described above. The so-called 'anxious' bully can be recognised by the fact that they are victims as much as they are bullies. These are the bullies who are cowards at heart and usually have a strong feeling of failure. The combination of low self-esteem and provocative aggression is an indication of a disturbed child. The motivation for the bullying is likely to be due to abnormal psychopathology rather than the pure excitement derived from aggressive display and having power over others. The motivations are complex and may include:

- anger against someone other than the victim (who makes an easier target);
- low self-esteem that is improved by having power over another person;
- poor self-image that is confirmed by bad behaviour – the bully is reassured that the self-image fits with reality;
- a desperate need for success even if only to be a successful bully;
- a desire to be noticed and to have attention – whatever the cost.

Clearly the motivation of the anxious bully is both unusual and indicative of some abnormality of personal functioning. Unless this deficit is attended to it will be very difficult to stop further bullying because the motivation is pathological. Expert professional help may well be required.

The passive bully

Children who become involved in bullying by being led into it or by wishing to seem one of the gang are generally easy to deal with. The desire for self-protection and the easy option is usually the driving force behind the bullying rather than a purely aggressive motive. In the case of an easily-led, passive bully it is usually particularly effective to increase the child's feelings of guilt and so exaggerate the possible costs of bullying that it no longer seems the easy option.

It is very easy for children to join in group bullying because the responsibility is dissipated between them and it is easy to shift the blame to someone else. To hold each group member fully responsible for what has happened may seem unreasonable, but it deals with the undermining effect of shared responsibility and increases personal accountability to the point where children will think twice before joining a bully gang again.

Making amends

Punishment in the normal sense of extracting a penalty for bullying can be effective. Bullying should never be allowed to pay, but all too often punishment involves the use of anger, aggression and humiliation – precisely what is not wanted. Aggressive punishment is more likely to be ineffective and may even encourage further bullying. By far the most effective punishment is to insist that the bully makes amends for the distress that has been caused. Exactly how this is best done will depend on the circumstances. However, it is important to try to achieve a balance between the distress caused and the reparation by the bully. There are a number of ways that a bully might make amends to a victim, for example:

- a public apology;
- a private apology, face to face;
- an apology in writing;
- a gift or a special favour for the victim.

Care has to be taken that any contact between the bully and the victim is with the victim's agreement and is closely supervised to make sure that it is successfully completed. This type of reparation by the bully is not an easy option. But it can be surprisingly effective and gets to the heart of the matter by showing that bullying is unacceptable, that it has a cost and should not be repeated.

Summary

The optimistic message of this chapter is that although bullying is a serious matter and bullies left untreated have a poor prognosis, there is a lot that can be done, provided that the problem is taken seriously and there is agreed and concerted action involving parents, teachers and children.

References

Abramson, L. Y., Seligman, M. E. P. and Teasdale, J. D. (1987) 'Learned helplessness in humans: critique and reformulation', *Journal of Abnormal Psychology*, Vol 87, pp 49–74.

Besag, V. E. (1995) *Bullies and Victims in Schools: a guide to understanding and management*. Milton Keynes: Open University Press.

Billman, J. and McDevitt, S. C. (1980) 'Convergence of parent and observer ratings of temperament with observations of peer interaction in nursery schools', *Child Development*, Vol 51, pp 395–400.

Day, R. C. and Ghandour, M. (1984) 'The effect of television-mediated aggression and real-life aggression on the behaviour of Lebanese children', *Journal of Experimental Child Psychology*, Vol 38, pp 7–18.

Elliott, M. (2001) *The Kidscape Primary Kit*. Kidscape, 2 Grosvenor Gardens, London SW1W 0DH.

Eron, L. D., Huesmann, R., Dubow, E., Romanoff, R. and Yarmel, P. W. (1987) 'Aggression and its correlates over 22 years', in D. H. Crowell, I. M. Evans and C. P. O'Connell (eds), *Childhood Aggression and Violence*. Plenum Publications.

Friedrich, L. K. and Stein, A. H. (1973) 'Aggressive and prosocial television programs and the natural behaviour of preschool children', *Monographs in Social Research and Child Development*, Vol 38, No 151.

Galloway, D. M., Ball, T., Blomfield, D. and Boyd, R. (1982) *Schools and Disruptive Pupils*. London: Longman.

Goldstein, A. P. and Keller, H. (1987) *Aggressive Behaviour: Assessment and Intervention*. Oxford: Pergamon Press.

Graham, P., Rutter, M. and George, S. (1973) 'Temperamental characteristics as predictors of behaviour problems in children', *American Journal of Orthopsychiatry*, Vol 43, pp 328–39.

Henningham, K. D., Del Rosario, M. L., Heath, L., Cook, T. D., Wharton, J. D. and Calder, B. J. (1982) 'Impact of the introduction of television on crime in the United States: Empirical findings and theoretical implications', *Journal of Personal Social Psychology*, Vol 42, pp 461–77.

Maccoby, E. E. and Jacklin, C. N. (1974) *The Psychology of Sex Differences*. California: Stanford University Press.

Nicol, A. R., Wilicox, C. and Hibbert, K. (1985) 'What sort of children are suspended from school and what can we do for them?' in A. R. Nicol (ed), *Longitudinal Studies in Child Psychology and Psychiatry*. Chichester: Wiley.

Olweus, D. (1978) *Aggression in Schools: Bullies and Whipping Boys.* Washington, DC: Hemisphere.

Olweus, D. (1979) 'Stability of aggressive reaction patterns in males: a review', *Psychological Bulletin*, Vol 86, pp 862–75.

Olweus, D. (1984) 'Aggressors and their victims: bullying at school', in N. Frude and H. Gault (eds), *Disruptive Behaviour in Schools.* New York: Wiley.

Olweus, D. (1987) 'Bully/victim problems among school children in Scandinavia', in J. P. Myklebust and R. Ommundsen (eds), *Psykologprofesjonen mot ar2000.* Oslo: Universitetsforlaget.

Olweus, D. (1989) 'Bully/victim problems among school children: basic facts and effects of a school based intervention program', in K. Rubin and D. Pepler (eds), *The Development and Treatment of Childhood Aggression.* Hillsdale, NJ: Erlbaum.

Olweus, D. (1993) *Bullying at School: What We Know and What We Can Do.* Oxford: Blackwell.

Patterson, G. R. (1982) *Coersive Family Process.* Oregon: Castalia Publishing.

Pfeffer, C. R., Zuckerman, S., Plutchik, R. and Mizruchi, M. S. (1987) 'Assaultive behaviour in normal school children', *Child Psychiatry and Human Development*, Vol 17, pp 166–76.

Pikas, A. (1975) 'Treatment of mobbing in school: principles for and the results of the work of an anti mobbing group', *Scandinavian Journal of Educational Research*, Vol 19, pp 1–12.

Richman, N., Stevenson, J. and Graham, P. (1982) *Preschool to School: a behavioural study.* London: Academic Press.

Robins, L. N. (1978) 'Sturdy childhood predictors of adult antisocial behaviour: replication from longitudinal studies', *Psychological Medicine*, Vol 8, pp 611–22.

Rutter, M. (1987) 'Psychosocial resilience and protective mechanisms', *American Journal of Orthopsychiatry*, Vol 57, pp 317–31.

Rutter, M., Tizard, J. and Whitmore, K. (eds) (1970) *Education, Health and Behaviour.* London: Longman.

Shaffer, D., Meyer-Bahlburg, H. F. L. and Stokman, C. L. J. (1980) 'The development of aggression', in M. Rutter (ed), *Scientific Foundations of Developmental Psychiatry.* London: Heinemann.

Stephenson, P. and Smith, D. (1988) 'Bullying in the junior school', in D. Tattum and D. Lane (eds), *Bullying in Schools.* Stoke-on-Trent: Trentham Books.

Thomas, A. and Chess, S. (1977) *Temperament and Development.* New York: Brunner/Mazel.

Whiting, B. and Edwards, C. P. (1973) 'A cross cultural analysis of sex differences in the behaviour of children aged three through eleven', *Journal of Social Psychology*, Vol 91, pp 171–88.

Wolff, S. (1985) 'Non-delinquent disturbance of conduct', in M. Rutter and L. Hersov (eds), *Child and Adolescent Psychiatry: Modern Approaches.* Oxford: Blackwell Scientific.

8

■ ■ ■

Bullying and school non-attendance

KEVIN BROWN

- ▶ Bullying is neither exclusively nor even primarily a child-related activity
- ▶ There is a strong link between bullying and school non-attendance
- ▶ Any attempts to change the permeating culture need to be demonstrated in the practices – not merely articulated in the policies – of those in power and authority
- ▶ Bullying is a part of a cycle involving all of us, so we must all change our behaviours
- ▶ Some of the ways we respond to bullying and non-attendance perpetuate or exacerbate the problem
- ▶ School non-attendance has to be recategorised – and I introduce the DARE model
- ▶ We really can make an impact on both bullying and school non-attendance, but do we really want to?

This chapter will be uncomfortable reading.

Whose problem is it anyway?

There is a danger that bullying is linked indelibly with children and schools. This association is unhelpful, as:

- it is not either exclusively or even predominantly a young person's activity but a cultural, societally-wide and pervasive problem;
- it assumes that schools are the locus for its occurrence and its eradication;
- there is thereby an unchallenged threat from bad examples from politicians and other societal leaders.

But first, what is bullying? In the anti-bullying industry we all have our favourite definitions. Mine originally (in the early 1990s when I entered this field) was 'the use of power by one or more people intentionally to harm, hurt or adversely affect the rights and needs of another or others'.

Power seems crucial. Bullying is the use – or, to be more precise, the abuse – of power. Power can be based on age, physical size, intellect, status, position. So teachers and parents can be considered prime candidates to be bullies as they are older, bigger, have greater knowledge, have status as adults and the position of legal authority in their societal roles. They have the necessary power to be bullies. It is how that power is used or abused that determines whether they turn their potential to abuse into actuality.

But power can also be based on a different kind of knowledge, where age, size, intellect and status are irrelevant. Position may still be important though, as the knowledge I am referring to is personal knowledge of the potential victim.

Is age important in another respect? Do we continue to assume that bullying is an activity almost exclusively confined to people of a certain age and status within the population, namely, school-age children? If so, is this based on evidence of bullying or on our beliefs?

Certainly bullying happens among children. And certainly, in a variety of ways, it prevails among adults. Unless bullying is considered an innate or genetic behaviour, like the infant's constantly beseeching demand for succour, it must be learned. So where do children learn it? Every time we see politicians insulting each other, footballers fouling each other, world leaders retaliating – through military reprisals or outright war – for actual or perceived wrongs, children learn that the way to obtain power is by putting down, verbally or physically, other people.

Likewise, we have ambiguous ideas of who is responsible for children attending school. Legally it is the parents who must educate their child. But if we fail to make schools relevant and inviting to pupils, are we colluding with their non-attendance? If we coerce them, or indeed punish them for not attending (and I still know of schools that exclude children who truant!), then what messages are we giving about the experience of schooling and the power we will exert to enforce conformity?

Learning about bullying from children

I regularly work with children in schools. One day, in a not untypical 'teacher-ish' way (that is, I knew the answer but I'd let them have a stab at it first, and then I'd tell them what it really was!), I asked a group of children what bullying was. An 11-year-old boy replied calmly that he knew what bullying was. I indulged him and he stated simply:

Bullying is knowing what hurts someone and deliberately doing it.

My thinking has, then, been interrupted on a number of occasions, including when I listened to this boy's definition of bullying. His definition seems to encapsulate simply the real essence of what bullying is. I never use any other definition now.

Often I have been taken aback by what children tell me, as it interrupts my assumptions or confounds me. But I listen and struggle to understand. The greatest influence on my work on bullying has been due to asking children questions that previously I had assumed need not be asked. I will share some of that understanding with you, and particularly as it links bullying to school non-attendance.

Bullying is learned behaviour – I am confident in that assertion. If it isn't – if it is genetic, for example – we might as well all pack up and go home as we could do nothing about it. 'Bullying is knowing what hurts someone and deliberately doing it' implies that it has these aspects:

- Bullying is learned behaviour.
- Bullying is undertaken within a relationship.

Furthermore, children are clear there are several ways that they can and do 'act' – they can be victims, they can be 'watchers' (by which they mean they see or know of bullying happening) and they can be bullies. What is crucial is that, in contradiction to the usual adult versions of bullying, children almost all acknowledge that they have been or are, at times, bullies.

We need, then, to replace our characterisations and caricatures of certain pupils as bullies and others as victims and recognise that bullying involves people in various roles. Roles are what people play, it is not who they are.

'Nobody loves me, everybody hates me, I think I'll go and eat worms ...'

We may have some assumptions about how people feel about bullying and I will share with you an exercise I undertake with participants on my Bully No More! courses.

First, I ask, 'What does bullying feel like?' The common response to this question is for the adult respondents implicitly to adopt the position of victim and articulate what one course participant poignantly described as an 'inventory of negative emotions'. These adults – mostly teachers and other professionals in the educational arena – are then asked to identify the feelings that bullies (as opposed to victims) may have. This produces a mixed bag.

Sometimes participants fall into two camps – those who feel (perhaps as erstwhile or current victims) angry and punitive towards bullies whom they see as destructive of the innocence and opportunities of other people, and those who identify with the caring, compassionate components of their profession and who wish to uncover reasons for the bullying behaviour (and in some instances they feel concerned to rescue the bullies from their bullying, to make them 'better').

Table 8.1 Feelings lists: adults' version

Bully	Victim	Watcher
angry	sad	scared
strong	angry	worried
clever	guilty	excited
happy	scared	sad
confident	lonely	embarrassed
smart	trapped	confused
guilty	worried	angry
sad	ashamed	relieved
lonely	confused	frustrated
scared	frustrated	guilty
big	embarrassed	amused

The feelings of the third category, which I usually refer to generically as 'watchers', are again a mixed bag. Course participants sometimes find it harder to identify these feelings, partly because they begin to realise the term 'watchers' covers a number of possible roles. Table 8.1 shows the typical adults' version.

Compare this with the kinds of responses I obtain from children when I undertake the same exercise – Table 8.2.

Table 8.2 Feelings lists: children's version

Bully	Victim	Watcher
angry	sad	scared
lonely	angry	worried
sad	guilty	lonely
scared	embarrassed	angry
trapped	scared	sad
ashamed	lonely	embarrassed
confused	trapped	confused
guilty	worried	ashamed
frustrated	ashamed	trapped
worried	confused	frustrated
embarrassed	frustrated	guilty
excited	excited	excited

The lists are different. Why? This confounded for me for some time until, by asking 'who are you thinking of when you compile the lists?', teachers said 'children' and children said 'ourselves'. That is, teachers were making assumptions about how children felt and meanwhile not acknowledging the roles of their own feelings (and that they actually played these roles) when they were victims, bullies and watchers.

What children tell us is that:

- no one involved in bullying feels good about themselves.

'I don't want to go to school any more'

I will now focus on the impact of bullying on school attendance. Why do children go to school? They tell me there is a very strong pull. It is generally neither the lessons nor the teachers. It is partly to do with not letting parents down and not getting into trouble. But mostly it is so that they can feel they belong because the most frightening thing for them is to be excluded from normal situations. They need their group identity.

It is interesting that, in our version of civilised behaviour, we have replaced the sanction of caning or belting children (one form of bullying) with exclusion (another and, according to children, more devastating form of bullying). So much for the UN Rights of the Child.

It is, then, a very significant statement if a child does not attend school. I refuse to label this either 'truancy' or 'school refusal', as such distinctions are adult-generated and do not tie in with how children see non-attendance.

Why don't children come to school?

Patrick Whitaker (1995) has produced an interesting list of reasons why children don't come to school:

- feelings of inadequacy;
- inability to express oneself;
- inability to influence anyone;
- feelings of being shut out;
- increase in cynicism;
- increase in destructive feelings;
- feeling that one has either to dominate or be dominated;
- feeling that to conform is the safest way forward;
- feeling that intolerance and exploitation have to be accepted;
- feeling that new ideas must only come from teachers;
- feeling that teachers are not interested in these feelings and that there are no easy ways of communicating with them.

Note that it is feelings that predominate. Alternative research has sometimes tried to identify comprehensive reasons for non-attendance (Ken Reid (1999), for instance, has produced pages upon pages of typologies and categories) and this has often lost sense of this essential element in attempting to concoct a set of psychological profiles.

Based upon what children told me, I started to categorise school attendance and non-attendance in the following way:

- Negative non-attendance (not attending and not gaining anything positive out of this).
- Negative attendance (attending and not gaining anything positive out of this).
- Positive non-attendance (not attending and gaining something worthwhile).
- Positive attendance (attending and gaining something worthwhile).

However, I recognised that this needed refining to glean the essence of the feelings that lay behind these categories. I have introduced the concept of engagement, which combines and integrates the most constructive aspects of positive non-attendance and positive attendance. Hence I now reframe and recategorise schools within the *DARE* framework, as follows:

The DARE model of attendance and non-attendance

D(etached)   *A*(ttached)

R(ejected)   *E*(ngaged)

The Detached pupil has low expectations and does not experience the positive message generally articulated in the school ethos statement. This pupil may suppress feelings, acquiesce, conform and play the game. The pupil will be passive and learn to survive. Survival may be a very important lesson, but it's a long way from the explicit values of the ethos. For this pupil, much of school won't 'touch the sides'. This is an image of negative attendance.

The Attached pupil not only finds it possible to survive but can develop skills in carving out a route through the system which provides rewards and status, in comparison with peers. Modelling on teachers, this pupil strives to emulate the superiority that comes from better academic marks, prowess in sport or music and avoidance of negative attention. The markers set out to define a good pupil will be recognised. It's possible a fair degree of self-esteem and confidence will emanate from succeeding in this environment, albeit in competition with and at the expense of others, and to that extent this may be seen as positive attendance.

The Rejected pupil is able to experience feelings, but these may well be those of sadness and anger at dismissal, and feelings of worthlessness and rejection. 'Don't you want me?' The pupil might test this out, already half expecting the answer: 'No.' This pupil conforms in another way, to the label that says 'Reject'. This is likely to lead to negative non-attendance.

The Engaged pupil is a powerful actor on the environment. Engagement is not defined in terms of stark figures of attendance. Engagement is a qualitative concept, not a quantitative one. For me, engagement implies a different ethos, a different concept of educational outcomes. It implies ownership of learning opportunities, of assertiveness, of questioning and challenging behaviour. Often, it is perceived – wrongly – as a threat and can lead to efforts to reduce the self-esteem and influence of the Engaged pupil. Perhaps the pupil is ignored, belittled or sidelined – or punished. Such bullying behaviour can lead to the pupil adopting a different role – conforming in an acceptable way (Attached), cowed into becoming Detached, or pushed (represented through non-attendance or exclusion) into rejecting the school or being Rejected.

We are all involved in perpetuating the culture – 'the way we do things round here' – and of course an Engaged pupil challenges that.

The essential common underpinnings of bullying and non-attendance

Another of the questions I asked both children and teachers – again one which I did not think needed asking – produced another jolt to my assumptions. I used a questionnaire to seek out all the reasons why children did not attend school and then to list those reasons in order of importance (in terms of which reason led to the most number of days being missed).

The lists of reasons were very similar – sickness, parental holidays, family crises or bereavements, moving house, bullying, and so on. But what was different was the main reason. One hundred per cent of teachers stated that sickness was the highest single cause of absence; 75% of children agreed, but the other 25% put bullying as the number one cause of non-attendance. Teachers disputed this minority perception – after all, they register the reasons for non-attendance. How did the children respond to that? They were perfectly clear – neither parents (who sign the notes) nor the teachers were generally told the real reasons when bullying was the actual cause for fear that the adults would make the situation worse! So the children would convince the parents they were ill.

What do children feel when they deliberately stay away from school? Is it similar to what they feel when they are bullies, victims and watchers?

Here are two young people's reflections on both bullying and school non-attendance, which indicate they link both inextricably.

Jane's story

Jane was quite happy at primary school. She was academically able and very competent in physical activities. Indeed, she showed such promise at PE that she was noted as a future potential national athletic competitor. But things went wrong soon after she started high school, and increasingly so when she entered the second year. She began to leave school during certain classes (particularly PE) and thereafter begin to miss whole days. Eventually she became a persistent non-attender.

Let's ask the usual questions:

- Why did this happen?
- What explanations can we find?
- Is there a family background to non-attendance?
- Were her peers missing school too?

Jane gave the following reasons. She didn't feel valued by the teachers at the school. Especially in PE she felt the male teacher consistently overlooked the girls and got boys to demonstrate exercises. She felt he was only interested in male sports and boys' achievements. He made derogatory comments about her and ridiculed other girls' attempts. She felt that her complaints about this to her guidance teacher were dismissed. She went from 'Engaged' to 'Detached'.

There were others non-attending school, but not her friends. What Jane did was begin to associate with them, to try to find a new identity, to find a place she felt she was wanted, valued and belonged, and gradually she slipped into 'Rejected'.

When I visited her family, I found that the mother was very keen to get Jane to attend school. Indeed, she did not realise the extent of the absence. She was worried that Jane, as the third eldest, would set a bad example for the youngest child. Upon further examination of family patterns, Jane's oldest sister was at university – but unbeknown to her mother she had deliberately missed quite a lot of schooling. Meanwhile, her older brother had attended regularly. He left school at 16, without much in the way of qualifications.

My work with Jane was to help her re-invest in school, which meant that she needed to see that the 'put-downs' were addressed. The school was prepared to accept that the PE teacher was discriminatory in his work with pupils, and somewhat grudgingly acknowledged too that they had not taken Jane's complaints seriously. They were reluctant initially to tackle the PE teacher. They suggested another PE teacher could take Jane and that this would be sufficient accommodation of her needs. Eventually they realised that for Jane to feel she had been taken seriously (let alone actually address the bullying that was being perpetrated by the PE teacher) they had to raise the matter as an issue of equal opportunities.

Jane then returned. She had missed most of the year's work – indeed she had burnt her school books on one of her out-of-school 'excursions'. She was subsequently mostly present, but remained in the 'Detached' category. She never fulfilled her potential at school either academically or in sports.

Lisa's story

Lisa did not really look much different from any other girl. But a slightly darker skin colour was commented upon and – noting this was a vulnerable issue for her – this became the thing commented on derogatorily by some other pupils who 'knew it would hurt her, and deliberately did it'.

She told me that she had the support of her parents, who helped her become hardened against these comments. But then the comments focused on her clothes. Her parents bought her new clothes. She was struggling to concentrate on her lessons and her poor marks were commented on. She was given specialist help. This then became the target of comments. She missed school. This too was commented on when she returned. As she told me, 'It was one thing, then it was another. I have no idea why it started, but it just carried on. It was always me; teachers said I was looking for the comments and that they were no big deal, I should ignore them. Well, it was hard. The teachers never understood what it was like and then they made me feel like I was just weak or making excuses for not doing my work properly. I tried to go to school, but I couldn't face it. I just stayed at home.'

Was it easy for her to stay at home? She was adamant it caused her a lot of upset. She felt really different, and she knew it was upsetting her parents (who faced court action for not sending her). She became very depressed.

The solution was that she had to change schools and start year to make up for the work she had missed. But this was not successful. She carried the sense of failure, she became the target of bullying comments in the new school, and never attended during the last two years of her compulsory education. She felt 'Rejected'.

She believed that if the school had taken her seriously initially she might have got through it.

The predominance of feelings

In the same way that I came to realise the issue of feelings had to be pre-eminent in any approach that addressed bullying, so I have recognised that this is true of approaches that address non-attendance. As a way of illustrating again the overlap, I was once asked (as an 'expert') to work with a girl who had absented herself for some days, allegedly due to bullying. I went to see her at home. My first question, after the preliminary niceties, was why she didn't go to school. 'Because of the bullying,' she replied. My next question was predictable – but her response wasn't. I asked her who was bullying her and she replied – almost with disdain – that no one was. I was confused and tried to clarify what she meant. She repeated that she was not going to school because of the bullying. But she assured me again that she was not being bullied. She looked at me as if she could not comprehend my lack of understanding.

Then the penny dropped. It is not only victims who are affected by bullying, and we should not assume that they are always affected most. She was a 'watcher' and was profoundly disturbed by what she saw and knew was going on. It led to her not attending school, and teachers who were dismissive of her reason (because, they assumed, if it wasn't happening to her it couldn't affect her) were perpetuating the problem.

What can perpetuate the problem?

The reaction to bullying and school non-attendance can often be problematic. This is not necessarily because it is not taken seriously (as in the examples above). Indeed, it may be because it is taken seriously but from a perspective that perpetuates – or even exacerbates – the problem. I refer to this as the RIP syndrome.

The RIP syndrome

The three most common responses to allegations of bullying are: Rescuing (the victim); Indifference ('they'll grow out of it'); and Punishment (of the bully). Children consistently tell me that each of these responses is unhelpful and leads them to keep bullying secretive.

A very similar response arises from non-attendance – Rescuing (of the school refuser); Indifference (either by not noticing they are absent or having no interest in their return); or Punishment (of the truant – 'how dare they thumb their nose at authority').

Each of these responses perpetuates a power relationship whereby the Rescuer, the Indifferent and the Punisher adopt a position of superiority. There are more appropriate responses which do not convey that superiority – they require collaboration on an equal footing and are best framed as 'helping/caring', 'interested/supporting' and 'challenging/inquiring'.

What young people say is the problem – and what they want

The problem identified by children is that adults have preconceived ideas of what solutions and the process leading to solution may look like. But these do not accord with what children state that they need. Children want justice. But justice for them is a different concept. For adults, it is reparation, retribution, punishment and vengeance. Children, on the contrary, want something much more important and much more positive.

- Children do not want retribution or vengeance – they want the bullying to stop.

Likewise, children are clear about attending school. They want to be at school, but under circumstances that are quite basic to all of us. These are the ABCs of social inclusion. Children need to feel they:

- are Accepted and valued;
- Belong and fit in;
- have some Control and choice over what happens to them.

What teachers and parents can do

Teachers and parents can now ask, how great a proportion of our pupils, our children are in each of these categories in their schools?

Detached?	?%
Attached?	?%
Rejected?	?%
Engaged?	?%

It is not only the non-attenders (the 'Rejected') whose needs are not being met. Moreover, if a child does not have the self-esteem and confidence that comes from being 'Engaged', then they are much more likely to become victims and bullies.

This seems to me a more important measure in any school than the typical breakdown of authorised absence and unauthorised absence figures. It can actually help teachers and parents address the causes of bullying.

Essential issues to address in engaging pupils

This is a brief recipe of issues that need to be addressed in meeting pupils' needs, in engaging them as partners in the education process.

- Social trust – children, parents and members of the community need to establish a relationship and rapport that treats the educational provision and its practitioners as trustworthy.
- Relevance – the method of delivery and the content have to make sense to children's identity and aspirations.
- Ethos – it needs to be genuine, positive and inclusive.
- Integration – there needs to be a connection between the curriculum and the 85% of young people's waking time spent in the home and social arenas.
- Ownership – the purpose of education is to enable children to find and make meaning of their lives.
- Being there – finally, I once saw scrawled as graffiti on a wall in a drug rehabilitation centre the following slogan. For me it encapsulates what children are telling us they need from us if we are to help them overcome bullying and engage them in schooling. It is about us 'being there' for them – listening, being open to new learning ourselves, being humble, not making judgements about them. And really wanting to be partners with them in making sense of the world.

**'I don't care what you know
until I know that you care'**

Summary

Bullying is 'knowing what hurts someone and deliberately doing it'.

- It is learned behaviour.
- It is undertaken within a relationship.
- It involves people in various roles.
- No one involved in bullying feels good about themselves.
- Children do not want retribution or vengeance – they want the bullying to stop.

The *DARE* model of attendance and non-attendance categorises pupils into *D*etached, *A*ttached, *R*ejected and *E*ngaged. 'Truant' and 'school refuser' are not helpful terms.

The RIP syndrome (the typical adult responses to bullying and school non-attendance – to be Rescuer, Indifferent or Punisher) leads to bullying and non-attendance being perpetuated and exacerbated.

The ABCs of social inclusion need to be in place. Children need to feel they:

- are Accepted and valued;
- Belong and fit in;
- have some Control and choice over what happens to them.

Both bullying and school non-attendance can best be tackled through helping young people to be 'Engaged'.

References

Brown, K. (1997) *Bullying – What Can Parents Do?* Crowborough: Monarch.

Reid, K. (1999) *Tackling Truancy in Schools: A Practical Manual for Primary and Secondary Schools.* Routledge.

Whitaker, P. (1995) *Managing to Learn. Aspects of Reflective and Experiential Learning in Schools.* London: Cassell.

9

■ ■ ■

Peer mentoring: what is it?

PAULINE MASKELL

▶ Peer mentors act as confidants, counsellors and sponsors
▶ Peer mentors have been used to help those who have been bullied and those who have been the bullies
▶ Peer mentors use friendship skills but they can be more objective than friends
▶ Peer mentors have the capability of changing the atmosphere in their school, group or club

Supporting one's peers is not a new idea but recently there has been new interest in its application. Peers have been shown to be effective in various supporting roles which often tend to merge into each other. Carr (1994) has counted more than 30 different terms defining peer helping systems in a survey of the Canadian National Peer network. Some of the most commonly used are peer tutor, peer helper, peer counsellor, peer support worker, peer facilitator, peer leader, peer mentor, befriender, mediator or coach. The terms do allow peer programmes to develop their own identities but they can create confusion. Perhaps the best term is that which is becoming most widely used: peer mentor.

Peers have taken on the roles of mediator, mentor, counsellor, tutor or friend. The role may progress from that of listener to that of tutor, helper, mentor and long-term befriender. A mentor acts as a confidant, counsellor and sponsor, encouraging those they are supporting to trust them, experience and understand feelings and take considered risks. The relationship is built on attraction and mutual trust and respect. It is similar to that of an elder sibling, who offers compassion but not competition.

Peer mentors have their own ideas of their role:

I'm like a mixture of big sister, teacher and friend, but not really any of them.

Carly

I'm not perfect, but I'm fun, acting as a friend to them and not giving advice.

Anthea

Development of the peer support movement

Peer support programmes in schools and colleges usually make use of students who are already seen as being helpful and trustworthy by their peers. This development has been due to several factors:

- research into and developing awareness of bullying in schools;
- diminishing resources available for assisting students;
- the more universal appeal and glamour associated with the idea of counselling;
- the willingness of adult counsellors, teachers and youth workers to work alongside students;
- educational reform and changes in school ethos to provide a wider support net.

In many cases peer support has been used to help those who have been bullied and those who have been the bullies. It has developed much further, to listen, mediate and mentor a whole range of problems because problems are seldom simple.

Why use peers?

A peer is defined as someone who has the same status, for example another student or a member of a self-help group. Peers do not have to be the same age. Often it is helpful if the supporting peer is older, more knowledgeable or more experienced. This may to some extent change their relative status but the relationship can remain on an equal and friendly footing.

The peer group has positive influences. They can listen to each other and accept each other's opinions, suggestions and strategies because they are peers. They have lived through situations and coped with them recently and as such have 'street credibility'.

As Ann explained:

I have lived through being bullied for several years and although I don't have much confidence, I can share what I've learnt with others.

Kathy explains that part of the relationship with those they are helping is based on the fact that they are treated as an experienced older peer.

If we ask them to do something they will trust us because we've already been there.

Peers have advantages over those who have authority or have to act in a prescribed or fairly rigid role. They can use and understand the same language as those whom they are helping. They understand the words and the ways in which they are used without tedious explanations. They can understand words such as 'pants', 'geek' and 'cool'. You do not have to 'watch your language' with peers because it is difficult to do so when you are upset.

You are more likely to remember peers' points of view because their strategies in social situations are more appropriate than those of adults. For example, they will not offer solutions but rather encourage those they are helping to come up with a range of possible strategies. They will then support them in their decisions. They are seen as less directive than the adults who want to help.

Tanya sums up the opinions of many peer mentors:

We are not really there to solve things, we are there to comfort. We are not really counsellors, we are listeners. We just listen, we might just hint. We encourage people to fall back on themselves and say things like, 'What would you do?' They usually say, 'Thank you for the advice.' We haven't given any.

They are aware that they are more likely to understand, not only because they are closer to the situations but also because they have reflected on their own experiences. These are comments which peer mentors have made about this aspect of their image.

Adults have forgotten what it is like to hurt so much.

Ryan

Teachers do not really want to talk about personal things in case they do not know the answers.

Stuart

They will not offer you their solutions or presume to think that they feel the same way that you do. Their experiences will help them think more flexibly and use a wide repertoire of communication skills. They are well aware of the skills which they need.

You have to be on the same wavelength and not patronise. You need to show them respect, be on the same level and not the enemy.

Helena

Peer mentors can act as a gateway to more specialist services. Young people will often tell peers their problems because this can be done informally, whereas many find the formal label of counselling daunting and it thus forms a barrier. Peer supporters can develop a relationship which gives their 'clients' the confidence to go further and seek more specialist help if necessary. It is important that the skills of appropriate referral are part of the training process for the peer supporters. However, a brief period of support may be all that is necessary to help the other person to cope.

Peer mentors are different from friends. They do use friendship skills but they can be more objective than friends. They can sum this up for themselves:

I am an understanding and considerate person with good listening skills.

Carol

I am a friend, but I can stand back from the problem and put my prejudices to one side.

Meena

They do not have preconceived ideas how individuals will behave and they can stand back from situations. The young people who come to see them find it easier to tell them about their problems because they do not know them well, although they may know them by repute. These young people say that it is easier to tell an unknown person because you know that you will not hurt them when you tell them about your pain.

Peer mentors have the capability of changing the atmosphere in their school, group or club. They can make a helping approach the norm which includes everyone. First, they are recruited from a representative sample of people. For example, some may be shy, some may be leaders, some will excel at sport, others at art, some will enjoy problem solving, others may prefer personal contacts. They will also represent the cultural background and gender balance. Active recruitment will be necessary to get this balanced sample.

How can peer support be useful in anti-bullying?

Peer supporters can, by training, enhance their innate communication skills. Training and support are needed to give them confidence so that they do not harm themselves or others, and this should continue for as long as the supporters are working with others. The personal development and self-awareness of peer mentors also develops over a period of time.

Peers will learn the basic counselling skills of active listening, good communication, both verbal and non-verbal, and the ability to encourage people to talk and use empathy in both the listening process and interpretation of what people are saying. Training will initially consist of activities, drama techniques and games which can be used to explore these skills. Later on, ideas can be put into practice to further develop awareness. Trainee peer mentors have different expectations of training:

I expect role-play and practice with past situations to help me to cope with those who need help.

Hannah

I am already a good listener but I want to learn how to step back and not get too involved.

Lee Mai

Peer mentors can use the skills developed to listen to 'bully' and 'victim', both of whom have needs. They can liaise with teachers and use their support in supervision sessions. They can learn and use mediation skills to help in situations. They can use mentoring to support and be a point of contact for people in the long term.

The most effective peer support systems are those which:

- are well publicised;
- address perceived needs;

- are available for everyone;
- are used for a variety of support needs;
- are run by students for students;
- are supported by adequate training and supervision;
- have the support of everyone connected with the school, college or club;
- are rooted in community links.

Publicity needs to be simple, straightforward, frequent and diverse. It can be carried out by peer mentors and their adult trainers, either in person or through group contact, through one-to-one contact or by performances or plays. Often in schools mentors are attached to a particular form or class so that the group can become familiar with them. Role-plays or performances about their role form a vivid way of putting over a message. However, people forget easily or take little notice if the message is not immediately applicable, so contact must be repeated frequently.

Publicity can also be conducted through a range of media, posters, individual information cards, student bulletin, e-mail, home website page, announcements, local radio and school or college newsletter. The messages put over in this way have to be simple and attractive enough to catch people's attention and must be changed sufficiently often so that they do not become boring. It is also helpful, as well as being a boost for the mentors' self-esteem, if local newspapers, magazines, journals and TV programmes report on their work. The most effective publicity ensures that everyone knows about the service because they have picked up information and knowledge in different ways from different people.

The needs for a peer support system must be those perceived by the students. They can bring these needs to the attention of adults through their school or college council representatives, personal tutors, PSHE tutors, school or college support or counselling structures. This can provide the impetus for a needs analysis (the simple questionnaire on page 112 can be used). It is more effective to focus on one particular issue when peer support structures are being set up. There is an optimum time for this needs analysis to be effective. This is a time when there is an interest in what peers can offer and when there are adults who are prepared to facilitate this. Peer support will involve some staff directly, such as trainers, heads of year, pastoral staff, school counsellors, and all staff indirectly. It will involve the senior management team, parents, governors and community groups. The identified needs and the ways of addressing the problems of setting up peer mentoring groups as expressed by students and facilitators need to be explained to all those involved. (See Figure 9.1).

A peer mentoring system that is available for everyone has to be offered in different ways. Peer supporters usually work in pairs. They can attach themselves to a particular group as mentioned, so that they become well known. They then work with small groups on different topics such as friendships until everyone in the group has worked with them. When problems arise, group members have a 'buddy' to contact. They can offer specialist services which students or their teachers can request, such as anger management, coping with

Figure 9.1: Identifying needs and ways of addressing the problems of setting up peer mentoring groups

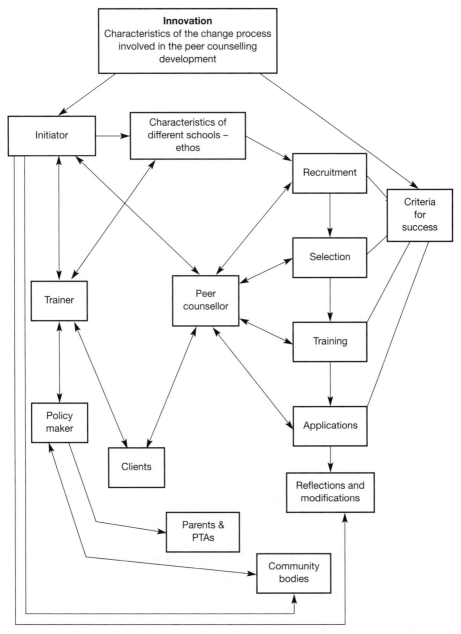

stress, self-esteem skills. They can be contacted at a drop-in centre or by post via the 'buddy postbox'. They take part in school events helping groups and individuals, such as health days and open evenings. In this way they can make it clear that support is available for all and can model supportive behaviour which others can learn. Peer supporters explain how this works:

They can see that it is not a service for the sad but there for everyone to use when they need it.

Becka

We don't want them to think that we have nothing better to do with our time than listening to people with problems. It is fun to learn and train and help others.

Simon

Students need training:

- in order to support;
- to learn strategies for working with people;
- to become more self-aware;
- to help them to come to terms with their own particular problems;
- to apply and adapt what they have learnt.

The training needs will change with each group of students because they will have different initial skills. Trainees need to have an input into their training and be able to adapt it to their needs. It is also useful and empowering if students who have already done training can take over the training process with new trainees. Trainers need to develop a basic training programme which can be adapted by the group. It is also vital that community groups are involved and aware of the peer mentoring programme. Young people's counselling groups, community health and mental health, health clinics, drug and alcohol help groups are just some of the groups which can have valuable input into the training and can work with the peer mentors on joint projects. For example, one of the groups with which I work, 'Buddy' peer counselling group, wrote, directed, produced and acted in a play together with Community Mental Health for National Mental Health Day. This play was also used as input to the regional mental health conference on services for young people.

Rewards are also important to peer mentors. When they volunteer they express a natural desire to help. They develop and change, become more confident and capable. In many evaluative studies it has been seen that their personal development is accelerated. They say that one of their greatest rewards is that of working alongside adults in an equal and responsible relationship. They also appreciate the certificates they receive, the references, a high profile within the school or college or youth group and community, personal satisfaction, and the doughnuts and jelly babies which form an integral part of the training sessions.

Summary

Peer mentoring, properly instituted, can be very useful in helping to alleviate bullying. The peer group can be a positive influence and peer mentoring can enhance that by encouraging a friendly, respectful, supportive atmosphere in the school. Peer mentoring has benefits for victims, bullies, other students and for the peer mentors themselves. The final word should go to one of the peer mentors, Carly. She says:

It is the most important thing that I have ever done. It's like ripples in a pond, the effects spread.

References

Carr, R. (1994) 'Peer helping in Canada' *Peer Counseling*, 11 (1), pp 6–9.

PEER SUPPORT QUESTIONNAIRE

1. Which of these cause anxiety to young people?

School work/problems ☐

Bullying ☐

Family problems ☐

Friends/peer pressure ☐

Teachers/staff ☐

Drugs/alcohol ☐

Sex/health/body image ☐

Bereavement/loss ☐

Other ☐

2. Which issues are most important?

1. _____

2. _____

3. _____

3. Who would young people confide in?

Friends ☐

Peer counsellors/Buddy/ABC ☐

Family ☐

Teachers/staff ☐

Someone outside school ☐

4. Why do you think peers could help with problems?

_____

_____

5. What training would help young people be more effective in helping other young people?

_____

_____

6. How could young people take a bigger part in providing a good environment in school?

_____

_____

Needs analysis

The context

Describe the culture of your organisation.

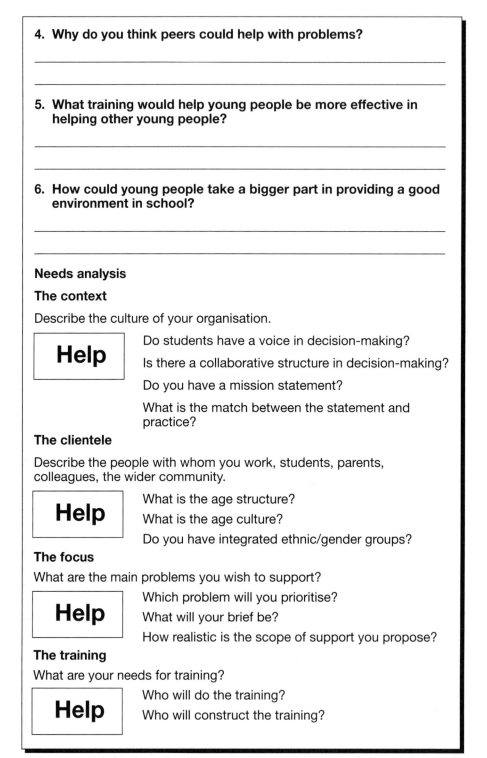

Help

Do students have a voice in decision-making?

Is there a collaborative structure in decision-making?

Do you have a mission statement?

What is the match between the statement and practice?

The clientele

Describe the people with whom you work, students, parents, colleagues, the wider community.

Help

What is the age structure?

What is the age culture?

Do you have integrated ethnic/gender groups?

The focus

What are the main problems you wish to support?

Help

Which problem will you prioritise?

What will your brief be?

How realistic is the scope of support you propose?

The training

What are your needs for training?

Help

Who will do the training?

Who will construct the training?

Is the training appropriate to the focus?

How will you recruit people to train?

The strength analysis

What are the strengths and weaknesses in your scheme?

What are the present strengths of your team of young people and trainers?

What are the potential blocks to your goals?

How can you make blocks into strengths?

The evaluation

How will you monitor what you have done?

How will you evaluate whether or not you are achieving your goals?

What will you do if your evaluation does not produce the results you hoped for?

Buddy   Year 12 group will offer a package over four sessions of the following:

(Please tick which ones)

Group skills   ☐

Drug awareness   ☐

Sex education   ☐

Self-awareness   ☐

Communication skills   ☐

Organisation & planning   ☐

Positive thinking   ☐

Friendship   ☐

Active listening   ☐

Other – chosen by group or form tutor   ☐

Please indicate if you would like them to
work with a small group from your form   ☐

Date   . . . .

Signed . . . .

10

■ ■ ■

Parents and teachers working together

VALERIE BESAG

▶ The advantages of parents and teachers working together
▶ Getting the best from a meeting
▶ Gathering appropriate information
▶ Preventative work
▶ Communicating with the bullies and victims
▶ Understanding the immediate and long-term emotional effects of bullying
▶ Helping children survive bullying

It is every child's democratic right to attend school in safety. As education is one of the very few compulsory activities we impose on our children, it behoves all adults, in whatever capacity, to ensure that this is possible. Parents and teachers, being the most closely involved with children, have the most valuable role to play. In this chapter, the term parent includes all those who care for young people in the role of parent.

There are many advantages in parents and teachers working in partnership (Besag, 1989, 1992, 1999; Randall, 1996). One of the most obvious is that in this way the two halves of the child's life can be put together. This eliminates the risk of a tiny, but essential, piece of information being overlooked. Children may live several miles away from their secondary school and have different friends there from those in their home location. Parents and teachers may know only the set of friends relevant to their own situation and have no knowledge or understanding of other areas of the child's life.

Parents as partners

Parents can offer valuable insights and information, not only concerning the child but also on family matters that may be causing distress (Elliott, 1996).

Family discord, bereavement, sibling relationships, financial stress and health concerns are only a few of the problems that can result in a child becoming insecure and vulnerable or, conversely, a bully (Besag, 1999). If there is a serious level of tension in the home, it is worth checking with school that all is well. Younger children especially find it difficult to put their worries and concerns into words. They express themselves through their behaviour, although this is not always on a conscious level. In addition, there are often more opportunities to offer rewards in the home environment than in school. So, by teachers and parents working together, behaviour in school, for example, could be successfully reinforced and rewarded at home.

Parents are often extremely anxious to have a bullying situation resolved speedily and so will offer the highest level of commitment to any suggested course of action. Inviting them to become actively involved in any planning can help reduce their stress and anxiety – feelings of helplessness may be increasing their concern (Besag, 1989).

It may be easier for a bullied child to confide in a teacher than in parents who are often bewildered by the child's reluctance to discuss the matter and refusal of their offers of help. The situation, in such cases, remains shrouded in mystery, and parents rely heavily on teachers to support the child and communicate with them appropriately.

There are several reasons why children may be reluctant to confide in their parents (Lewis, 1988; Rigby, 1997). Frightened victims often fear reprisals from the bullies, or even those classmates not involved in the bullying, if reporting an attack is viewed as 'telling tales'. If the bullying is severe or prolonged, they may not wish to worry their parents, especially if they feel that parents are unable to bring about effective change. Children are sometimes wary of admitting that they have given money or expensive items to bullies. Bullied children feel rejected and unpopular and may feel ashamed to talk about this to their parents. Although it is widely accepted that many parents are eager for the academic success of their children, we are perhaps less aware that parents can be equally sensitive to the social success and popularity of their offspring. Most of us are ashamed when we cannot cope, especially if we are made to feel foolish in front of our peers.

In the case of adolescents, it may be that with a growing and necessary sense of independence, victims feel that they should be able to cope alone without turning to their parents for help. Often, at this stage, the links between young people and their parents become loosened. They spend less time in the company of parents and relationships may become strained as social norms are flaunted or challenged. At this age, the peer group is the most influential. It is from this source that social mores and attitudes are copied (Harris, 1995).

This is a difficult time but an essential part of moving towards independent living. The pathways of family communication are often subtle and can easily fall into disuse. The family habit, once widespread, of eating and relaxing together has faded for a variety of reasons. Nowadays, young people often have their own 'territory' established in the family home. They may spend much of their time in their own room engaged with a range of expensive equipment; casual chatter and banter with trusted members of the extended family may not be as prevalent as was once the case. In summary, there are many reasons why children may prefer to disclose the bullying to a trusted teacher who is less emotionally involved than their parents (Myers, 1992).

Good parent and teacher communication is required, particularly in the case of children with special educational needs. Children with a range of problems may become the target of stigmatisation, name-calling and rejection (Nabuzoka and Smith, 1993). Other children do not understand the root cause of many behaviour difficulties such as may be attendant in children with Attention Deficit Disorder and Hyperactivity. They may view these children as deliberately aggressive. Children with language and communication difficulties may be misunderstood and ridiculed. Shy children may be considered unfriendly. Even older children, both the bullied and the bullies, may not understand the processes of bullying and the severe adverse effects of this behaviour, thinking of it as just a bit of fun (Salmon et al., 1998). Adults need to be especially vigilant when supervising these children. They need to ensure that relevant targets for their emotional and social development are included in their individual educational plans.

Given that many bullied children find it difficult to approach their parents for help, the optimum situation must be that all parents are alerted to the possibility of bullying occurring and are made aware of the warning signs (Besag, 1989, page 132; Elliott, 1994; Smith and Myron-Wilson, 1998). Parents should be encouraged to approach the school if they suspect anything untoward.

The quality of the initial contact made between home and school, should bullying be suspected, is of the utmost importance. It is essential that clear signals are given that all parties are taking the problem seriously and that a resolution is to be sought with the utmost urgency. Once all are alerted to the problem, the most appropriate course of action may be for the school to set up an informal meeting for all those concerned so that all viewpoints are represented. It may be feasible to invite the parents of both victim and bully to meet together, but this would serve no purpose if their views are known to differ radically and there is no common ground from which to work (Besag, 1992). Staff present at the meeting need to be aware of the severe tension and distress many parents experience on realising that their child is being bullied or is bullying others. Anxious parents may appear truculent, aggressive or even threaten litigation. However, once assured that all appropriate action will be taken to resolve the situation, most parents will calm down and be willing to support the school in developing an action plan.

Gathering information

The first thing to consider is whether or not bullying is the root problem. It may be that the child is using this claim to avoid school for some other reason. A general fear of separation from the parents, or of leaving the home, may well go unnoticed. Other situations are easier to avoid, but such fears are highlighted when the child must leave home to attend school (Besag, 1989, page 159; Green, 1984). Depression may lead to isolation and refusal to attend school or leave the home. Even primary-age children may suffer from depression. Parents noticing a change of behaviour, indicating that their child may be depressed, need to consult their GP or local educational psychology service for advice and appropriate assessment.

Before an initial meeting between parents and teachers, it may be useful for parents to be advised of some of the points to be raised so that they have time to reflect, observe and discuss with each other in private beforehand (Besag, 1989). Having guidelines to focus their thoughts could result in them coming better prepared and with more valuable information. The meeting should be of a problem-solving format, with the outcome being a positive line of action for all to follow, so allowing little room for an over-emotional response from any party.

The role of the school will be to collate all school-based information, even contacting schools the pupils involved attended previously if that is considered relevant. Every way possible should be used to collect information as direct questioning of the bullies or bullied may result in sparse or inaccurate accounts. Sensible observation carried out by staff, or reliable pupils, can result in startling revelations. Training all pupils that to alert staff to others in trouble is not 'telling tales' but is taking responsible action is imperative. Young people react differently to individual people and situations. A child may feel comfortable in some lessons but extremely vulnerable in others. Only by effective lines of communication being in place throughout the school will such situations come to light.

Asking well-chosen pupils to observe and report back may be thought of as controversial, but this could be necessary for the wellbeing and safety of all. It is difficult for teachers to supervise situations such as the toilet or school bus (Boulton, 1995), so the peer group may be the only source of important information. The peer group or older pupils can support vulnerable pupils in many ways. Such programmes include mediation, peer counselling and mentoring systems (Besag, 1992, 1999). In recent years these have been developed to address a range of specific problems such as playground conflicts, depression, friendlessness and the transition period between primary and secondary school. Information from the peer group may be gained informally. Teachers can gain valuable information by listening to pupils chatter among themselves. Once alerted to the suspicion of a child being bullied, they could glean useful insights from overhearing these conversations.

The value in gathering and collating information in this indirect manner cannot be underestimated as bullying is a covert activity, hidden in that curriculum organised by the pupils themselves which may be more pertinent than that organised by the school (Besag, 1986). Adults do not witness bullying, but the peer group does. Boys in particular may actively seek out an audience to gain kudos (Ekman, 1977, quoted in Olweus, 1978). An emphasis on a community ethos, where all have a responsibility for the welfare of all, is an essential element in any successful programme. The development of effective and trusted lines of communication between pupils and staff could lead to pupils becoming more forthcoming in protecting the vulnerable. On questioning pupils in one secondary school, I found that they were able to identify those among them who had bullied others repeatedly since their first years in school. The work of Harris (1995) shows that the peer group have a more accurate and detailed knowledge of each other than their adult caretakers. The research of Cowen (1973) found that in the group studied, the young people were able to predict each other's future mental welfare better than professionals.

In collecting information more directly from staff, attention needs to be drawn to such things as the quality of the child's peer interactions:

- evidence of rejection by peers;
- timid and submissive behaviour;
- isolation from the peer group;
- vulnerable presentation;
- evidence of confidence and resilience.

Parents need to be aware that the collection and collation of information takes time, especially when at least 70 teachers work in all but the smallest secondary school. Often parents expect the situation to be resolved on the spot, although they are aware that any other system of justice can be slow. Once clearly identified, bullying often stops almost immediately, having thrived on secrecy, but the stage of identification takes time. This being so, it is imperative that parents contact the school immediately if they suspect bullying is taking place, even if their own child is not directly involved.

We know now that children merely witnessing bullying can be very distressed and anxious (Glover et al., 1997; Measor and Woods, 1984). In the case of the victim, a speedy resolution is essential as the situation can easily escalate and their confidence can be rapidly reduced (Lewis, 1988). Parents should encourage their children to approach those teachers they feel most comfortable with first, rather than a designated teacher such as the year tutor. It is important that some responsible adult is alerted to the situation rather than a child being left feeling helpless and guilty due to a reluctance to approach a less familiar teacher.

It is to everyone's advantage that some form of written record is kept of the meeting – who is to be the key person, the proposed course of action and the date set for a review meeting. The latter is essential to ensure that the situation has been resolved satisfactorily. Parents may be hesitant to contact the school a second time if the bullying is continuing, yet the school may assume that all is well. It is particularly important to keep detailed notes as legal challenges can be made years later. The situation will need monitoring for some time, especially to reassure the bullied child who may have lost confidence in the level of adult protection. If the parents of the bully were not at the meeting, they should be advised by letter of any proposed action concerning their child. All parents should be made aware if their child has been involved in any bullying, either as bully or victim.

If parents approaching a school receive a negative response, they are able to turn for support to other bodies such as school governors, doctors, nurses, educational psychologists and advisers, who all work to support children in school. All can be contacted directly by parents through the education department of the local authority. The administrators in this sector of any local authority are also able to offer guidance and support to parents. Depending on the age of the child (ten or over) and the severity of the attack, it may be appropriate for parents to contact the local police. If the child is at risk in the community, parents should discuss this informally with designated police officers.

In one secondary school, the young people who had left recently frequently hung around the school gate taunting and bullying the current pupils on their way home. At the request of the head teacher, the local police informally approached these young people and supervised the area. This resolved the situation speedily and, contrary to the fears of parents, the bullying did not re-emerge elsewhere. In addition, the head teacher took photographs of the gang at the school gate. This encouraged their fast dispersal. Victims of community bullying may be helped by organisations such as Victim Support.

In any discussion, within school or with outside agencies, it is essential to take care over the vocabulary used. It is advisable to describe the behaviour as bullying and not the child as a bully. Describing a child as a bully could lead to litigation. Describing a child as a victim may encourage feelings of helplessness and inadequacy. It is always best to keep to behavioural terms rather than to label individuals. It is easier to talk in terms of behavioural change than changing personalities.

Prevention

All the above suggestions concern liaison work between parents and teachers once a bullying problem has been identified. The optimum approach, however, is the type of preventative work carried out in Norway where Professor Dan Olweus brought bullying in school to the attention of the public (Olweus, 1978). The preventative programme designed by Olweus involves booklets, discussion groups, videos and workshops for pupils, parents and teachers. It is important that parents, as well as teachers, have the opportunity to receive this type of training for they have more contact hours with their children than professionals, but receive little advice or support (Olweus, 1993b).

Michele Elliott pioneered similar preventative work in schools in the UK with the Kidscape programmes. These are taught by teachers in the context of the curriculum and involve discussions, role-play and parent meetings (Elliott, 2001a). An excellent book on all aspects of parenting, not just bullying, is *501 Ways To Be a Good Parent* by Michele Elliott (1996).

Good literature is now available for parents to buy for children to read about bullying. Any good bookshop or library will have a selection of stories and poems in stock or will be able to offer advice. These may be sourced from a computer website. Literature could be used as a way into discussions with children on the sensitive topic of bullying. It is often easier to talk in the third person about distressing issues. Anxious and threatened children may be able to discuss what is happening to them in school in terms of characters in a book, even though they are unable to talk directly about their own experiences.

Supporting parents and children

One aspect of the problem of bullying that could be dealt with in workshops for parents is the emotional and behavioural effects bullying can have on a child. Parents need to be able to identify what is happening to their child and be able to respond appropriately to what can be difficult behaviour. A bullied child can become irritable, volatile and fearful (Lewis, 1988). In the words of one victim, he used his younger sister as his 'personal punch bag'. Parents, too, may be the butt of pent-up rage and frustration.

The sudden lack of confidence many victims experience may bewilder parents (Olweus, 1993a). It is not uncommon for a bullied child to avoid any contact with others. For example, a fearful child may cross the road on the approach of even an unknown peer group, or wait for a bus several yards away from a queue. This avoidance of others, perhaps to avoid their rejection, leaves many bullied children isolated in school. If they are not included in the network of informal chatter, they miss the constant reminders and cues passing among the peer group. This could result in them being in the wrong place, at the wrong time, with wrong equipment and materials. Parents and teachers need to be particularly patient and supportive at this time (Besag, 1992, pp. 41–44; Myers, 1992).

The parents of a child being bullied may approach the school for advice on how to support the child at home during this difficult period (Besag, 1989, 1992). They need to be advised to remain calm and confident in front of the child and to resist persistent questioning which may add to their stress. The child must be assured that the bullying will be stopped and helped to understand that this taunting is something that many people encounter in some form or other at some time. The child needs to feel confident that help is available to develop coping skills in case they should encounter bullying again, as well as to manage the current trauma.

It may be helpful to discuss name-calling (Besag, 1989, 1992, 1999). This is often the most distressing aspect of bullying (Besag, 1989; Elliott, 2001b). Busy adults can underestimate the damaging, long-term effect of name-calling and other verbal abuse. Ways of coping with such attacks can be taught. Children can rehearse keeping calm, laughing it off and ignoring it. These strategies can help the child shrug off a potentially distressing situation (Besag, 1989). It is easy to tell a child to ignore bullying, but ignoring is a skill that may not come easily to all. Parents can help children by talking through potential bullying situations such as name-calling and rehearsing ways in which they could respond.

One useful technique is to appear to remain calm and relaxed while fending off the verbal attacks with casual or humorous responses. An example of this could be when the bully calls the target child 'fatso'. The amicable response could be 'Yeah, I'm really lucky. My Mum's a marvellous cook.' A red-haired child name-called 'Carrots' could be helped to respond calmly by his parents gently desensitising him to the name by using it affectionately around the home.

If caught in a difficult situation such as bullying, it is useful for the children to be able to draw on specific strategies to enable them to walk away without losing face. Concentrating on something external to the situation helps, such as a proposed visit to a favourite cousin, a model being planned, a new game, a trip to the shops with pocket money – anything that helps the child to walk away giving the external appearance of remaining calm. Crying, shouting or any other dramatic response may encourage the bullies to repeat the attack.

However, while some children find such strategies helpful, others may not. Parents should help the child find a strategy that helps. Ignoring and similar techniques need adequate rehearsal at home in order for the child to feel confident in applying them to a real-life situation. Just to advise a child to 'ignore it', without showing them how to do so, leaves them undefended and vulnerable.

It is always helpful for parents to talk to others whose children have had similar experiences in order to share ideas and solutions. They need to be reassured that this is something that can happen to anyone and that the bullying has not occurred because of any defect in the victim. The best outcome would be for bullied children to reach a solution for themselves. This may be brought about with the involvement of the peer group, or with the support of concerned adults, so that they feel confident in their ability to cope.

It must be stressed that research shows that victims left to struggle with the problem alone are unlikely to extricate themselves from the bullying, which can continue for years (Cole, 1977; Cowen et al., 1973; Stephenson and Smith, 1988). With adult support, victims can gain in confidence and self-esteem if they find that a resolution is within their grasp. It is important that the victims be encouraged, in a sensitive manner, to examine any behaviour, attitude or response of their own that could be irritating or exacerbating the bullying. It is essential, however, that this work is approached in a practical manner, where victims identify for themselves how they could best work towards resolving the problem. If approached in a prescriptive way, they could feel that they have 'deserved' the bullying and they have been solely at fault (Besag, 1992, 1999).

One of the ways in which liaison work between home and school can be most effective is in restoring the self-esteem and confidence of victims (Lewis, 1988). Positive comments and praise help to do this but, in addition, mastering a skill leads to a sense of achievement, giving tangible proof of self-worth. Encouraging young people to take up an individual activity such as swimming or chess gets them out of the house. They are in the company of others although there are few social demands made upon them in these activities. They may feel that they are able to handle such situations. Faced with more socially demanding activities, they may prefer to sit in a bedroom, turning increasingly to solitary occupations.

On examination of the profiles of those children at high risk of becoming involved in bullying (Besag 1989, 1992, 1999), it can be seen that potential victims are often 'watchers' rather than 'doers' and may need a lot of encouragement to join in groups and make new friends, even before the experience of being bullied. It is, however, easier for a shy and hesitant person to join a skill-based group where adults are present, for example a dance class or tennis club, as adults are more tolerant than the peer group. Importantly, in a skill-based group there is less emphasis on social skills. This is one way in which those who have been bullied, and so become wary, can be eased back into functioning happily within the peer group. Once the vulnerable child is functioning comfortably within a mixed adult and peer group, moves can be made towards similar skill-based groups attended by peers but under adult supervision. An example of this would be a badminton club in after-school hours. Lastly, the child could progress to less supervised and purely social peer groups such as a youth club or disco. Details of such programmes of work for both bullies and victims can be found in Besag (1989).

It is unfortunate that many clubs and activities organised by schools, such as football and tennis, demand good co-ordination skills. Many young people who are bullied, especially boys, are not proficient in these skills. For profiles of children with these difficulties, see Besag (1989). Children with poor co-ordination and organisational difficulties may be assessed as Developmentally Dyspraxic (see Chapter 16). Teachers may misunderstand their presentation and consider such children lazy or stupid. Such negative attitudes are quickly picked up by other children and used to taunt the vulnerable when out of sight of adults.

Once made aware of the range of opportunities schools can offer to develop the social confidence of socially vulnerable children, parents and teachers could work in liaison. Vulnerable young people could learn to interact within the peer groups with confidence and without fear of ridicule and rejection. The long-term value of such work is that even in adult life, those who are naturally shy may find that a bank of skills such as chess, photography or swimming can help them join groups in unfamiliar situations, so enabling them to make friends and develop confidence. A boy diagnosed as dyspraxic may have appropriate muscle strength and enjoy working out at the gym. Skill in this area could lead to peer acceptance and 'street cred'. Research indicates that those who are socially vulnerable in childhood are at high risk of remaining so in later years if left to cope alone and unsupported (Lewis, 1988; Olweus, 1993a).

The style of work attempted between concerned teachers and the parents of a child bullying others depends largely on the attitude and reaction of the parents. If the parents admit that this behaviour is unacceptable, the prognosis for change will be more favourable. Many parents, finding themselves in this situation, feel under considerable stress and experience feelings of shame, guilt and confusion. A child, however, may be bullying others for a variety of reasons independent of parental guidance, for example, jealousy of a sibling or confusion between leadership and dominance (Elliott, 1994). Children being bullied may bully others due to frustration. In cases such as the above, if parents and school have a common approach, the situation can be resolved speedily.

However, bullies may not be behaving in this way as a reaction to stress or trauma. Recent research shows that many have good social skills and know how to manipulate the peer group to their own advantage (Sutton *et al.* 1999a, 1999b). In such cases, it is essential that parents and teachers ensure that they are all giving the same message to these young people: that bullying in any form will not be tolerated.

Aggression

There are, however, those parents who ignore repeated reports and warnings from the school that their children's bullying behaviour will not be tolerated. Such parents may consider that aggressive behaviour is an acceptable means of settling disputes or expressing frustration. Having taught their children to 'stick up for themselves' they feel others should behave in a similar way. Children from such families are modelling behaviour they have witnessed at home (Besag, 1999). In such families, it is not uncommon for one parent to be the disciplinarian, using a harsh and punitive style, and the other to be lax, inconsistent, or ineffective (Olweus, 1993b).

It would appear that, in whatever form, unpredictable swings from harsh to lax parental style of discipline cause problem behaviour (Olweus, 1993b; Patterson *et al.*, 1973). Depending on whether or not the parents are co-operative, the school could have a valuable role to play in directing the attention of such parents to alternative styles of management, either directly in discussions or indirectly in workshops and parent meetings (Elliott, 1996). Patterson *et al.* (1973) show the damaging effects of harsh discipline. The child learns to model the aggressive behaviour and the relationship between child and parent can rapidly deteriorate. A positive style of management can help to strengthen parent–child bonds (Elliott, 1996).

If young people are accustomed to using aggression as a means to an end, whether it be material gain, kudos or entertainment, the use of models such as persuasion, advice or counselling may be found to be ineffective to counter such deviant behaviour as bullying. Any behaviour only continues if rewarded. The bully has been gaining in some manner from the bullying behaviour. There may be no guilt or remorse from the bully whereas all others involved may have found the experience destructive and distressing and urgently seek a successful resolution.

Nowadays parents and professionals can look to resources other than books for advice and support. The CD ROM *Coping with Bullying* (Besag, 1999) is available at minimum cost due to support from a number of funding and charitable agencies. This is designed to help parents, teachers and young people understand how they can help themselves and each other counteract this destructive behaviour.

Summary

In conclusion, we are now aware that bullying is a form of abuse, child-to-child abuse. As such, it can be a most damaging experience. In the short term it can be a traumatic experience for a child of any age, whereas the long-term prognosis for both bullies and bullied is poor. Those bullying during their school years are known to go on to young adulthood at higher risk of embarking on a deviant career than others (Olweus, 1973), whereas those who have been bullied and left alone to cope can be expected to lead a life of impoverished social experience and all that entails.

We now have profiles of those at high risk of becoming involved in bullying (Besag, 1989). This being so, adults can embark on a variety of preventative work. Teachers and parents have the most contact hours with young people. Parents, in most cases, are the most committed to their own children. This means that, by working together, they have the best prognosis for positive change. By working together on preventative programmes (Elliott, 2001a) or in liaison in an identified situation, we should eventually be able to ensure that all pupils feel that they are able to attend school in safety. Bullying is a complex behaviour that requires a sophisticated and comprehensive approach where parents and teachers are working closely together.

References

Besag, V. E. (1986) 'Bullies, victims and the silent majority', *Times Educational Supplement*, 5 December, Times Newspapers Limited, pp 22–3.

Besag, V. E. (1989) *Bullies and Victims in Schools*. Open University Press.

Besag, V. E. (1999) *Coping with Bullying*. Available from SMS Multimedia (P.O. Box 40, Ashington, NE63 8YR).

Besag, V. E. (1992) *We Don't Have Bullies Here*! valbesag (Training and Publications). Available from 3 Jesmond Dene Terrace, Jesmond, Newcastle upon Tyne, NE2 2ET.

Boulton, M. J. (1995) 'Playground behaviour and peer interaction of primary school boys classified as bullies, victims and not involved', *British Journal of Educational Psychology*, 65, pp 165–77.

Cole, R. J. (1977) 'The bullied child in school', unpublished MSc dissertation, University of Sheffield.

Cowen, E. L. *et al.* (1973) 'Long-term follow-up of early-detected vulnerable children', *Journal of Consulting and Clinical Psychology*, Vol 41, pp 438–46.

Ekman, P. (1977) 'Stability of aggressive reaction patterns in males – a review', *Psychological Bulletin*, 86 (4), pp 852–75.

Elliott, M. (2001b) Bully leaflet, Kidscape.

Elliott, M. (2001a) Kidscape Primary Kit, Kidscape.

Elliott, M. (1994) *Keeping Safe: A practical guide to talking with children*. Hodder and Stoughton.

Elliott, M. (1996) *501 Ways to be a Good Parent*. Hodder and Stoughton.

Glover, D., Cartwright, N. and Gleeson, D. (1997) *Towards Bully-free Schools: interventions in action*. Open University Press.

Green, C. (1984) *Toddler Training*. Century Hutchinson.

Harris, J. R. (1995) 'Where is the child's environment? – A group theory of socialisation', *Psychological Review*, 97, pp 114–21.

Lewis, D. (1988) *Helping Your Anxious Child*. Methuen.

Measor, L. and Woods, P. (1984) *Changing Schools – pupil perspectives on transfer to a secondary school*. Open University Press.

Myers, B. (1992) *Parenting Teenagers*. Jessica Kingsley Publishers Ltd.

Nabuzoka, D. and Smith, P. K. (1993) 'Sociometric status and social behaviour of children with and without learning difficulties', *Journal of Child Psychology and Psychiatry*, 34 (8), pp 1435–48.

Olweus, D. (1978) *Aggression in the Schools – Bullies and Whipping Boys*. Hemisphere.

Olweus, D. (1993b) *Bullying at School – what we know and what we can do*. Blackwell.

Olweus, D. (1973) *Hackycklingar och oversittare – Forskning om skilmobbring*. Almqvist and Wikzell.

Olweus, D. (1993a) 'Victimisation by peers – antecedents and long-term outcomes' in Rubin, N. A. and Asendorg, J. A. (eds) *Social Withdrawal, Inhibition and Shyness in Childhood*. Hellidale.

Patterson, G. R., Cobb, J. A. and Ray, R. S. (1973) 'A social engineering technology for retraining families of aggressive boys' in Adams, H. E. and Unikel, I. P. (eds) *Issues and Trends in Behaviour Therapy*. C.C. Thomas.

Randall, P. E. (1996) *A Community Approach to Bullying*. Trentham Books.

Rigby, K. (1997) *Bullying in Schools: and what to do about it*. Jessica Kingsley.

Salmon, G., James, A. and Smith, D. M. (1998) 'Bullying in schools – self reported anxiety, depression, and self esteem in secondary school children', *British Medical Journal*, 317, 7163, pp 924–5.

Smith, P. K. and Myron-Wilson, R. (1998) 'Parenting and school bullying', *Clinical Child Psychology and Psychiatry*, 3, pp 405–17.

Stephenson, P. and Smith, D. (1988) 'Bullying in the junior school' in Tattum, D. and Lane, D. (eds) *Bullying in Schools*. Trentham Books.

Sutton, J., Smith, P. K. and Swettenham, J. (1999a) 'Bullying and theory of mind: a critique of the "social skills deficit" approach to anti-social behaviour', *Social Development*, 8, pp 117–27.

Sutton, J., Smith, P. K. and Swettenham, J. (1999b) 'Social cognition and bullying – social inadequacy or skilled manipulation', *British Journal of Developmental Psychology*, 17, pp 435–50.

11

■ ■ ■

20 Anti-bullying exercises to use with students

MICHELE ELLIOTT

▶ Tried and tested ideas that work
▶ Exercises for children and young people

Beleaguered teachers with too much to do and too little time to do it in may welcome the following ideas which have been used successfully with students. With a couple of exceptions, the exercises are not labelled for particular ages as most can be adapted for students of different ages and abilities.

Collage

Collages are a non-threatening way for students to express their feelings about bullying. You will need a variety of magazines (lots) with pictures to cut out, paper to paste pictures on, glue, scissors.

Ask the students to work on a 'bullying' theme to make collages. They go through the magazines and cut or tear out pictures which reflect the theme. Some suggestion for themes are:

- When I am bullied I feel ...
- When I see someone being bullied ...
- People who bully are ...
- Victims are ...
- What I would like to do to people who bully ...
- How people who bully feel ...
- How victims feel ...
- What adults do about bullying ...
- Bullying is ...
- Ways to stop bullying ...
- The way I see myself ...

- The way others see me ...
- The way I wish I was ...
- The way parents/teachers/students see me ...

Display the collages, if appropriate, or ask the students to discuss them in small groups. This exercise does not depend upon artistic talent and students of all ages seem to enjoy the hands-on approach of making collages (Elliott and Kilpatrick, 2002).

Making friends

Although we ask students to become friends, we seldom help them to think of how to go about it. Bullying is sometimes the result of misguided attempts of children or young people trying to become part of a group or trying to approach someone to become a friend.

Ask the students to discuss ways to make friends. Have them work in small groups and come up with a list of ten ways to make a friend. Then ask them to report to the larger group and write the suggestions on the board, avoiding duplication.

These suggestions were compiled by a group of 13-year-olds:

- Showing an interest in what people do.
- Being complimentary without going over the top.
- Having a pleasant expression on your face.
- Laughing at people's jokes.
- Being kind.
- Asking to join in.
- Offering to help.
- Inviting people to do something.
- Going to places where other students are.
- Being welcoming to new students.
- Bringing something interesting to do.
- Being willing to share.
- Being humorous/telling jokes.
- Being fair.
- Organising games or activities.
- Thinking of new ideas.

Using the same method, ask the students to think about ways *not* to make friends. One group thought of the following:

- Being bossy.
- Telling others how to play.
- Telling others they are doing things wrong.
- Talking about yourself all the time.
- Being mean.

- Talking about other students behind their backs.
- Being negative and sarcastic.
- Being too intense or serious all the time.
- Bragging.
- Moaning all the time.
- Being a bully.
- Claiming credit for something you didn't do.
- Lying or cheating.

Ask the students to draw up a Friendship Charter and post it in the school where it can be seen and discussed.

Follow-up exercises

Ask the students to role-play someone trying to make friends the wrong way and then another role-play showing the right way.

Ask the students to conduct a survey asking students and staff for their ideas on making friends. Chart the results and discuss.

Write a paper about an imaginary new student trying to make friends in your school – what obstacles might she or he encounter? What things would help? Include suggestions which the school might use to change for the better.

Story/play

There are several books about bullying listed in 'Resources' on pages 324–27. The teacher can either choose one to read or ask children to read a story or prepare a short play about bullying. Some teachers have asked older children to read to younger children or to put on a play for young children.

Letter

Use an English class to ask the students to write a letter to a pen pal (real or imaginary) or a new friend describing what they like to do, what kind of a person they are, what they hope to do when they leave school. Ask them to talk about their life in school and to bring in the theme of bullying from either a victim or bully viewpoint. For example, they can write about a typical day in school and include a bullying situation.

Body outline

This exercise is for younger children. Ask the children to lie down on a large piece of paper (rolls of heavy lining paper from a DIY shop are perfect for this and quite cheap) and trace an outline of their bodies. Ask them to cut out their outline and colour it in as they wish. Get a pad of Post-it notes and write something good about each child and attach the note to the outline, perhaps on the hand. Change the message as often as possible – the children will be delighted.

Nicknames

Ask the students what nickname they would like to be called if they had a choice. Often hurtful nicknames are given to children and young people and then used to bully them. Help each student find a positive nickname for him/herself. This might be a good opportunity to use words from other languages, such as Solecito (Spanish for little sun), Shaina (Yiddish for beautiful), Leoncito (Spanish for little lion). Ask the students for other suggestions. Come up with a list and let the students decide on their own names, but don't let anyone pick a negative nickname.

Student of the Week

This exercise works very well with younger children. Each week put up the picture of one student. Ask each of the other students to say one good thing about the student and make a list of five statements to put under the picture. If you want to speed up the exercise, have a Student of the Day. Try to have all the pictures and comments up on parents' evening and ask the parents to add a comment (if all the parents can't come, try to get a good comment either in writing or over the telephone and add it to the child's list).

Poem

Ask the students to write a poem about bullying. Display the poems and choose some to be read at assembly. Alternatively, have a contest in which judges from outside the school choose the winners and give book tokens (donated by the local bookshop?) as prizes.

Perfect school

This is fun and can lead to noisy discussions. Ask the students to design a school that is perfect for bullies. They should think about the buildings, the playground, the attitude of the students and staff towards bullying. Alternatively, they can design a perfect school in which there is no bullying. For younger pupils, give them a plan of the school and grounds and ask them to colour in green for where they feel safe, red for where they don't, or have them use different colours or circle these areas if colour-blindness is a problem. This could also be used as a computer-based activity.

Positive/negative

Ask the students to draw a line down the centre of a piece of paper and write Positive at the top on one side and Negative on the other. Ask them to write in three positive things about themselves in the first column and three negative things in the second. The ground rule is that none of the traits can be physical, but should be things that have been developed by the student and therefore could be changed. For example:

Positive	Negative
Honest	Bad temper
Fast runner	Don't do homework
Like pets	Untidy

Ask the students if they could work on changing one negative trait into a positive one over the next week or month. This exercise is best done individually and not with other students unless a trusting relationship has been built up; otherwise the 'negatives' could be used to bully.

Class newspaper

Ask each student to contribute an article, drawing, puzzle or poem about bullying to a class newsletter. Get the students to put together the newsletter and photocopy it for parents, students and staff.

Millionaire

Tell the students that they have each inherited £1 million, of which they must use 90% to eradicate bullying. After they have stopped all bullying, they can then use the remaining 10% of the money for personal use and must use that 10% to make their own lives happier. How would they use the money? The students can either work individually and write about what they would do or work in small groups and report back to the class what they would do as a group.

Puppet play

This exercise is for younger children. Using socks decorated by the children (buttons for eyes, felt mouths, wool for hair and whiskers) or paper cut-outs of characters, ask the children to make up a puppet play about a child who is being bullied and how sad the child feels. Ask them to think of a positive way to end the play so that the child who is bullying gets help and so does the victim – a happy ending!

Mural

Ask the students to co-operate on drawing and decorating a class mural depicting on one panel a playground where bullying is happening and on another panel a playground where everyone is having a good time and where there is no bullying. Discuss your own playground and think of ways which could make it more like the 'No bullying' panel.

Make someone feel good

Ask the students to agree to each do or say at least one thing a day to make someone else feel good. Have a rule that it has to be a different person each day that they make feel good. You may want to make this a month-long project and ask each student to do or say something to each member of the class or group. Ask each student to keep a journal or record of what they do and discuss it with them.

Wish list

This exercise is best done on an individual basis and discussed with the teacher or a trusted friend. Ask students to write down on one side of paper five words which describe them. On the other side of the paper they should write down five words which they wished described them.

Ask them to take one of the words on their Wish List and describe what it means to be like that. For example, if they said they wished they were 'happy', what does it mean to them to be happy?

People who seem to be happy:
Smile
Have friends
Do well in school
Have money
Come from nice families
Feel good about themselves

Then ask the students to look at the list they have just made to see which things it might be possible for them to work on to become happy. It might not be possible to have money (or necessarily even true that you need it to be happy) or to come from a nice family, but it might be possible to work on smiling, having friends, doing well in school and feeling good about themselves.

Ask the students to make it a goal to work on attaining at least one of the ideals on their Wish List. Help them work out an action plan to achieve their goal: for example, if the goal is to 'be popular', the student needs to think about how they can make friends and adopt welcoming and friendly behaviour (see 'Making friends' exercise above). Their action plan might start something like this:

- Try to smile at people whenever possible.
- Be kind to other people and helpful.
- Invite someone home.
- Be ready to listen to others.

For 'Doing well in school', the action plan might look like this:

- Choose one subject to work on to start with.
- Ask the teacher for extra help.
- Set aside more time to work on that subject.
- Study with someone who might be able to help you understand it better.
- Don't get discouraged if it takes some time to get better in the subject.
- Tell yourself that you will improve and believe that you can do it.
- Ignore anyone who attempts to discourage you, even a well-meaning parent who says, 'I never did very well in that either'.
- Reward yourself for getting better.

This exercise helps people to develop self-esteem if they follow through and actually are able to change the goal from a wish to a reality (Elliott and Kilpatrick, 2002). Although it does take lots of help and encouragement, it is worth it to achieve the goal. The students can do this exercise with parents and other adults, if they are supportive.

Bully gang

Ask the students to write a story about a child or young person who suddenly finds that they are being pulled into a bully gang and being pressured to start bullying a person they have been friends with in the past. Ask them to write about what the character might be thinking and feeling and how he or she resolves the problem. Use these stories as a springboard to discuss how hard it is to resist peer pressure and how many people who bully others might not really want to but are frightened or led into this type of behaviour and how they can get help to stop.

Follow-up exercise: Victim viewpoint

After the students have completed the exercise above, ask them to write the same story from the viewpoint of the victim. She/he will be confused, frightened and worried, especially when one of their friends joins in the gang bullying. Again follow this with discussion about how the victims of bullying can feel and how they can get help.

Bulletin board

Using the media, ask students to look for references to bullying, including racist attacks or attacks on gay or lesbian people or incidents of suicide or suicide attempts attributed to bullying in the press over a month and use these stories to create a bulletin board and to discuss the issue of bullying and ideas about stopping it.

Mystery person

Give each student the name of another student and tell them to keep the name of their person a secret. Ask them to telephone each other or talk away from school to students to find out 'different' facts about their Mystery Person – not just biographical details but names of pets, kinds of food they like, secret ambitions, etc. Have the students write about their Mystery Person without giving their name, then read aloud their writing to see if the class can guess who the person is. Start with general information like:

- My Mystery Person loves chocolate ice cream and Chinese food (not mixed together). My Mystery Person secretly wants to become a famous rock star and dye his/her hair blue.
- My Mystery Person likes to go swimming in the holidays. She/he nearly got run over by a car at the age of three.
- My Mystery Person likes to draw, make plasticine models and take things apart to see how they work.
- My Mystery Person is known to smile a lot.
- My Mystery Person has two brothers, a cat, a dog and a gerbil. She/he likes the pets, but sometimes can't stand the brothers.
- My Mystery Person has brown hair and brown eyes and is 4 feet 10 inches (145cm) tall. Who is she/he?

At various points before the end of the reading, ask the students to raise their hands if they think they know who the Mystery Person is – the comments being read out should all be positive (you may wish to check the stories) and gradually get specific so that the identity of the Mystery Person becomes apparent. This is a good way to focus positively on a student, making them the centre of attention in a nice way and revealing new information about him/her which might be interesting.

Bully letter

Ask the students to write a letter to an imaginary bully to try to explain why she/he should try to change and give some suggestions on how to change.

Follow-up exercise: Dear Bullied Person letter

Ask the students to write to an imaginary victim of bullying telling the victim how they will personally help him/her to stop being a victim and giving advice about how the victim might get some help.

Summary

Some of these exercises could be adapted for assemblies or plays. Schools that have successfully combated bullying find that the more time they devote to keeping bullying on the agenda, the fewer incidents of bullying are reported. So the time spent on exercises like these which promote good citizenship actually save time in the end.

References

Elliott, M. and Kilpatrick, J. (2002) *How to Stop Bullying: A Kidscape Training Guide*. Kidscape. (See address under 'Help Organisations' on page 317)

12

■ ■ ■

Positive behaviour: strategies for infant and junior schools

EVE HALBERT

▶ Creating a safe classroom environment
▶ Activities for infants and juniors

Teaching is not a soft option – the problems faced by teachers can be immense. In schools I have taught in, many of the children suffered from poor self-esteem, with little or no support from home. This caused some of them to try to win respect and status from their peer group by acting in an aggressive way. Creating a warm, supportive atmosphere, a place of safety for children and teachers alike, was a priority if we were to ensure that bullying was stopped. These activities are some that I used successfully over many years working with children, some of whom had very disturbed behaviour.

Schools can become battlegrounds where skills of intimidation and bullying are learned. The aggressive children usually have the highest profiles. In our attempts to deal with them, we often overlook the quiet, overly adapted child who has the 'faint soul' look in their eyes. As a result, victims and those who become withdrawn develop unhealthy patterns of behaviour that last a lifetime. Hopefully the strategies included here will help redress these patterns.

Smart and stupid behaviour

I have linked *smart* and *stupid* behaviour with happy and sad faces as it is the simplest way to enhance understanding of behaviour.

The terms *smart* and *stupid* have been used for very specific reasons. First, 'naughty' and 'bad' carry status within the peer group. Both carry the kudos of defiance and, within the school system, the peer group often admires the individual or individuals who dare to defy authority. The pupil who answers back, storms out of a classroom, throws books across a room, etc. is often seen as some kind of hero or heroine.

This is often true in adult life. We have well-used phrases such as 'naughty but nice'. But there is another side to the use of 'naughty' or 'bad'. Most human beings, be they adult or child, would like to defy powerful figures like employers or traffic police but dare not. They tend to admire those who do and often actively encourage others to play that role. This is sad for children labelled as disruptive when they try to change and be 'good'. The peer group taunts them for 'turning chicken' or 'losing their bottle'.

The word *stupid* has been substituted for 'naughty' or 'bad' because it carries no status or kudos. Stupid behaviour carries only penalties, e.g. loss of privileges, parents having to come into school, etc.

The word *good* also carries disadvantages. The child who is seen as 'good' in the teacher's eyes is often disparaged for being the teacher's pet, the creep. Many children who would wish to please the teacher by being helpful cannot afford to do it for fear of mockery or bullying. This also applies to adult life. Anyone who brings their boss flowers or chocolates is seen as a creep looking for promotion or someone not to be trusted in the staff room. Therefore, the word *smart* is used as it does carry status and kudos. Every child wants to be seen as streetwise or sharp.

When working with children we must strive to be constructive, not destructive. No child should ever be categorised as being stupid. That is demoralising and damaging, leading to poor self-esteem. Being categorised as stupid is a fixed state. If a pupil believes that he or she is stupid, then it will become a self-fulfilling prophecy and behaviour will deteriorate.

However, we are all capable from time to time of actions that are unwise, to say the least. Actions are about behaviour and can be changed in an instant given a choice of alternative behaviours. The choice of *smart* and *stupid* behaviour is thrown open to the class. They decide and give reasons for the choices. For example, if smart behaviour is seen as lining up quietly after the bell has rung, this has to carry a benefit, e.g. you don't have to spend more than a few moments standing in the cold playground. That is smart thinking.

Stupid behaviour is similarly categorised. For example, stealing from the teacher's desk is seen as stupid behaviour because the penalty for the whole class is that access to the classroom may no longer be an option during break times and, if it happens to be a cold day or if it is raining, it is far more unpleasant to be left in the playground or in the crowded school hall than to be in the warmth of one's own classroom.

The whole class also suggests penalties and privileges. These can be seen as additional art lessons, a special activity time or extended playtime. Teachers must always look for opportunities to reward smart behaviour. This massively increases the self-worth of the child.

This system reduces teacher stress, as there is rarely a need to be a lion tamer. External methods of control are extremely wearing on the body and soul. Shouting, bawling and scolding are exhausting methods of keeping control. It also encourages negative behavioural patterns. Some children become disaffected and shut off. Others, who experience violence at home, may become further traumatised even if the teacher is shouting at someone else.

Children are more than able to select appropriate behaviour given the chance and the choice. If choice is given to the peer group, behaviour will change, as it is one of the most powerful influences in a child's life. Most children would rather defy you than their friends.

Acceptance and approval is not dependent on academic achievement

A pupil with learning difficulties can easily be the smartest child in the class, earning praise and reward for him or herself or privileges for the class. Children with learning difficulties often have disruptive behavioural patterns. These strategies often help academic performance and give status in a positive way.

Smart and *stupid* need not always be used. Children have their own way of expressing behaviour. For example, pupils from ethnic minority groups often prefer the word 'cool' for smart behaviour or 'foo foo' for foolish behaviour.

The only time that I would use the word 'good' is when referring to work done by a pupil. Nothing pleases a child more than the comment 'Good work, Lisa!' on their books and projects.

If peer influence was going to work, I had to allow the class to decide what behaviour was relevant for them without interference from the class teacher or me. The following is a list of smart behaviour drawn up by the class. They chose the categories without help from me.

Smart behaviour:

1 Lining up quietly.
2 Helping others with their work.
3 Working quietly when the teacher is busy.
4 Raising your hand when you want to ask a question.
5 Knocking on the door before entering the classroom.
6 Remembering to say please and thank you.
7 Waiting your turn.
8 Going to the toilet at break time.
9 Bringing a sharp pencil, ruler and rubber each day.
10 Minding your manners.

Benefits:

1 The teacher will be smiling.
2 Extra art lessons.
3 Pottery.
4 We will learn quicker.
5 Parents will be pleased with the stars on our work.
6 More trips out.
7 There will be no bullying.

8 We will have more fun in the class.

9 The teacher will trust us to stay in the class at break time.

Stupid behaviour:

1 Fighting.
2 Name-calling.
3 Stealing.
4 Bullying.
5 Shouting out in class.
6 Forgetting PE kit.
7 Not saying please and thank you.
8 Wandering about the classroom annoying other people.
9 Talking when the teacher is trying to explain things.
10 Being rude.
11 Hitting a teacher.
12 Messing about in class.

Penalties for stupid behaviour:

1 Writing lines.
2 Parents having to come into school.
3 Losing playtime.
4 Missing football and games.
5 Having to go to the deputy or head teacher.
6 No TV.
7 No activity afternoon.
8 No trips to museums or special things.
9 Suspended from school.
10 Having to go to another school.

Teddy Bears and Thorns

Children who bully often have little idea of the effects that they are having on others. The bully normally carries status within the peer group so it can be a difficult role to eradicate. Many boys are expected to be tough, not to be a sissy and not to cry.

The bully girls are just as bad, if not worse in some instances. Having worked with girl gangs, I found a viciousness that matched the boys in every way. This seems to be a frightening trend in our society.

There is not much point in trying to persuade a child to stop one type of behaviour unless they can see some better alternative.

The focus of Teddy Bears and Thorns was to help the class understand the effects of cruel behaviour while giving them the choice to be strong yet sensitive too. It also gave them the chance to look at their own behaviour.

I brought a big bag of soft, fluffy teddy bears into the class and invited the children to pass them round. They had to touch them and tell me how it felt. They had to rub the bears against their faces and on the backs of their arms. Both boys and girls loved this. Words like soft, gentle, warm, comfortable and cuddly were used.

The bears were gathered back in and a bag of thorns from a wild bramble bush was produced. The class were asked if they would like to put the thorns against their faces. There was a resounding 'No!'. When asked why not, I was told that they hurt you, scratch you, make you bleed, were horrid.

This was compared to behaviour. What type of children gave you the same feelings as a teddy bear? The penny soon dropped. Here is their list.

1　Makes you feel good when you are sad.
2　Shares things with you.
3　Lets you play with them when you have no friends.
4　Is kind to you.
5　Laughs a lot and cheers you up.
6　Takes you to the teacher when you have hurt yourself.
7　Helps you with your work when you are stuck.
8　Is a good friend whom you can trust.

These are all strong characteristics in any personality. It is the combination of strength and sensitivity.

The class had no trouble in defining Thorn behaviour.

1　Bullying other people.
2　Hurting you.
3　Fighting.
4　Tripping you up.
5　Saying nasty things about you.
6　Calling you names.
7　Spitting and scratching.
8　Stealing your things.

This had quite an effect on behaviour. No pupils wanted to see themselves as nasty thorn bushes and it helped the bullies to understand how others perceived them. You cannot change behaviour if you do not know the choices. Thorn bushes do not have status.

However, it was the teddy bears that had the lasting effect. I only came in once a week but they had no intentions of doing without something soft to touch and cuddle. This amazed me. These were tough boys from a huge, sprawling council estate, yet every one had a soft toy. Some took the form of gorillas or monkeys or football mascots. They admitted that they took them to bed at night. That was a well-kept secret!

They developed their own system of showing kindness. When any child was hurting or upset, the children offered their soft toys to them to hold till they felt better. That was a powerful way of developing empathy. It allowed the boys to show their vulnerability which, in terms of mental health, is vital.

Nobody thought that this was a sissy activity. It is hard to bully in this kind of atmosphere.

A 'cuddle corner' soon evolved with a whole pile of soft toys. If a child was really upset, they could sit in the 'cuddle corner' either on their own or with a friend. This was a sanctuary and a place of safety in the classroom. Many children have wretched lives outside of school. We rarely get to know what happens to them in terms of emotional, physical and sexual abuse. These strategies can give them coping skills in the present and for adult life. You have to feel kindness and empathy to know that it exists and that someone really cares about how you are feeling.

However, much depends on the teacher. Many will not allow toys in school, but it is a small price to pay for mental health – there is nothing more painful to watch than a suffering child. It also gives the opportunity for others to develop skills of compassion and care.

Butterflies and Wasps

It is distressing to watch infant children hurt each other by kicking, biting and hitting. Feelings of rage erupt like mini volcanoes. Unchecked, these tendencies grow until we have aggressive adolescents and adults. It is not uncommon to have infant children excluded from school for this kind of behaviour. At the same time, infants can show a great deal of tenderness, compassion and love for one another. It is our responsibility, as educators, to foster this kind of behaviour.

In terms of mental health, infant children can learn skills of congruence, empathy and unconditional positive regard if we show them by example. To do this I used the analogy of Butterflies and Wasps.

The room was filled with posters and pictures of brightly coloured butterflies. The class then discussed what was beautiful about butterflies. They were soft, gentle, exciting, pretty. They then discussed how they would feel if the room was filled with butterflies and how the children would feel if butterflies landed on their heads or their shoulders. The prospect made them ecstatic.

Then we discussed how strong and courageous the butterflies had to be. They started as caterpillars, then had to go into a chrysalis before emerging with beautiful wings. What a transformation from a crawling grub to a magnificent creature. But the butterfly also had to be very strong and clever to survive wind and rain.

This analogy, in terms of personality, was the goal of human beings – strong, clever, yet gentle and nice to have around.

The wasp was differentiated from the hard-working bee which goes about its business of collecting nectar to make honey and serve the good of all in the hive. The bee never stings or attacks unless someone tries to hurt the hive. The bee is too busy to be nasty. The busy honeybee does not look for trouble.

The wasp is a different creature. It is often bad tempered and nasty and stings people for no reason. Many of the children told of how they, their friends or people in their family had been stung by wasps. They had done nothing to hurt the wasp, it just picked on them for no reason. That was why our poster of the wasp had it firmly trapped in a bottle so that it could not get out and hurt anyone. We then discussed what it would be like if the classroom was filled with wasps or even had just one wasp in it. The class were horrified.

We then discussed why some children behaved like butterflies, i.e. were kind, gentle, exciting and nice to have as friends. We were not afraid of them and they were also strong – they would help us if we hurt ourselves or we were unhappy. Next we discussed why some children behaved like wasps, i.e. they hurt us for no reason by bullying, name-calling, kicking, etc. We did not feel safe with them and they hurt us.

The teacher was asked to identify some boys and girls who behaved like butterflies and who were nice to have around because their behaviour was kind. They were given a butterfly badge. There were enough badges for everyone but they had to choose the right behaviour to wear one.

This had a stunning effect on the class. One little boy who was on the verge of exclusion for kicking and biting started to cry and said that he wanted to be a butterfly. His behaviour changed overnight because he wanted one of the coveted badges! He came from an aggressive family but the butterflies and wasps gave no kudos to this kind of behaviour. You could still be very strong and be kind at the same time.

One of the teachers came up with a superb idea. She got the class to paint their own portrait in terms of a butterfly. Every morning the butterflies were pinned to the wall. It was a fresh start for each child no matter what had happened on the previous day. All children had an opportunity to be the brightest and best and have high status. This was particularly helpful for statemented children with special educational needs. They blossomed with this. One little girl with Down's syndrome was consistently a butterfly and it pleased her mother no end.

Children who hurt other children at playtime or in class time had to sit on the Thinking Chair – the way of putting 'the wasp in the bottle' to keep others safe. Remarkably, the chair was usually empty. No one wanted their butterfly that was so carefully painted removed from the wall or to have their special badge taken away.

This is how we, as educators, create an ethos where children have pride in themselves, gain mastery over their lives and acquire skills for adult life. It is our duty to provide a sanctuary where these skills can be practised, especially if the home and community environments are lacking in warmth and compassion.

(N.B. The Butterflies and Wasps exercise is for bullying and unkindness only. It is not fair to use it for laziness or silly behaviour. There are other strategies for these issues.)

Class council

If children are to be encouraged to make decisions and gain self-esteem through self-discipline, then responsibility must follow their actions. The class council allows the peer group to make good citizenship decisions about behaviour which is negative and damaging to others. This usually involves issues such as bullying, racial abuse, etc.

Many children are frightened by bullying, are humiliated by name-calling, are saddened by personal possessions being stolen, are angry and frustrated when a PE lesson is stopped because of the stupid behaviour of others.

The class council allows the peer group to draw its own boundaries for behaviour modification. This is very important, as it is seen as just and fair. This system gives the problem back to the peer group and, as the peer group is the dominant influence, that judgement is more effective than all the shouting, nagging, pleading and cajoling that a teacher can muster.

The class, by this time, have become used to decision-making. They will have decided already their criteria for smart and stupid behaviour. This allows them to provide a framework for behaviour management in the class.

The teacher has the role of negotiator and will also deliver the decision of the peer group. This is an unbiased role where help can be given to weigh up all the evidence. It is normally wise to remove the offender while the discussions are going on to allow the more timid children to make their views known without fear of intimidation. Their voices must also be heard. Although bullies can pick off individuals, it is difficult to withstand the displeasure of their behaviour by the peer group.

It is also important to find all the witnesses to the event, as it must be seen to be fair if it is to work properly. The role of the witnesses is crucial because what appears to have happened may be far from the truth and no one needs a witch-hunt. For example, two pupils have been involved in a nasty fight. One appears to be the victim – they have come off worst in the skirmish. After listening to the witnesses it may become clear that the child who seems to be the 'winner' was severely provoked or was being systematically bullied and turned and fought back. (Listening to children is a skill which we all need to develop. Being able to express feelings is essential and children need to be taught how to listen to each other as well.)

Pupils can be very harsh when given the power to judge their peers. It can lead up to wanting the offender 'hanged by the neck till dead'. The easiest way to deal with this is to remind them to pass judgement with mercy, as they may be the next ones to stand before the class council. They must first consider how they would feel if that penalty was imposed on them and then pass judgement as they would wish to be judged. The teacher is there to ensure moderation and fairness.

Once the decision is made, I flick the solution back to them and give them responsibility for solving the problem. Bullies are also victims, e.g., 'You tell me that John bullies other children at break time. How do you think that we can help him change his behaviour?' In one case four children volunteered to stay with the bully every break time and show him how he should behave. The children were primed to treat the bully in a supportive and friendly manner so that he felt changing his behaviour was a good idea. In a sense, these volunteers offered the bully a lifeline back into the mainstream of the class.

Many of us like standing in judgement on others. It is the 'I'm OK, you are not OK' syndrome. Being part of the solution is more positive. Bullies have needs too. Intimidators can change and every opportunity must be taken to praise the aggressive child for taking responsibility for changing in a positive way.

The children drew up a class council 'not allowed' list:

1 Bullying.
2 Fighting.
3 Name-calling.
4 Stealing.
5 Spoiling a trip out.
6 Fighting at the swimming baths.
7 Stuffing toilet paper in the sinks and turning on the taps.
8 Constantly disturbing the work of the class.

Possible suggestions from the class for offences included:

1 No break times for a week.
2 Going home for dinner.
3 Lines.
4 No swimming lessons.
5 Going to the head teacher.
6 Bringing parents into school.
7 Working in the corridor away from the rest of the class.
8 No TV programmes for one week.
9 No tuck shop.

These may not be the solutions that I would have chosen, but that is not the point. The pupils were learning valuable lessons and they actually worked. I was not the only one who had choices in this matter. Their voices had to be heard and I got far more co-operation in other matters because I allowed them the freedom to make their own decisions and establish their own behaviour management strategies. Of course, I ensured that positive behaviour was rewarded so that children who bullied had an incentive to change.

Class clown

No class is complete without the class clown. All teachers know this character. It is the pupil who demands attention or takes energy by shouting out, making silly comments, showing off, falling off chairs, etc. and is often the bane of any teacher's life. This character has immense power within the peer group. Most pupils love distraction and illicit humour, often at the teacher's expense.

As with stupid behaviour, the status and kudos has to be removed from this character. That is why the clown has tears in his eyes.

The clown is both loved and loathed. If we look at the adult world, the person seen as the joker, the life and soul of the party or as a riot is used for entertainment value. When they are not cheering up the dull lives of others, they are often discarded. Rarely are their views taken seriously – they are rigidly typecast as being purely of entertainment value and are often goaded and encouraged by others to maintain that role.

When a child takes this role it is difficult to break. First, the whole class is on the clown's side, at least for a time. If the child wants to change they often run the gauntlet of the peer group with comments such as 'You have become really boring' or 'You are not fun any more'.

Second, the behaviour maintains his or her position and status. Without that role they would be nothing. It is also an unstable position because one minute they can be in favour, e.g when the class wants entertaining, and the next minute out of favour if the class wants to concentrate on something.

I have watched children be devastated by this as they are often desperate for approval and to be told to shut up because they are spoiling things usually upsets them. This also applies to adult life. Those seen as jokers in some situations are often seen as a pain in others by the same people.

When discussing the behaviour related to this, it is very important that neither the teacher nor the class actually names the class clown as this is very damaging to the child. The class should be encouraged to discuss the role of a class clown, not *the* class clown. For example, it makes us laugh, it breaks the boredom, etc. They can then discuss why the clown is crying, e.g. the clown is unhappy underneath – it has to make people laugh or it would be ignored, people get fed up with it if they are busy. Maybe it would like to be like other people.

The penalties of being a clown are always being in trouble, getting sent out of the class and not being wanted when the class wants to do something serious. This can now be identified as stupid behaviour, which can change at any time.

The class are now invited to help the clown by offering good advice, e.g. just tell them that if they want a laugh they should make the jokes themselves and let them get into trouble for a change; if someone calls you boring just ignore them and come and play with us, etc. This is essential because:

- it allows the child who has taken this role to re-evaluate his or her position without being identified by name;
- it makes the peer group take responsibility for smart behaviour rather than encouraging stupid behaviour;
- it reduces teacher stress as the child who constantly shows off and distracts and disrupts the class wastes vital emotional energy and stamina.

Class identification of class clown behaviour:

1 Shows off.
2 Makes funny faces.
3 Makes rude noises.
4 Tells jokes when the teacher is talking.
5 Falls off the chair.
6 Makes you laugh.
7 Throws things around the class.

8 Interrupts the teacher and other children.
9 Tickles you in the line.
10 Puts water on the teacher's chair.
11 Crawls under desks.

Penalties:

1 Gets lines.
2 Has to sit outside the head's office.
3 Gets kept in at break.
4 Their parents have to come into school.
5 Sit on their own at dinnertime.

Once the class can identify the behaviour they can ignore it and see it for what it is – a way of getting energy and attention from others. If the class refuse to respond to the class clown, the behaviour stops because there is little point in performing without an audience. It also allows the child to change without goading from the peer group. Again, reward the clown for better behaviour.

Sneaky rat

Of all the classroom characters this is the hardest one to pin down. Teachers often know that, when there is trouble, a particular child is always there but never seems to be involved – the Iago of the school, the co-partner in crime.

Fights often start in the playground as a result of a pupil spreading gossip into a vulnerable ear, usually the ear of a volatile child who does not stop to think of the consequences. Whereas the class clown is an overt character, sneaky rat is covert and manipulative. Class clown is often encouraged by sneaky rat for his or her own amusement while sneaking into the background to watch the fireworks start.

The guise of this character is often self-righteousness, being the first to inform the teacher of any misdemeanour, constantly telling tales and using every opportunity to gloat over the downfall of a classmate. The information that they pass is often spurious, e.g. ' I heard Donna call your mother a dog in the toilets' or 'Darren says he's going to punch your little brother', etc.

The sneaky rat can also destroy the ethos of trust in a classroom, creating suspicion between pupil and pupil or teacher and pupil. Money can go missing from pockets in the cloakroom; things can be stolen from the teacher's desk or stockroom. This creates a real dilemma for the teacher when the culprit cannot be found and the whole class is under suspicion. It is also uncomfortable when school satchels and bags have to be turned out for inspection. It creates a very uneasy atmosphere.

To deal with this character the class discussed the sneaky, underhand nature of this behaviour and brought the problem out into the open, particularly in the case of telling tales where a fight ensues. It is not enough to punish the obvious miscreants. A little time spent on information gathering sometimes reveals a manipulative stirring behind the scenes.

Another useful tip for the teacher is to ask any pupil who is telling tales what their motive is. 'Why are you telling me this? What do you hope happens to Mary?'

Sneaky rat behaviour includes:

1 Tells tales to the teacher to get people into trouble.
2 Tells tales to put the blame on someone else.
3 Spreads rumours and gossip.
4 Steals from the classroom when the teacher is out.
5 Steals from coat pockets in the cloakroom.
6 Encourages others to give cheek to the teacher.
7 Tells lies to their mother and father when they get home from school.
8 Says things which are only partly true to make others look bad and them look good.

Penalties include:

1 They get found out.
2 Others in the class won't trust them any more.
3 The teacher will be angry because they have caused trouble.
4 They won't have any friends.
5 Their parents will have to come into school.
6 They will lose privileges.

There was another very interesting aspect raised by the pupils themselves that I had not thought of and it was to do with motivation. They were concerned with what they would do when they really had to tell the teacher something but it was not telling tales. They worked out their own system based on smart and stupid behaviour.

Smart reasons for telling the teacher:
1 To keep myself safe from bullies.
2 If someone is doing something dangerous which could hurt themselves or others.
3 If a friend is upset and will not tell the teacher on his or her own.
4 If there are racial insults or serious name-calling.
5 If you are afraid of anything at home or in school.

Stupid reasons for telling tales:

1 If you are being spiteful.
2 If you are trying to get someone into trouble and make yourself look good.
3 If you know it is not true.
4 If you have done it and are trying to blame someone else.
5 If you exaggerate.

I was astonished that they had used the smart and stupid behaviour principle so effectively and they had worked it out well before me. These were children from a huge, disadvantaged housing estate in an inner city area. De Bono was right. We need to look at our education system which seems to spend so much time and effort on academic tail chasing and meetings stuffed with high-sounding nonsense by those who have never done the job.

It is essential to find the balance between the safety and protection of children and identifying the subversive forces which operate within the peer group. Having done this, the teacher will have helped the pupils to look for motives, a strategy which will stand them in good stead for adult life. There is nothing more malicious than gossip. Within this, the doors are open for children who are hurt or frightened to come for help and support.

For the persistent tell-tale, I found that three questions helped.

1 Why do you want me to know this?
2 What do you want me to do to Mary? Alan? Peter? Lizzie?
3 What do you think will happen if you have been using 'sneaky rat'?

A bright child came up with this. 'If you always tell tales, one day you might be telling the truth but nobody will believe you!' Smart kid! Trust, once lost, is hard to re-establish.

The Good Newspaper: dealing with the 'looking good syndrome'

The 'looking good' syndrome is prevalent in everyday life. In a competitive society it is necessary to be perceived as 'looking good' in order to avoid rejection. Sadly, this usually involves comparing ourselves with others. If we can point out faults in others, then we assume that we will look better than them, e.g. 'There is always such a din from Miss Bell's class!' or 'Have you noticed that Mr Jones's class is always late for assembly?' or 'Mrs Smith and Mr Johnston always shoot out of school as soon as the bell rings.'

This negativity seems to permeate our society. We have become a weary nation of complainers. There are signs everywhere of 'How to Complain' about schools, hospitals, gas, electricity, doctors, water board and even on the back of lorries. Why do we not just add, 'How to complain about each other.'? Is it any wonder that one in four of us will suffer from depression or some other mental illness at some point in our lives?

This 'looking good' syndrome is prevalent in classrooms and is probably one of the most wearing things that a teacher has to endure. It is part of human nature to tell tales and gossip. This leads to bullying, but it can be discouraged. Energy follows thought. If we focus on negative thoughts then our behaviour will become negative and vice versa.

The Good Newspaper solved this for me. There was no great psychological theory behind this. I just got fed up of belly aching and whining. When a child ran up, desperate to tell me something bad about another child, I simply replied, 'Tell me three nice things about Joe or Anna or Deiroy, then I will listen to what you have to say' It worked!

The Good Newspaper worked in other ways. Not every child can be top of the class, but every child can be kind, loving, helpful, funny, etc. This simple exercise allowed children with special needs to gain recognition and esteem. Their merits, in terms of human values, were nothing short of astonishing. The Good Newspaper covered every aspect of the children's lives – home, school and the community.

First, we discussed some articles in newspapers, e.g. 'Shopkeeper Mugged', 'Four People Killed in Car Crash', 'Baby Found Dead in Field', 'Boy Drowned in Canal'. After this, I put the newspapers ceremoniously in the bin because the stories made us all depressed and sad. Clean sheets were put up on the wall and all our good news was recorded, e.g. 'Lisa has stopped calling people names', 'James has played without bullying anybody', 'Tom takes care of his little brother because his mum is in hospital', 'Marie can read a whole page now', etc. The list became endless and changed the behaviour of the class radically.

Children want to please and need approval and recognition. If they know that positive good news will make you happy, that is what you will get. Each entry was met by a round of applause and a pat on the back.

This actually took the status out of disruptive behaviour. Many disruptive pupils have learning difficulties, undetected hearing or visual problems, and struggle academically. The Good Newspaper let them be 'top of the league' any time they wanted. Perhaps the greatest reward was to take the paper to the head teacher who displayed it on the wall outside her office for everyone to see.

Bad news can be good

This may seem to be a contradiction. Not so. My work always involved difficult pupils and difficult classes. My objective was to keep pupils in school, not throw them out. That entailed understanding and working with the whole class as a community and reshaping the dynamics of the class.

The disruptive child is often viewed as the hero or the heroine. They do things that others would not dare do but would like to do, so are therefore encouraged and celebrated by the class. If a disruptive child is excluded, the class will soon find another hero or heroine to step into their shoes.

Disruptive children look for and need excitement. To understand this concept, you will need to understand 'the buzz' that comes with it. Ask any bank official or stockbroker who leads an ordered professional life yet becomes a football hooligan at weekends or becomes a drunken lout abroad on holiday.

It is 'the buzz' of breaking the rules and defying authority. With the disruptive child, it becomes a way of life. In terms of the dynamics of a classroom, it must become a class issue.

Bad news is part of life and part of problem solving. If negative behaviour appears, give the class a chance to solve it. For example, 'Ryan and Sam were fighting in the playground.' Give the problem back to the class and ask the class to come up with constructive solutions to help Ryan and Sam to change their behaviour. Ask what advice the class would give them, e.g. 'How can you help Ryan and Sam to keep out of trouble?', 'Who is going to include them in their games so that there will be no need for them to fight?', 'What can you tell them about smart and stupid behaviour at break time?'

Tell the class that they have to report all the things that they notice about Ryan and Sam that are smart. The real triumph in this one is when such pupils have turned their behaviour around, they can become the 'guardians' of weaker children. They still get 'the buzz' but their power is used for you instead of against you.

They are not vigilantes. They become partners in helping other children. This is a real status position. If I could get the most difficult ones on my side, my job was easy. It works only if they have your respect and approval. That is the right of every child.

Today is a new day

Sometimes it is useful to have a newspaper of things that made us unhappy on the previous day. But don't dwell on it! Note it, then bin it. Ask two simple questions. 'Do we need this behaviour today?' 'Can we leave it with yesterday and start a new day?' Tear up the sheet of paper in front of the class. Stupid behaviour trashes the class and deserves to be in the bin. A fresh start gives everybody the opportunity to change their behaviour.

Sometimes a teacher can have a bad day. So we, too, can say sorry. After all, we are supposed to lead by example and they will love us for it. It is OK to be human!

Liquorice allsorts: personality

This is the best way that I can describe personality and it works well with a class. Take a big box of liquorice allsorts and spread them on a table. Sort them into three piles. The first pile should contain your favourites. The second pile is the ones that are OK. The third pile are the ones that you don't like and give to the dog. If you don't like liquorice allsorts, use a box of chocolates. In my case the 'don't likes' include coffee creams and rum truffles.

This is like personality. Some bits of us are wonderful, some bits are OK, and some bits really need looking at. It is just the same for our pupils. Now we start to make choices. Do we start a witch-hunt for the coffee creams and the rum truffles or do we really enjoy the chocolate fudge and hazelnut whirls? If we spend all our time looking for the rubbish in ourselves and others, that is exactly what we will find. All you have to do is change your attitude and look for the best bits.

Do a deal with your class. Agree to concentrate on their best bits and let them find yours. That is the beginning of helping children to be truly autonomous and it is the best thing that you can do for yourself. None of us is perfect but there are always some really good bits if we look for them. It makes sense.

Never be afraid to ask children what they like about you and what they dislike. We are quick enough to do it to them. If you do this you may get some pleasant surprises. Some children told me that they liked the way I smelled! It is not what would have immediately come to mind as one of my outstanding characteristics. We spend most of our working lives with other people's children and partners so we may as well make it good.

We know from statistics and research that far too many children lead unhappy lives, being the victims of emotional, physical and sexual abuse. Even those with happy home lives can have a miserable school life. A safe place is the best gift that you can give any child and a classroom as a place of safety is the best gift that you can give to yourself.

Call out your dead: preventing exclusion

This is going into special measures but is sometimes necessary to prevent exclusion. It is also used to prevent the rights of other pupils being violated and abused.

Every child has the right to an education, but extremely disruptive pupils stop that process. They are often powerful and exert a negative influence on the work of the class. That has to stop. 'Call out your dead' is never used until all other strategies have been exhausted. I did this for a whole morning a week with persistently disruptive pupils. The criteria were strict. No teacher was allowed to use this facility unless they could persuade me that they had tried to turn the situation round.

The class council was useful. Children expressed their exasperation at the behaviour of the miscreant. They were allowed to have a voice and their complaints were listened to and acted upon. Disrupting a class of children who want to work is just another form of bullying.

Although the EBD child has problems that have to be dealt with, there is another element. There is a real 'buzz' in defying authority. It becomes a power game, but all psychological games are stupid and destructive because someone has to lose. There is no better way of getting energy and attention than by 'kicking off'. An immense euphoria comes with it – just ask football hooligans or rioters. There is no 'buzz' like it. When you work in approved schools or residential care establishments, you become well aware of that factor.

Children or adolescents who wreck rooms or destroy property will tell you that they were not angry – they did it for a laugh. That is their way of expressing the 'buzz'. At that stage, they are in the position of having 'nothing left to lose', which is dangerous for us and dangerous for them.

The aim and objective is to stop any child going that far. We have to respond in a way that ends the game. 'Call out your dead' is one such strategy.

One head teacher gave me the old music room which stored chairs for assembly. There was nothing else in the room except for some cardboard boxes. The chairs were put in a circle. The rules were strict. The pupils aged from 6 to 11 sat in silence. I did not want to talk to them. That was my choice. It was thinking time. They had to think why they were sitting in this dingy room, missing break times and being bored to death. I told them that I did not care, as I would be paid whether I worked hard with a whole class or sat reading my book while they did some thinking.

They found that hard as they were used to me being warm and friendly and having fun with them. I think that is important. If you build the bridges in the good times you have something to negotiate with. If you are seen as aloof and unfriendly, children do not care if they lose your approval. They never had it in the first place. The same goes for parents, and a smile costs nothing.

I think that the reality of exclusion had escaped them. It was time to think about it.

Disruptive children rarely truant. They need the peer group and the community of the school to operate in. Isolation is the quickest way to end disruption. Exclusion can be a misery for any child. They lose their friends, their sense of identity, education and status. Parents get fed up with them home all day.

Starting a new school, if one can be found, is often traumatic, as they have to travel longer distances, have to start at the bottom of the pecking order and have to try to catch up on missed lessons in a new group. Often they are not accepted by their new set of peers, especially if the new school is not in their neighbourhood. This is particularly true if they come from a large housing estate which is territorial.

After sitting in silence till the first break, the discussion started. These were their conclusions about the stupidity of being excluded:

Penalties:

1 You will lose all your mates.
2 You could get bullied at another school.
3 You would have no friends to walk home with.
4 Other schools would not want you if you were a troublemaker.
5 Your mum might have to give up her job to look after you.
6 Your parents would ground you and stop your pocket money.
7 You would get bored being alone all day.
8 You would have to do more chores in the house.

The first week that I did this I had 17 pupils. On the second week there were only four. By the third week there were none.

Make sure they realise they have something to lose. Spell out the reality to them. Then respond in a way that ends the game.

Transition: Humpty Dumpty

Education involves the process of transition from nursery to infant to junior then secondary school. For many, the process continues on to college or university and into the adult world of work. At each stage new skills have to be learned as there are different expectations and work levels to be achieved. This is particularly difficult in infant education. Many children find the change traumatic. Leaving the security of home to join the large group of nursery children can sometimes be met with tears from both mother and child. No sooner does the child find his or her niche than they are moved to another world of more bigger, boisterous children in the infant school.

But the biggest fear comes when they leave to go to the junior school. The transition is rather like snakes and ladders. From being Year 2 top infants, children have their world turned upside down and become bottom of the heap again. This is also true when juniors go to secondary school. The experience can be overwhelming when fears start to be articulated, i.e. 'Will I get bullied?', 'Will I still have my friends with me?', 'How will I know what to do?', 'Are the teachers very strict?'

As expectations increase with more challenging work, so does the need for discipline and understanding of appropriate behaviour. It is helpful if time is spent in letting the infant children express their fears. By doing this they can then define what skills are needed for transition. We all know what happens if a child has had a difficult time in infant school. Labels such as 'disruptive', 'unco-operative', etc. start to be gathered. Without appropriate transition skills, these children can end up like Humpty Dumpty – they fall off the wall. If they have a great fall, it culminates in exclusion, transfer to another school and the merry-go-round starts. Nothing puts Humpty together again.

The following list of transition skills was drawn up by a group of children as suggestions to help them transfer to their new junior school.

1 Help other people.
2 Ignore stupid behaviour of other people.
3 Keep your own behaviour smart.
4 Go to the toilet at break time.
5 Listen to the teachers.
6 Do neat, tidy, beautiful work.
7 Tell the teacher if something is wrong instead of fighting.
8 Keep still when you are working.
9 Be smart in assembly.
10 Be good to the teacher and the teacher will be good to you.

11 Share with others.
12 Help others to keep out of trouble and your school will be a safe place.
13 Be kind to each other and be a friend to children who are sad.
14 Always tell an adult if you are being bullied.
15 Always tell an adult if you see someone else being bullied.

These rules may seem strange to us as adults but we are not undergoing transition, the children are. It is empowering for them to realise that they have choices in their own destiny and can find their own solutions to problems. When children are allowed to be part of the decision-making process, the outcome is more likely to work and be effective. In this case it was.

As the junior school already used the strategies of a safe place, the flow through from the infants was much easier as all children were in tune with the ideas. It saved the junior teachers having to train the younger children as the process had already been started before they arrived.

Summary

These are just a few of the activities I have used with children over many years. The main message is that children often behave badly, bully others or lash out in order to gain respect from their peers or to deal with their internal problems. They need us to teach them positive ways to get respect and how to turn their self-destructive behaviour into 'smart' behaviour. Good luck!

13

■ ■ ■

Teachers hold the key to change

ASTRID MONA O'MOORE

▶ Teachers, through their own behaviours and interactions with pupils, are central in shaping the values and attitudes of children

▶ Research indicates that teachers greatly underestimate the amount of bullying that goes on in their schools

▶ Teachers with high self-esteem have been found to produce pupils with high self-esteem

▶ This chapter deepens understanding of bullying by presenting data from a nationwide study carried out in Ireland

All I can remember is being hit and called names and never getting a chance to learn anything. When I told teachers they just told me to stand up for myself.
Observer 19 March, 1989

It is hard to believe that sentiments such as those expressed above are still to be found today. However, only a few months ago the Anti-Bullying Research and Resource Centre at Trinity College, Dublin received a letter from a very distressed mother. It read as follows.

Dear Dr O'Moore,

I wonder if you would send me some information on how to handle bullying. My son, who loved school for two years, suddenly began to hate it and pleaded with me to let him stay at home. This went on for a while until eventually he woke up at night and I'd hold him and he began to tell me when he was half asleep 'They are at me.' I asked him who they were and he gave me two names. When I followed it up the day after, he told me not to do anything as they would kill him. He really believed it. I could see myself that they were getting great mileage out of his fear, working on it to their advantage with control and manipulation, because my son loved to be friends with all children.

154

I told the principal and all he said was, 'Your son cannot socialise, toughen him up.' When I asked him how bullying is handled in the school he said it was not my business and I was trying to tell him how to run his school. I asked him about procedures. He didn't want to know. He denied that there was a problem even though many parents came to him individually. He then said to me that this conversation was now ended, pointing to the door.

She went on to describe the nature of the bullying in more detail and also the attitudes of the individual staff, which were equally as defensive. She ended her letter with 'Please, please, please. I need help. I am at my wits' end about it.'

Unfortunately, this letter is not an isolated one. The Anti-Bullying Centre deals with many such calls for information, advice and guidance. Since the first European Teacher's Seminar on Bullying in Schools, which was held in Stavanger in August 1987 (O'Moore, 1989, 1990), there has been a tremendous growth in awareness of the problems of bullying.

Internationally at present, there are many books, journals, articles, websites, conferences, educational packs, television programmes and newspaper reports devoted to the subject of bullying. Initially our understanding of victimisation and bullying was limited to pioneering studies emanating from the Nordic countries (Pikas, 1975; Olweus, 1978; Bjorkqvist *et al.*, 1982; Lagerspetz *et al.*, 1982; Roland, 1988). However, Smith and Brain (2000) have pointed out the lessons that have been learned from a further two decades of research.

Parent pressure groups have also been founded with the aim of introducing an anti-bullying ethos in all schools. Just recently, Ireland has seen yet another group emerge, the Concerned Parents against Bullying (CPAB). This was in response to a suicide that was attributed to school bullying (*Irish Examiner*, 11 October, 2001).

However, in spite of the widespread publicity that bullying receives from professional and lay audiences, there are still, as demonstrated by the above letter and similar calls to the Anti-Bullying Centre, individual teachers and school management authorities who fail to recognise bullying as a problem.

As part of a nationwide study of bullying in Irish schools (O'Moore *et al.*, 1997) it was found that there were teachers in one quarter of the primary schools and one half of the secondary schools who did not recognise bullying as a serious issue. Obviously teachers need to become more sensitive to the ill effects of bullying.

The present author is of the opinion that teachers hold the key to change (O'Moore, 2000). In Europe and in other parts of the world there are few children and few parents who have not had contact with teachers. Few will deny that teachers, through their behaviours and interactions with pupils, are central in shaping the values and attitudes of children. Thus, if all teachers could become sensitised to the ill effects of bullying behaviour, they should, through their commitment to prevent and counter bullying, sensitise future generations of children and parents.

The aim of this chapter is to further deepen our present understanding of bullying by presenting data from a nationwide study that was carried out in

Ireland. It is hoped that the results will help teachers and other professionals involved with children to further prevent, reduce and counter bullying in their school communities.

As Smith and Brain (2000) point out: 'Given the normative nature of bullying, it will be a continued struggle to keep it to within acceptable limits – limits such that suicides caused by bullying, actual physical harm to victims, or life-long depression and feelings of low self-worth in those victimised are rare indeed. Such a goal will, however, be a most worthwhile one for the combined efforts of researchers and practitioners to achieve.'

The nationwide study

The study comprised a total of 20,442 school children (11,118 girls and 9,324 boys) aged 8 to 18 years. Of these, 9,599 children were primary school pupils (4,485 girls and 5,114 boys) aged 8 to 11 years attending 320 primary schools in the Republic of Ireland. There were also 10,843 post-primary school children (6,633 girls and 4,210 boys) aged 12 to 18 years drawn from 211 schools in the Republic of Ireland. A detailed account of how the schools were selected is given in O'Moore *et al.* (1997). The schools represented a cross-section of the schools in all 26 counties of Ireland.

All the pupils were tested in class by their own teachers. The extent to which children bully others or are themselves bullied was assessed by the modified version of the Olweus self-report questionnaire (Whitney and Smith, 1993).

The definition of bullying which was used with the present sample was:

We say a pupil is being bullied, or picked on, when another pupil, or group of pupils, say nasty and unpleasant things to him or her. It is also bullying when a pupil is hit, kicked, threatened, locked inside a room, sent nasty notes, when no one ever talks to them or things like that. These things can happen frequently and it is difficult for the pupil being bullied to defend himself or herself. It is also bullying when a pupil is teased repeatedly in a nasty way. But it is not bullying when two pupils of about the same strength have the odd fight or quarrel.

The questionnaires were administered in class by class teachers. Standardised instructions were issued to all teachers. These were the same as those used by Whitney and Smith (1993) in their Sheffield study. Accordingly, teachers were asked to seat the pupils in such a way as to avoid conferring or copying. They were also asked to explain to the pupils that the questionnaire was about life in school and how much bullying takes place in schools. The importance of answering the questions truthfully was also communicated to the pupils. The questions were answered anonymously. Pupils needed to provide only the name of their school, class and the date at the time of completing the questionnaire.

The questionnaires were administered without a time limit. After completion they were placed in an envelope and forwarded for analysis.

The Piers-Harris Self Concept (Piers, 1984) was used to examine the self-esteem of pupils. The questionnaire is an 80-item self-report questionnaire designed to assess how children and adolescents feel about themselves. The responses provide a measure of global self-esteem and six 'cluster scales', namely behaviour (16 items), intellectual and school status (17 items), physical appearance and attributes (13 items), anxiety (14 items), popularity (12 items) and happiness and satisfaction (10 items).

The questionnaire was administered as part of the second stage of the nationwide study. There were 13,112 school children (7,313 girls and 5,799 boys) aged 8 to 18 years involved in the second stage. Of these, 7,315 were primary school children (3,652 boys and 3,663 girls) in 259 primary schools and 5,797 post-primary school children (2,147 boys and 3,650 girls) in 135 post-primary schools. A more detailed account of this sample is given in O'Moore and Kirkham (2001).

Results of the nationwide study

In reply to the questions on bullying in the modified Olweus questionnaire, the children could use the following response categories: 'It has only happened once or twice', 'sometimes', 'once a week' and 'several times a week'.

Not to risk under-reporting, the pupils' response category to the Olweus questionnaire 'it has happened once or twice' (referred to in this study as occasional bullying or victimisation) was included in estimating the level of school bullying and victimisation. It was felt that by excluding those who answer 'I have been bullied once or twice' was to ignore those who have been subjected to a possible one or two episodes of bullying. Unfortunately there is no data on the duration of bullying. However, as the questions relate to the school term that the study took place, there is no knowing whether the bullying in which the pupils were allegedly involved was successfully resolved or whether it reflected the embryonic stages of greater conflict. Moreover, it is possible that the response option 'once or twice' may be used by children who are reluctant to admit that they are being bullied or bully others.

There is evidence of under-reporting of children (Neary and Joseph, 1994; O'Moore et al., 1997) and of girls in particular (Roland, 1988). In the present study the response category 'sometimes' will be taken to indicate moderate bullying. Combining the response categories 'about once a week' and 'several times a week' will be considered as frequent serious bullying.

Extent of peer bullying and victimisation

Primary school

In primary school, the results indicated that 18.6% of children were bullied occasionally and 19.9% had bullied others once or twice. Another 8.4%

reported that they were moderately bullied and 5.1% claimed that they had bullied others sometimes. A further 4.3% claimed that they had been frequently bullied (once a week/daily) and 1.4% admitted to bullying others with the same frequency. Table 13.1 shows that the boys report a significantly greater level of victimisation and bullying than do the girls.

Table 13.1 Percentage of boys and girls in primary and post-primary schools being bullied or bullying others during this school term

	Primary		Post-primary	
Been bullied	**Girls N=4,485**	**Boys N=5,114**	**Girls N=6,633**	**Boys N=4,210**
Occasional	15.8	21.0	8.4	14.7
Moderate	6.8	9.9	2.1	4.3
Frequent	3.2	5.2	1.0	3.4
Bullied others				
Occasional	13.6	25.8	7.0	18.5
Moderate	2.9	7.1	1.5	3.9
Frequent	0.6	2.2	0.3	2.0

Post-primary school

In post-primary school a lower incidence of victimisation and bullying was reported than in the primary schools. Approximately one in ten (10.8%) reported that they had been bullied occasionally and one in seven claimed that they had bullied others on occasion. Another 2.9% were bullied sometimes and 5.1% stated that they bullied others to the same degree. One in fifty pupils approximately (1.9%) claimed they had been bullied frequently. In addition, 1.4% admitted to bullying other pupils about once a week or more often. From Table 13.1 it can be seen that boys report being involved in problems of victimisation and bullying to a much greater degree than do girls.

It should be emphasised that the incidence of victimisation which was found among the primary school children (31.3%) in the present national study contrasts sharply with that which was found (42.1%) in the earlier small-scale Dublin study (O'Moore and Hillery, 1989).

The decline in the reported victimisation may reflect the efforts which have been made in Ireland in the intervening years to prevent and counter bullying behaviour. This is most encouraging. The details of the initiatives taken in Ireland during the 1990s have been detailed by Byrne (1999).

Year differences in peer victimisation and bullying

Victims

Results for the national study indicated that the proportion of pupils who reported that they were bullied decreased steadily from third class in primary school to sixth year in post-primary school. However, from Figure 13.1, we can see that there is an increase in moderate and frequent victimisation for both boys and girls in the second year of senior school (ages 13/14 years). The figure further shows that there was another increase in victimisation among boys in fifth year and for girls in sixth year.

Figure 13.1 Percentage of boys and girls who have been bullied in each class/year sometimes or more often

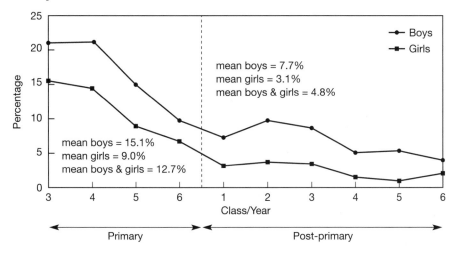

Bullies

Figure 13.2 shows a decrease of reported bullying with age. However, while there was a dramatic fall in the extent of bullying others in first year of post-primary school as compared with sixth year in primary school, it rose again in the second year. The incidence of bullying others dropped again in third and fourth years. However, in fifth year there was a further escalation before it dropped to its lowest level in sixth year.

For each class or school year it can be seen from Figure 13.2 that boys 'bullied others' more often than did the girls. It can also be seen that there was an earlier decline among girls than among boys of bullying others. However, whereas the bullying tended to decline among the boys from fourth to sixth year (16 to 18 years), it escalated among the girls in their final school year (17 to 18 years).

The decrease in victimisation and bullying behaviour with age that was found in the present study has also been found in other international school-based surveys (Smith et al., 1999). Smith and Madsen (1999) have given four

159

Figure 13.2 Percentage of boys and girls who have bullied others in each class/year sometimes or more often

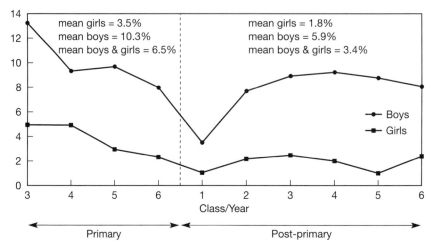

main reasons for the age decline. The first of these, that younger pupils are outnumbered and thus children in the higher classes have more scope to bully them, finds support in the present study.

More than one third of the victims in the Irish sample reported that they were bullied by their peers in higher grades to themselves. However, the lower incidence of bullying behaviour which was found among the first years as compared with subsequent years in the present sample does not support Smith and Madsen's (1999) second hypothesis that they may bully less as they become more socialised.

The low prevalence of victimisation and bullying that was found among first-year pupils has been attributed by O'Moore et al. (1997) to the greater supervision and mentoring that first-year pupils in Irish post-primary schools experience. The authors also advance the view that the increase in bullying as the pupils advance through senior school may reflect the increased pressure to achieve academically.

It was felt the increase, in particular among sixth-year post-primary girls, reflected the strong competitive climate that characterises the final year of school. Results presented later in the chapter show that the pupils in the present sample who bullied suffered from feelings of inadequacy in relation to scholastic achievement and success.

The other two hypotheses of Smith and Madsen (1999) for the age decline of victimisation – namely that potential victims are becoming more socially skilled and that changing definitions may influence pupils' self-reports – would appear to have something to offer. However, the present study is not in a position to offer any statistical data which can support these hypotheses. Still, the qualitative data that emerged from the questionnaires indicated that there were pupils at primary level who were in doubt, in spite of the definition given, as to whether the negative experiences that they had had constituted bullying.

Extent of bully victims

Much international reporting (Smith *et al.*, 1999) of incidences of bullying behaviour omits to distinguish bullies and victims from children who both bully and are bullied (bully/victims). Yet whenever typologies of bullying behaviour have been linked with psychological traits, children who are classified as bully/victims tend to have greater problems, as compared with 'pure bullies' and 'pure victims', on measures of behavioural conduct and global self-esteem (O'Moore and Hillery, 1991; Austin and Joseph, 1996; Mynard and Joseph, 1997).

In the earlier editions of this book, the present author presented evidence which indicated that children of primary school age who were classified as bully/victims were rated by their teachers to have more conduct disorders than children who were 'pure victims' and 'pure bullies' only. A summary of the results are given in Table 13.2.

Table 13.2 Teacher ratings (Rulter's Behaviour Questionnaire) of the frequency and nature of conduct disorders for victims, bullies and controls

Children (7–13yrs)	No.	Antisocial		Neurotic		Undifferentiated*		Total	
		No.	%	No	%	No	%	No	%
Controls	376	21	5.5	14	3.7	2	0.5	37	11.5
Pure victims	178	26	14.5	8	4.5	6	3.4	4	22.5
Victims/occ. bully	139	32	23.0	8	5.8	4	2.8	44	31.7
Victims/freq. bully	12	6	50.0	1	8.3	0	0.0	7	58.3
Pure bullies	77	18	23.4	2	2.6	1	2.6	22	28.6
Bully/occ. victim	124	29	23.4	9	7.3	4	3.2	42	33.9
Bully/freq. victim	27	9	33.3	0	0.0	0	0.0	9	33.3

*Undifferentiated means that the total score of the antisocial and neurotic clusters are the same

As Table 13.3 shows, the present national sample of 20,452 children and adolescents indicated that 14.1% of primary pupils and 4.1% of post-primary pupils were both bullying others at school and being bullied.

The fact that there were 2.8% of pupils of primary and post-primary school age who were moderate to frequent bully victims (being bullied sometimes

Table 13.3 The typology of bullying behaviour and the percentage of pupils in each category

Typology	Primary pupils 8–11 yrs	Post-primary pupils 12–18 yrs
Pure bullies	12.3	10.8
Pure victims	17.1	11.5
Bully/victims	14.1	4.1
Total involved	43.5	26.4

and more frequently and bullying others sometimes and more frequently) suggests that in Ireland there may be 13,480 pupils of primary and post-primary age who are in serious need of psychological intervention.

Later in the chapter we will present evidence to show that the distinctions of pure victim, pure bully and bully/victims have important predictive value in relation to self-esteem. Particularly vulnerable, it seems, are the bully/victims.

Teacher awareness of bullying

Research has indicated that teachers greatly underestimate the amount of bullying that goes on in their schools. The Dublin study of 7 to 13-year-olds indicated that teachers identified only 22.1% of the self-confessed pure bullies and 38% of the bully/victims. Thus, only 24% of the total number of bullies were identified by teachers (O'Moore, 1997).

One can only speculate as to why teachers are so unaware of bullying. Indeed, 23.1% of all children in the Dublin study reported that their teachers did not know that bullying goes on.

There are undoubtedly many reasons. Clearly teachers cannot be everywhere at once. A major factor is undoubtedly the covert nature of bullying and the subtle manner which bullies use to intimidate their victims. Sullivan (2000) outlines the very gradual and purposeful steps that children who bully take before they confer victim status on a potential victim.

Another reason which makes it difficult for teachers to detect children who bully is the taboo that exists among school children on telling tales. Obviously, much value is lost to teachers as a result of pupils' reluctance to inform teachers about bullying incidents that they have witnessed, though it must also be pointed out that many teachers are unsympathetic to pupils telling tales. For example, it is not uncommon to hear children say, 'When I told my teacher that I was being bullied, he/she did not believe me.' Or, 'I was made to feel stupid.'

In the present nationwide study, 65% of victims in primary schools had not told any of their teachers. The reluctance to tell was even greater among post-primary pupils. As many as 84% claimed that they had not told their teachers of their victimisation. While more children told someone at home that they were bullied at school, as many as 46% of primary school pupils and 66% of post-primary pupils did not tell anyone at home.

Table 13.4 shows the increasing reluctance of pupils as they advance through primary and post-primary schools to tell either their teachers or anyone at home of their victimisation. This is a trend that has also been found among Scottish and English school children (Mellor, 1991; Whitney and Smith, 1993). However, in sixth year of Irish post-primary schools there appears to be an easing among some pupils in relation to telling teachers.

Table 13.4 Percentages of 'victims' in primary classes and post-primary years who report not having told their teacher or anyone at home about being bullied

	No. of victims	Have not told teachers	No. of victims	Have not told anyone at home
Primary				
3	303	53.8	320	33.7
4	1075	62.0	1091	41.2
5	975	65.8	996	49.7
6	726	74.0	730	53.7
Post-primary				
1	714	82.2	714	60.9
2	550	83.3	550	69.3
3	185	82.7	714	63.5
4	73	87.7	550	68.1
5	89	92.2	189	78.9
6	46	84.8	72	79.9

It is of note that the reluctance to tell was more marked in the present nation-wide study, particularly in relation to telling parents, than it was in the earlier Irish study reported on by O'Moore (1997). While the differences may reflect a worsening situation, it is more likely that they are due to the fact that in the earlier study pupils were asked to respond to a hypothetical situation, i.e. 'Would you tell if you were bullied?' In the present study the pupils were asked if they *had* told that they *had* been bullied.

Teacher intervention

A very worrying feature of the results of the recent Irish national study was the apparent lack of intervention of teachers when they are witness to bullying behaviour. Only a little more than half of pupils in primary schools (54%) reported that teachers tried to intervene.

Fifteen per cent reported that teachers 'intervened sometimes' and 39% claimed that they intervened 'almost always'. Post-primary pupils perceived their teachers to intervene even less than primary school pupils. Just over one third of the post-primary pupils (36%) stated that 'the teachers tried to put a stop to it when a pupil is being bullied at school'. Twelve per cent reported that teachers 'intervened sometimes' while 24% claimed that they intervened 'almost always'.

To effect a significant change in attitudes to bullying, children need to see their teachers consistently challenging all incidents of bullying that come to their attention. This will help to convey the message to pupils that bullying is not to be tolerated. Also teachers need to be aware of the effect that their own behaviour might have on their pupils. One mother who wrote to the Anti-Bullying Centre at Trinity College, Dublin had this to say:

> *Teachers in almost every school in Ireland bully children. They pick on certain children and give them a terrible time. That is a well-known fact for years now. They make a laugh of them in class if they cannot keep up with the good ones. Teachers have their favourites and they give them the most attention. The ones they dislike are exploited and ignored ... it's no wonder children bully each other in schools as that is what they see their teachers doing to them, and then they bully each other.*

In view of the poor level of teacher intervention it was perhaps not surprising to find that in the present study there was an equally unsatisfactory level of intervention by pupils. From Table 13.5 it can be seen that only half of the primary school pupils (59%) and less than half of the post-primary pupils (47%) reported that they had tried to help someone they saw being bullied. Table 13.5 shows that approximately one in seven primary and post-primary pupils did not intervene because they felt it was none of their business.

The research findings confirm the findings of Rigby and Slee (1991) on age trends in attitudes to bullying. With the exception of pupils in their final year of post-primary school, children as they advance through primary and post-primary school appear to become less inclined to help someone who is bullied. Readiness to help dropped by 21% from third class in primary school (8/9-year-olds) to fifth year in post-primary (16/17-year-olds).

Table 13.5 Percentage of pupils in primary and post-primary schools who report what they usually do when they see a pupil of their own age being bullied at school

Actions	Primary pupils	Post-primary pupils
Nothing, it's none of my business	14	15
Nothing, but I think I ought to help	27	38
I try to help in some way	59	47

Figure 13.3 shows that boys are less willing than girls in each class or year group to help a fellow pupil who is bullied. It can also be seen that the growing reluctance to help eases earlier for girls than it does for boys. A growing lack of sympathy and hardening of attitudes was found among pupils when they were asked whether they could join in bullying a pupil they didn't like (see Table 13.6.)

From the table it can be seen that a greater percentage of second-level pupils than first-level pupils responded that they could join in bullying someone they didn't like.

Figure 13.3 Percentage of boys and girls who reported that they would try to help a pupil of their age being bullied at school

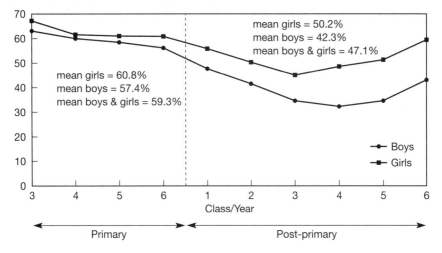

Table 13.6 Percentage of pupils who reported that they could join in bullying a pupil they didn't like

Response	Primary school pupils N=9,599	Post-primary pupils N=10,843
Yes	6	9
Yes, maybe	10	12
I don't know	18	19
No, I don't think so	12	15
No	21	20
Definitely no	33	26

Gender and year differences which have been detailed by O'Moore *et al.* (1997) showed that there was a steady increase in the readiness to bully a fellow pupil right up until fifth year in post-primary school. Girls, however, were less prepared to bully someone they didn't like than were the boys.

There was further evidence that children care less about bullying as they grow older when the pupils in the study were asked what they thought of pupils who bully others. In primary schools there were 33% of girls and 21% of boys who reported that bullying behaviour upset them a lot. In post-primary schools there were 6% fewer girls and boys who stated that they were uncomfortable with bullying. However, by sixth year the pupils reflected a greater sensitivity. A more detailed breakdown of the year and gender differences can be gained from O'Moore *et al.* (1998).

The rather casual attitude that was reflected in the children's responses to bullying behaviour was mirrored by an equally nonchalant attitude in parents and teachers. The children who had bullied were asked whether anyone at home or their teachers had spoken to them about their bullying. From Table 13.7 it can be seen that less than half of children at primary school and approximately only one third of post-primary pupils have been spoken to by their teachers.

Table 13.7 Percentage of children and adolescents who bully but who have not been spoken to about their behaviour by teachers or parents

	Primary pupils N=2,503	Post-primary pupils N=1,700
Have not been spoken to by teachers	52	67
Have not been spoken to by anyone at home	57	73

In sixth year in post-primary school only 14% stated that they had been spoken to by their teachers. Table 13.7 further shows that there is an inadequate level of communication about bullying behaviour in the homes of children who bully. It is, of course, uncertain whether this situation reflects that parents do not know that their children engage in bullying behaviour in school or whether they simply hold a non-caring attitude to bullying behaviour. Whatever the reason the findings point to a strong need to increase the level of communication between parents and teachers in relation to bullying behaviour.

There is evidence which points to the fact that parents do wish to be informed by teachers if their child is involved in bully/victim problems, either as bully or victim, even if it is only a suspicion (Olweus, 1993).

The author is very much of the opinion that teachers should alert parents of alleged incidents of bullying sooner rather than later. This gives parents the opportunity not only to reinforce the school's policy on bullying but also to correct the inappropriate behaviour. All too often parents are not notified until behaviour has so deteriorated that the child is advised of suspension or expulsion from school.

If, on the other hand, the problem is one of victimisation, then equally parents can take the necessary steps to support their child and stop the bullying.

Moreover, there is research which indicates that young offenders might have been spared judicial correction and sentencing had bullying behaviour that characterised them in their schooldays been challenged and corrected effectively rather than ignored (Kilpatrick, 1997).

Self-esteem and bullying behaviour

There is a growth of data which indicates that a high level of self-esteem protects children and adolescents from involvement in bullying. Salmivalli (1999) in her study of participant roles of bullying found in particular that it was the children with the highest level of self-esteem who were able to take on the role of defender of children whom they witnessed being bullied. Thus one of the keys to reducing the level of school bullying is for teachers to initiate programmes which will encourage children to help each other when there is potential threat to them.

Analysis of the present data concerning the self-esteem of the children and adolescents in the Irish nationwide study produced findings which have considerable implications for teachers.

Victims

Children of both primary and post-primary school age who reported that they had been victims of bullying had significantly lower global self-esteem than those who stated that they had never been bullied.

From Table 13.8 it can be seen that the greater the frequency with which the children and adolescents were bullied, the lower the global self-esteem. Analysis of the six cluster scales of the Piers-Harris Self Concept Scale suggests that both primary and post-primary victims saw themselves as more troublesome, more anxious, less popular, less physically attractive and as having lower intellectual and school status than children and adolescents who were not victimised. The more frequently the pupils were victimised, the more inadequate were their feelings in the individual domains of self-esteem. A more detailed cluster scale analysis can be found in O'Moore and Kirkham (2001).

When a distinction was made between children who were bullied only (pure victims) and children who were bullied but also bullied others, it was found that the pure victims of all ages had significantly higher global self-esteem than victims who also bully.

The only cluster scale among the primary school children not to reach statistical significance between the pure victims and the victims who bully was

Table 13.8 Mean scores for each of the self-esteem cluster scales for victims and their non-victimised peers of primary and post-primary age

Cluster scale	Primary (8–11 years)				Post-primary (12–18 years)			
	Not been bullied (n=5,123)	Occasional/ moderate (n=1,873)	Frequent (n=294)	F ratio	Not been bullied (n=5,123)	Occasional/ moderate (n=1,873)	Frequent (n=294)	F ratio
Behaviour	13.3	11.8	10.5	252.1*	12.8	11.7	10.8	67.3*
Intellectual and school status	12.3	10.9	9.5	172.6*	11.6	10.6	9.5	53.9*
Physical appearance and attributes	8.9	7.8	6.1	180.9*	8.1	7.0	6.1	75.1*
Anxiety	10.6	8.5	6.2	499.9*	9.4	7.8	6.0	157.5*
Popularity	9.8	7.6	5.2	947.9*	9.4	7.8	6.0	157.5*
Happiness and satisfaction	8.7	7.7	5.9	432.2*	8.1	7.1	5.5	168.6*

*$P<.001$

physical appearance and attributes. Among the post-primary group, only two of the six domains – behaviour and intellectual status – reached statistical significance.

Statistical details are included in O'Moore and Kirkham (2001). These results confirm the earlier findings of O'Moore and Hillery's small-scale study in relation to the children's self-reports and of their behaviour (O'Moore, 1997).

Bullies

The total group of children and adolescents who reported that they had bullied their peers in school during the term of the study were found to have significantly lower global self-esteem scores than children who had not bullied others (see Table 13.9). The results indicate further, as the table shows, that the more frequently the children bullied others, the lower was their global self-esteem.

The table also shows that the children of primary school age who bullied most often had significantly greater feelings of inadequacy in relation to behaviour, intellectual and school status, physical appearances, anxiety, popularity and happiness and satisfaction than children who did not bully. However, with the two cluster scales, physical appearance and anxiety, there was a tendency for the mean cluster scale scores to be higher, although not statistically significant among children who bullied frequently compared with those who bullied once or twice or sometimes.

Also the higher mean score of the frequent bullies as compared with the occasional/moderate bullies in respect of their attitudes toward their popularity was not statistically different.

From Table 13.9 it can further be seen that post-primary pupils who bullied had lower mean cluster scores in four of the six clusters compared with pupils who did not bully. Thus the results indicated that post-primary children who bullied had lower mean cluster scale scores in four of the six clusters compared with pupils who did not bully. The results further indicated that post-primary children who bully perceive themselves to be more troublesome, to have lower intellectual and school status, to be less popular, and to be more unhappy and dissatisfied.

When the distinction was made between children and adolescents who only bully (pure bullies) and those who have never been involved in bullying others, the pure bullies of primary school age also have significantly lower global self-esteem and have significantly greater negative feelings with respect to behaviour, intellectual and school status, and happiness and satisfaction.

However, the pure bullies did not feel significantly less adequate than did the control children in relation to their physical appearance, popularity and level of anxiety. Indeed, the results indicated that adolescents who bully – whether only once, twice, sometimes or frequently (i.e. once a week or more) – are significantly less anxious than those who do not bully.

Table 13.9 Mean scores for each of the self-esteem cluster scales for bullies and their non-bullying peers of primary and post-primary age

Cluster scale	Primary (8–11 years)				Post-primary (12–18 years)			
	Have not bullied (n=5,510)	Occasional/ moderate (n=1,622)	Frequent (n=126)	F ratio	Have not bullied (n=4,679)	Occasional/ moderate (n=1,017)	Frequent (n=78)	F ratio
Behaviour	13.4	11.1	8.1	547.6*	13.1	10.8	8.0	322.1*
Intellectual and school status	12.2	10.7	9.6	135.9*	11.6	10.6	9.7	41.7*
Physical appearance and attributes	8.6	8.1	8.2	13.3*	7.9	7.8	8.2	0.4NS (not significant)
Anxiety	10.1	9.2	9.3	44.3*	9.1	9.1	9.5	0.6NS (not significant)
Popularity	9.2	8.5	8.4	59.2*	9.1	8.8	8.4	5.2**
Happiness and satisfaction	8.5	7.9	7.2	80.7*	7.9	7.6	7.3	11.8**

*P<.001

**P<.01

Table 13.10 Mean global and cluster self-esteem scores for pure bullies and moderate and frequent bully victims of primary and post-primary age

Cluster scale	Primary (8–11 years)				Post-primary (12–18 years)			
	Pure bullies (n=828)	Bullies/ moderate victims (n=100)	Bullies/ frequent victims (n=47)	F ratio	Pure bullies (n=730)	Bullies/ moderate victims (n=42)	Bullies/ frequent victims (n=22)	F ratio
Global	57.5	45.8	39.4	89.4*	54.7	44.5	40.1	6.1**
Behaviour	11.4	8.8	8.2	38.6*	10.6	9.6	8.0	7.1*
Intellectual and school status	11.2	9.2	8.3	25.1*	10.8	9.1	8.6	13.0*
Physical appearance and attributes	8.8	7.4	6.1	24.3*	8.3	7.2	5.8	22.8*
Anxiety	10.4	7.9	6.1	70.9*	9.7	7.0	6.2	62.5*
Popularity	9.7	7.0	5.3	151.4*	9.5	6.7	5.4	16.2*
Happiness and satisfaction	8.4	7.2	5.7	57.4*	7.9	6.7	5.7	28.1*

*P<.001
**P<.01

171

The lower anxiety levels among the pure bullies of adolescent age may mask the feelings of inadequacy and explain why bullies are often rated by others as confident, tough and popular (Olweus, 1993).

When comparison was made between pure bullies and bullies who also admitted to being a victim, the results indicated that pupils of primary and post-primary age who both bully moderately and frequently and are also victimised moderately and frequently have significantly lower global self-esteem and harbour significantly more feelings of inadequacy than pure bullies.

Thus, bully/victims see themselves in comparison to pure bullies as being more troublesome, having lower intellectual and school status, and being less physically attractive, more anxious, less popular and more unhappy and dissatisfied. As Table 13.10 shows, the more frequently they bullied others and were bullied, the lower was their global self-esteem and the greater were their feelings of inadequacy in relation to the individual domains.

These results of children who bully either as pure bullies or bully/victims, while reported in more detail in O'Moore and Kirkham (2001), are again in agreement with the earlier small-scale study reported on by O'Moore (1997). In the latter study 32% of all the children who bullied had conduct disorders, 22.4% of whom were bully/victims; 77% of the conduct disorders were antisocial in nature, 15% were neurotic and 8% were undifferentiated.

Discussion

The results from the nationwide Irish study strongly indicate that bullying is widespread and that children and adolescents who bully or who are bullied have lower global self-esteem than peers of similar age who neither bully or are bullied. The results also indicate that bullies and victims of primary and post-primary school who have bullied or been bullied frequently have a lower global self-esteem than those who have been subjected to occasional or moderate bullying, or who have bullied others once or twice or sometimes.

Furthermore, children and adolescents who are involved in the dual role of bully and victim have significantly lower levels of global self-esteem than their peers who are classified as either pure bullies or pure victims.

The findings with respect to the victims in the study confirm those of the literature (Austin and Joseph, 1996; Salmivalli, 1999). However, the results presented in relation to pupils who bully contradict earlier studies involving Swedish and Australian children (Olweus, 1993; Slee and Rigby, 1993). They also contradict Pearce and Thompson (1998) who are emphatic that bullies do not lack confidence.

However, if one considers that the global self-esteem of the 'frequent pure bullies' in the present Irish sample lies within the 50th percentile for the primary school children and just short of it for the post-primary children, then it might be reasonable to claim that they also have adequate self-esteem. However, their self-esteem is significantly lower than that of those who do not bully. Also it must be noted that pure bullies made up only 32% of all primary school children who bullied and 40% of post-primary bullies. Thus, the majority of children who bully have lower self-esteem than those who do not bully.

It does seem reasonable therefore to speculate that the differences in self-esteem between children who bully and those who don't act as a contributory factor in bullying behaviour. There is evidence that children who do not bully but rather defend victims have genuine self-esteem (Salmivalli, 1999). As a result the author inferred that a healthy self-esteem is needed before an adolescent dares to defend a victim. Thus, to effect prevention and intervention of bullying behaviour our concern should be to determine the antecedents to the 'lower' self-esteem of children who bully.

Home factors undoubtedly play a significant part (Roland and Munthe 1989; Bowers et al., 1992; Olweus, 1993). However, the role of the school is more contentious. Olweus (1996) believes that bullies' aggressive behaviour cannot be explained as a consequence of frustrations and failures in school. Nevertheless, the present results indicate that feelings of inadequacy (such as those expressed in relation to their academic and school status and their popularity among peers) could be a strong contributory factor in their behaviour as bullies. The study found that 72% of pupils in primary and 71% of pupils in post-primary who reported that they bullied once a week or several times a week stated that they hated school. Rigby and Slee (1992) have also found that pupils who bully are less happy than most students and dislike school more.

How children react to feelings of low self-esteem will depend on the temperament of the child. If children are inclined to extroversion, they are more likely to compensate and fight back at the source of frustration. On the other hand, if introverted by temperament, the child is more likely to demonstrate shy, timid behaviour (Lawrence, 1996). There is evidence to indicate that children who bully are indeed more extroverted than pure victims (O'Moore, 1995; Mynard and Joseph, 1997; Connolly and O'Moore 2002).

Thus the stereotype of bullies as confident and tough might be a 'cover' for feelings of inadequacy. By making others feel helpless and isolated they make themselves out to be powerful and in control. Such a show of strength, particularly if they are also fearless as was the case for the adolescent pure bullies in the present sample, helps to disguise the fact that they harbour negative feelings of self-worth.

It is to be expected that as long as the factors contributing to the self-esteem or threatened egoism of bullies remain (Baumeister et al., 1996), the compensatory behaviour will not cease.

A review by Salmivalli et al. (1998) of follow-up studies of children who bully indicates that their aggressive behaviour is quite stable over time. However, as the children involved in the studies were for the most part retested while they were still at schools, their situations may not have changed. For example, the same sources of frustration which might have contributed to their initial behaviour, such as heavy emphasis on competition and pressures from teachers to achieve academically, might also have been operating at the time of retesting. Thus it can be argued that the aggressive behaviour was not so much an indication of a stable trait as it was situation specific. Indeed, Pollack et al. (1989) have found evidence to support the hypothesis that aggressive behaviours will depend on the circumstances in which a child finds himself at a particular time.

More recently, Salmivalli *et al.* (1998) have found that among girls, in particular, bullying is more situation specific. They found that the bullying behaviour of girls was connected more to their prevailing social situations and social relationships than being 'an aggressive, dominating, antisocial personality pattern'.

The lack of popularity that characterises self-reports and peer nominations of victims has long been debated as being either a cause or effect of continuous bullying (Roland, 1988). However, the same argument can be applied to the relationship between popularity and bullying others. Rigby and Slee (1992) have argued that bullying may have the effect of maintaining self-esteem, in so much as the behaviour is effective in producing feelings of dominance and power.

If this were the case, it might be reasonable to expect that the children who bully frequently or over a long period of time might have higher levels of self-esteem than those who bully occasionally. However, the results of the present study indicated that the reverse was true. It may be that bullying others may positively affect only specific domains, popularity being one of these.

Some evidence for this may be found in the present study in relation to the pure bullies who viewed their popularity as positively as did the children who were not involved in bullying. However, the bullies' view of their popularity may not be entirely objective (Salmivalli, 1998).

The lower levels of self-esteem and the feelings of inadequacy that characterised the victims, bullies and in particular bully/victims in this study have important implications for the prevention and treatment of bullying behaviour. There is evidence that inadequacy in children and adolescents with regard to a cluster of domains that include appearance, likeability and athletic competence provokes low levels of peer support and leads to a combination of low self-esteem, depressed effect and hopelessness.

Harter (1993) also claims that inadequacy with regard to a cluster of scholastic competence and behavioural conduct diminishes the level of parent support and that both these also provoke a constellation of depressive reactions. She reports that these reactions in turn are highly predictive of suicidal ideation. Findings of the present Irish sample indicate that this places all children involved in bully/victim problems at risk, in particular those who are most frequently involved.

It is to be noted that all the subgroups in the present study shared feelings of inadequacy in relation to scholastic competence and behaviour. Thus teachers, together with parents and other professionals who work with children and young people, need to become ever more sensitive to factors that place children and young people at risk of developing inadequate self-esteem.

Schools should also try to plan for a considerable number of pupils who may need psychological intervention above and beyond that which the staff can provide. It would seem from this and earlier studies reported on by O'Moore (2000) that most in need of such help due to their unhealthy psychological qualities are pupils who are frequently involved in bullying either as pure bully or bully/victims.

A conservative estimate based on the figures in the present study would indicate that there may be at least 4% of the school-going population aged 8 to 18 years who need professional intervention in addition to what school staff can provide in order that the long-term psychopathological sequelae associated with bullying at school may be prevented.

What can be done?

In the light of the findings from the present study there is absolutely no doubt that teachers hold the key to the successful prevention and treatment of bullying.

Essentially, bullying and victimisation is not a normal phase of development through which children pass unscathed. On the contrary, it is symptomatic of social and emotional difficulties which require attention if the welfare of the children is at heart. For school authorities to respond to approaches made by concerned parents of bullied children in the manner illustrated at the outset of this chapter is to behave irresponsibly. Furthermore, for staff, principals and boards of management to assert that 'there is no bullying in their schools' is to ignore all the current research on the subject of bullying.

Evidence clearly indicates that no school is immune to bullying. Initiating an anti-bullying policy in schools should not be seen as an admission of failure or as a poor reflection on the school but instead should be viewed as a positive step in creating an education in an environment of mutual support and caring. Social, emotional and academic growth is optimised in a supportive environment that is free from feelings of humiliation, distress and despair. Thus, to allow bullying to go unchallenged is effectively to prevent children from realising their full potential which is, after all, the aim of education.

There is at present no shortage of valuable suggestions and guidelines for creating a school ethos and organisation which repudiates bullying (Tattum and Herbert, 1997; and Department of Education Ireland, 1993; Elliott, 2002; SCRE, 1993; HMSO, 1994–2001; Newman *et al.*, 2000; Sharp and Smith, 1994).

However, many of the recommendations are of short-term value. Robin Chambers, one of the pioneers of an anti-bullying policy, gave some evidence of this when after strenuous efforts at challenging bullying in his school, he commented that he was working against the tide. He stated, 'If you take your eye off it for two days, well, it's like a weed. You keep having to pluck it out, and always will, so long as we've got the society we've got.' (St. John Brooks, 1985).

The author believes that in order to effect any real change in bullying behaviour one must tackle the root cause of the problem. From our results we have reason to believe that low self-esteem is a contributory factor in bullying. Indeed, this lends support to the existing strong body of evidence which indicates that self-esteem is central to determining behaviour (Baumeister, 1993). Thus the emphasis in the alleviation and prevention of bullying should be on enhancing self-esteem. Self-esteem begins in the family, and before entry to school each pupil is, to quote Burns (1982), 'invisibly tagged, some enhancingly by a diet of nourishing interest and affection, and others crippled by a steady downpour of psychic blows from significant others, denting, weakening and distorting their self-concepts'. However, once at school, peers and teachers take precedence over parents.

In schools even more evaluation takes place than the child has already experienced at home. There is daily appraisal of academic work, of sporting ability and of social behaviour. This is particularly true of schools where there is a heavy emphasis on competition. Thus the majority of pupils experience daily reminders of their potential and limitations. They are constantly being ranked and evaluated. Frequently, the superior achievement of one child is used to debase the achievements of others. Thus for every child whose self-esteem is boosted there is another whose feeling of self-worth is potentially diminished. Whereas a few successful or unsuccessful experiences may not have a major effect on the self concept, it is the frequency and consistency of feelings of adequacy or inadequacy over a period of years which leaves its mark on the self concept.

It has been repeatedly shown that whether or not children come to school with a firm picture of their self-worth, teachers have the potential to employ the academic and social learning experiences of school to either reinforce or reteach children a positive view of themselves. This includes competence, worth and belonging (Tattum and Tattum, 1992; Kaplan, 1997; Smyth, 1999).

All too often, however, schools overlook the emotional needs of the child in their efforts to achieve academic results. For example, it is not uncommon to hear teachers express the view that 'due to curricular and examination pressure we have no time to spend on the social and emotional problems of students'. Yet self concept contributes positively towards both academic success and social and emotional adjustment. There is considerable evidence to indicate that reported self concept of ability is a better predictor of academic success than is the intelligence quotient (Thomas, 1980).

It is a terrible indictment on schools when school leavers report that the post-school period was a time when they recovered from the emotional and devaluing effects of schools (Burns, 1982).

It should be noted that teachers with high self-esteem have been found to produce pupils with high self-esteem. The converse has also been found to be true (Lawrence, 1996). For example, Lawrence reports that in addition to qualities of empathy, acceptance and genuineness, teachers of high self-esteem are (a) able to delegate routine jobs, (b) able to find time to relate personally to pupils, (c) tolerant of pupils' conversations and (d) generally relaxed in teaching. This implies that they are able to present a high self-esteem model with which the pupils identify. Lawrence further explains that this process of identification with the teacher is strongest where the pupils perceive the teacher as establishing a 'growth-producing atmosphere'.

It is therefore timely to reconsider the stimulating view held by Thomas (1980) that 'only by seeing teaching as one of the helping professions and less an elitist procedure for purveying knowledge can we encourage a positive sense of worth not only in our pupils but in ourselves'.

Summary

To conclude it must be stressed that by placing so much emphasis on the school with teachers holding the key to the alleviation and treatment of problems in schools is not to deny the influence of the home, as has been demonstrated by both Olweus (1983) and Roland (1988). However, there is clear evidence to show that the incidence of behavioural difficulties has a stronger association with the quality of the teacher–pupil relationships in a school than with the pupil's socio-economic background (Rutter *et al.*, 1979; Weissbourd, 1996; Bemak and Keys, 2000). In other words, schools do make a difference. Thus it is no longer justifiable for schools when faced with behavioural difficulties such as bullying or victimisation to apportion all the blame on the child's home background. The evidence is clearly in favour of the view that a positive school ethos does contribute significantly to the good behaviour of pupils.

References

Austin, S. and Joseph, S. (1996) 'Assessment of bully/victim problems in 8- to 12-year-olds.', *British Journal of Psychology*, Vol 66, pp 447–56.

Baumeister, R. F. (1993) *Self-esteem the puzzle of low self-regard*. New York: Plenum Press.

Baumeister, R. F., Smart, L. and Boden, J. M. (1996) 'Relation of threatened egotism to violence and aggression: the dark side of high self-esteem', *Psychological Review*, Vol 103, No 1, pp 5–33.

Bemak, F. and Keys, S. (2000) *Violent and Aggressive Youth: Intervention and Prevention Strategies for Changing Times*. California: Corwin Press Inc.

Bjorkvist, K., Ekman, K. and Lagerspetz, K. (1982) 'Bullies and victims: Their ego picture, ideal ego and normative ego picture', *Scandinavian Journal of Psychology*, No 23, pp 307–13.

Boulton, M. J. and Underwood, K. (1992) 'Bully/victim problems among middle school children', *British Journal of Educational Psychology*, Vol 62, pp 73–87.

Bowers, L., Smith, P. K. and Binney, V. (1992) 'Cohesion and power in the families of children involved in bully/victim problems at school', *Journal of Family Therapy*, Vol 14, pp 371–87.

Burns, R. B. (1982) *Self-concept development and education*. London: Holt-Rinehart & Winston.

Byrne, B. (1999) 'Ireland' in Smith, P. K., Morita, J., Junker-Tas., Olweus, D., Catalano, R. and Slee, P. (eds) *The Nature of School Bullying: A Cross Cultural Perspective*. London: Routledge.

Connolly, I. and O'Moore, A. M.(2002) *Personality and Family Relations of Children who Bully*. (Submitted for publication).

Department of Education (1993) 'Guidelines on countering bullying behaviour in primary and post-primary schools'. Ireland: Stationary Office, Department of Education.

Elliott, M. (1988) *Keeping Safe, A practical guide to talking with children*. Hodder & Stoughton.

Elliott, M. (2002) 'Booklet for parents and children and material for teachers', Kidscape, 2 Grosvenor Gardens, London SW1W 0DH.

Harter, S. (1993) 'Causes and consequences of low self-esteem in children and adolescents' in Baumeister, R. F. (ed) *Self-esteem, the puzzle of low self-regard*. New York: Plenum Press, pp 87–116.

HMSO (1994) (2001) 'Bullying: Don't suffer in silence, an anti-bullying pack for schools', London: HMSO.

Kaplan, P. S. (1997) *Educational Psychology for tomorrow's teacher*. New York: West Publishing Company.

Kilpatrick, J. (1997) 'Bullying pays' in M.Elliot (ed), *Bullying: A practical guide to coping for schools*. London: Pearson, pp 89–96.

Lagerspetz, K., Bjorkqvist, B. and King, E. (1982) 'Group aggression among school children in three schools', *Scandinavian Journal of Psychology*, No 23, pp 45–52.

Lawrence, D. (1996) *Enhancing self-esteem in the classroom*. London: Chapman.

Mellor, A. (1991) 'Bullying in Scottish secondary schools'. Spotlights 23, Edinburgh: Scottish Council for Research in Education.

Mynard, H., Joseph, S. (1997) 'Bully/Victim problems and their association with Eysenck Personality Dimensions in 8- to 13-year-olds', *British Journal of Educational Psychology*, Vol 67, pp 51–4.

Neary, A. and Joseph, S. (1994) 'Peer victimisation and its relationship to self concept and depression among school girls', *Personality and Individual Differences*, Vol 16, pp 183–6.

Newman, D. A., Home, A. M. and Bartolomucci, C. L. (2000) *Bully Busters: A teacher's manual for helping bullies, victims and bystanders*. Illinois: Research Press.

Olweus, D. (1978) *Aggression in Schools: Bullies and whipping boys*. Washington DC: Hemisphere.

Olweus, D. (1979) 'Stability of aggressive reaction patterns in males: A review', *Psychological Bulletin*, No 94, pp 852–75.

Olweus, D. and Roland, E. (1983) *Mobbing, bakgrunn og titlak*. Oslo: Kirke og Undervisningsdepartementet.

Olweus, D. (1993) *Bullying in schools: What we know and what we can do*. London: Blackwell.

Olweus, D. (1996) 'Bully/victim problems in school', *Prospects*, (Paris/UNESCO) Vol 26, No 2, pp 331–59.

O'Moore, A. M. and Hillery, B. (1989) 'Bullying in Dublin Schools', *The Irish Journal of Psychology*, Vol 3, No 10, pp 426–41.

O'Moore, A. M. (1990) 'Bullying in Schools' in Socialisation of Youth in a Changing World, Western European Education, *A Journal of Translations*, Spring 1990, pp 92–117.

O'Moore, A. M. and Hillery, B. (1991) 'What do teachers need to know?' in M. Elliott (ed) *A Practical Guide to Coping For Schools*. London: Longman.

O'Moore, A. M. (1994) 'Bullying behaviour in children and adolescents', *Journal of the Irish Association for Counselling and Therapy*, Vol 1, No 30, pp 23–30.

O'Moore, A. M. (1995) 'Bullying behaviour in children and adolescents in Ireland', *Children and Society*, Vol 9, No 2, pp 54–72.

O'Moore, A. M. (1997) 'What do teachers need to know' in Elliott, M. (ed) *Bullying: A practical guide to coping for schools*, pp 151–66 London: Pitman in association with Kidscape.

O'Moore, A. M., Kirkham, C. and Smith. M. (1997) 'Bullying behaviour in Irish schools: A nationwide study', *Irish Journal of Psychology*, Vol 18, No 2, pp 141–69.

O'Moore, A. M. (2000) 'Critical issues for teacher training to counter bullying and victimisation in Ireland', *Aggressive Behaviour*, Vol 26, pp 99–111.

O'Moore, A. M., Kirkham, C. and Smith. M. (1998) 'Bullying in Schools in Ireland: A nationwide study', *Irish Educational Studies*, Vol 17, pp 254–71.

O'Moore, A. M. and Kirkham, C. (2001) 'Self-esteem and its relationship to bullying behaviour,' *Aggressive Behaviour*, Vol 27, pp 269–83.

Pearce, J. B and Thompson, A. E. (1998) 'Practical approaches to reduce the impact of bullying', *Archives of Disabled Children*, Vol 79, pp 528–31.

Pepler, D., Craig, W., Ziegler, S. and Charach, W. (1993) 'A school based anti-bullying intervention: preliminary evaluation' in D. Tattum (ed.) *Understanding and Managing Bullying*. Oxford: Heinemann.

Piers, E. V. (1984) 'Piers-Harris Children's Self-Concept Scale'. California: Western Psychological Services.

Pikas, A. (1975) *Sa stopper vi mobbing*. Stockholm: Prisma.

Pollack, G., Gilmore, C. Steward, J. and Mattison, S. (1989) 'A follow-up of aggressive behaviour in children', *Educational Review*, 41, 3, pp 263–70.

Randall, P. (1996) *A Community Approach to Bullying*. London: Trentham Books.

Rigby, K. and Slee, P. (1992) 'Dimensions of interpersonal relations among Australian children and implications of psychological well-being', *Journal of Social Psychology*, Vol 133, No 1, pp 33–42.

Rigby, K. and Slee, P. (1991) 'Bullying among Australian school children: Reported behaviour and attitudes towards victims', *The Journal of Psychology*, 131, pp 615–27.

Roland, E. (1988) 'Bullying: The Scandinavian research tradition', in D. P. Tattum and D. A. Lane (eds) *Bullying in Schools*. London: Trentham Books.

Roland, E. and Munthe, E. (eds) (1989) *Bullying: An International Perspective*. London: Fulton Press.

Rutter, M. (1967) 'A children's behaviour questionnaire for completetion by teachers: Preliminary findings', *Journal of Child Psychology and Psychiatry*, No 8, pp 1–11.

Rutter, M., Maughan, B., Mortimore, P. and Owston, J. (1979) *Fifteen Thousand Hours: Secondary schools and their effects on children*. London: Open Books.

Salmivalli, C. (1998) 'Intelligent, attractive, well-behaving, unhappy: The structure of adolescents, self-concept and its relation to their social behaviour', *Journal of Research of.Adolescence*, Vol 3, pp 333–54.

Salmivalli, C. (1999) 'Participant role approach to school bullying: Implications for interventions', *Journal of Adolescence*, Vol 22, pp 453–59.

Salmivalli, C., Lappalainen, M. and Lagerspetz, M. J. (1998) 'Stability and change of behaviour in connection with bullying in schools: A two year follow up', *Aggressive Behaviour*, 24, pp 205–18.

SCRE (1993) *Supporting Schools Against Bullying*. The Scottish Council for Research in Education.

Sharp, S. and Smith, P. K. (1994) *Tackling Bullying in your School: A Practical Handbook*. London: Routledge.

Siann, G., Callaghan, M., Glissov, P., Lockhart, R. and Rawson, L. (1994) 'Who gets bullied? The effect of school gender and ethnic group', *Educational Research*, Vol 36, No 2, pp 123–34.

Slee, P.T. (1995) 'Peer victimisation and its relationship to depression among Australian primary school students', *Personality and Individual Differences*, Vol.18, No.1, pp 57–82.

Slee, P.T. and Rigby, K. (1993) 'The relationship of Eysenck's personality factors and self-esteem to bully-victim behaviour in Australia', *Personality and Individual Differences*, Vol 14, pp 371–73.

Smith, P.K. and Brain, P. (2000) 'Bullying in schools: Lessons from two decades of research', *Aggressive Behaviour*, 26, pp 1–9.

Smith, P. K. and Madsen, K. C. (1999) 'What causes the age decline in reports of being bullied at school? Towards a developmental analysis of risks of being bullied', *Educational Research*, Vol 14, No 3, pp 267–85.

Smith, P. K., Morita, J., Junker-Tas., Olweus, D. and Slee, P. (1999) *The Nature of School Bullying: A cross cultural perspective*. London: Routledge.

Smyth, E. (1999) *Do schools differ? Academic and personal development among pupils in the second level sector*. Dublin: Oak Tree Press in association with The Economic and Social Research Institute.

St. John Brooks, C. (1985) 'The school bullies', *New Society*, 6 December, pp 262–65.

Sullivan, K. (2000) *The Anti-Bullying Handbook*. New Zealand: Oxford University Press.

Tattum, D. P. and Herbert, G. (1990) *Bullying: A positive response*. South Glamorgan Institute of Higher Education.

Tattum, D. P. and Herbert, G. (1997) *Bullying, Home, School and Community*. London: David Fulton.

Tattum, D. P. and Tattum, E. (1992) *Social Education and Personal Development*. London: David Fulton.

Thomas, J. B. (1980) *The Self in Education*. Slough: NFER.

Weissbourd, R. (1996) *The Vulnerable Child, What Really Hurts America's Children and What We Can Do About It*. New York: Addison-Wesley.

Whitney, I. and Smith, P. K. (1993) 'A survey of the nature and extent of bullying in junior/middle and secondary schools', *Educational Research*, Vol 35, No 1, pp 3–25.

14
■ ■ ■

How drama can help

FRANCIS GOBEY

(This chapter concentrates on general PSHE curriculum work with class groups, not on more specialised or therapeutic work with individuals.)

▶ Drama is a good resource for the anti-bullying curriculum

▶ Resource materials work best within a whole-school initiative

▶ Students need to be active participants as well as spectators of plays and videos

▶ Process and practice in drama/workshops hold key messages about bullying

▶ Group work develops learning about bullying, not bullying and resisting bullying within a social context, and builds consensus

▶ With more drama and video resources on bullying available, it is a question of making best use of them

Drama as a resource

Over the past ten years many Young People's Theatre, Theatre in Education and TV companies have produced work on bullying, and the theme has emerged as a popular topic in children's programmes and soap operas. Artists, academics, educationalists and pressure groups have together succeeded in lifting the taboo. Few schools now claim that bullying does not exist or that not talking about it helps it go away; more young people now take part in anti-bullying initiatives or do curriculum work in the area.

Learning about and dealing with bullying is built into the Personal, Social and Health Education and Citizenship framework of the 1999 National Curriculum for England: from Key Stage 1 knowledge that there are 'different types of teasing and bullying, and that bullying is wrong', through Key Stage 2 understanding of 'the consequences of antisocial and aggressive behaviours, such as bullying and racism, on individuals and communities', to Key Stage 3 skills to 'challenge offending behaviour, prejudice, bullying, racism and discrimination assertively and take the initiative in giving and receiving support'. Schools are also now asked to enable pupils to be participants in 'developing and putting into practice school policies about anti-bullying'.

Within this framework, though, schools still face the challenge of bringing the curriculum to life and many will choose to use video and drama. Many stories about bullying, whether of lonely victimhood, alienated aggression, group action or eventual comeuppance, make for powerful entertainment, but this can remain at the level at which they are perceived – entertainment. I would hope, however, that they could also be starting points for effective, experiential learning.

Teachers who are not specialists sometimes shy away from drama work that involves participation as well as spectating. Remembering how drama perhaps was taught in their own schooldays, they might feel that asking a group to 'go away and make a sketch about bullying' would probably be chaotic and perhaps actually reinforce bullying behaviour. And I think they'd be right.

But it needn't be like this. Participatory drama offers:

- a variety of expressive languages, forms and techniques;
- the safety of structures, styles and time limits;
- the protection of acting a role in someone else's story;
- a chance to rehearse alternative behaviours safely;
- exploration of the social context, as well as the individual;
- ways of exploring distressing experiences without exposing personal vulnerabilities;
- a basis for including 'real' feelings in working towards consensus about sensitive issues;
- opportunities for less forthcoming students to make a full contribution;
- a model of working practice that is implicitly anti-bullying.

Good practice – a checklist

In choosing, using and adapting published drama materials on bullying – whether plays, videos, excerpts or exercises – a school needs to be attentive to the social as well as the learning context in which they are to be used. This is because bullying, not bullying and resisting bullying are socially learned behaviours; the whole social structure of the community, school, class or group is implicated in the learning process. An anti-bullying curriculum is likely to be effective only within a whole-school approach to 'prejudice, bullying, racism and discrimination'.

Schools might like to bear in mind the following questions:

- Does the material try to do justice to the full range of experiences: emotional, physical and psychological?
- Are the overlapping interests of the individual, group and community all addressed?

- Is the material accessible in terms of languages, language level and other special needs?
- Is the material 'closed' or 'open' in the way it allows people to use and interact with it?
- Are cultural differences and differences of value and belief acknowledged and respected?
- Is the material suitable on its own? As part of a course? After a recent incident?
- How might the material become part of the curriculum or part of a whole-school initiative on dealing with bullying?

The emphasis here is on reflection and preparation. Much of my work has been in preparing staff groups for working on difficult and sensitive issues affecting young people's self-esteem and mental health, such as bullying, abuse and grief. The first step is for the staff group to work on the issues themselves. This is because understanding one's own experience is a prerequisite for understanding that of others, and because the group needs to build its own consensus. After all, bullying, abuse and grief are not confined to young people, nor do adults have the 'solutions'.

The second step is to try out the same participatory drama tools and exercises that the young people are going to use. This is because it is only fair, and because it builds awareness of, and confidence in, the active learning methods most suited to the anti-bullying curriculum. Staff will also then be able to judge what works for them and what is appropriate for direct work with those bullying and being bullied. As Andrew Mellor of the Anti-Bullying Network says, in any drama work it is important 'to be clear about the messages that you want to promote, and to be aware of the possible effects that the release of powerful emotions can have on children, some of whom may already be struggling with the emotional consequences of being bullied or abused'.

A workshop approach with a staff group uses exercises, role-plays and powerful video drama extracts to reawaken the full dramatic reality of bullying as it affects all those involved, in physical, emotional or psychological ways. The message of this is that any practice or intervention, however well intentioned, that does not address the difficult feelings, numbing ambivalences and sometimes buried horror of the bullying situation cannot hope to achieve lasting positive change. The workshop is substantially the same as that for young people, but with more analytical discussion of ways and means.

A workshop begins with brief exercises, designed both as warm-ups for the group and pointers to the way even the shortest and most artificial games can have a bearing on promoting an anti-bullying ethos. Partners then use each other as mirrors to get ready in front of and to see their feelings reflected. In another exercise, partners conduct a dialogue consisting only of yes and no. The results of these games are fed back to the whole group and it soon becomes clear that links can be made with issues around bullying.

In the next exercise groups form – one by one but without prior discussion or allocation of roles – into frozen pictures of 'some aspect of bullying'. These pictures are considered in turn. What can be seen to be going on? What roles are involved? This process brings with it the suggestion that bullying is a behaviour each of us is capable of engaging in and one which occurs in a social group. By means of adopting different roles, participants also get an experience of how far their own behaviour is chosen and how what they do affects the group.

In developing this exercise I use a technique called 'Feelings Balloons', whereby an advocate from among those watching goes to one character in the frozen picture, stands behind them and articulates the emotion or thought being experienced (often acutely) at that moment. There is a safety factor in this 'advocacy' as well as a liberation: feelings can be expressed that it would be difficult to say on one's own. With each group showing in turn, all participants get a chance to try this role. At this stage of the workshop the debriefing often includes remarks on how accurate and sensitive the advocates have been – a message about the possibility of empathy. One further development of these frozen pictures is for another spectator to intervene and make one small, physical change to a character's position, stance or gesture, and then to unfreeze and refreeze the picture to test out how the group responds.

Another role-play technique I use is called 'Dilemmas'. Following a 'Frozen Picture', a video or script excerpt showing a bullying situation, three participants enact the drama of the inner conflict of one of the various characters involved: one in role as the character, and the others as two opposed, alternating 'voices'. The drama is most effective if the 'voices' position themselves at each shoulder, a little behind the person in role, out of sight but not out of mind as it were. The person in role says what their dilemma is, but then lets the voices express and test all the conflicting feelings and thoughts and worries it entails: those watching the dilemma can also contribute suggestions. In the case of the character being bullied, these voices could be one of fear and one of anger; the inner conflicts of the person bullying, the side-kick, the witness, the friends, the teacher, etc. are also dramatised.

'Dilemmas' brings out the mental anguish bullying can cause, but can also be used to show who (among the many roles involved) might be in the position to make a decision, to begin a resolution. Again debriefing from the exercise can make these links – it is also important for participants to come out of role.

In this spirit the active part of the workshop always ends with a group 'deroling' exercise to gather and rechannel the energy in a positive direction. Such intense and interactive drama work can release powerful feelings – especially if they resonate with current or remembered experiences – and a responsible workshop, I feel, needs to locate these within a relatively whole, emancipatory experience.

Drama work with young people

These exercises derive from my work in the 1990s with the Neti-Neti Theatre Company, supporting the play, and then video, *Only Playing, Miss*. Written by Penny Casdagli, this play about bullying is performed multilingually in English, Sign Language and Bengali, and is aimed mainly at Years 7 to 9.

Initially my work was exploratory and aimed at developing writing work for the project. I approached bullying as a type of behaviour actual or potential in most people's lives and sought to embed it within a wider framework of feelings and empathy, power, communication, friendship, ethical choice and consensus.

These workshops were small-scale, practical and participatory. They began with drama, acting games and role-play, with a record being kept or tape, in writing or on video. They first explored individual feelings of powerfulness and vulnerability before moving on to social relations and the dilemmas caused by abuses of power. The issue of bullying was then drawn out of this context, looked at in its various guises at home, in communities and in school, and broken down into its constituent parts, such as name-calling, teasing, exclusion, intimidation, assault, etc.

Some work was more direct in tackling the dynamic within the group. Such workshops tried to create an atmosphere in which pupils could be honest about their experiences and tell their stories without fear of ridicule – not always easy if there was bullying within the group. Consensus about what bullying is, let alone what can be done about it, cannot be assumed from the start: a group works slowly towards admitting that certain behaviour, such as teasing or 'blanking', is really bullying. Individuals – and this applies equally to staff – gradually open up as they feel supported.

Other workshops had the specific goal of making a help and advice pack for new pupils. Everything achieved in the workshop in discussion, on paper or on tape was put together and presented as the group's consensus. We would then make a video to show the rest of the year group. In this way one group of 15–18 students could pass on their experience and conclusions.

Only Playing, Miss

This play on video takes as its subject the story of Eugene Hickey who returns to his class following the death of his father. Some of his classmates see his behaviour as out of order, and one of them, David Rant, begins to bully him. In this he is joined by Sam, who also turns her friends against Becky, Eugene's ally.

The cycle of ritual violence and cruel taunting escalates, despite the best efforts of Eugene's wise friend Jo, until Becky gets the others to help her tell their teacher, Mrs Richards. The audience witnesses Mrs Richards confronting the bullies but only later learns of her work with the respective parents. It is only in the final scene that Eugene and his friends find the courage to stand up to David Rant, and Rant to share the story of his own bereavement with Eugene.

This story, presented in varied dramatic ways as narrative, naturalistic action and song, can be seen as the *content* of the play, with meanings readily accessible to the school audience. But the full impact of the play owes much to Neti-Neti's *practice* as a company. Multilingual presentation by a mixed and fully integrated cast of differently abled actors adds a particular resonance to a story about bullying, which often has its roots in the fear of difference. With black, Asian and deaf performers playing substantially positive roles, *Only Playing, Miss* implicitly challenges those racist and ablist attitudes which bullying often exploits.

Only Playing, Miss is only a play. It offers no easy solutions but uses the real-life nature of the story to make an impact and all the resources of drama to break down the silence that bullying relies on.

Initially within the play there is much that is familiar to those watching. The school depicted is mixed and multicultural; there's an unsympathetic teacher as well as a supportive one; the main incident of bullying occurs in an unsupervised changing room; the boys are more physical than the girls; the girls behave and talk more as a group. Anyone watching who has themselves been bullied immediately recognises Eugene's or Becky's situation and feelings.

At the same time, though, there are elements in the dramatic world of the play that are not at all familiar, or rather operate in a different context. The songs, for instance, which punctuate the action allow for a much greater expression of individual feeling than could be found in the school playground.

In fact, all the language of the play is rather special. In the fictional school of the play all pupils and teachers use Sign to support their English; some of them also speak Bengali with the Bengali-speaking character Hashi. It appears (as is the case with the performers) that one pupil and one teacher are deaf; and they sometimes use their first language, BSL (British Sign Language). Communication between pupils and with teachers then, provided the will is there, is not only possible but *abundant*. In contrast, when the action moves to David and Eugene's homes, the characters are restricted to only one language, English.

There is a message in this about the problems and possibilities of communication, which is reinforced by the events of the play. Eugene's silence and complicity in the bullying is challenged by Jo, who speaks from his own history and shares what he has learned; the silence of the whole class is broken by Becky when she unites the girls and informs Mrs Richards; and David Rant's silence over the death of his mother finally cracks as Eugene and friends stand up to him.

It is the value of friendship which emerges as the strongest motivation for change: more powerful in the end than the assaults of the toughest bully. Affection between boys is shown in a confirming way, as is the expression and sharing of strong feelings, which friendship allows.

In *Only Playing, Miss* the loss of a parent and the troubled grief this causes has to stand for all the other vulnerabilities that bullying behaviour latches on to. These, however, can be talked about in workshops or follow-up classes.

Using the video

I have found that the video and script of *Only Playing, Miss* can be used in many fruitful ways in workshops as a stimulus to acting, discussion and decision-making:

- scenes can be acted before viewing and then compared;
- scenes can be interrupted so that predictions can be made or acted;
- key moments can be acted in slow motion or with 'forum' techniques;
- the viewpoints of different characters can be traced;
- the changes in characters can be assessed from beginning to end;
- scenes of characters can be compared with real life, etc.

In follow-up pair or small-group work, the students could concentrate on a different character in the play, answering questions such as:

- What is Eugene like at the start?
- How does he feel about himself?
- What does he think of Rant?
- What do you think is the turning point for him?
- How has he changed by the end?
- How has the group changed?

At this stage the focus can move from the play to the young people's own experience, with questions such as:

- In this school what are people who bully like?
- And people who get bullied?
- And people who see bullying going on but don't do anything – what are they like?

In each case a questionnaire could give a range of options to circle in agreement: honest/tough/scared/mentally strong/sensitive/babyish/brave/weak/unlucky/like anybody else/cowardly/good at making friends/in need of help/don't trust teachers, etc.

The next task would be an exercise asking the pair or group to imagine that their friend is being bullied (a better question at this stage than asking: What would you do if you were being bullied?), with questions such as:

- How do you feel about your friend?
- How do you feel about the people bullying them?
- What do you do?
- Who helps you?
- What problems do you have?
- What happens in the end?

Working on this scenario, the students offer their own strategies for dealing with bullying in their school. The workshop leader may advise and, if necessary, challenge fantasy or violent 'solutions'.

Spokespeople from each of the work groups then report on their opinions and strategies in the plenary session. If the workshop has gone well there is often a high degree of consensus both about the characters in the play and about the most effective ways of dealing with the problem of bullying in the school.

The plenary session now functions as a reunion of the characters in the play at the point where the bullying drama has been resolved – resolved because in each of the characters there has been some change: an insight, a decision, an access of courage, a new valuing of friendship.

But it also offers an enlightening and perhaps surprising opportunity to see a problem approached from different perspectives producing a more or less consensus outcome.

Summary

In each case, at the plenary, students hear the same message coming from their peers:

- Bullying is bad for everyone.
- Speaking out and stopping it is good for everyone.
- Preventing it is a job for everyone – parents, teachers, support staff, managers and every pupil in the school.

And, perhaps too,

- The drama workshop approach has worked!

References

Casdagli, Penny and Gobey, Francis (1990) *Only Playing, Miss: Playscript/Workshops in Schools.* Trentham Books.

DfEE (1999) 'Non-statutory frameworks for personal, social and health education and citizenship at key stages 1 and 2; personal, social and health education at key stages 3 and 4', *The National Curriculum for England*, DfEE/QCA.

Gobey, Francis and Casdagli, Penny (2001) *Grief, Bereavement and Change: Guidance for teachers in PSHE.* Heinemann.

Gobey, Francis (1995) 'Conflict, knowledge and transformation – three drama techniques for use in conflict resolution', in Marian Liebmann (ed.) *Arts Approaches to Conflict*. Jessica Kingsley.

15

■ ■ ■

Bully 'courts'

MICHELE ELLIOTT

▶ Example of student council to deal with bullying – bully 'court'
▶ Bully 'court' as part of a whole-school policy
▶ Suggestions for students to deal with bullying
▶ Using bully 'courts' as drama

Jennifer was curled up in a corner of the girls' toilet, sobbing. Suniti and Hattie giggled as Marina continued her onslaught.

'You're such a baby – why don't you drink from a bottle?'

'Yeah,' Hattie chimed in, 'maybe you need nappies, too.'

Jennifer said nothing and tried to stop, but she was too upset. She tried to avoid going anywhere the bullies might be, but she'd made a fatal mistake today.

'You're the ugliest …' Marina stopped suddenly as two girls came in the door.

'What's the matter, Jennifer?' said Kirsty.

Zahida bent down to help Jennifer up.

'Oh, she's just stupid, aren't you, Jennifer?' taunted Suniti.

Kirsty turned on her. "Lay off! Leave her alone."

'You wanna fight?' Hattie stepped in front of Kirsty.

Zahida stood up and intervened. 'Come on Kirsty. Come on Jennifer, let's leave these 'ladies' in the loo, where they belong.'

Zahida went directly to their form tutor, Mrs Clarke. 'I am fed up with these girls acting like this – Jennifer is not the only one they bully.'

'Is Jennifer willing to take it to the council?' asked Mrs Clarke.

'You mean the bully court?' said Zahida.

'Well, the students call it that, but the teachers don't like to call it that. In any event, do you think it is a good idea?'

'I'll ask Jennifer. I'm willing to testify and I know Kirsty will as well.'

The 'court' met two days later.

'Why were you bullying Jennifer?' asked Mark in a solemn tone. He peered across the table at Marina.

'I wasn't, replied Marina, indignantly.

'Tell us what happened, then,' said Lucy.

'Well, I was just putting on make-up and Jennifer came in and looked at me. You know, just her dumb look. I said "Who you lookin' at?" She said no one, but I knew she was lookin' at me. I told her to shove off, but she didn't move. I was there first. I only told her to shove off, nothin' more. She's such a wimp to come and tell.'

'Did you touch her at all?'

'No!'

'You sure?'

'Well ... maybe I accidentally brushed against her, but I didn't hit her or nothin.'

'Did you say anything to her.'

'No.'

'Why was she crying?'

Marina shrugged. 'Who knows – she's always crying about something. You'd think she was three, not 14.'

'Is there anything you'd like to say before we talk to the other girls?'

'No.'

For the next 15 minutes, the bullies, the victim and the witnesses individually told the teacher and the four children on the court what happened. The teacher and four young people who comprised the bully 'court' then retired to discuss the case. Was Marina being a bully? What about Hattie and Suniti? Did Kirsty, Jennifer and Zahida tell the truth? Did Jennifer cause what happened? What sentences could the court suggest to the head teacher if Marina and the others were guilty of bullying? Why did Marina seem to be a ringleader in bullying her classmates? She had been accused of bullying before. Did she have problems? Could anyone on the court help her? What about the contract they had all signed agreeing that they would not bully? (See Chapter 25).

The court decided that Marina, Hattie and Suniti did bully Jennifer. In fact, Jennifer had a bruise from being pushed on to the floor. Now it remained to decide what solutions or punishments they would recommend. The debate was intense.

'I think that she should be suspended for a week,' said Mark.

'She's been a problem ever since she came to this school.'

'I don't agree,' argued Shofig. 'Suspending her won't prove anything – she'll still be a bully when she comes back.'

'But at least she won't be able to give anyone a hard time for a week,' replied Mark.

The teacher, Mrs Clarke, intervened. 'We can only recommend suspension to the head teacher. The court has no power to suspend her.'

'I know,' said Mark, 'but I still think we should recommend it.'

'It would be better to make her do something around school during break,' contributed Susan. 'Don't let her have a break for a week, but make her work instead.'

'Yeah, like clean the loos', said Lucy.

'That would be appropriate,' said Shofig.

'Stop, this is serious,' said Mark reproachfully.

Suggestions came more quickly. 'Let's forbid her to go on the school outing next week. That would make her think.'

'No break time for a month.'

'Too long – not fair.'

'How about the "long and tedious" penalty?' said Shofig.

'What's that?' asked Lucy.

'You know, tearing up ten pieces of paper, throwing them into the air and then picking them all up again.'

'That's dumb,' said Lucy.

'Of course it's dumb – most punishments are dumb.'

'Like writing lines,' said Mark.

The discussion went on fast and furious for another ten minutes. Mrs Clarke pointed out that they had to come to a conclusion. They finally decided that Marina should:

- apologise to Jennifer; then
- stay away from Jennifer and not speak to or even 'look' at her for two weeks;
- write a story about bullying from a victim's point of view;
- not be allowed a break for a week; and
- if she was reported for bullying again and found 'guilty', the court would recommend to the head teacher that she be suspended.

They also decided that Hattie and Suniti should apologise to Jennifer and stay away from her, as well as not have time at school with Marina or each other. They felt that Hattie and Suniti needed a break from Marina and each other to think about their behaviour. Neither girl had been a bully until they started hanging around with Marina.

Jennifer, Marina, Hattie and Suniti were called in separately and told of the decision. Marina, Hattie and Suniti, who had the option of appealing to the head teacher, accepted the court's ruling instead. They knew that the head teacher might have suspended them, so felt it better to take their punishment from the court.

This bully court was held in a London inner-city secondary school. The students, teachers and parents had all agreed to try the bully courts because the problem of bullying was getting worse. The courts were set up with the help of Kidscape, which had pioneered the idea with some 30 pilot schools, both primary and secondary.

The original idea came from a student who was fed up with the petty verbal bullying going on in her school. The teachers and parents were enthusiastic if the courts could be set up in a sensitive and effective way. After deciding on a whole-school philosophy about bullying (see Chapter 25), the students elected two representatives and the teachers nominated two more. One of the teachers agreed to be the adviser and the 'court' was set up.

The idea spread and Kidscape monitored 8 schools out of 30 which took part in a pilot scheme. The students were surveyed to determine the extent of the problem. More than 70% of the students said that they had been bullied at some time; 35% of the bullying happened either at school or travelling to school. At the end of the three-month trial period, 6% of the children said they had been bullied, a dramatic drop in reported cases. It appeared that the courts had been a major factor in reducing bullying, so why not introduce them everywhere?

That could be a disaster. Bully courts will only work in schools which have a strong anti-bullying policy which is supported by parents, teachers, staff and children. The court system has only the authority that is given to it by the people. The danger is that it will otherwise become a place of revenge for one group against another. Without the school policy, the bully courts become simply a way of bullying the bullies. The court is the final link in the chain of setting up a complete school anti-bullying strategy involving everyone. It takes time to forge the chain, to build the self-esteem of children and young people, to deal with themes of safety and caring for one another, to ensure that the relationship between staff and pupils is one of trust, and then gradually move on to role-playing ways to cope and to role-playing the court itself.

A crucial test of a school's readiness for bully courts is when pupils have grasped the principle that there are no bystanders in bullying. You have to foster in children and young people a sense of community and responsibility so they know that if an incident comes to light in which they didn't take part but just walked by, they are culpable. They are just as guilty as if they had taken part in it. Even if they don't like the person being bullied, they can't walk by. When that point is reached, putting children or young people in charge of justice through a bully court is feasible. You may wish to ask the parents to a meeting, show them a mock court and ask if they approve. If they do, work out the best way forward in your school.

Kidscape suggests the following guidelines.

1 Agree guidelines for behaviour with students.
2 Sign individual contracts with each student re guidelines.
3 Post the guidelines on bulletin boards throughout the school.
4 Call a school assembly and have students present guidelines; include all staff, as well as playground supervisors.
5 As part of the guidelines, set up an arbitration court.
6 The court could comprise four students, two elected by the student body and two appointed (as an honour) by the teachers.
7 One teacher would sit on the court (which could be called an 'honour court').
8 The term of office depends upon the agreement of the students – one school term would be suggested.
9 Unless there was an emergency, the court would meet once a week at a set time.
10 The court would be responsible for most infractions, unless they were serious enough to involve the police (i.e assault) or there was a family problem which made it inappropriate.
11 Solutions and/or penalties would be binding on all parties, with the right of appeal.
12 The verdict of the court would be written down and filed, with copies going to all concerned parties.
13 School governors and parents would receive information about the court and be invited to a meeting to see a mock case and to discuss the issues.
14 The effectiveness of the court would be evaluated by students, parents and teachers.

Suggestions for students

Bully courts have also been useful in coming up with suggestions for students on how to deal with bullies. The following are some of the suggestions for the victims generated by the students and teachers involved.

1 Laugh at or ignore comments or teasing. Remember that these people are ignorant. They want your scared reaction, so humour or silence might throw them off. You have to keep it up for a while until they get bored.
2 You can tell them to bug off, elephant breath, or something to that effect. But you must say it angrily and walk away immediately. Practise in the mirror.
3 If it is a group bothering you, look the weakest one in the eye and say 'This isn't funny' and then walk away.

4 You can sign up for self-defence courses which will give you more confidence. These lessons don't necessarily mean you 'fight back' and they can help your confidence.

5 Stay with a crowd – bullies usually pick on kids alone.

6 Ask one of the gang members when they are alone why they find it necessary to gang up on one person.

7 It might help to ring one of the bullies and ask how they would like it if this was happening to them. This will work only if you have some sort of relationship with that person.

8 Seek the advice of your parents and if they have any ideas, give them a try. You need their advice and support.

9 Do not stop if they confront you. Keep on walking. Get someone to witness what they are doing so that a teacher intervenes without you telling on them.

10 Stop thinking like a victim – you do not deserve this. Walk tall, pretend you are confident, even if you are not. Look at the bullies and smile as if they are not frightening you to death, even if you do not feel this way inside. Keep walking away and ignoring them if nothing else. They will get bored eventually.

11 Keep a diary of all the events – time, place and what is said.
Have your parents contact the head teacher or school parent-governors (ask the secretary for the names) and tell them what is happening. It is not right that bullying is allowed to go on, nor is it right that the bullies should be allowed to get away with it.

12 Make sure that your case comes before the bully court so that all can work on the problem together.

The bully courts may not be the right answer for every school. If the groundwork of co-operation has not been laid, they will fail. One head teacher saw the 'courts' as just another form of bullying. Patricia Godfrey, a teacher of over 20 years' experience, disagrees. 'Children see bullying from a different level – they're at eye-level height with others. Their insight can be fresher; they can offer more genuine ideas than adults' (Knuppe, 1990).

Soon after the publicity in the newspapers about the courts, Kidscape received a letter from Robert Laslett, who has set up a children's court for bullies in 1961 at a school for maladjusted children. The court continued to meet twice a week until 1985. He noted that the idea was as old as Homer Lane and his New Commonwealth and that David Wills had a court at Barns in 1940. Robert Laslett confirmed Kidscape findings about the courts.

The success of the court was really due to the relationships between the staff and the children at the school – in a way the court exemplified these relationships. Young people and children knew that we were concerned about bullying and they also knew that they could be quite open about their feelings and behaviour.

Laslett (1975)

Drama

Bully 'courts' can also be used as a drama exercise. If the children are secondary school age, ask them to come up with their own scene and characters. If the children are younger, the teacher may have to set the scene. It is possible to use an incident of bullying which has occurred in the past as the basis of the drama, as long as the children involved are no longer in the school. The *Sticks and Stones* video, listed in the Resources section (see page 324), portrays a fictional bully incident and a 'court' which meets to discuss what to do. It serves as an example of how to use bully courts as an effective drama exercise with students.

Summary

If not properly monitored, any system is open to abuse, including the bully courts. Properly used, the courts (we prefer the name councils or arbitration panels, but children like calling them courts) have proven to be an effective way of getting students involved in solving their own problems in a positive and constructive manner.

References

Knuppe, J. (1990) 'Pupils put bullies in the dock', *The Sunday Times*, 6 May.
Laslett, R. (1975) 'A children's court for bullies', *Special Education*, Vol 9, No 1, pp 9–11.

16

■ ■ ■

The playground

VALERIE BESAG

▶ Playground bullying can be difficult to identify. Good quality supervision is essential

▶ Children learn the skills essential for emotional development through play

▶ Recent research helps us understand gender differences in play, bullying and the dynamics of groups and gangs

▶ Non-physical bullying can be the most distressing and can have severe long-term impact

▶ Children lacking social and physical skills are often targets for bullying

▶ Older students can make a positive difference

The Playground

Friends, Pals, Mates, Companions
Someone to help you
Someone to tell you things
Where would we be without friends?

Someone to boost your confidence
Someone to give you inspiration
Someone to lend you things
Someone to have fun with
Friends, Pals, Mates, Companions.

Nicholas English (age 10)

The poem above illustrates how important most young people consider friendships and positive peer interactions to be. Traditionally, it has been assumed that children love playtimes and rush out of class in joyous anticipation. It is salutary to contrast this picture of childhood with that given in another poem, *The Killing Ground*, by Adrian Mitchell. Mitchell's poem offers a view of playgrounds that, sadly, is a more realistic picture for many young people attending our schools today.

I heard a deep voice talking, it had that iceberg sound
'It prepares them for Life' – but I have never found
Any place in my life worse than The Killing Ground.

Adrian Mitchell (1984)

Studies involving large cohorts of children show that bullying occurs across cultures. The research of Smith and Sharp (1994) in England, Craig and Pepler (1995) in Canada, Rigby and Slee (1991) in Australia and Olweus (1978, 1993) in Scandinavian schools illustrates that this is an aspect of human behaviour rather than a fault in our education system. However, this does not mean that as parents and professionals we can remain passive. Most bullying occurs in playgrounds, where children spend a quarter of their school day. There is now a greater understanding of what goes on there, including both negative and positive interactions, and what can be done to remedy untoward behaviour.

Hard to identify

Bullying among school children is hard to identify, even within a supervised classroom setting. The name-calling, abusive remarks, pushes, thumps and snatching of equipment can all occur behind the teacher's back. In the bustle of a large playground it becomes extremely hard to distinguish behaviour causing distress from rough and tumble play. However, children from the age of three can distinguish rough and tumble play from deliberate aggression (Pelligrini, 1988). It is adults who are easily confused – or fooled. Commonly, in playground disputes, aggressors accused of bullying claim to have 'only been playing'. However, by definition, games are enjoyed by all participants. If any one child is not taking pleasure in the activity it cannot be defined as a game.

Bullying can be a covert behaviour, often causing severe stress and fear, yet leaving little visible evidence and rarely anyone willing to act as witness. Extreme vigilance is required when supervising children at play. The occasional use of a hidden video camera can pick up untoward behaviours before they become established and habitual. The occasional filming of children in the playground, for in-house research purposes, can throw up the most surprising behaviours, not always from expected sources. Children wishing to hide their aggressive behaviour can employ the most devious means. Most young people are agreeable to such research if it leads to them feeling more secure around school. It may be advisable to discuss this with parents and school governors before filming. Such a meeting could be used to begin, or complement, a realistic whole-school approach to bullying where all those concerned with the school can work together to develop a comprehensive approach to this problem.

Normal interactions

There is a place for some degree of teasing, challenging and critical comment in the normal interactions of childhood play. Young people use these strategies to shape the behaviour of individuals to the standard common to the group. This process continues through life, whether in the form of gentle cues from friends or more direct criticism from elsewhere. It is possible to become over-protective of young people. They need to be able to meet challenges and justifiable criticism to prepare them for the teasing, taunting and the range of other challenges they will undoubtedly meet later in life. Childhood is the time to try out and hone appropriate responses. The cut and thrust of the playground is the place to develop embryonic social skills.

One aspect of training for playground supervisors and teachers which is often overlooked is experience in defining what is rough and tumble play and what is aggression and bullying. It is not always easy to decide and adults may intervene unnecessarily. Premature intervention by adults may inhibit the natural learning process whereby young people develop the skills of mediation, resolution, negotiation and argument. Not all argument is bad. Challenge and controversy offer opportunity for emotional and linguistic development. Over-involvement and direction by adults may thwart the emerging skills of decision-taking, imaginative play and creativity. If adults intervene too quickly, they not only thwart opportunities for children to become independent, but the quality of play and language used decreases. We now have an understanding of the wide range of skills young people need to develop (Goleman, 1996). These emotional literacy skills are best learnt in the naturalistic setting of the playground. The role of adults in the playground is to be vigilant and supportive, ready to step in, but only where necessary.

Unfortunately, some young people get more than their fair share of negative attention from their peers. This can be damaging at the time and in the long term (Boulton and Smith, 1994). Even as adults we remain watchful of our behaviour in order to maintain social acceptance, but in the case of children it is essential to identify those repeatedly singled out for negative comment and at risk of becoming the group scapegoat. Once relegated to that unfortunate role, the child can quickly become the target for all (Besag, 1989).

Boys versus girls

In considering playground behaviour, it is relevant to note the difference between the play of boys and girls as this relates to the gender difference in bullying behaviour. Boys are considered more physical and boisterous in their play (Maccoby and Jacklin, 1980). Correspondingly, bullying among boys is characterised by overt physical and verbal abuse (Roland, 1988). Boys appear to form larger and looser groups than girls, whether as an organised team or in an informal gang playing a chasing game (Omark *et al.*, 1975). For boys, it appears to be the activity rather than the relationship that is the focus of the group.

In contrast to boys playing an organised group game, girls most often gather in twos or threes, with the third most likely on the periphery (Douvan and Adelson, 1966). Girls place a stronger emphasis on the quality of their relationships. Their interactions are characterised by conversation and the exchange of opinions. More modelling of the attitudes, presentation and behaviour of each other takes place. Due to this bonding process, jealousy, possessiveness and loyalty are often in evidence and the inter-relationships can be constantly under review. These dyads of young girls have been compared to lovers due to the intensity of the relationships. There is often the need for frequent contact by telephone or the exchange of notes, and physical contact such as holding hands (Lever, 1976). Rumour, malicious gossip and social ostracism are the preferred modes of bullying among girls. This perhaps reflects the importance and vulnerability of these close relationships. Besag (2000) shows that close friendships are very important to girls. Many of these young girls were afraid of being absent from school in case their friend was 'sneaked' away by another girl.

Name-calling

However, one aspect of bullying common to both boys and girls, and reported by both to be the most distressing, is name-calling. Young people of all ages appear to be imaginative and astute in identifying the Achilles heel of their target, and in choosing an apt and humorous name, qualities which ensure the durability of these abusive names.

Our names are personal to us and are used to distinguish us from others. Allport (1954) refers to them as 'labels of primary potency', a term still relevant today. Abusive names are often dehumanising as in 'cow, pig, bitch'. Without our name, we have no identity. It is significant that names are replaced by numbers in situations such as prisons and the armed forces where there is an intention to impose a group identity to further discipline and control. Graphic illustrations of this process in action can be seen in the novel *1984* by Orwell (1995) and the cult television programme *The Prisoner*.

Adults supervising a busy playground may underestimate the distress caused by abusive names, yet children report them causing more distress than physical assault. Name-calling is often used in the initial stages of bullying to test the response of those suspected of being vulnerable. Good supervision at this stage could prevent an escalation to crisis. Adults need to be aware that the power of a threat or insult lies not in what is said but how it is said; the manner in which it is delivered and received. It is a two-way process. It may be that only the recipient understands what is implied or intended and can make the appropriate choice as to how to react. Hearing about an abusive incident from a third party could diminish the impact and the episode could wrongly be dismissed as trivial. Nicknames and diminutives may be used in a benign fashion. For example, it has been a tradition to allocate the name

'Chalky' to males with the surname White. This is often a sign of affection or used to signify inclusion in a group as in membership of a cricket team. However, we have come to understand the destructive power of name-calling and police and legal action can now be taken on behalf of those stigmatised or attacked verbally because of cultural, racial or presentation differences.

From the profiles of those at risk of becoming involved in a bullying situation, it can be seen that many victims fall into the category of passive 'watchers' who remain on the sidelines of playground fun, whereas bullies tend to be the 'doers', confident and fully involved in all activities (Besag, 1992; pp 18–19). A child may be on the fringe of playground activities for many reasons. Recently, we have become more aware of a significantly large category of children neglected or rejected by the peer group.

One group of children, mainly boys, who frequently fall foul of playground bullies are those now referred to as Developmentally Dyspraxic (Besag, 1989, pp 50–51; see also Besag, 1992, pp 42–6 for a case study). These children experience co-ordination problems. As boys tend to be more robust and physically active in their play than girls, the problems these children have with running, catching and balancing skills, for example, are more noticeable among boys and their rejection more common. In addition, these children may display mannerisms which give rise to taunts (Besag, 1989, p 177). These boys are especially at risk of playground bullying as they are often actively rejected or, at best, ignored.

If confident and well supported by adults, these children can overcome many of their difficulties and find success with specific activities. One such activity is swimming as the water supports the body so that attention can be concentrated on the arm and leg movements. Another possibility is table tennis which has a restricted repertoire of movement, unlike other forms of tennis. Opportunities for these children to gain recognition and prestige in any way should be sought, as feelings of rejection and fear can exaggerate their co-ordination problems, so compounding their physical and social difficulties. Dyspraxia is a complex and pervasive difficulty affecting a wide range of functioning. Vigilance and the identification of Dyspraxia in the playground may alert teachers to problems a student has in tackling the academic programme successfully.

Pupils often appear to use teachers as role models so that the dismissive attitude of a teacher towards a boy who is poor at sport and playground games can encourage the rejection and bullying of the boy by the group. A teacher may make a joking remark in class in an innocent fashion. This can be picked up by the class and later used to taunt the victim in the playground in the teacher's absence.

Supervision

Most bullying appears to start with the spontaneous teasing out of those suspected of being vulnerable for the entertainment of the individual or the group. This can quickly escalate to a distressing level if the opportunity occurs. There are times and places throughout the school day when the quality of supervision can be poor due to no teacher being nominated as responsible for oversight of an area. Examples of this are changing rooms, toilets, corridors, bus queues and lunch queues. Young people congregate in such places in their free time and the less robust could be at risk. These unsupervised areas become unofficial playgrounds with all the risks but little protection.

Good supervision over play breaks is not only necessary for the safety and wellbeing of all pupils but is in the best interests of the school as a whole. Disputes arising in the playground are often carried over into class, causing disruption (Blatchford and Sharp, 1994). Attention needs to be given not only to the quantity of supervision but also to the quality. The style of supervision, firm and friendly or authoritarian and rigorous, may reflect the ethos of the school. If there is a mismatch, the supervision could enhance or detract from the work done elsewhere throughout the school day (Blatchford and Sharp, 1994).

Play breaks demand more than the casual oversight of a couple of adults wandering around the playground. One boy in his first year at secondary school suddenly refused to attend without explanation. Only when an older boy was asked to shadow him did it become known that if he went to the cloakroom to get his coat, he would be locked in by other pupils. His only option was to play out in the winter weather without a coat. Staff had been conscientiously patrolling the playground unaware of the distress of this young boy (Besag, 1992, p 86).

One method of identifying weaknesses in a supervision system is by a member of staff tracking pupils and noting problems. One school adopting this method found that pupils allowed in school five minutes before the bell, when staff left the staff room, were congregating on the stairs, outside registration rooms and in various nooks and crannies around the building. The joking and jostling in these unattended groups caused many pupils to enter class in either a truculent or excitable mood. In another school, a teacher doing a similar exercise discovered that, for some considerable time, non-white pupils had been forbidden by others from using the stairs and were forced to wait for the arrival of a teacher for protection. No one had alerted staff to this situation (Riley, 1988). Punctuality of teachers is imperative – this means being well in advance of pupil arrival.

Staff absences can also cause problems if not identified until playtime has begun, for it is by then too late to reallocate the duty. The tracking exercise also found unsupervised, crowded corridors to be prime locations for disputes and fights. The crush gave cover for deliberate attacks made on vulnerable pupils. Seemingly playful pushing, jostling and bag swinging could be covert, targeted aggression.

The school tackled the problems outlined as a team committed to upgrading the quality of supervision (Besag, 1992, p 56). Teachers are now in class at least five minutes before the pupils enter the building. The corridors are supervised by teachers informally chatting to pupils or among themselves. Entering school from play, the pupils are met with a net of positive, welcoming comments, informally offered by several teachers standing around the entrances and corridors. The outside play areas are observed from second-storey classroom windows so that the bird's eye view supports the supervision offered from staff in the playground. Staff absences are routinely dealt with first thing at the same time that lesson cover is arranged. Older pupils are allowed to remain inside in designated areas to chat among themselves or with staff, to prevent overcrowding in the play areas. Most older pupils do not want to play boisterous games, nor do they want to stand around in the cold.

Activities

Some schools are able to offer a variety of activities for pupils of all ages to help make best use of the play breaks. Activities such as art and craft work, the library, computers, gymnastics, football, videos and comics can be arranged with volunteer adult support. These are especially valuable for 'wet' break times. Once there is recognition of the value of good leisure experiences and the danger of poorly supervised playtimes is highlighted, it may be that voluntary help will become more readily available. One school in Australia has a gifted school librarian who encourages all to visit the school library at breaks. The room is overflowing every lunchtime with young people busily engaged in a range of activities, reading being only one on offer.

There are many ways in which older pupils are able to support other pupils in school. Older pupils in both primary and secondary schools can be responsible for easing new entrants through the difficult transition period by chatting in small groups about such issues as bullying, which many pupils feel wary about discussing with adults. Vulnerable pupils could be paired with slightly older or more confident ones, who are able to take on the role often undertaken by older siblings or neighbourhood friends.

Games groups organised by older pupils have been found to be very useful in helping pupils overcome their feelings of vulnerability and in supporting them in developing a range of social skills (Besag 1989, p 186; 1992, pp 56, 57). Elizabeth Campbell devised a peer support programme for secondary school pupils in Sydney that has now been adopted by most schools throughout Australia and New Zealand. This programme, run by older pupils, aims to help younger ones to settle into the secondary school. It would appear that the interaction between the older and younger pupils is just as important to the success of the programme as are the activities on the programme. This type of work encourages good social interactions between pupils.

Training

Those supervising children during the longest break, the lunch hour, are often untrained and poorly paid. Many schools now support training schemes for these supervisors so that, instead of concentrating on the negative role of stopping trouble, they are able to help pupils maximise the valuable time during play breaks when they are free from the restrictions of curriculum demands. For the quality of supervision our children need, it may be that we must consider training supervisors to a professional standard and offer a qualification and an appropriate salary for those working with pupils during these key periods in the school day. An overview of training schemes can be found in Blatchford and Sharp (1994).

It is not simply a matter of providing more staff and more equipment. Key skills for supervisors have been identified by the Sheffield Bullying Project (Smith and Sharp, 1994) as:

- the ability to keep calm and not rise to provocation;
- a willingness to listen carefully to all sides of an argument;
- a refusal to be sidetracked;
- care in avoiding sarcasm and personal criticism;
- labelling the behaviour, and not the child, as unwanted;
- the use of a hierarchy of sanctions well known to all adults and children;
- willingness to implement sanctions rather than relying on calling upon a teacher.

Schools introducing schemes where extra play equipment is taken into the playground find that this can lead to even more quarrels and upsets. With thought, simple strategies can be employed to avoid this, e.g. only the pupils in the class of the teacher on duty that day are allowed to use the equipment and are responsible for its safe return. It is important not to relinquish an idea at the first hurdle. Pupil suggestions to make the idea workable are often forthcoming. Pupils are more likely to stick to the ideas and strategies they have suggested themselves.

Friendship skills

Schools can play a major role in supporting good playground behaviour by encouraging friendship skills. The ability to initiate and maintain friendships is a skill which some children appear to assimilate without help, whereas others require well-planned support. As we are social animals, the ability to uphold relationships is essential to our continued wellbeing and success. Research indicates that those children unable to resolve relationship difficulties in childhood are at high risk of continuing to have similar problems throughout the adult years (Cowen *et al.*, 1973; Olweus, 1987). The value of friendship skills cannot be underestimated.

Children use friendships for companionship and emotional support. In the safe relationship they also learn to challenge, debate, concede and accept strengths and weaknesses in themselves and others. Friends offer guidelines to acceptable behaviour and attitudes, vicarious experiences and a wealth of knowledge about the world. The isolated child not only misses out on companionship but is also denied a valuable learning medium.

Having friends and being socially successful is more important to many young people than academic success. The rewards are more immediate than academic success and rejection can lead to shame and embarrassment. Parents too can experience these negative feelings if they sense that their child is unpopular. This contributes to the reluctance of many parents to approach a school if a bullying problem is detected.

Those identified as popular by their peers appear to possess clearly defined qualities. This information can be used to design programmes for those in difficulties for the school day and contains a wealth of formal and informal opportunities for social interactions (Jersild, 1966; Ginsberg et al., 1986; Dygdon et al. and 1987; Boulton and Smith, 1994).

The work of Gottman Parker (1986) and others has shown that the skills of making and keeping friends may be learnt. Just teaching group entry skills is not enough as, once in the group, the child will need to have a battery of social skills to hand to maintain and sustain the friendship links. In addition, the peer group can be trained to be aware of those who need emotional support. A programme such as Circle of Friends, which provides mutual support and protection for vunerable children, is an effective way of helping peers accept a child into a friendship group. However, the child will need the skills often subsumed under the umbrella of emotional literacy (Goleman, 1996) to establish and maintain firm friendship bonds.

The qualities highly prized by the majority of children include the ability to be supportive and complimentary, and to show an interest in others and to display an obvious desire for friendship. Independence and maturity, mediation and leadership skills are valued, and the ability to generate ideas for games and activities is attractive to young people of all ages (Lagerspetz, et al., 1982; Besag, 2000).

From research in the field of sociolinguistics, we are able to identify the features of language and posture in the approach behaviour of children which influence the chance of a child being accepted or rejected by the group. We are becoming increasingly aware that there are many pupils in our schools with some hidden communication problem. These pupils are especially at risk, as they do not appreciate the nuances of verbal communication, the differences in intonation, sarcasm and innuendo. The problem may not be simply a matter of shyness or timidity. Before this type of work can be attempted, however, an isolated or rejected child may need help to develop feelings of self-worth and confidence as many are unwilling to approach others due to fear of further rejection. (For details of this type of work, see Besag, 1989, pp 143–7). As with other programmes aiming to enhance social skills, it is not enough to implement the programme. Careful monitoring, amending and evaluating of progress will be necessary over a long period, often years.

The current curriculum work in school lends itself to small groups or pairs of pupils working together in a co-operative rather than a competitive mode. When choosing pairs of children, teachers should be aware of the extra dimension of relationship building and use the opportunity to initiate suitable friendships. There are many opportunities for this type of work even within the curriculum material. A topic such as 'names' could encompass historical, mythological, geographical, art and craft material (Besag, 1992). Names such as Joiner or Smith are based on jobs; names such as York on places. The emotional intent and effect on the recipient of affectionate and abusive names could be explored. Genealogies could be traced, enhancing research and library skills. This type of work can effectively reduce the amount of aggression and name-calling in groups, and contribute to more rewarding playtime experiences.

Mediation

Older pupils trained in mediation skills can support both bullies and victims in resolving difficulties. Mediation schemes have proved to be successful in both primary and secondary schools. There are many advantages to enlisting the support of peers to help disputants reach an acceptable resolution, e.g. peer counselling, mediation, mentoring systems (Besag, 1992, pp 123–6). There is a range of schemes used in schools to support appropriate playground behaviour, whether to reduce bullying or to enhance social interactions. Such schemes include befriending and buddy systems where vulnerable pupils are paired up, formally or informally, with others. Some schools have a designated place in the playground where young people go who are looking for a friend to play with. Some young mediators, befrienders and buddies wear special caps for identification. Not all young boys enjoy popular games such as football. A range of activities should be on offer so that all can enjoy and benefit from their free time.

Parents of isolated or rejected children could be guided by teachers to those of children experiencing similar problems or those with confident children willing to befriend a child less fortunate. Many parents may be anxious for their child to make friends but feel unable to find a way forward. Workshops held in school, supported by a range of literature, could alert parents to the valuable role they can play in helping their own child, and others, to become socially skilled and confident in a variety of settings (Besag, 1992, p 126).

Parents can alert teachers to other children in distress. One case of bullying was stopped when a young girl, witnessing the repeated attacks on a classmate in the playground and being too afraid to alert the school staff, reported the incidents to her parents. The parents contacted the school staff and the young victim's parents. Once the bullying was exposed and the bullies taken to task, it stopped and did not recur (Besag, 1992, pp 42–5).

Summary

An awareness of the long-term effects of bullying on both the victim and bully should encourage adults, in whatever capacity, to address themselves to the problem of the physical and emotional distress occurring daily in our playgrounds so that we offer our children the quality of protection we enjoy ourselves as adults (Olweus, 1993).

Not only do we need to be aware of the safety and wellbeing of our children during non-teaching hours, but also there is a growing recognition of the opportunity available for young people to develop socially and to learn with and from each other, away from the restriction of rigorous curriculum demands. Current job adverts more often than not stress the need for 'good interpersonal and communication skills'. Where better can young people learn and develop these essential life skills? The playground needs to be viewed as a learning forum, an opportunity to be maximised where the energy, enthusiasm and good nature of young people relaxed and at play can be used to enhance social opportunities for all.

Some schools have curtailed playtime in a bid to reduce aggression, but this may be preventing children from having the opportunity to develop social skills. By interacting with a wide range of peers, meeting challenges and learning skills of assertiveness, confidence and negotiation, social development can come to maturity. Role-play allows young people to 'try on' a range of personalities, attitudes and behaviours, so developing understanding of the viewpoint of others. The playground offers the opportunity for the skills of empathy and reciprocity to be developed. These skills are essential to an understanding of others. The playground can be considered as a training ground where young people prepare themselves and others for adult life.

Playground bullying can be difficult to identify as it can be carried out in a covert manner hidden in the guise of a game or accident. Conversely, a genuine game may be misinterpreted as bullying by a child or playground supervisor. Therefore, there is a need for all to be able to identify and understand the dynamics of bullying behaviour.

Time spent in play is a valuable opportunity for young people to learn and hone the social skills necessary for full emotional growth. Recently, we have come to understand the differences in play and bullying behaviour of boys and girls as individuals and in groups and gangs. Boys tend to use more physical means to dominate others, whereas girls tend to use a range of verbal, emotional and psychological techniques that can be at least as destructive. The manipulation of friendship bonds is a technique used frequently by girls. This can cause long-term distress, anxiety and loss of confidence and self-esteem. More sophisticated methods of dealing with bullying have been developed based on our knowledge of these gender differences.

Older students can make a positive difference to playground interactions by modelling appropriate behaviour, helping with quality supervision and using a range of specialist techniques to resolve differences amicably.

In summary, playgrounds can be considered as extensions of classrooms; as areas of opportunity for physical, social and emotional development. The special quality of a playground is that, with appropriate care and supervision, these skills can be learnt in the most enjoyable way.

References

Allport, G. W. (1954) *The Nature of Prejudice*. Addison-Wesley.

Besag, V. E. (1989) *Bullies and Victims in Schools*. Open University Press.

Besag, V. E. (1992) *We Don't Have Bullies Here!* valbesag (Training and Publications), 3 Jesmond Dene Terrace, Jesmond, Newcastle upon Tyne, NE2 2ET.

Besag, V. E. (2000) *A Study in the Changing Relationships in a Group of Primary Age Girls* (manuscript submitted for publication).

Blatchford, P. and Sharp, S. (1994) *Understanding and Changing Playground Behaviour*. Routledge.

Boulton, M. J. and Smith, P. K. (1994) 'Bullying/victim problems among middle school children: stability, self-perceived competence and peer acceptance', *British Journal of Developmental Psychology*, Vol 12, pp 315–29.

Cowen, E. L. *et al.* (1973) 'Long-term follow-up of early detected vulnerable children', *Journal of Consulting and Clinical Psychology*, Vol 41, pp 438–46.

Craig, W. M. and Pepler, D. J. (1995) 'Surviving the playground: self reports and observations of bullying at school', in K. Covell (ed) *Readings in Child Development*. John Wiley.

Douvan, E. and Adelson, J. (1996) *The Adolescent Experience*. John Wiley.

Dygdon, J. A., Conger, A. J. and Keane, S. P. (1987) 'Children's perceptions of the behavioural correlates of social acceptance, rejection and neglect in their peers', *Journal of Clinical Child Psychology*, Vol 16, pp 2–8.

Ginsberg, D., Gottman, J. and Parker J. (1986) 'The importance of friendship', in Gottman, J. M. and Parker, J. G. (eds), *Conversations of Friends*. Cambridge University Press.

Goleman, D. (1996) *Emotional Intelligence*. Bloomsbury.

Gottman, J. M. and Parker, J. G. (eds) (1986) *Conversations of Friends*, Cambridge University Press.

Jersild, A. T. (1966) *Child Psychology*, 5th Edition. Staples Press.

Jersild, A. T. and Markey, F. V. (1935) 'Conflicts between pre-school children', *Child Development Monograph*, Vol 21.

Lagerspetz, K. M., Bjorkqvist, K., Berts, M. and King, E. (1982) 'Group aggression among children in three schools', *Scandinavian Journal of Psychology*, Vol 23, pp 45–52.

Lever, J. (1976) 'Sex differences in the games children play', *Social Problems*, No 23, p 487.

Maccoby, E. E. and Jacklin, C. N. (1980) 'Sex differences in aggression: a rejoinder and a reprise', *Child Development*, No 51, pp 964–80.

McKinley, I. and Gordon, N. (1980) *Helping Clumsy Children*. Churchill Livingstone.

Mitchell, A. (1984) *On the Beach at Cambridge*. London: Alison and Busby.

Olweus, D. (1978) 'Aggression in the Schools', *Bullies and Whipping Boys*, Washington, D. C.: Hemisphere Press (Wiley).

Olweus, D. (1993) *Bullying at School – what we know and what we can do*, Blackwell.

Olweus, D. (1987) 'Bully/victim problems among school children in Scandinavia', in J. P. Myklebust and R. Ommundsen (eds) *Psykolog-prefesjonen mot ar 2000*, Universitetsforlaget.

Olweus, D. (1980) 'Familial and temperamental determinants of aggressive behaviour in adolescent boys – a causal analysis', *Developmental Psychology*, Vol 16, pp 644–60.

Olweus, D. (1979) 'Stability of aggressive reaction patterns in males – a review', *Psychological Bulletin*, 86 (4), pp 852–75.

Omark, D. R., Omark, M. and Edelman, M. S. (1975) 'Formation of dominance hierarchies in young children', in T. R. Williams, *Action and Perception in Psychological Anthropology*. Mouton.

Orwell, G. (1995) *1984*. Penguin Books.

Pelligrini, A. D. (1988) 'Elementary school children's rough and tumble play and social competence', *Developmental Psychology*, 24, 802–6.

Rigby, K. and Slee, P. T. (1991) 'Bullying among Australian school children: reported behaviour and attitudes to victims', *Journal of Social Psychology*, 131, pp 615–27.

Rigby, K. (1996) *Bullying in Schools: And what to do about it*. Jessica Kingsley Publishers Ltd.

Riley, D. (1988) 'Bullying – a study of victim and victimisers within one inner-city school', Inservice BEd, Inquiry Report, Crewe and Alsager College of Higher Education.

Roland, E. (1988) Report of the European teachers' seminar on bullying in schools. Council for Cultural Cooperation.

Rubin, K. H. and Pepler, D. J. (1980) 'The relationship of play to social-cognitive growth and development', in H. Foot, A. J. Chapman and J. R. Smith (eds) *Friendship and Social Relations in Childhood*. pp 209–34, Chichester: Wiley.

Sharp, S. and Smith, P. K. (1994) *Tackling Bullying in Your School – a practical handbook for teachers*. Routledge.

Smith, P. K. and Sharp, S. (1994) *School Bullying – Insights and Perspectives*. Routledge.

17

■ ■ ■

What teachers can do to tackle bullying

WENDY STAINTON ROGERS

Teachers can tackle bullying by:

► avoiding actions that, however unintentionally, promote bullying

► avoiding actions that permit bullying

► taking actions that make it harder for children to bully

► taking actions that help children to be resilient to bullying

This chapter is about how individual teachers can help to tackle bullying, using the framework below. They can do this both in the *way* they teach and in *what* they teach. In both cases it is helpful to think of a spectrum:

Actions that are bullying-**promoting** – that actually *encourage* bullying	→	Actions that are bullying-**permitting** – that *collude with* bullying and allow it to go on unchecked	→	Actions that are bullying-**preventive** – that actively seek to *reduce* or prevent bullying

How teachers can stop actively promoting bullying

When adults talk about their experiences of mistreatment when they were at school, it is surprising how often they give examples of teachers who humiliated them. What stands out from the accounts they give is the apparent 'triviality' of the event and yet the enormous pain caused, sometimes remembered vividly for 40 or 50 years. For example, one man in his sixties, describing what happened to him when he was nine, spoke about how he got some help from a cousin with maths, his worst subject, in order to prepare for a test at school. With her sympathy, patience and skill, his confidence was restored. However, this did not last long:

The ... day came, I tried hard on the ten sums presented and knew I had not done excellently, but reasonably well. A few days later our results were read out from the teacher's dais. Mr B—'s declaration ran something like this: 'Reynolds – seven out of ten. If you had done as I expected you might have got five out of ten; it is obvious that you have cheated, so I'm giving you three out of ten.' That remained my recorded mark. It was a terrible, humiliating, bitter experience.

(Kitzinger, 1988, pp 1–2)

Whenever a teacher humiliates a pupil, the teacher is, quite simply, engaging in bullying. It really does not matter to the pupil whether the intention is merely to exert control or to gain personal gratification. Kitzinger describes the core of humiliation as being made to feel powerless, of 'having our noses rubbed in our own powerlessness, being forced to accept that we are without power' (Kitzinger, 1988, p 11). Bullying is about the misuse of power.

It would be nice to assume that this kind of bullying by teachers was something that happened only in the past. Unfortunately most secondary school pupils, at least, will tell you that in their school there are one or two teachers who regularly use intimidation, sarcasm, belittling or harassment towards pupils, and that even the best of teachers can, on occasion, resort to this kind of behaviour (Lawson, 1994).

At the risk of moralising then (and if it makes it any better, I will plead guilty for my time as a school teacher) the most obvious – but crucial – point is that to tackle bullying, teachers have to stop doing it themselves. Young people are highly sensitive to hypocrisy and will soon tumble teachers who claim to be against bullying but are actually bullies themselves, or a school with an anti-bullying policy that continues to tolerate teachers who are bullies.

However, I would argue that as well as *being* bullying, such behaviour also *promotes* bullying. It does this by conveying a clear message that such behaviour is 'all right': that it's acceptable to exploit your superior power to get your own way. Teachers who themselves bully are saying, in their actions, 'powerful people are those who get their own way by abusing their power' or, possibly more insidiously, 'it's all right to gain satisfaction or the approval of others by making a weak person feel humiliated'. And whether they do this by wielding individual power or whether it occurs via a climate in the whole school of collective intimidation, pupils are being explicitly and directly shown a role model of oppression.

However, even where explicit bullying itself is not involved, similar messages may be conveyed by behaviour that implies that some people are 'fair game'. What is often passed off as 'teasing' can, in fact, be just a rather subtle way of singling out a child who is unconventional in some way, or just plain irritating. Such behaviour encourages bullying, because the message here is that certain pupils are legitimate targets for ridicule. Often such behaviour is presented as 'just a lark' in order to cover up its intent. This reminds me of a Turkish saying that says: 'When the cat wants to eat her kittens, she calls them mice.' In other words, one way to pretend you are not mistreating others is to redefine them as 'fair game' and redefine what you are doing as a joke and hence as something not to be taken seriously.

For example, some male teachers make suggestive comments to girls to 'put them in their place'. Outside of an appropriate context, drawing attention to a woman or a girl's sexuality is a potent strategy for undermining her. It portrays her – and usually makes her feel – as somebody not to be taken seriously and hence not competent to present a challenge. And because what is going on is presented as 'just a bit of fun', if the 'victim' objects, she is portrayed as lacking a sense of humour. Jaqui Halson, in a study of gender relations in schools, stresses just how common this sexual harassment is in schools:

> Some of the more common forms of sexual harassment are often trivialised or dismissed as 'inoffensive' or 'friendly'; 'just teasing' or 'just larking around'.
>
> (Halson, 1989, pp 131–2)

Of course, boys can be on the receiving end too from women teachers. Or the target may be the child who is overweight or bad at sports. On the surface this may seem a long way from bullying. In truth the message is more subtle, but much the same as with overt racism or sexism: 'This person's discomfort is really rather a joke,' and, 'It's OK to get amusement out of another person's uneasiness.' Such tactics are often used in training athletes, where bullying is passed off as 'toughening up'. But the effects can be the same.

To avoid actively encouraging bullying, teachers need to become much more reflective about their own behaviour towards pupils. First, they must become more sensitive to their own use of power, especially when they convince themselves that they are 'only joking'. Much humour centres around making *someone* the butt of the 'joke' – and for that 'someone' the joke is often far from funny. Second, even mildly sexist or racist 'jokes' or seemingly innocuous comments about children's predilection for eating sweets or clumsiness can identify them as 'fair game', even if it does not directly humiliate them. In so doing, teachers can 'set up' a child as a target for bullying by other pupils.

How teachers can stop allowing bullying to happen

Teachers who strive to promote and maintain rigid status differentials between themselves and their pupils thereby provide the conditions under which bullying can flourish. They do this in two ways. First, by giving out the message that status and power are legitimate mechanisms for control, they create the conditions where the *misuse* of power can thrive. Second, they make it very difficult for pupils to seek help if they are being victimised.

When children are being bullied, they need to be able to turn to someone they can trust. They need to know that this person will listen to their fears, take them seriously and do something about the problem. But such conditions cannot comfortably coexist where there is mutual mistrust between teacher and pupil, or where the pupil who reports bullying is treated like a 'sneak' or a 'cissy'. A teacher who treats a request for help as an admission of weakness is a teacher who allows bullies to prosper.

But equally as bad is the teacher who denies the possibility that bullying may be happening, who claims 'it isn't a problem in *my* class, in *our* school'. It can be easy to be taken in by pupils who have an apparent charisma – who are popular, amusing and self-confident – and not to recognise that they may be bullies. They too may pass off their bullying as 'larking around' when, in truth, their 'jokes' are at the expense of another pupil's anguish. Equally, the child who is the bully's target may well be one the teacher, too, finds irritating or inept, and it can be hard to recognise this child as a victim. Even where bullying is more direct, it is often carried out in private – bullies can be incredibly skilful at covering up what they are doing. All that may be apparent is the victim's behaviour, and if this is a child who is already withdrawn, the effects of bullying can be very difficult to spot.

To avoid colluding with bullying and ignoring it, teachers need to be clear about the thin dividing line between harmless joking and teasing between one pupil and another, and behaviour which is intimidating and tormenting. It's not always easy to spot, and you will need to develop acute observation skills. The key is not to be distracted by the comic dexterity of the trickster but to look at their impact on the other pupil. Maybe the pupil being teased cheerfully goes along with the prank or even joins in. Even so, can you detect signs of unease and discomfort?

It isn't necessary – and often it's not helpful – to intervene in any hard-hitting way. A straight accusation of bullying is unlikely to work. And it's critical not to make the situation worse by presenting the target as a weakling who needs to be offered special protection. Your focus needs to be on the behaviour and its inappropriateness. Great skill is needed to explain why *this* joke is not funny. It's not a joke at all but intimidation, dressed up as 'harmless' when it is far from being so. Hard it may be, but getting this message across and vigilantly maintaining it can, over time, radically change the atmosphere to one where bullying cannot flourish.

For children to be able to seek help when they need it, it is essential for the school to have policies that treat their concerns seriously and for there to be clear procedures to follow whenever a pupil reports bullying. But individual teachers also need to work at building sufficient trust for pupils to feel they can confide in them. A teacher who is seen to sensitively but reliably intervene whenever a child is being made the butt of a 'joke' is well on the way to being trusted. Also necessary is a reputation for confidentiality and for 'seeing through' any complaints that are made. Once a teacher is known to be willing and able to deal diplomatically but firmly with reports about bullying, they will become one whom pupils will trust.

Bullying-preventive teaching

The contrast comes when we consider bullying-*preventive* teaching. I would suggest this is of two kinds. The first is, straightforwardly, an approach to teaching which treats all pupils with a level of respect, and avoiding (whatever the temptation) making jokes at the expense of the weakest. It is about not contributing to a pupil's vulnerability, about not setting up victims, and acting as a good role model, as somebody who does not misuse the power they have.

More proactively, bullying-preventive teaching is about:

- publicly acknowledging that bullying is not acceptable;
- having the courage to identify bullying whenever you observe it happening;
- putting it specifically on the agenda at your school and in your class;
- responding sensitively and effectively whenever pupils seek your help;
- creating opportunities which will help staff and pupils to develop strategies to counteract bullying.

Overall what is needed is to change the way that pupils behave towards each other. To do this the pupils themselves must *want* to change. And they need strategies – they must *know* how to change.

Wanting to change

Wanting to change comes down to 'changing hearts and minds' – to alter what people do, you need to get them to alter the way they see the world. To reduce bullying we need to make such actions 'unthinkable'. Unfortunately, the processes which underpin changing minds are not at all easy to influence – if they were, advertisers would not spend the massive sums they do. Getting somebody to change their perception or opinion takes a lot more than simply telling them to.

Knowing how to change

Elsewhere in this book are a number of suggestions for classroom activities designed to help pupils tackle bullying. Here I will focus instead on what teachers can do within the ordinary, everyday settings of the classroom and the school more generally.

First, to get pupils to change their behaviour you need to take a long, hard look at your own. Consider carefully how you exert your authority. It is crucial to distinguish between a teacher's legitimate and necessary use of the power of their position and the misuse of this power. Teachers who are known to get things done by negotiation and taking pupils with them, rather than by intimidation or coercion, have already won much of the battle by setting the ground rules for appropriate behaviour. Pupils will learn by your example and will discover that life is much more pleasant in an atmosphere where people treat each other with respect. In other words, pupils need to see that there are benefits for everybody in creating and working to maintain a bullying-free environment.

Second, you should develop a greater vigilance towards pupils who pass off bullying as mere teasing, and create the sense that their target lacks a sense of humour if they get upset. It is never going to be easy to 'take on' such pupils – it requires self-confidence and considerable social skills to intervene effectively. It can be even harder to have the courage to directly challenge the more aggressive bully, and harder still to take on a group of bullies working in concert. But leaving them unchallenged does not solve the problem. Indeed, it's likely to exacerbate it in the long term. If you get known as a teacher who is 'soft' on bullying, then it will certainly not go away. Your strategy here has to be to get support from your colleagues, not to 'go it alone'. Your aim should be to be seen as a teacher who will not tolerate bullying, within a school where bullying is not tolerated. Pupils who are prey to bullying will gain confidence in such a setting, and potential bullies will learn that they cannot 'get away with it'.

Third, take pro-active steps to reward behaviour that counters bullying. Whenever pupils treat each other with empathy and respect, let them know such behaviour is valued. It's important not to be heavy-handed, and often a smile will be enough, or a look of approval. Actively seek to promote inclusiveness. Get the less able students working together with the more able, in ways that allow an otherwise less competent child to shine. Distract potential bullies by giving them, too, opportunities to gain approval in ways that don't involve putting another pupil down.

Summary

None of these strategies will work immediately, so my final message is to be patient and to keep at it. Changing behaviour takes time – there are no magic solutions to something as insidious as bullying. It can be easy to become disillusioned and feel you are getting nowhere. But do keep trying, and be prepared to make small steps. The rewards will be worth it, both for you and for the pupils you teach.

References

Halson, J. (1989) 'The sexual harassment of young women', in L. Holly (ed), *'Girls and sexuality', Teachers and Learning*, Open University Press, pp 1–2.

Kitzinger, C. (1988) 'Humiliation', paper presented to the British Psychological Society London Conference, December.

Lawson, S. (1994) *Helping Children Cope with Bullying*. London: Sheldon Press.

18

■ ■ ■

Bullying: a guide to the law

CAROLYN HAMILTON

- ▶ Head teachers have a legal duty to take measures to prevent all forms of bullying among pupils
- ▶ Advice for parents from the Children's Legal Centre (CLC) that schools need to know
- ▶ Guide through the complaints procedure – how parents approach the school

What is bullying?

Bullying has been defined as the dominance of one pupil by another[1] and is generally part of a pattern of behaviour rather than an isolated incident[2]. It includes a whole range of behaviour: name-calling and teasing, malicious gossip, stealing from the victim, physical violence, threats, coercion and isolating individuals from group activities.

Must schools take measures to stop bullying?

Both the head teacher and the governing body of a school have a duty to ensure good discipline within their school and to prevent bullying.

It is up to the head teacher to determine measures with a view to encouraging good behaviour and respect for others on the part of pupils and, *in particular, preventing all forms of bullying among pupils*. The measures taken by the head teacher must be publicised in a written document and made known within the school to parents of pupils, as well as to people employed or working as volunteers within the school.[3]

The governing body also has a role in framing the school's discipline policy. Under s. 61(1) School Standards and Framework Act (SSFA) 1998, the governing body must ensure that policies designed to promote good behaviour and discipline are pursued at the school. In particular the governing body should make and, from time to time review, a written statement of general principles to which the head teacher should have regard in drawing up a written discipline policy. The governing body may also bring to the head teacher's notice any particular measures that they want him or her to have regard to, and may provide such guidance as they consider appropriate.

The governing body should not act in isolation. The School Standards and Framework Act[4] requires governing bodies to consult the parents of all pupils at the school before making or revising the statements of general principles. If parents believe that there are omissions in the policy or that alterations should be made – for example with reference to bullying – they have the opportunity to make their views known to the governing body (although no specific format is laid down in law for this process of consultation). The head teacher must, in addition, at least once every year take steps to bring the measures adopted to prevent bullying to the attention of all pupils and parents as well as to all those who are employed or who provide services to the school.

Tackling bullying

There are many different ways of tackling bullying and schools are bound to differ in their approach. However, the DfES guidance stresses that bullying is an issue that should be addressed by the whole school:

> *'Head teachers have a legal duty to take measures to prevent all forms of bullying among pupils. All teaching and non-teaching staff, including lunchtime supervisors, should be alert to signs of bullying and act promptly and firmly.'*

(DfEE Circular 10/99, Social Inclusion: Pupil Support, July 1999, para 4.30)

Although schools are under an explicit legal duty to take action against bullying, the numbers of calls to the Children's Legal Centre's advice line have not dropped. This suggests that bullying is still a major issue and that many schools are still failing to confront and deal with bullies. In these circumstances, it may be necessary for parents to make a formal complaint.

The advice in this chapter is aimed at parents. However, teachers too need to be aware of the procedures suggested to parents by the Children's Legal Centre.

Complaints

This section provides a step-by-step guide through the complaints procedure. If your child is being bullied at school, you should first make an informal complaint.

Making an informal complaint

Step 1: Talk to the class teacher

You should:

- talk calmly with your child about his/her experiences;
- make a note of what your child says, particularly of who was involved, how often the bullying has occurred, where it happened and what happened;
- reassure your child that he/she has done the right thing in telling you about the bullying;
- explain to your child that, should any further incident occur, he/she should report it to a teacher straight away and tell you about it;
- make an appointment to see your child's class teacher or form tutor;
- explain to the teacher the problems your child is experiencing;
- be realistic when talking to the teacher – the school will not be willing to exclude the 'bully' from the class or the school immediately on a first allegation of bullying. However, the teacher should investigate your allegations and take reasonable steps to protect your child.

REMEMBER:

When talking to your child's teacher to:

- try to be as specific as possible – the teacher may have no idea that your child is being bullied and will need dates, places, times and the names of the other children involved in order to take effective action to stop the bullying;
- make a note of what the teacher has said to you and the action that he or she intends to take;
- stay in touch with the school after this meeting (let them know if things improve as well as if problems continue).

If you are not satisfied with the class teacher or tutor's response, you will need to speak to the head teacher.

Step 2: Talk to the head teacher

The head teacher has day-to-day responsibility for discipline and for ensuring that standards of behaviour are acceptable. This is equally true of independent (private) and maintained (state) schools. The head teacher does not, however, have a completely free hand. The head must comply with the statutory duties laid down in the School Standards and Framework Act 1998 and he or she must act in accordance with any written statement of general principles that has been provided by the governing body (s. 61(1) SSFA).

Before a parent meets the head teacher it is a good idea for him or her to request and read a copy of the school's disciplinary policy and specifically the anti-bullying policy. If the head teacher is unable to resolve a parent's complaint, or the parent feels that the action taken to stop the bullying is insufficient, the parent may need to take matters further by making a formal complaint.

Making a formal complaint

Step 3: Finding out about formal complaints procedures

There is now a legal requirement for maintained (state) schools to have a written complaints policy. Section 39(1) SSFA requires the governing bodies of all maintained school to establish procedures for dealing with complaints and to publicise these procedures. Schools may, however, draft their own complaints procedures, which do not have to conform to any standard criteria. Before making a complaint, parents should ask to see a copy of the school's complaints policy.

Complaints procedures may differ substantially from school to school, depending on the procedures adopted. Each school has the power to set its own procedures. A complainant should ask the school to whom a formal complaint should be addressed. Any written complaint should state clearly that the parent(s) wish to make a formal complaint and wish to be informed of the way in which the complaint will be dealt with. The following letter of complaint to the chair of governors highlights the points that the letter should contain.

Mr/Ms

Chair of Governors

……….. School

Dear Chair,

I wish to make a formal complaint. My daughter, S, has been bullied over a period of ... months/weeks by X, Y and Z. The incidents complained of are as follows:

(parent should list the bullying incidents)

I have complained to the teacher and the head teacher on numerous occasions. These are listed below:

(parent should list the occasions on which he/she has spoken to the teacher and head teacher)

My daughter is now suffering anxiety and depression and is frightened to attend school. I would like a full and thorough investigation of these bullying incidents. Please let me know what action you will be taking, both in relation to the bullying which has occurred and to ensure that my child is not bullied in the future.

Yours faithfully

A. N. Other

Step 4: How to make a formal complaint

It may be advisable to ask to see a copy of your child's educational record before making a formal complaint. This is particularly useful where there is a dispute about letters written previously or a query about dates that informal discussions about the bullying have taken place.

When making an application to see your child's educational record, you should state that you are doing so under the Education (Pupil Information) (England) Regulations 2000 or the Education (Pupil Records) (Wales) Regulations 2001. The application should be made in writing to the head teacher. The school should make the child's school record available within 15 days. There is no charge for inspecting the report. However, if a parent wishes to have a copy made, there may be a charge for photocopying.

There are some limited circumstances in which these records can be withheld by the school:

- Where a pupil makes his or her own application, they will not be allowed to see their educational records if it is obvious that they do not understand what they are asking for. (However, a parent can request the record.)
- Schools will not disclose anything from an educational record which is likely to cause serious harm to the mental or physical health of the pupil or anyone else (for example, information which discloses that the pupil has been abused or is at risk of abuse).

Despite the legal requirement to have a written complaints policy, procedures may differ substantially from school to school. Some require that the letter be sent to the head teacher while others require that it be sent to the chair of governors.

Step 5: The response of the governors

The response of the governors will vary from school to school as each school has the power to set its own procedures. However, there are some common elements:

- As a matter of good practice, most complaints procedures will contain time limits (usually between 7 and 21 days) within which the governors should reply to the letter initiating the complaints procedure.
- Commonly, the governors will appoint a sub-committee of between three and five governors to hear the complaint and determine what action should be taken.
- Normally, parents will be allowed to attend and present evidence to the sub-committee, although some governing bodies make a decision on paper submissions alone.
- Usually, parents are allowed to take a friend or representative (which could be a legal representative) with them to the meeting.
- Generally, either the head teacher or another teacher with responsibility for investigating the evidence will be invited to give a report on the incidents complained of (the parent may be allowed to question or cross-examine the head teacher and vice versa).

It is rare for children, especially those at primary school, to be allowed to appear before the governors' sub-committee, give evidence or to present a complaint on their own behalf.

Step 6: Complaints to the local education authority

Note: This section is not applicable to independent schools.

If the governing body appears inefficient or obstructive, a complaint can be made to the Director of Education via the LEA. This is done through the local town or county hall. The Director should respond to any complaint and can contact the school on a parent's behalf. It is, however, important to be aware that the LEA will not usually interfere in the internal management of the school and is unlikely to instruct a school to take any specific action.

There is some legal provision for the LEA to intervene in schools that are causing concern (s. 15 SSFA 1998). However, this is concerned with situations where the safety of the pupils or staff is threatened by a breakdown of discipline. It is unlikely to apply in most bullying cases, since schools will probably maintain that they are containing the problem.

Step 7: Complaint to the Secretary of State for Education

Before a formal complaint can be made to the Secretary of State for Education, the complainant must have exhausted all other procedures.

The grounds for complaint to the Secretary of State for Education are as follows:

- A complaint can be made against the LEA, or the governing body of any maintained school, that has acted unreasonably with respect to the exercise of any power or the performance of any duty imposed by the Education Act 1996 (s. 496 Education Act 1996 as amended by the SSFA).
- A complaint can be made against the LEA or the governing body of any maintained school if they have failed to discharge any duty imposed on them by or for the purposes of the Education Act 1996 (s. 497 Education Act 1996 as amended by the SSFA).

If the Secretary of State is satisfied that either of the above two criteria are met, then the complaint will be investigated. Parents should be warned that the above two grounds are very difficult to fulfil and few complaints have resulted in action by the Secretary of State. Furthermore, it can take up to six months to get any response to a letter of complaint.

Step 8: Complaints to the Local Government Ombudsman (LGO)

Parents can also complain to the LGO. However, the LGO can investigate only in very limited circumstances and does not deal with complaints:

- about the internal management of the school (for example where the school has heard a complaint but the complainant is unhappy with its decision);
- about the actions of independent schools;

- about something that happened over 12 months ago unless he or she thinks it is reasonable to look into the matter despite the delay;
- where the case has already been heard by a court or a tribunal.

It is also unlikely that the LGO would investigate where a complaint had been made to the Secretary of State for Education.

In general, the LGO can only investigate complaints about the way the LEA or school has done or failed to do something – where there has been 'maladministration' by a school or LEA. It will not get involved where parents simply disagree with the action that has been taken by the LEA or school.

Maladministration, in this sense, will have occurred only where the school or LEA:

- has taken too long to take action without good reason;
- does not follow its own rules or the law;
- breaks its own promises;
- gives the wrong information; or
- does not make a decision in the correct way.

REMEMBER:
Before complaining to the LGO:

- a parent must give the LEA the opportunity to deal with the complaint;
- it is worth checking with the LGO that your complaint is one that they can investigate.

Parents must make the complaint in writing and sign the letter themselves. If the LGO decides to investigate, the parents will be kept informed. Once the investigation is completed, a formal report will be produced. This will say whether there has been maladministration by the LEA and/or school. Where there has been, the LGO may recommend that compensation be paid or that some other action be taken to put matters right.

Although most schools and LEAs comply with the LGO's recommendations, it cannot force the school or LEA to pay compensation or comply with any other recommendations it makes.

Withdrawing children from school

Under s. 7 Education Act 1996, parents have a legal duty to ensure their child receives an efficient full-time education suitable to the child's age, ability and aptitude and any special educational needs. There is no legal requirement that this education be provided at school. The law allows parents to educate their child at home provided that the standard of education is satisfactory. There are a number of organisations that can assist parents by providing both materials and moral support.

Choosing home education

Parents should be warned that, if they decide to home educate, they have opted out of the state education system and should not expect any assistance from the LEA in educating their child.

It is advisable to contact the LEA before asking for your child's name to be removed from the school roll to ascertain whether the programme of home education that is planned would meet with LEA approval. The LEA has an obligation to ensure that the child is receiving a suitable education. If the LEA is of the view that the home education parents are providing is unsuitable, parents could face legal action (see below).

It is also important to remember that if you decide to withdraw your child from school and provide education at home, you must inform the school and LEA to ensure that your child ceases to be registered at his or her school. Failure to deregister the child may result in action for non-attendance at school being taken (s. 444 (1) Education Act 1996).

Informing the LEA

The Director of Education
Education Department
ABC County Council

Dear Sir/Madam,
This letter is to inform you that as from (date), I shall be removing my child (name of child) from (name of school) and educating him/her at home as is my right under section 7 Education Act 1996.
Please ensure that my child is no longer registered as a pupil at (name of school).
Yours faithfully,

A. N. Other.

Flexi-education

Some parents feel that their child should only return to school part-time for a certain period – perhaps while they build up their confidence and problems are resolved. If the school agrees to this, the child will attend for just part of the week. The parents must provide education at home for the rest of the week. It is up to the head teacher and the governing body to decide whether they are prepared to agree to such an arrangement. The school is under no legal obligation to do so and the parent has no right to insist. Furthermore, if the school does agree, the parents have a responsibility to ensure that their child keeps up with other pupils in the class.

LEA duties to provide education otherwise than at school

Under s. 19(1) Education Act 1996, the LEA has a duty to provide suitable education for children unable to attend school, whether because of illness, exclusion or otherwise. A child may be entitled to home tuition or education at a special unit such as a pupil referral unit if:

- a parent decides not to send a child to school because of extreme physical danger;
- the child refuses to return to school; or
- the child is suffering from anxiety and/or depression and is failing to cope.

A medical or psychological assessment may be necessary to convince the LEA that a bullied child falls within these categories.

Education provided under s. 19 (1) Education Act 1996 may not be of the quality or quantity provided by schools. Research has found that home tuition that is funded by LEAs can be as little as two hours a week and is rarely more than ten hours. *In R v East Sussex county Council ex parte Tandy* [1998] ELR 251 the LEA, for financial reasons, attempted to reduce the hours of home tuition given to a child. The House of Lords stated that what constituted 'suitable education' must be determined by educational considerations and not resources, and that the local authority could not reduce the home tuition given to the child on the basis that the authority wanted to save money. The case did not, however, determine what constituted 'suitable education' in terms of the number of hours of teaching necessary.

Parents should not keep their child away from school unless the circumstances are serious enough to warrant such action. The CLC has dealt with cases where parents have been threatened with legal action unless they return a bullied child to school (see Case Study 1).

Case study 1

Mrs K called the CLC advice line having removed her child from school. Her daughter, J, had been bullied over a period of 14 months. J was a special needs child and had a statement of special educational needs. The school had failed to deal with the bullying despite both informal discussions and formal written complaints. Not only was Mrs K frustrated at the school's failure to take action, she was also worried about J's state of anxiety. She decided that her only course of action was to remove J from school. She hoped that this would spur the school into taking action against the bullies.

However, the LEA threatened Mrs K with prosecution for non-attendance of J at school. Furthermore, the LEA notified social services,

---

who decided that they must investigate under s. 47 Children Act 1989. Mrs K was unwilling to co-operate with the social worker. The social worker threatened Mrs K, saying that the local authority would make an application to the courts for an interim care order if J was not returned to school forthwith.

When Mrs K rang the CLC, the advice officer suggested that Mrs K should co-operate with the social worker in her investigations. Mrs K was also advised to obtain medical and psychological reports to support her withdrawal of J from school. In the event, medical and professional backing was obtained and the LEA agreed to provide some home tuition for J, as is their duty under s. 19 Education Act 1996, until another school was found that was more suitable to her special needs.

What can LEAs do to enforce attendance?

LEAs often fail to say what form of legal action they are going to take if a child fails to attend school. It could be any of the following.

School attendance order

If it appears that a child is not registered at a school and is not receiving suitable education, a school attendance order may be served under s. 437 Education Act 1996.

Step 1: Before serving a school attendance order on a parent, the LEA must first serve a notice on the parent in writing requiring the parent to satisfy them that the child is receiving a suitable education. This will generally specify a time period within which the parent must reply.

Step 2: If the parent cannot satisfy the LEA (or the parent fails to answer) *and*, if, in the opinion of the LEA, it is expedient that the child should attend school, the authority must serve a school attendance order on the parent. This order requires that the child become a registered pupil at the school named in the order.

Step 3: Before serving a school attendance order, the LEA must serve a further notice on the parent, in writing, informing them that it intends to serve the order and the school it intends to name. The LEA may, if it wishes, name one or more schools that it regards as suitable alternatives. If the parent chooses one of these schools within the 15 days given for reply, that school will be named in the order. A parent can also apply to other schools not named in the notice. Provided that the parent can show the LEA within 15 days that the child has been offered a place by the school, that school can be named in the order instead. The school can be any registered school, including registered independent schools (s. 438 (4), (5) Education Act 1996).

Step 4: If a parent fails to comply with a school attendance order, he or she will be guilty of an offence (unless they can prove that the child is receiving suitable education otherwise than at school (s. 443 (1) Education Act 1996). Parents can be prosecuted in the magistrates' court and fined. However, a parent cannot be imprisoned for a child's non-attendance at school.

Failure to attend school regularly

Where the child is registered at a school but is not attending regularly, the LEA may decide to prosecute the parent (s. 444 (1) Education Act 1996). Prosecution can result in a fine. There are a number of defences for parents prosecuted for this offence: no offence is committed if the child was away from school for a religious holiday or as a result of sickness or some other unavoidable cause (s. 444 (3) Education Act 1996). Where relevant, parents will probably need to produce evidence to the court in the form of medical or psychological reports.

Education supervision orders

If the child is not receiving a suitable education, then, following consultation with social services, the LEA may also apply for an education supervision order (s. 36 Children Act 1989; s. 447 (1) Education Act 1996). This order lasts for one year. A supervisor will be appointed to advise, assist and befriend the child and parents. The supervisor can also give directions to the child and parents to ensure that the child is being properly educated (Sch. 3 Part III para. 12 Children Act 1989). Failure to comply with these directions is a criminal offence, which can result in the prosecution of the parents and the imposition of a fine (Sch. 3 Part III para. 18 Children Act 1989).

Care order

Where a child persistently fails to attend school and is not receiving a suitable education out of school, it is not unknown for local authorities to initiate proceedings to take the child into care. The local authority will have to prove in court that:

- the child is suffering or is likely to suffer significant harm; and
- this is attributable to the child being beyond parental control; or
- the child was not receiving the care it is reasonable to expect (s. 31 Children Act 1989).

If granted by the court, the effect of a care order is that the local authority gains parental responsibility for the child (in addition to the parents) and has the power to remove the child from the parents (see Case Study 2).

Case study 2

A care order was made over a 15-year-old who had persistently truanted from school over a three-year period. In one year she had attended school for only 28 days. The court agreed with the local authority that there was little point in making an education supervision order since, despite regular visits by the education welfare officer, who offered to take the child to school, the child still refused to attend. The court decided to make a care order.

O's lack of attendance at school impeded her intellectual and social development and she was likely to suffer significant harm as a result. O was removed from home so that a pattern of school attendance could be achieved. (**Re O** (A minor) (care order: Education Procedure)[1992] 2 FLR 7.)

Taking action – the criminal law

Where all else fails, parents may wish to consider legal action. Before starting any form of legal action it is wise to consult a solicitor. It is worth finding out whether there are solicitors in your area who specialise in education law by contacting either the local Citizens Advice Bureau, the Law Society, the Children's Legal Centre (which provides a specialist education legal service) or an organisation of education lawyers called ELAS (see 'Help Organisations', page 318).

Some forms of bullying may amount to criminal behaviour. Where a child who has been bullied has been threatened, the bully may have committed the offence of 'threatening behaviour' under s. 4 Public Order Act 1986. This provides that:

A person will be guilty of threatening behaviour if he or she uses threatening, abusive or insulting words or behaviour, or distributes or displays to another person any threatening, abusive or insulting written material, sign or other 'visible representation' to

(i) cause another person to fear violence: or to

(ii) provoke the immediate use of unlawful violence by another person.

If the bullied child is physically or sexually assaulted, the bullies may have committed the criminal offence of common assault or indecent assault. Both offences can be committed without actually touching the victim. However, in practice the police are unlikely to act unless physical contact has been made.

Children under the age of ten cannot be prosecuted for a criminal offence. This means that the police cannot charge a child under the age of ten, no matter what he or she does. Any child over ten can be charged with committing a criminal offence. However, the police cannot charge a bully with committing a criminal offence unless they have evidence that the incident occurred. If a child has been injured, parents should take the child to a doctor to obtain medical evidence. As soon as possible the child should write down the details of all the bullying incidents. This is important because this record, if made immediately after the event, can be used in court. This means that should the child be required to give evidence, this evidence can be given by simply reading from the original document (rather than giving evidence from memory).

It is advisable to contact the police in cases where the assault is of a serious nature and the school and LEA have consistently failed to deal with the bullying. The experience of advice workers at the CLC shows that the mere threat of informing the police is sometimes enough to spur the school or LEA into action.

The Protection from Harassment Act 1997

Under this Act it may be possible for injunctions to be put in place to restrict the bullying child's behaviour and for damages to be claimed for the harm suffered by the bullied child. Applications are normally made via a solicitor.

The Act also contains two criminal offences which may apply in cases of bullying:

- criminal harassment; and
- putting people in fear of violence.

Parents contacting the police should ask about the possibility of prosecution under this Act. However, it should be noted that a criminal prosecution cannot proceed unless the harassment has taken place on at least two separate occasions.

Private prosecution

Parents may be frustrated if the Crown Prosecution Service (CPS) or police decide not to prosecute where there has been a physical or sexual assault. In these circumstances, and provided there is sufficient evidence, it may be possible to bring a private prosecution against the bully. However, there may be good reasons why the CPS or police have decided not to prosecute. Under s. 10 Prosecution of Offences Act 1986, there are two possible justifications for deciding not to prosecute in such a case: that there is insufficient evidence and that it would be against the public interest. The latter ground is most commonly used to prevent prosecution in bullying cases. For example, it might be decided that it would be against the public interest to prosecute where the bully is a special needs child.

Parents are entitled to know the reason why the authorities are not proceeding with a prosecution and should ask for an explanation.

Taking action – using civil proceedings

Judicial review

It may be possible to seek a judicial review of the school or LEA's decision not to take appropriate action to deal with the bullying situation. As a result, the school or LEA may be forced to act.

Judicial review is a public law action. It can only be taken against public bodies or private bodies that perform a public duty. LEAs are susceptible to judicial review. So too are boards of governors of LEA-maintained schools, (*R v Haberdasher Aske's Hatcham Schools*, ex parte ILEA [1989] 1 Admin. LR 22).

Judicial review is not an option where the complaint is against an independent school. These are not public bodies and the relationship between those paying the fees and the school is founded upon the law of contract (*R v Fernhill Manor School*, ex-parte a [1993] 1 FLR 620). (For claims against independent schools, see 'Breach of contract' on page 229.)

An application for judicial review can be made only once all rights of appeal against the school and LEA have been exhausted. Furthermore, parents must act promptly. Applications for judicial review must be made within three months from the date when the grounds for the application arose, although this time limit can be extended where the court considers that there is good reason for doing so.

In judicial review, the court examines the way in which a decision has been reached and not the merits of the decision as such. An application may be successful, for example, under the following circumstances:

- the school or LEA failed to follow proper or correct procedures;
- they did not apply the law correctly; or
- they acted so unreasonably that no other school or LEA would have reached such a decision.

A child can apply for judicial review, provided the court believes that he/she has sufficient interest to apply. If a child has left the school complained of and is settled at a new school, he/she is unlikely to have sufficient interest. The application is made in the name of the child. However, it is brought on behalf of the child by a 'litigation friend', usually one of the parents. The advantage of the child making the application is that he or she may pass the financial tests for community legal services funding (formally legal aid) in circumstances where the parent would not.

Unless it is proved that the LEA, school or teacher has also been negligent, a successful application is unlikely to result in the payment of damages. However, a successful judicial review action may have the effect of forcing the school or LEA to act to stop the bullying.

Negligence

Parents, acting on behalf of the bullied child, may be able to sue the school, teacher or LEA for damages as compensation for psychiatric damage or physical injuries suffered as a result of a school or teacher negligently failing to act to protect pupils from bullying. Negligence arises where a duty of care is owed to the child and that duty of care is breached, resulting in damage to the child.

The law of negligence is very complex. For a case to be successful, it would be necessary to prove the following things.

- **That the child has been bullied**. There is no legal definition of bullying. In deciding whether bullying has occurred, the court will look at all the circumstances. It will be necessary to prove that the bullying went beyond normal social interaction between children and was of a serious nature; *and*
- **That the teacher or school owes the pupils a duty of care**. It is well settled in law that a school owes its pupils a general duty of care. However, it is far less clear in law how far a school must go to protect a pupil against bullying; *and*
- **That the bullied child has suffered harm as a result of the bullying incidents**. This could be physical injuries or psychiatric damage. Expert evidence would be needed to prove the damage in court. For psychiatric damage it would be necessary to prove that the person bringing the claim was suffering, or had suffered from, a recognised form of psychiatric illness. The harm must also have been a consequence of the bullying incidents.
- **It will also be necessary to show that the harm was foreseeable**. It must have been reasonable to expect that the teacher or school could foresee that the child might suffer harm or damage; and that the harm suffered was a direct result of the teacher and school negligently failing to act to protect the bullied child. It would need to be shown, not only that the teacher or school knew what was going on but also that they failed to take reasonable steps to stop it. Schools are not legally required to guarantee the absolute safety of children. However, they must ensure that pupils receive the same level of care and supervision that a reasonably prudent parent would take of his or her own children (*Beaumont v Surrey County* [1968] 66 LGR 580). In the Beaumont case, the court provided further explanation of the standard expected of head teachers. The judge said that a head teacher should take 'all reasonable and proper steps to prevent any of the pupils under his care from suffering injury from inanimate objects, the actions of their fellow pupils, or from a combination of the two'.

There have been a few negligence actions relating to bullying in schools. Whether a claim is likely to succeed depends very much on the individual circumstances of the case (see Case Studies 3 and 4).

If the school is a maintained school, a claim for damages will usually be against the LEA which, as an employer, will be vicariously liable for the acts of the teachers it employs. If the school is independent, the claim will be against the governors.

Case study 3

Becky Walker took legal action, claiming damages for psychological harm caused by bullying while at school. She claimed that Derbyshire County Council was negligent in that they failed to stop the bullying.

Becky was born with cerebral palsy. Although physically disabled, she was academically able and took part in school activities, including playing in the school band. She was subject to bullying from three other members of the band during the two-hour band practice each week over a 15-month period. The incidents amounted to taunts, disapproving glares from the bullies, snide comments that she sometimes overheard, and generally making life difficult for her. Becky eventually left the band.

Both she and her parents complained to the school about the bullying. After failing to get any satisfaction from the school, Becky started legal action. Her claim that the school had been negligent was unsuccessful. The county court held that the incidents complained of were not sufficiently distressing so that a teacher could foresee psychiatric damage to the claimant, particularly as the bullying occurred for only two hours a week at band practice and did not impinge upon Becky's whole school life. (Walker v Derbyshire County Council, *The Times*, 7 June 1994, childRIGHT, Nos 108 and 109, 1994.)

Case study 4

In 1996 Sebastian Sharp accepted £30,000 in damages from Shene School in Richmond, London. He had been bullied for a number of years between the ages of 12 and 15. The bullying was verbal and physical and on one occasion he was thrown through a glass door. The school did not admit liability but the case was settled in Sebastian's favour before reaching the High Court.

It is possible to make a claim against individual teachers. However, this may not be worthwhile. Teachers are unlikely to be covered by insurance and may not be able to afford to pay damages. The child him/herself may also sue a teacher, school or LEA for negligence. The application will normally be made in the name of the child but brought on behalf of the child by a 'litigation friend', usually a parent. Children will only qualify for community legal services funding in certain circumstances. Without it such actions can be extremely costly, although it is possible to obtain insurance to cover the costs of the case.

Trespass to the person

A civil action claiming damages for trespass to the person may be brought against a bully. For the action to be successful, it would be necessary to prove that the bully:

- threatened the use of immediate force; or
- hit the victim; or
- threw something at the victim.

Practical jokes may also be covered (for example, pulling a chair away so that the bullied child falls to the floor, see *Purcell v Horn* [1838] 8 Ad & E 602). Unlike the law of negligence, it is not necessary to prove that the harm or damage was actually inflicted on the bullied child. It is necessary to prove that the bully intended to cause harm. While there are no age limits to prevent a civil action of this kind, it may be difficult to prove that the bully is capable of having the necessary intent where he or she is very young.

An action of this kind would normally have to be brought on behalf of the bullied child by a 'litigation friend'. Proceedings would be brought against the bully rather than his or her parents. If successful, the court might award damages against the bully to compensate for any injury inflicted. However, if the bullied child suffered no harm or damage, the damages would not be high. The bully would be responsible for paying the damages. However, he or she might be unable to do so because of lack of money.

It is also possible to obtain an injunction to prevent the bully continuing with his or her behaviour. However, the courts are normally reluctant to grant injunctions against teenagers who are still at school. If an injunction is granted against a bully who is under 17, there is little the court can do if the bully breaks it. The bully cannot be given a custodial sentence.

Breach of contract

Parents of children who attend an independent (private) school enter into a contract with the school on behalf of their child. The school agrees to provide services to the child and may be sued if it fails to provide such services. Such obligations are reciprocal. The parent may be sued for failing to pay fees and so on. Such a contract is no different from the type of contract which might be entered into with any other supplier of services bought by a consumer.

A private school contract may include an express obligation on the school to provide a reasonably safe environment for the child. Even if not expressly stated, such an obligation would be considered by the courts to be implied in the contract. A school which failed to provide such an environment could be sued for breach of contract in the civil courts. For example, this might happen where a school fails to provide supervision adequate to prevent serious bullying and a child suffers physical or psychological harm as a result.

Bullying out of school

Often the most frightening and severe bullying takes place outside school. Schools are able to take action against pupils in such circumstances. However, it is unclear to what extent the school must take action to stop the bullying.

Bullying incidents on the way to and from school

Parents are often told that the school cannot deal with bullying that takes place out of school hours (for example, on the way to and from school). In fact, the courts have held that a teacher does have the power to discipline a pupil for bad behaviour outside the school premises (*R v Newport Salop JJ ex p Wright* [1929] 2 KB 416, *R v London Borough of Newham*, *The Times*, 15 November 1994).

While it is possible for a school to exclude a child because of behaviour outside school, the law is less clear in relation to other disciplinary measures. For instance, if the parent expressly withdraws their consent to the school disciplining their child for incidents off the school premises, it may be that schools are unable to take disciplinary action.

Where bullying has occurred outside school, particularly on the way to and from school, a complaint should be made to the teacher or school according to the steps laid out earlier in this information sheet.

Negligence

To make a successful negligence claim against a school or LEA for damages to a child arising from bullying off the school premises/outside school hours, it is necessary to show that the school or LEA was negligent. The parent or child would have to prove in court that the duty of care owed to pupils extends to incidents that occur outside school hours and that the damage was foreseeable. The law is unclear whether a duty of care is owed in these circumstances, although case law does provide some guidance.

Bullying incidents on school premises before and after school hours

It is unlikely that schools will owe a duty of care to supervise pupils who arrive on the school premises before the start of the school day, unless the school voluntarily accepts responsibility for them (*Ward v Hertfordshire County Council* [1969] 114 Sol. J 87).

Bullying incidents on the school bus

If transport to and from school is provided by the LEA or school, then it is likely that there is a duty to supervise pupils (*Jacques v Oxfordshire County Council* [1967] 66 LGR 440). If pupils travel to school using public transport, then while the bus company is responsible for ensuring the safety of passengers, it is unclear whether this extends to a duty to supervise pupils.

Bullying incidents on the way to and from school

While the law would seem to allow teachers and schools to discipline pupils for incidents off the school premises, it is by no means clear that they have a duty to do so and, if there is no duty, then it is not possible to make a claim for negligence.

Human Rights Act and bullying

The Human Rights Act 1998 (HRA), which came into force on 2 October 2000, incorporates the European Convention for the Protection of Human Rights and Fundamental Freedoms (ECHR). These rights can be found in Schedule 1 of the Act. All public authorities must act in compliance with convention rights (HRA s. 6) and all legislation must be interpreted to comply with them. If a public authority acts in a way that is incompatible with a convention right, the victim may take legal action against that authority. The term public authority will include local education authorities, maintained schools and possibly private schools.

There are two rights that may be of particular assistance to a bullied child who fails to obtain protection against bullying. Article 3 of the ECHR states: 'No one shall be subjected to torture or to inhuman or degrading treatment or punishment.' Corporal punishment has been banned in British schools as a consequence of European Court decisions that physical punishment of a child within school could amount to a violation of Article 3. Where a school consistently fails to protect a child from bullying by another child or a teacher this could constitute a failure to uphold a child's right under Article 3. It should be remembered, however, that the threshold for Article 3 is quite high, and that the majority of bullying cases would probably not be severe enough to reach that threshold.

Article 8 of the ECHR states: 'Everyone has the right of respect for his private and family life, his home and his correspondence.' Where children are forced to strip in public changing rooms against their will or to have their bags and lockers searched, their belongings removed or are exposed to video surveillance, this may not amount to inhuman or degrading treatment but it may infringe their right to respect for their private life.

There will, however, be limitations on the use of the HRA. Public authorities will have an element of discretion before they are considered to have violated a right. In enforcing all the rights under the convention a balance must be struck between the requirements and interest of society at large and the requirement to protect the individual's rights. The principle of the 'efficient use of education resources' is a factor which LEAs and schools may take into account when considering their duty to comply with convention rights. Thus to expect a school to commit vast resources to employ large numbers of teachers in an effort to stop bullying would be unreasonable.

The victim need not have suffered any actual detriment; so even if a child only risks being bullied at school, there may be a violation of a human right. It is possible that a child may take action against a school or authority where bullying occurs even if he or she is not the victim.

Under the HRA a bullied child does not have to remain at the school in order to pursue a legal action against the school or LEA for any bullying which occurred while the child was at school (*McIntyre v UK* 1998).

No one is certain as yet of the full scope and power of the HRA, particularly in relation to bullying, but it is certainly an issue which should be considered when contemplating legal action.

Conclusion

Parents contact the Children's Legal Centre when they feel teachers have not listened to or responded to their concerns about bullying. Most schools foster a climate of co-operation between parents and teachers, making it unnecessary for parents to seek legal advice. The Children's Legal Centre encourages this co-operation and is there to help ensure that children can go to school without fear of bullying.

Notes

1 This was the definition of bullying provided in the now superseded DfEE Circ. 8/94. Although the definition is not repeated in the new DfEE Circular 10/99 it is still an appropriate definition.
2 DfEE Circular 10/99 para. 4.29.
3 SSFA 1998 s. 61 (7).
4 s. 61 (3) (b).

19

■ ■ ■

A child's view – how ChildLine UK helps

HEREWARD HARRISON

▸ Bullying now represents the largest number of calls to ChildLine
▸ Children feel more able to report bullying
▸ Speaking up does not always end the bullying
▸ Children tell about being bullied

Introduction

ChildLine had counselled almost 1,200,000 children and young people and given help and advice to 105,000 adults from its launch in October 1986 to March 2001. Of these calls from children and adults, 153,000 were about bullying.

Bullying now represents the largest number of calls to ChildLine. From April 2000 to March 2001 almost 20,300 children and young people (15,400 girls and 4,900 boys) rang to talk about being bullied and the difficulties they were having in trying to stop it.

When ChildLine ran its two special Bullying Lines in 1990 and 1994, the response from children and parents exceeded all predictions. The first Bullying Line, open for three months in 1990, counselled 2,054 children, and counsellors on the second line, open for six months in 1994, spoke to 4,494 children. After each line closed, ChildLine published a report on what children said about bullying. For the second report, *Why Me?*, we supplemented the data with questionnaires and interviews with parents, teachers and children of all ages.

Our first report, *Bullying: The Child's View*, showed that children adopt a broad and inclusive definition of bullying, including verbal bullying, excluding or ignoring, physical violence, extortion and intimidation. The report looked at how and why children do or do not report being bullied.

Why Me? describes how children perceive bullying and their views on how it should be tackled. A few years on in the debate on bullying, there was evidence that children now feel more able to report bullying, but it was clear that speaking up did not always end the problem. The messages from children emerged loud and clear: children want to be involved in tackling bullying. *Why Me?* focused on practical suggestions for children, parents and teachers on strategies for effective action against bullying.

ChildLine was responsible for a landmark Conference on Bullying in November 2001, which focused on symptoms, strategies and solutions that work. The conference emphasised the essential role of young people themselves in helping others who are being bullied at home, at school and in the community.

Sandra's story

My name's Sandra. I'm 14 and in the third year at a comprehensive school in our town. I don't say much to the other girls in my form and don't have a lot of friends. I'm not what you would call a sociable person; my Mum describes me as shy and arty and she's probably right. A lot of the time I can't think why anyone would want to be friends with me. I don't have a spectacular personality or get a lot of attention from boys, and I'm not very good at schoolwork. I've just got one friend, Sarah, who lives on my street, but she doesn't talk to me much at school. She wouldn't dare, because she's afraid of them too.

It started at the beginning of this school year when my closest friend, Jess, moved away. Jess was pretty popular at school and because she made friends easily there were a group of us who could hang around together. I didn't always get on with the other girls as well as Jess did, but it did feel like I was part of a crowd. After a while I felt comfortable with our little group, and I told them all lots of things about me and my family which I wish now I hadn't.

When Jess left, the others started ignoring me. Then they started teasing me and calling me names, and then they started doing things much worse. At first they would snigger if I got something wrong in class and they'd take the mickey about it during break. One time I was really nervous in geometry class because they all kept smiling at me and giving each other knowing looks. I found out later that they'd stuck a sanitary towel to my blazer. (Later they soaked a whole package of tampons in ketchup and left them in my desk.) When the teacher asked me a question about the homework I got flustered and said something about circumcising a triangle. I'd meant to say 'circumscribing'. Ever since that they make motions with their fingers like scissors and whisper 'Snip, snip' at me.

They decided that the reason I missed Jess so much was because I'd been in love with her. They went from calling me 'rat-face' to calling me a 'rat-faced lesbian'. While they stood in queue to buy dinner they'd sing, or rather scream:

Sandra and Jess were up in a tree
K-I-S-S-I-N-G

First comes love, then comes marriage

Then comes Little Sandra in the baby carriage.

I think that the teachers on dinner duty thought it was just a joke. Some of them probably thought we were all still good friends, and some of them might even have thought I deserved it, because the girls who were picking on me were good students and I wasn't. One teacher bent over the table where I was sitting and said, 'It'll blow over.' It was like having someone say, 'There, there, keep your chin up. It's not that big a deal.' But it was a big deal to me.

I tried ignoring them. I thought that maybe they were looking for some kind of a reaction from me and that if they didn't get it they might get bored and stop. It didn't work; in fact, they got worse.

I feel really lonely at school now. No one talks to me, except for them, and if any of them approach me I know it's because they're setting me up for something. I spend my break times in the loo, or anywhere else where I think they won't find me. I feel very isolated, like I'm completely cut off from every other person at the school. Sometimes it's really difficult to keep from crying. I've thought about killing myself.

Recently things have got really bad. They tore up all my textbooks last week, and they ruined my uniform by covering it in make-up. My Dad will go mad if he finds out. A few days ago they waited for me outside the loo. It was time to go home, and I was hoping they'd go first. 'Snip, snip, Sandra,' they giggled as they poked me with their fingers. 'Tell us, Lesbo, how do you circumcise a triangle?'

'Speaking of lesbos, do you know that she made a pass at me in the dinner queue yesterday? She pinched my bum. Next she'll be sticking her tongue in my ear!'

'Maybe we should leave the circumcision to someone else and just give her a lesbo haircut.'

'I think we need to teach her a lesson.'

They held my hands behind my back and punched me in the stomach a couple of times. One of them slapped me across the face and called me a dirty-minded slag. I was glad that school was over and that I didn't have to go back into a class. I waited a bit and headed home.

I don't know what I can do about this any more. I can't tell anybody at school about it. That would make it worse, because I'd be a grass then as well as a wimp. And besides, who'd believe me? My Dad would be really angry if he had any idea at all. And my Mum – well, I couldn't bother her with it. She thinks I'm doing OK at school. Worst of all is my brother, who lives with his wife a few miles from us. He used to make me feel really special, but last week it was my birthday and he forgot.

That was the story I told a counsellor at ChildLine the first time I rang. I was surprised that I told him all those things. A lot of it was embarrassing, like admitting that the girls had stuck a sanitary towel to my clothes. He made it easy for me to tell him about what was happening at school, because he encouraged me to talk about it and sounded like he believed me. I was half expecting him to tell me to pull myself together or to fight back or something, but he didn't say anything like that. He listened, mostly. I found that at the end of the call I had a lot to think about. He told me, for instance, that it wasn't my fault that this gang were hassling me. They weren't picking on me because I was ugly or stupid or worthless, but because it made them feel good to give someone a hard time. Maybe they didn't think much of themselves either. He also suggested that being bullied didn't *make* me ugly or stupid or worthless, but it may take some time before I can really believe that. Most of the time I still feel like people wouldn't like me. I think it will be a while before I feel like I have any confidence.

The counsellor started me thinking about other things as well, like the fact that I felt really angry with these people at school but didn't sound very angry when I talked about them. He said that I sounded really flat and hurt, almost like I was feeling that I didn't have any right to speak about it at all. When the counsellor pointed that out to me and said that it was OK for me to feel pissed off with what was going on, I started talking faster, like there was a lot of bottled-up stuff inside that came pouring out. I realised that I was really afraid of these girls, and also that I was really afraid of letting any emotions show. In the past whenever I told anybody about how I was feeling, I always lived to regret it. They would either stop being friends with me or they'd use my feelings against me.

I was surprised when the counsellor said that we'd been talking for nearly an hour and that maybe I should go away and think about what we'd said so far before we started looking for a solution. I wasn't expecting him to say that, but in a way I was relieved, because I felt pretty tired after telling the whole story to someone. I think as well that I actually appreciated the fact that some-one was telling me that there was no easy answer to the situation I was in. Though it would have been nice to have left the phone box feeling like it was all sorted out, I knew that *I* hadn't been able to come up with any answers, and it was nice to hear that that wasn't because I was just stupid. As well as going home with a lot of things to think about, I also had a practical sugges-tion to work on before I phoned and spoke to a counsellor again. I was going to work on expressing my feelings. I was going to tell my brother, who's the one person I might feel safe trying it out on, that I was hurt and annoyed that he'd forgotten my birthday.

I phoned ChildLine back a few days later, having worked things out with my brother (at the same time increasing my confidence just a little bit) but having left things at school to get worse. What I didn't say in my first call was that I didn't go back to school after the incident in the toilets. It was too diffi-cult to admit that I just couldn't cope with what had happened, especially when the counsellor had made me feel like there were some good things about me, so I just said that I could probably avoid that gang of girls for a few days while I thought about what I might do. That was a lie, because there was no way to avoid a group of people at my school, and the bullies showed no signs of leaving me alone. I bunked off for five days, and I knew that soon the school would contact my parents about it. I haven't told Mum and Dad anything. The first day I pretended I was sick and after that I spent my days walking around the town.

I'm really afraid of what my parents will do when they find out. Dad doesn't like me very much. Well, he doesn't like women much generally. When I was younger he used to beat Mum up pretty often. I remember spending a lot of time in women's refuges and staying with Mum's relations. She's gone back to him so many times now that they don't want to know any more. My Mum's sort of cut off from her family, and though Dad doesn't hit her as much as he used to, I can tell that she's still really unhappy. I used to tell Mum that things would be better if they just split up, but she'd get upset about it and I'd always have to apologise. She feels that she can't leave him. She doesn't have any money, for one thing, and he's threatened her about leaving. He says that he'll kill himself if she tries. Mum's still afraid of him, and I can't tell her anything that will add to her worries. Back when we were all friends, I told some of the girls at school about how tough things were at home sometimes. I'm afraid that they'll tell the whole school about it and that I'll end up in care. I couldn't bear leaving Mum with him.

I think I'm in big trouble. I always thought that Dad would go mad if he found out about the girls at school, and now it looks like there's no way he won't find out. Mum will be really worried and upset. I don't want to do that to her. She's got enough to worry about without me on top of it. I could lie and say that I was just skiving for a week, but that won't make much difference as far as my Dad's concerned.

Should I tell the head why I haven't been at school? I'm not sure that I could. It isn't right to tell on people, no matter who they are. And what if the head doesn't believe me anyway? I don't think he could do anything so horrid to them that they'd stop. They might just wait a few days and then really make sure that I didn't talk about it again. Worse still, if I get a reputation for being a grass, then everyone else at school might start being horrible to me. And what if the school decide that I'm a problem student and send me to meet with the social worker? I'd die if she found out about my Mum and Dad. But maybe things can't get any worse than they are now. Would it really make a difference if instead of everyone ignoring me they joined in with the name-calling and things? Either way, I should probably try to go to a different school. But I don't know if Dad would let me.

I was glad I got to talk to the same counsellor again. I was in real need of some help this time, and it might have been hard starting the whole story over again with someone new. I found that it was even easier telling him about things this time, because I was beginning to feel like I could trust him to keep what I was saying confidential, and because I knew from last time that he wouldn't start preaching about my bunking off. He listened to me go on for a while, and he helped me sort things out in my head. He helped me look at what I was saying. I realised that I was sounding really confused about what to do, and it seemed that was OK with him. Instead of telling me what to do, which would probably have cheesed me off a bit, he let *me* figure out what I might do. He didn't seem too annoyed that I kept whinging about how it seemed like nothing would work, or that I kept saying that nothing could make things at school change.

I found that, like the last call, this call helped me to start looking at some of what was going on in a different way. I'd never thought, for example, about how alike my situation at home and my situation at school were. Thinking about it now, my Dad does sound like a bit of a bully. In some ways I guess it's not too surprising that I haven't been able to stand up to the bullies at school. I never saw my mother really get angry with Dad, and I've never really been able to tell him what I think about it. Mum must be scared of him in the same way that I'm scared of these girls at school. She's probably humiliated about it too, which is a lot of what I've been feeling. I could always see that what was happening at home wasn't my Mum's fault, and having it pointed out to me helped me see that I wasn't to blame for the girls at school, either. Though to be honest, I think that I've let them hassle me to some extent just by not doing anything about it.

I was surprised, and probably lucky, that things went as well as they did. I went to school the next day so that I could talk to Miss Lee, my English teacher, about bunking off. I knew that it would be hard to tell her everything that I wanted to, but maybe it was a bit easier because I'd been able to practise what I was going to say with the counsellor at ChildLine. I went into her office before school started, told her that I needed to talk about why I hadn't been to school, and admitted to her that it was difficult for me to say what I needed to. I'd never had to talk to a teacher before, so I really wasn't sure what to expect. She seemed concerned by the things I told her. I didn't tell her the names of the girls right off; I waited to see if I felt OK about doing that. In the end I decided to trust her and I told her the names. She called my parents in, though my Dad wouldn't come, and we all had to see the head. He said he would need to wait a few days before he made any decisions so that he could meet with the other pupils' parents. In the meantime he put them all on litter duty, so that they'd have plenty to do in break times besides pick on me.

The first time I saw the lot of them trudging around with the rubbish, I was afraid of what they might do to me. One of them said, 'Phew! I thought the rubbish smelled bad,' and another added, as she picked up some used napkins with the gloves she was wearing, 'Look, Lesbo, you've, uh, misplaced your towels again.'

'Come on, Lesbo, if you like girls so much, surely you're not going to get squeamish at the sight of some female blood.'

They all started to giggle, though I could tell that a couple of them didn't feel as good about doing it as they had done before. The leader encouraged the others with, 'Come on, girls, let's shower her with love,' and as she tried to fling the towels across the lawn towards me, 'It's your bridal bouquet, Rat-face, flowers for you and your girlfriend.'

The missiles didn't hit me, but fell between us on the grass. I, for once, didn't budge.

'You really do think you're clever, don't you?' I said. Then I got angry and told her that I found her pathetic. Then I walked off, and I don't think any of them noticed that I was trembling.

After the head met with their parents a few days later, they were all suspended from school for two weeks. I was surprised that the school had decided to take it so seriously. I thought that they might get a stiff talking to if anything at all. Since none of them has been around this week it's been a lot easier for me to answer in class, and yesterday Sarah sat down to eat her dinner with me. The other kids haven't acted as horrid as I thought they might. Though some of them did start the week by giving me really filthy looks, others seem to think a bit more of me for what I did. It isn't that things are all rosy. I don't know what they'll be like when they come back, whether they'll give up altogether or just try to torture me in less obvious ways. Miss Lee said that she's going to be watching them all closely, though I think it would be too optimistic of me to think it's all over.

Things at home are the same as they ever were. We don't talk about the bullying or about me not going to class that week. Mum and Dad still have lots of problems, and Dad still takes things out on us. Maybe when it's all settled down I might try talking to someone a bit more about home. I'll have to wait and see what happens when the girls get back.

Summary

Unfortunately, Sandra's story is not unique and it shows how bullying can blight a child's life. On the positive side, it also highlights how children have the ability to think through situations and take actions to help themselves with careful advice from adults. We must encourage children and young people to tell so that we can assist them to overcome the effects of bullying. We know that victims often suffer in silence and that bullying thrives on secrecy. If a child does not feel confident enough to talk to parents, friends or teachers, then ChildLine is there to help.

20

■ ■ ■

Long-term effects of bullying: Kidscape survey

MICHELE ELLIOTT

▶ Survey of 1,000 adults – most were bullied at school

▶ The long-term effects of sustained bullying are horrific

▶ If bullying is allowed to go on, it will blight more lives

▶ Stories from those taking part

▶ This survey could be used as a basis for lessons about the harm bullying does to its victims

Introduction

The Kidscape helpline often took calls from adults who were still suffering the effects of bullying which happened in their school days. The bullying they talked about was sustained and destroyed their confidence. We decided to find out how bullying affected people after they left school to investigate the old adage: 'I was bullied at school and it never did me any harm.' That may be the case for some, but our survey found otherwise.

Kidscape children's charity has conducted the first ever retrospective survey of adults to discover whether bullying at school affects people in later life. The survey, funded by The National Lottery, shows that being badly bullied as a child has a dramatic, negative, knock-on effect throughout life.

The extensive survey of over 1,000 adults shows that bullying affects not only your self-esteem as an adult but your ability to make friends, succeed in education and in work and social relationships. Nearly half (46%) of those who were bullied contemplated suicide, compared with only 7% of those who were not bullied. The majority of the adults reported feeling angry and bitter now about the bullying they suffered as children. Most received no help at the time to stop the bullying and telling either made matters worse or had no effect.

The questionnaire

The questionnaire was devised and refined with help of leading psychologists, teachers, trainers and university professors working in research. Dr Dan Olweus, Professor of Psychology at The University of Bergen, Norway and the internationally recognised expert in the field of behaviour management, and Dr Kevin Browne, Forensic Psychologist at the University of Birmingham, were consulted.

The questionnaire consisted of 16 set questions, plus open space to reply in a fuller way if the respondent wished. A significant majority added several pages of details about the bullying and how it had affected them. Some of the participants were self-selecting, having responded to requests in the broadcast or print media to take part in the survey. Others were randomly selected in the street, at Victoria Coach station and in other public places. In addition to compiling the questionnaire for adults who were bullied as children, a questionnaire for adults who were not bullied was devised as a control to compare the experiences of both groups.

Respondents

Of the 1,044 adults who took part in the survey, 828 were bullied at school; 216 were not.

Gender

- 70% of the bullied respondents were women, 30% men.
- 49% of the non-bullied respondents were women, 51% men.

The probable explanation of the larger number of females is that the radio and television programmes on which the survey was mentioned took place almost exclusively during the day. Also, it may be that women are more inclined to share emotional experiences than men. It is unlikely that women were bullied more as children than men. Most bully surveys, including several by Kidscape, indicate that boys are more likely to be bullied. So although the survey could be seen to indicate that girls were bullied more in the past, this is unlikely. Therefore the gender of the respondents should not be taken as representative of the total picture of bullying in bygone days.

We attempted to correct the gender response by advertising in magazines which catered for men and mentioning the survey on radio programmes focusing on male interests. This generated at least 100 surveys, but not enough to redress the balance.

Age now

The participants ranged in age from 18 to 81. The majority of the bullied female respondents were between the ages of 28 and 40. The majority of the bullied male respondents were between the ages of 22 and 40.

Age leaving school

Of the 828 respondents who were bullied, the overwhelming majority left school at or before the age of 16, many citing the bullying as the main reason (see Figure 20.1). As one 51-year-old man said:

I left school when I was 14 because I could not face the torture I knew was waiting for me behind the school gates. I used to be physically ill at the thought of going to school, but my Dad would force me out the door. I would get my books and pretend to go to school, but the minute I turned the corner I was off to a secret place I could hide. I spent most days there until they (the bully gang) caught up with me and then I got a good hiding. My Dad said to stand up to them – easier said than done when they were older, stronger and more cunning than me.

A 37-year-old woman wrote:

I knew I would die, either at the hands of the bullies or by my own hand. I left school as soon as I could, aged 16. Although I was bright, I left with no qualifications and ended up in a series of dead-end jobs.

Figure 20.1 Ages victims left school

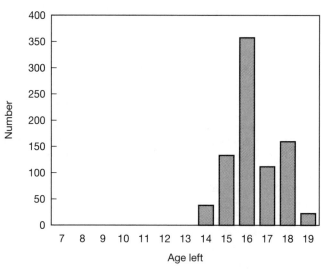

Further education

Of the bullied respondents, 40% said that the bullying had affected their plans for further education. Many wrote that they were afraid that the bullying would continue if they continued their education.

A 29-year-old man said:

The fifth year bullies at my comprehensive school went to the college where I wanted to study. I didn't have the courage to be at the same place, so I never did go on to further education. I have always regretted not continuing my studies and feel bitter about it. Who knows how my life would have been different if those boys had not been allowed to make my life such an unending misery.

A 46-year-old woman wrote:

The girls who were bullying me all went to a local college to study and I was terrified that, if I went, the bullying would just go on and on. I had to get away from them. I had already attempted suicide because of their taunting and I just couldn't face the idea that it would go on and on. Instead I went to work in a store. I worked in several stores and I am still a cashier to this day. I know I should have had more courage, but years of bullying made me think that I was stupid, ugly and would never amount to much. If someone tells you that often enough, you end up believing it. I did.

Age when bullying started

For the overwhelming majority of the bullied respondents, the bullying started between the ages of 7 and 13 (Figure 20.2). The highest peaks seem to correspond with the ages of children entering secondary school, ages of 11 or 12. A significant minority related bullying starting at a very young age – five or six, as soon as they entered primary school.

Figure 20.2 Age victims were first bullied

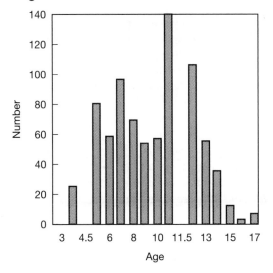

243

Why they thought they were bullied

Most adults thought they were bullied because they were:

- shy, didn't answer back;
- too short or too tall;
- good or bad looking;
- not interested in or bad at sports;
- too sensitive or cried easily;
- from parents who had divorced, died or were in prison;
- too intelligent or too stupid;
- a minority race or religion in their school or neighbourhood;
- skinny or fat;
- talented in music, art or poetry;
- too poor or too rich;
- speaking with a posh or 'lower class' accent;
- wearing the wrong type of clothes.

How long did it go on?

On average the bullying reported in this survey went on for between two and six years (Figure 20.3). Several respondents were bullied throughout their entire school careers (9 to 11 years), making one man, aged 44, comment that he did not know if:

> ... I was a natural victim or if I developed a victim mentality from the bullying I experienced. It is true that I was probably not very socially adept to begin with, but 11 years of bullying certainly did nothing to increase my ability to socialise. I suspect that, had the bullying been promptly dealt with when I was six, I would have been better at relating to people and being social. Eleven years of my life were taken away by the bullies – may they rot in hell.

A 34-year-old woman wrote:

> I was bullied for four years by the same group of girls, from the time I started secondary school until they left. They were two years older than me and I wasn't the only one they targeted. The two years after they left the school were my happiest memories. If only it all could have been like that.

Numbers of bullies involved

Approximately 17% of respondents were bullied by gangs of bullies who hung around together. Another 57% were bullied by more than one person (Figure 20.4). The respondents felt powerless against the combined forces of

Figure 20.3 Length of time bullied

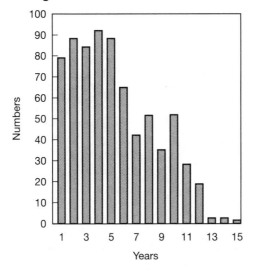

the gang or their numerous bullies. In only a small minority of cases was the bully operating alone. It would seem that the bullies needed one another to persist in their hurtful, cowardly behaviour.

A 27-year-old man wrote:

The three of them would wait for me after school and ambush me on the way home. I tried leaving school late, changing my route, riding my bike – nothing worked. They always found me and pushed me around.

Several respondents (2%) mentioned being bullied by teachers, even though the survey was designed to talk about child on child bullying. Most said they remembered teachers who were overly punitive or sarcastic and who hit them. One 70-year-old woman said that her maths teacher bullied her so badly that she only has to see a column of numbers 'to break into a cold sweat'.

Figure 20.4 Number of bullies involved

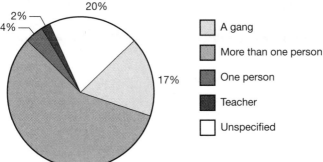

245

Figure 20.5 Ages of bullies

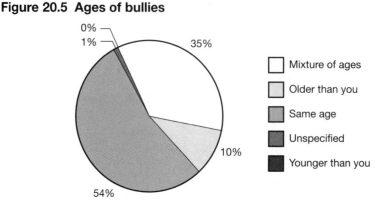

Most people were bullied either by children the same age or older (Figure 20.5). Unsurprisingly, it was rare for someone to be bullied by a younger child. The participants report that, in later life, they often had difficulty making friends with and were wary of people in their own and older age groups, a correlative with the relative ages of their bullies to them.

Sex of bullies

The respondents were asked if the bullies were the same sex or different sex to them or if they were bullied by both sexes – 61% of the victims were bullied by children of the same sex, 34% by both sexes and a small number by only members of the opposite sex. It was very unusual for a boy to be bullied by girls, but girls were often bullied by mixed groups of children (Figure 20.6).

Figure 20.6 Sex of bullies

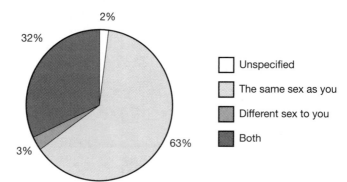

Type of bullying

Men

- 75% were physically bullied.
- 85% were verbally bullied.
- 30% were excluded or ostracised.

Men frequently reported being physically attacked as children by bullies and were less likely than girls to be ignored or ostracised. This mirrors all the research carried out thus far. The types of physical bullying reported, however, were nauseating to read and listen to: broken bones, internal injuries, scaring, operations to remove damaged testicles and kidneys, stabbings, being blinded in one eye, severe beating, being strung up upside down in toilets and almost drowning, being thrown down cliffs, into water and pushed onto the road in front of oncoming traffic, having objects inserted into various orifices, etc. The catalogue of abuse was horrifying.

It was surprising the number of men who reported that they were verbally bullied as children by boy bullies. Previous studies have indicated that verbal bullying was almost exclusively the domain of girl bullies. Perhaps younger boys now being bullied are unwilling to admit that they are called names as it may seem more acceptable to be physically bullied than verbally bullied. Either that or boy bullies today just kick and punch without verbally abusing their victims. It seems more feasible, however, that young boys today are just not reporting the verbal abuse.

Women

- 62% were physically bullied (see below).
- 93% were verbally bullied.
- 60% were excluded or ostracised.

The vast majority of women reported being verbally bullied, while a high percentage talked about being ostracised and excluded. This reflects earlier studies. The shocking finding was that so many younger women reported being violently physically bullied. Slightly over 60% of the respondents said that other girls had kicked and punched them, which is in direct contrast to previous studies of bullying behaviour.

Examining the figures more closely, we find that the reported patterns of bullying by girls appear to have changed over the past 5 to 15 years:

- Women between the ages of 30 and 50 who were reporting bullying that had taken place 20 years or more in the past described the physical attacks by girls as hair pulling, being tripped over and pushing as the most common. Other forms of physical bullying such as bruises, broken bones, black eyes or being stabbed with objects were not mentioned.

- Women between the ages of 18 and 30 reporting bullying that had taken place in the past 5 to 15 years said they had been severely physically attacked by girl bullies. The forms of violence included being stabbed, kicked in the head, having stones thrown, slapping, sticking pencils in arms, hands, legs, etc., being deliberately knocked down by bicyclists, broken bones, severe bruising from punching and black eyes, as well as other injuries requiring hospital treatment.

The copious written responses from women regarding physical assaults on them as children by other girls were unexpected. The Kidscape Helpline has received a considerable increase in calls regarding girls physically assaulting other girls. We thought this was a totally new phenomenon in the 1990s based on our previous calls and on all available research. What this survey highlights is that the increase in violence by girls to girls is indeed a recent occurrence, but one that seems to have been happening over the past 5 to 15 years. Older women who took part in the survey, though mentioning physical bullying, were talking about relatively minor events and none took the opportunity to write about more serious assaults.

Based on the data of kinds of bullying men and women endured in the past, the key factors seem to be:

- There has been a changing pattern of physical bullying by girls, one that has been going on since approximately the mid-1980s.
- Severe physically bullying by girls was rare before the 1980s and consisted almost exclusively of pushing and hair pulling.
- In the past 5 to 15 years, girls have been more likely to physically attack other girls, causing injury.
- Verbal bullying by girls was and still seems to be the most common form of girl-on-girl bullying (93%).
- Men reported a very high incidence of verbal bullying (85%) as children by boy bullies.
- Boys were still more likely to be violently physically bullied than girls, even with the reported changing patterns.

Did telling help?

Sixty-six per cent of the victims did tell someone that they were being bullied. Most often they told a parent or a teacher, sometimes a friend. The results of telling were dismal – 29% of the respondents said that telling made the bullying worse, 50% said it made no difference. In only 8% of cases did telling result in help for the victim (Figure 20.7).

A 47-year-old woman said:

When I told the teacher, she called the class together and told them not to pick on me. You can imagine what happened next. I was the butt of every joke, hurtful comment and was ostracised for the next two years. I never told anyone else. What was the point?

Figure 20.7 If bully reported, what effect did this have?

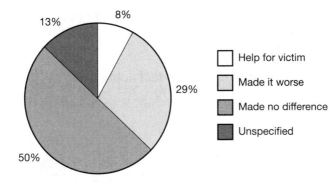

A 35-year-old man wrote:

I tried to tell my mum, but she didn't seem to understand. Telling made no difference and I decided not to try again because it would have hurt her to know how bad it was for me.

A 62-year-old man said:

The headmaster called me up to the front of the assembly. He announced that I was the shortest boy ever to attend that school (a private school of good reputation) and that he did not want anyone to harm me. The boys made it their business to ensure that my time in that school was pure torture. Perhaps the headmaster was trying to help as I had told a form tutor that I was being bullied, but all he did was exacerbate an already difficult situation.

How did the bullying make them feel?

Men, looking back on their feelings at the time of the bullying, were more likely to be angry and frustrated than the women. Women were more likely to be depressed, scared and vulnerable, although both sexes reported all of these feelings in varying proportions (Figure 20.8).

How does it make them feel now?

Men and women reported similar feelings now about the bullying, but they are more angry and bitter now, while the feelings of being scared and vulnerable have subsided (Figure 20.9).

One woman, aged 34, wrote:

I am bitter, but also feel great regret. I would have been capable of so much more had not my school years been so frightening. If I had enjoyed school I might have 'bloomed' into a more confident person. It makes me wish that I hadn't been born, as I have now wasted my life being too scared and nervous to try to succeed.

A man, aged 24, replied:

Yes, I am bitter and angry, but also annoyed that nothing was done about the bullying. Teachers had a chance to put it right and I look back partly with bitterness towards them, as well as the bullies.

Figure 20.8 How bullying made them feel at the time

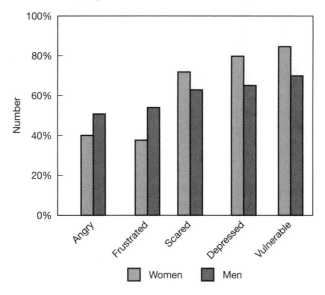

Figure 20.9 How bullying makes them feel now

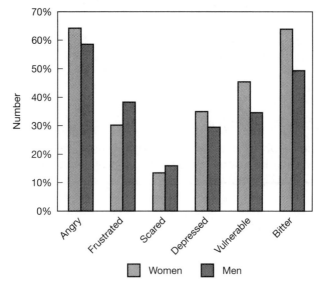

Suicide

Of the respondents, 46% contemplated suicide because of the bullying (Figure 20.10), while 20% attempted suicide because of it, some more than once (Figure 20.11). Compared with the non-bullied group, this is an incredibly high rate – 0.7% of the non-bullied adults had contemplated suicide and 0.3% had attempted it.

Figure 20.10 Victims who contemplated suicide

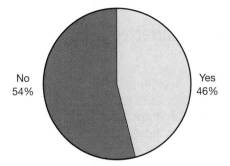

Figure 20.11 Of those contemplating suicide, who attempted it

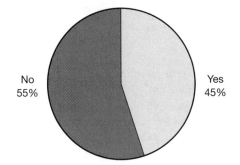

A man aged 35 wrote:

After one particularly bad day of bullying, I could stand it no longer. I got a rope and went into the woods to kill myself. I managed to secure the rope and put it around my neck and jump. I blacked out and thought I had finally managed to die. But I came to on the ground and realised that the rope had untied itself. I never told anyone about it and felt a failure because I couldn't even manage to kill myself properly.

A woman, aged 32, said:

It was a very childish suicide attempt when I was 12. I tried to drown myself in the bath. Of course I could not hold my breath and ended up choking up lots of water. This happened after a group of girls made me sing and dance while all the other children laughed. I was so humiliated that I decided to kill myself. I have never told anyone about this.

A 56-year-old woman wrote:

I tried to kill myself when I was 14 by swallowing every tablet in the bathroom cabinet. My Dad found me and took me to hospital. I then spent a long time in a psychiatric unit and suffered irreparable liver damage. I begged my parents not to make me go back to the school. It had and still has an excellent reputation for academics. My dad then took me to another school which was much better. I sometimes wonder if my old school has sorted out the problems in the intervening years.

How has the bullying affected people now?

Men and women report a wide variety of feelings about how the bullying has affected their lives. Women feel they cannot trust people and are afraid of new situations. They also feel they are easily victimised and are afraid to succeed. Men report similar feelings, but are more likely to feel uncommunicative, shy and to be loners than the women. Both men and women feel they have become worse people than they were in school and they did not feel good about themselves at school.

When the adults who were bullied as children are compared with those who were not bullied, the differences are dramatic. Adults who were not bullied are not afraid of new situations or uncommunicative or loners and they feel they are better people than when they left school.

One woman, aged 68, said:

The bullying has left me with an inability to cope with change or stress, severe depression and agoraphobia. I am afraid of anything new and most people think I am a recluse and they are probably right. I only trust myself. The bullying went on for years and years and it has left its mark on me.

A man, also aged 68, reported:

I am hypersensitive and raw to slights. I am constantly on the look-out for criticism and have the mentality of a perpetual victim. It is as if I am still waiting for those bullies to come around the corner and get me. I tell myself it is ridiculous ...

Self-esteem now

Some of the most dramatic results of the survey are evident in the area of self-esteem. Adults who were bullied as children report significantly lower levels of self-esteem than those who were not bullied; 43% report very low, low or below-average self-esteem (Figure 20.12). Only 0.6% of those who were not bullied report low or below-average self-esteem. None reported very low self-esteem.

In contrast, 43% of adults not bullied say their self-esteem is high or very high compared with 26% of those adults who were bullied.

Figure 20.12 Victims' feelings of self-esteem

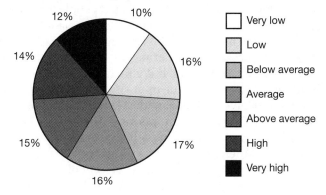

Making friends

Difficulty in making friends was one of the outcomes of being bullied. Nearly three quarters of the respondents, 73%, reported that they had problems. This compares with 11% of the non-bullied adults.

One 70-year-old woman said:

I was so unhappy as a child being bullied that I have never really trusted people. I prefer my animals, who never say an unkind word and who can always be trusted.

A 39-year-old man wrote:

I cannot make friends with anyone my own age. I think it is because the bullies were in my form. I have always sought out older friends, usually adults, whom I felt safer with – people who had gone past the 'bullying stage'.

Continued bullying

Thirty-six per cent said they were now or had been bullied in further education or at work. In the group of people who had not been bullied as children, only 0.3% reported bullying either in further education or at work. Still, it was encouraging that 64% of those bullied as children had not experienced further bullying.

Summary

This is the first time adults have been questioned about their experiences of being bullied as children and how this might have affected their lives. Kidscape planned to include 300 people in The National Lottery-funded research, but found that many more people wanted to take part so that the total numbers reached over 800, plus over 200 people who were not bullied. This brought the numbers to more than 1,000 people taking part.

Some of the conclusions are not surprising. For example, bullying is obviously not a new problem but one that has affected people for generations. The oldest respondent was 81, but as with the rest of the people who took part, time had not dimmed the memories. The feelings of fear had diminished, but not the anger and bitterness at the unfairness of what the children suffered.

Contrary to some popular opinion, bullying does *not* help children to cope better with adult life. In fact, it has the opposite effect. Adults who were bullied as children tend to have problems with self-esteem, feelings of anger and bitterness, suicidal thoughts and attempts, and difficulty relating to people. Many were afraid of new situations and felt shy and easily victimised. Over half of the men and women said they were loners, while less than 20% felt they were better people now than when they left school.

Compare this to those adults who were not bullied and you can see the dramatic differences. Adults not bullied as children generally have high self-esteem, are not loners, make friends easily and definitely feel they are better people now than they were at school.

The duration and severity of the bullying was heartbreaking. People wrote volumes about bullying that had gone on for years, causing them untold misery. They left school early because of it. Many had health problems and were bullied in later life because they had no self-worth. The bullies' harsh messages stuck with them and shaped them. When they tried to get help as children, only 8% were given any help that stopped the bullying. For the rest, telling either made no difference or made the bullying worse.

The lessons for us today are clear. If we allow bullying to go on, we are condemning another generation of children to the same sort of problems that most of the adults in the survey told us they had encountered. These adults had some recommendations for us. Many said that children should be given counselling to help them overcome the effects of the bullying. Others told us that the 'trendy' idea that bullies should not be blamed and suffer no consequences to their actions made them furious. 'Bullies need to apologise and make amends', wrote one woman, aged 54. 'If they (the bullies) do not do this, they will just grow up thinking they can do anything they want and become big bullies'. She knew because she was working for a bully boss.

The vexed problem of bullies who are teachers was raised by 16 of the respondents. 'Tell children to go to another teacher or their parents.' One man said, 'Teacher bullies are the worst because everyone seems to turn a blind eye to them. Yet they have the power to make your life even more of a misery than the pupils. One signal from my PE teacher and I was bait for the mob. For five years he bullied me and so did everyone else. I hated, correction, still hate him to this day.'

It should be kept in mind that this survey is the tip of the iceberg. Many people suffered worse bullying than those who took part in the survey. They have had nervous breakdowns. They have succeeded in their suicide attempts.

It should also be noted that some people have overcome the bullying they endured. They were determined to succeed and did. They did not allow the bullying to stop their education. One man said that he got so angry about the bullying that he became an aggressive and highly successful business man. 'I may not be a better person than I was back then, but I certainly am a success in my job and I owe it all to those boys in the sixth form. I hope they are having a miserable life.'

They probably are. Professor Dan Olweus, in a long-term study, found that boys who were bullies were twice as likely as their peers to have criminal convictions and four times more likely to be multiple offenders. Typically convictions were for aggression and violence and were often alcohol-related (Olweus, 1997). In a survey of young offenders conducted by Kidscape, it was found that 92% of the young offenders had engaged in bullying behaviour while at school (Elliott and Kilpatrick, 2002).

The message is simple. Bullied children and bullies alike are badly affected when bullying is allowed to thrive. Bullying must never be tolerated.

I'm 34, self-employed, married with two children. I have an adoring husband, beautiful children, a job I love and a nice home. Yet there is always this lingering fear that I don't deserve my home, that my husband and children don't love me, that my friends are only nice to me to my face because they want something from me and that they run me down behind my back. This is the legacy I have inherited from bullying.

References

Elliott, M. and Kilpatrick, J. (2002) 'Kidscape Survey of Young Offenders, 1994' in *How to Stop Bullying: A KIDSCAPE Training Guide*.

Olweus, D. (1997) 'Bullying/victim problems among school children' in K. Rubin and D. Pepler (eds) *The Development and Treatment of Childhood Aggression*.

21

■ ■ ■

Treatment of bullying in a therapeutic community

DR L. F. LOWENSTEIN

► Creating awareness that bullying is wrong because it causes distress to others

► Helping bullies form personal relationships along alternative lines

► Working with children from very disturbed backgrounds

► Making bullying an unsuccessful way of gaining satisfaction

► Helping children develop self-confidence and independence to deal with problems which will arise in life

Allington Manor is a residential school and therapeutic community for children in need of special assistance. The school accepts girls and boys between the ages of 11 and 16 with a range of learning, emotional and behavioural difficulties. The emphasis of the school is on rehabilitation for the child, socially, emotionally and educationally.

Introduction to the problem

Patrick and Robert (names have been changed) were two boys with serious problems who were admitted to Allington Manor, Eastley, Hants. Their main disturbing behaviour was bullying other children and the distress this produced in the bullied children and the community as a whole. Patrick and Robert bullied through a combination of verbal threats and unprovoked sadistic and physical attacks on those children who were in fear of them. Naturally, this produced stress and frustration in the tormented children who already had their own problems, which necessitated their being placed in a therapeutic community for schooling, care and treatment.

Thus the problem of aggressive, sadistic, bullying behaviour affected the whole community and reinforced the negative behaviour of the two boys. It was vital to intervene, both for the sake of the two boys and the community as a whole, and in particular the victims of bullying.

As can be imagined, many methods for dealing with Patrick's and Robert's bullying had been tried in the past with little or no positive results, hence their placement at Allington Manor.

As we will see from the background history which follows, both boys had experienced a considerable amount of bullying themselves from parents, siblings and other children. They had therefore taken for granted that the world consisted essentially of two types of individuals: bullies and the bullied. Having themselves experienced the distress and pain of being the victims of bullying, they had chosen now that they were stronger and older to be the perpetrators instead of the victims of aggression.

While this obviously satisfied *their* needs, it was causing serious problems to the victims and to the community as a whole. It was equally not in the long-term best interests of the perpetrators of bullying for them to be allowed to continue to behave in this way.

The goal was to create a feeling of awareness in the two boys that what they were doing was wrong because it was causing distress to others. It was also the aim to develop some positive feelings of care towards others and hence to promote kind behaviour rather than sadistic behaviour. It was the aim also to help them form personal relationships along alternative lines with all children. This would, of course, constitute an asset for the compulsive bully and the therapeutic community as a whole.

Patrick's background history

Patrick had come from an extremely disturbed background where a considerable amount of violence had taken place in the home, mostly by the father physically attacking the children and his wife from time to time, usually under the influence of alcohol. Patrick therefore suffered from child abuse at a very early age. Both parents had been in care themselves.

Even at the age of four, bruising was frequently noted while Patrick attended school and an NSPCC office was notified. There were many subsequent injuries and eventually Patrick was removed from the home at the age of eight to a place of safety. Patrick's father was convicted of assault about the same time. There were many subsequent changes in placement for Patrick, but he was returned home on a trial basis at the age of 14.

This broke down less than a year later. He had gone missing several times from home. He was finally rejected from home by his parents because of his abusive behaviour towards his mother and also his threatened violence. No contact with home has been made since that time and Patrick has no desire to seek any contact whatsoever. The social worker described Patrick as 'a difficult and quite damaged boy who is capable of producing some quite bizarre behaviour. A return home in the foreseeable future is unlikely and this leaves him with no real aim for his future'.

Patrick also had great difficulty in relating to the school situation. He was frequently quite unco-operative and even when tested by the psychologist refused to perform in certain of the test items. He was totally unco-operative in most lessons and not expected to do anything that could be loosely termed academic. He frequently refused to go to school and once there tended to run away. He was also disruptive and abusive to both staff and other children. He gave the impression of hating and despising all around him. He always had a surly, aggressive look on his face and was very uncouth in every way and lacking in manners, grasping at everything, self-centred and uncaring. He seemed to be going out of his way to make everybody hate him.

His relationship with his peer group was poor and almost non-existent, but so was his relationship with adults. Patrick's first reaction to requests was an ignorant 'Hmph' and often unco-operative behaviour, ignoring what was being said. When disciplining measures were taken he would often become stubborn and argue, saying he was being victimised and 'picked on'. A great deal of pressure had to be exerted before he would comply to any sort of structure.

Robert's background history

Robert's personal history before he attended the therapeutic community was described as 'verbally and physically aggressive'. Outbursts were directed towards peer groups and staff in general. Community homes in most of Wales where he was placed were unable to contain him. He was also noted to be hyperactive. At five feet one inch tall and weighing seven stone, he was of slim build but very energetic and strong.

At a case conference held shortly before his coming to the therapeutic community, a number of the staff felt considerable reservations about Robert's long-term prognosis due to his difficult behaviour, disrespect for staff, and also his temper with a high degree of aggression following.

Robert comes from a Welsh background and could converse equally well in Welsh and English. The results of the testing indicated that his ability was in the low-average range. Further reports by the psychologist who investigated him clearly showed that there was a lack of emotional bonding between himself and his parents. Robert was described as being very much like a 'demanding, egocentric three-year-old'.

Robert was placed in care at the age of three due to home difficulties in managing him. He was also placed with foster parents but this lasted only three months before he was placed in a children's home with his elder twin brothers. He was then returned home but this again broke down when Robert was aged eight.

There were no sleep problems and his appetite was good. He appeared to need some form of firm control over him for as soon as it was removed he would become insecure and aggressive. His behaviour was described prior to coming to the therapeutic community as moody and unpredictable. At the same time there was a considerable warm, helpful and caring side to his personality. He expressed affection through hostility and could be very affectionate towards adults, especially when he wanted something. He accepted discipline and punishment but only if he considered it fair.

Although he frequently expressed the view that he would like to be at home with his mother, to whom he claimed to be close, he found it difficult to live in that environment due to her lack of control over him.

In the peer relationship in his younger years he was considered to be the 'group clown' and scapegoat and was frequently in conflict with other children due to his attention seeking towards the staff and the stressful interaction this caused with the others. Robert tended to be a major source of irritation to the group.

His relationship with adults varied considerably. He appeared to be more relaxed with staff who were able to control him and who, in a sense, could be in charge of him, but he was abusive to those he felt weak. He related superficially to many people and appeared on the whole to be self-centred.

Robert was one of five illegitimate children. Mother was, at the time, cohabiting with the same person she has been with for six years. The problems within the family were chronic and long-standing and this had been damaging to Robert. As already mentioned, the prognosis for Robert was not good and there was some possibility that he might become involved in crime. This crime was likely to be of a violent nature because of his temper outbursts against people and objects.

In the therapeutic community his behaviour continued very much as previously. His behaviour was very challenging, demanding, violently provocative, bullying and threatening.

Treating or dealing with the problem

In dealing with the problem of bullying, a number of specific treatment measures were simultaneously instituted. These were at least in part based on the specific problems and diagnosis carried out earlier. Useful methods were also gleaned from such theoretical bases as rational emotive therapy.

Let us look at a summary of some of the strategies used to remedy or eliminate the process of bullying:

1 Creating awareness in the community and in the individuals involved, i.e. in the bully and the victim, and making certain bullying is discovered every time or most of the time.
2 Making certain that bullying can never be used successfully to gain ends since it results in the victim suffering distress.
3 Making certain that the community as a whole is against the bullying and takes actions against such behaviour by reporting it and acting against it in any way necessary.

4 Making certain that bullying is punished.
5 Providing alternative socially acceptable ways towards which habitual bullies can turn and use to achieve their ends if this does not conflict with the rights and welfare of others.
6 Drawing attention to the model of non-bullying behaviour and encouraging such alternative behaviour. This may be done by shaping improved behaviour.
7 Rewarding non-bullying type behaviour with tokens, praise and through extrinsic reinforcement.
8 Physically restraining the bully in the midst of his physically aggressive behaviour, causing him to experience similar pain, distress and frustration to that which he is foisting on his victim, albeit this method must be used sparingly.

It will be noted that all these aims are used simultaneously and are methods of combating bullying and similar antisocial behaviour. They will be discussed individually in detail despite the fact that they are interrelated.

Creating awareness of the bully in the community

It is an important role for the leader of the therapeutic community to create an awareness and a conscience within the community concerning the dangers of bullying. Similarly, the individual or individuals carrying out the activity of bullying must be made aware of how they are affecting others, be it through verbal threats or physical aggression.

This was done via individual encounters with Patrick and Robert as well as through group meetings. Here all members of the community are encouraged to have the confidence to express their feelings about the bullies, knowing their protection is ensured by the staff and the other children. In a group, individuals who are victims of bullying are encouraged to express what has happened and how it is affecting them emotionally and behaviourally.

In this way, three things happen concurrently:

1 The victim gets rid of his pent-up feelings of fear, anxiety, aggression and frustration.
2 The bully is made aware of how the victim feels as a human being through his sadistic behaviour. Bullies on the whole tend to dehumanise their victims.
3 The victim receives support from the group while the group condemns the actions of the bully.

All this brings pressure on the bully to stop his cruel behaviour. It may also provide the bully with the opportunity to release his or her tensions and frustrations concerning past experiences in other than bullying behaviour. Frequently, bullies will report having suffered a great deal in the past themselves and how this accounts for their present behaviour. This, in itself, provides the bully and the community with insight into why such behaviour occurs.

Sometimes it is necessary to conduct a 'poll' within the group anonymously by asking them as a body to write on a piece of paper whom they regard as the biggest bullies and victims of bullying in the group. The result is then collated and a bar graph is drawn, which is discussed by the group and hung up in a public place for everyone to see. The same poll is then repeated after a sufficient period of time has elapsed and changes, for the better or worse, noted. Then the bully is either praised or punished in some manner depending on the outcome of the group assessment. On the whole, these two assessments virtually always show an improvement in the bully's behaviour. This is possibly due to the fact that the bully himself feels ashamed of being thus noted for his antisocial behaviour and seeks to make amends for it.

Making bullying an unsuccessful way of gaining satisfaction

Bullies appear to gain some gratification from the sadistic act of threatening and/or actually carrying out acts of aggression against the victim. This in itself acts as a reward and encourages future acts of bullying. The inflicting of pain appears to trigger satisfaction. It is for this reason that the behaviour must be halted for the sake of the perpetrator as well as the victim.

For the victim, it becomes an immediate as well as a lasting source of torment, which has its effects long after the bullying has passed. For the bully, it is a maladaptive pattern which eventually brings him into conflict with society and the law. Behaviour such as assault, grievous bodily harm, mugging and violence towards wife, children and others is likely to follow, with the anticipated consequences that such behaviour must be terminated or reduced in any way possible.

These are but some of the reasons why the bully must be totally unsuccessful in his behaviour. Lack of success must also be engendered through the punishment that follows such behaviour. This will be discussed in greater detail later on.

Obtaining the support of the community (staff and children) in combating bullying

Allington Manor School and Therapeutic Community exists in part in order to produce a miniature society and one which, through the interaction of its members, seeks to produce change in those members who require it in positive and desired directions. The support of all or most of the membership, therefore, is vital in order to effect the optimum change in bullying behaviour.

The leader of the therapeutic community has a vital role in seeking to unify the group in condemning the cruel activities of bullies. In part, this is achieved by creating an awareness not merely that the problem exists but that something definite must be done about it. Knowing that the leader feels as he does and knowing that others can become victims of bullying, the membership is likely to back the goals and the other procedures that have been adopted in order to attain these goals.

Numerous group, as well as individual, meetings with children and staff create a climate which suggests the importance of each and everyone standing up against bullying and showing a positive care for others. This works from the top down, suffusing every member of the community, including new members who join it.

It is of course important to seek up-to-date information from the community to check on the bullying behaviour, such as whether it has changed for the better or worse. Such information is also important to the bully who obtains the appropriate reinforcement (negative or positive) based on his own behaviour during the interim period. It certainly makes the bully aware that he is being observed and checked and that reports are being provided. The victim can also act as reinforcer by his responses. It incidentally also provides the victim and others with the view that the staff and other children of the therapeutic community as a whole care about their welfare.

Ensuring that the bully is punished

Whenever punishment is used, ethical considerations come into play despite the suffering of the victim of the bully in this particular case. Any behaviour that is encouraged or even tolerated by a community is likely to continue, especially if it is rewarding to someone. If certain behaviour is considered 'outlawed' and is subsequently punished, there is every likelihood that it will in time be inhibited. It will occasionally reappear, unless substitute behaviour is found which takes the place of the maladaptive bullying behaviour.

In the first instance there may be the need to lower one's aim rather than expect a total inhibition of bullying. One way of decreasing problem behaviour is through differential reinforcement of other behaviour (DRO). This may be the avoidance of bullying without any truly friendly or warm relations towards victims of bullying. It may be accomplished by keeping the bully busy doing other things which he enjoys. Bullying behaviour is therefore less likely to occur.

Such methods may work for a time, but stress and frustration experienced by the bully sooner or later will lead to his resuming his negative behaviour. Therefore, other more severe ways must be found to combat bullying, including the physical restraint of the individual, which will be discussed in the final section (see page 265).

Whenever possible, the victim of bullying must be kept from the bully, since victims act almost as a trigger for the outlet of the bully's pent-up frustrations which then lead to aggression. Somehow, however, the bully always 'finds' the victim. For this reason certain areas of the school and community must be made 'no-go areas' for the bully. Places such as the communal television room, music room or dining room may have to be made inhospitable to the bully. In so doing there is a strong element of punishment since this constitutes a deprivation of privileges. It constitutes also a 'time-out' procedure. Having to eat alone constitutes an escalation in the ostracism by the staff and the community as a whole of the individual who is bullying.

The bully is in fact first warned of the impending 'natural time-out' procedure that will be adopted.

1 If you cannot stop bullying you will no longer be permitted to use the TV room, music room, etc. and eventually you will not be allowed to eat in the dining room with all the other members of the community.

2 If bullying continues, the threat is put into operation immediately.

3 This eventually affects the bully, though he may not show it for a time and may become even more aggressive in his bullying. It certainly affects the community and makes clear the standards expected of the therapeutic community. It also reduces the peer attention received by the bully.

4 Once the target behaviour of non-bullying has a chance of being reached, this 'time-out' procedure is reduced and then eliminated. This acts as a positive reinforcement of non-bullying and eventually caring behaviour may follow.

5 It is important to reintroduce all the sanctions if the bully has a relapse and it is sensible to expect that he will. Then the process of punishment and removal of punishment must continue until the bullying behaviour is extinct.

6 Extinction of bullying within the community means that such behaviour is less likely to occur outside the community.

7 Finally, the aim of the therapeutic community is to encourage 'over-correction' in the bully. This means the bully will eventually be required to make amends to the victim. This alternative behaviour is reinforced, first by the fact that there are no aversive repercussions and second by the fact that such behaviour is reinforced extensively by tokens, pocket money, privileges, etc. Ultimately, the alternative behaviour is likely to continue even when more obvious reinforcement ceases.

Providing opportunities to behave positively

As already mentioned, changing behaviour through aversive methods works best when combined with learning or conditioning in a positive direction. The objective therefore is to discourage and, if possible, eliminate maladaptive behaviour that is harmful to others and eventually to oneself. The individual is also encouraged to substitute attitudes and behaviour. Behavioural changes occur under optimum learning conditions, i.e. critical learning times, traumas, through practice leading to a new habit, and of course the individual's co-operation with such changes is important.

A good part of the work must be done by the individual himself to promote his capacity for self-control and redirection of behaviour. For this to occur he must be encouraged or induced over a long period of time to accept suggestions to change. Much depends on a combination of the suggestibility of the individual and the skill of the therapist or director.

Eventually, the influence of the therapist must take second place to the behaviour of the individual and his ability to use his own resources adaptively. Initially, the bully should do all he can to avoid being in the vicinity of the victim of his bullying, since in this way he reduces the temptation to bully. Later, however, to be truly over the need to bully, he must be able to interact in a neutral way or benevolently with his potential victim.

In the case of Patrick and Robert, suitable incentives or rewards were offered if, in the short term, bullying was reduced and if, in the final analysis, they would desist from bullying altogether. In the case of Patrick, the reward was a cigarette, given even for a slight improvement. For Robert it was the opportunity of having sweets and, if successful, being able to spend a week with a member of staff and her family, something he enjoyed very much.

Eventually Patrick and Robert became aware how much more pleasant life was when the rights of others were respected. They also became aware of the pressures upon them to change. This encouraged a more favourable attitude generally and this was ultimately also manifested by their behaviour. Much of this was achieved through the individual and group therapy sessions. The token system, which is described opposite, was also useful in reinforcing the other methods currently in use to reduce antisocial and asocial behaviour such as bullying. It meant eventually greater acceptance of the bullies by the other members of the community.

Perhaps one of the greatest difficulties for the two boys was to overcome the intrinsic reinforcement which they received from their bullying of others. Only a combination of punishment for this with positive reinforcement for socialised behaviour could dislodge eventually the gratification they got from their maladaptive action. It required the following:

- a commitment towards change in the desired direction;
- a lengthy period of practice of the new pattern of behaviour, with appropriate reinforcement being given;
- the feeling that one was rewarded or at least not punished by the change in behaviour.

Encouraging modelling (imitation) of non-bullying behaviour

As we have already established, individuals who bully have not merely frequently suffered from the effect of bullying themselves but have also identified and now imitate modes of bullying behaviour. It is therefore necessary when changing behaviour to find a model or models who can act as substitutes for such identification. It must be a model worthy of imitation, i.e. strong, benevolent, sympathetic and attractive.

More often than not, new behaviour needs to be shaped gradually by the method of successive approximations. This means initially reinforcing behaviour which falls far short of the standards one ideally wishes to inculcate. Hence, initially, one aims to bring about a lessening of the bullying behaviour rather than its total stoppage.

This inculcating of socialised behaviour is done through the model or direction which is received and continually reinforced through pressure from all directions. Factors which enhance modelling (imitation of behaviour) are the similarity of sex, age, race, attitude, prestige, competence, warmth and nurture of the directing model.

It should be remembered that the modelling approach should be seen merely as one approach to help the bully. Frequently, it is best to combine this technique with other methods and to use it as part of a total approach.

Reinforcing non-bullying and alternative behaviour

It is vital to reward non-bullying behaviour. This includes rewarding a neutral position of non-involvement by the former bully with victims. Later the expression of favourable comments and actions towards the real or potential victim must be reinforced. Hence, if the bully can actually learn to display caring and helping behaviour towards his former victim, treatment may be said to be almost successful. Total success is achieved when this attitude and behaviour generalise to other individuals elsewhere outside the community.

Equally, bullying behaviour must never be reinforced but the reverse attitude must be taken. It must be punished and discouraged in every possible way. One very useful method which has long been used is the Token Economy Programme (TEP), evaluated as being useful in modifying a number of disorders and maladaptive or unsocialised patterns of behaviour.

Tokens are conditioned reinforcers that are given immediately or as closely as possible to a response or behaviour which is deemed desirable. It is therefore reinforced or rewarded because it is socialised and hence desirable. There is then the expectation that non-bullying behaviour will recur with greater and greater frequency. The tokens, although symbolic in the first instance, can be spent 'to buy' or 'be exchanged for' extrinsic rewards such as sweets, privileges, cigarettes or even money.

Equally, failing to behave appropriately leads to minus tokens being awarded which places the individual into a kind of 'behavioural debt'. These minus tokens need to be 'worked off' before any kind of positive reward or privileges are provided. TEP need not and should not be continued once the improvement or total cessation of bullying has occurred. Gradually, the TEP method can be reduced.

Imposing physical restraints

In some cases where all the positive and aversive methods have been unsuccessful in reducing or stopping bullying behaviour, a final method must be contemplated. This consists of physically curtailing the negative behaviour of the bully directly and decisively. It may also be necessary to use this method when the bully circumvents or ignores the punitive aspects already described.

Obviously, the method of physical restraint should be used sparingly for optimum results, but when it is used, it must always be considered as one step, the next of which must lead to a positive direction. This might be illustrated when the action of restraint actually occurs.

A bully found in the act of viciously bullying another child should be firmly restrained by being forced to lie on the floor. This minimises injury to himself and to the member of staff, and also reduces the likelihood of damage to property. The bully must be gripped firmly and at the same time he must be told what is happening, i.e. his behaviour is being controlled because he is unable to do so on his own.

Frequently, the bully will claim, while he is being physically controlled, that the adult himself is a bully just like himself. This claim must quickly be discounted by the adult with a statement such as, 'I am not doing what you are doing. You're enjoying your threats and physical attacks against your victim. I don't enjoy what I have to do. I must do this and hold you because you are bullying other people. As soon as I know you will stop this behaviour, initially by your giving me your assurance, I will stop holding you. There is therefore a big difference between what you do and what I am doing. If you fail to keep your promise and bully again, I will be forced to do this again in order to protect your victim as well as yourself.'

Hence, while being physically restrained, the bully is actually forced to listen and gain information, possibly in a way which will make an impact. He benefits from the physical restraint and verbal communication simultaneously. It will of course be argued that 'treatment' thus carried out must be done by a reasonably fit and strong individual who will not abuse his power. Such an argument is absolutely correct. In the right hands, this method is very effective and often 'gets through' the message while other approaches will fail, because they are insufficiently basic or reality orientated.

Summary

The main object of these eight steps is to help the children develop the self-confidence and the independence to deal with problems which will arise in life. If we give these children a clear message that bullying behaviour is not acceptable and that there are more positive ways of dealing with their anger, then other children will be spared the pain of becoming their victims.

22
■ ■ ■

Bullying in children's homes

PETER STEPHENSON

- ▶ 55% of the young people reported that they were involved in bullying within children's homes
- ▶ 42% reported that they do something to stop bullying if they see it happening
- ▶ 76% of the staff reported that they do try to stop bullying if they find out it is happening

Introduction

The majority of research carried out on bullying among children has investigated bullying that takes place in schools. Relatively little research has been carried out on bullying that takes place in other settings.

Bullying is unacceptable wherever it occurs. It is unacceptable whether it takes place in a school, in a child's family, in a children's home or elsewhere. This chapter provides information on bullying that takes place in children's homes.

The survey

The survey was carried out in 1995 in Cleveland. The findings were disseminated widely in the Cleveland area but have not previously been published. At that time 101 young people were living in 14 children's homes within the county. All the young people were invited to take part in the survey. Information was obtained from 79 of the youngsters. The majority of the young people were between 15 and 17 years old, with a similar number of boys and girls.

Information was also obtained from 110 members of staff who worked in the homes – at least seven members of staff in each home. In all cases the information was obtained on an anonymous basis – staff and young people were asked not to put their names on the questionnaires.

Two definitions of bullying were provided. One was intended to be more suitable for staff:

- Bullying is a form of aggression in which a more dominant individual abuses the power he or she has over a less dominant individual.

The other was intended to be more suitable for the young people:

- Bullies set out to hurt or upset somebody, knowing that the other person will not be able to stand up for himself/herself.

Examples were also provided of verbal bullying (e.g. name-calling), of physical bullying (e.g. hitting) and of indirect bullying (e.g. exclusion from the group).

The survey carried out was exceptional in that we did not only ask about bullying that took place between the young people. We also enquired about bullying that took place between the staff and about bullying that took place between the staff and young people. It was considered that the issue of bullying needed to be addressed whoever was involved.

Bullying among the young people

How much bullying was there?

The few studies that have been reported suggest that bullying within children's homes is a common occurrence (see, for example, Sinclair and Gibbs, 1998). This was certainly our finding. More than half the young people (i.e. 55%) stated that they had been involved in bullying in the last month. Twenty-five per cent said they had been bullied by other youngsters, 20% said they had bullied other youngsters and 10% said they had been bullied and had also bullied others.

About a third of the 26 youngsters who reported that they had been bullied said that the bullying had happened no more than once or twice; about a third said it had happened three or four times and about a third said that it had happened every day.

The bullying was reported to occur at all times of the day and night and in all locations, both inside and outside the home. Evenings, bedtimes and after bedtime were the most frequently mentioned times of the day. Bedrooms were the most frequently mentioned location. These findings have implications for the staffing of children's homes.

The ratings by staff suggest a similar picture, though staff working in the same home frequently disagreed with each other. Staff were asked to specify how much bullying there was usually in the home. The most common response was that it was a minor problem from time to time (48%); the next most common response was that it was a major problem from time to time (19%). No member of staff said that it was never a problem.

Whereas 55% of the young people reported that they were involved in bullying within the children's home, 40% reported that they were involved in bullying at the school they currently or most recently attended. In effect, a relatively high proportion of the young people were involved in bullying when at home and when at school.

The findings suggest that a similar percentage of children were being bullied in the two settings. Twenty-five per cent of the young people said they were being bullied in the home; 24% said they were being bullied at school. It appears, however, that more of the youngsters engage in bullying other youngsters when in the home than when at school – 20% of the young people said that they bully other young people when in the children's home. Only 8% said that they bullied other children when at school.

These findings confirm that bullying is a common occurrence in children's homes. Given that over half the young people had been directly involved in bullying, the young people not directly involved are likely to have witnessed bullying or to have been involved in some way in its consequences. The implication is that bullying has an impact on all young people placed in children's homes.

The findings certainly suggest that bullying is more prevalent in children's homes than in mainstream schools. Between 10% and 20% of children in mainstream secondary schools are commonly reported to be involved in bullying. We did find that the level of bullying in two residential special schools for children with emotional and behavioural difficulties was similar to that found in the children's homes in the present study. It is possible that there is a similar level of bullying in children's homes and in this type of special school.

The finding that some young people are being bullied when they are in a children's home and also when they are at school is of concern. These young people are moving from one situation in which they are being bullied to another situation in which they are being bullied. They have no respite from the bullying. This finding underlines the need for an inter-agency co-ordinated approach to dealing with bullying problems.

What was the nature of the bullying?

We asked the young people who reported that they had been bullied to specify in what ways they had been bullied. The bullying most often took the form of name-calling and teasing, with physical bullying a close second. Their possessions being damaged or taken came third. The ratings made by staff were broadly similar.

The majority of staff reported that they considered physical bullying to be the most serious aspect of the problem. Some of the young people put forward the same view. It is of interest, however, that about half the young people reported that they thought name-calling was the most serious form, particularly when it took the form of insults directed at their parents or other members of their family. The children considered that name-calling directed at members of their families was particularly upsetting. It may be significant that children in children's homes have been separated from their families.

Action taken by the young people

Nearly all the young people who reported that they were being bullied said they had told somebody (22 out of the 26 youngsters). Most often they had told a member of staff in the home, their social worker, a member of their family or a friend. This is an encouraging finding. Surveys carried out in secondary schools indicate that relatively few pupils tell a teacher that they are being bullied.

Eighteen per cent of the young people said they had filled in complaint forms about being bullied; 64% of these youngsters said they were unhappy about the way the complaint was handled. According to them, either nothing happened or nothing happened that had not already happened, or the action taken did not lead to an improvement in the situation.

About a third of the young people who had been bullied said that they had run off from the children's home on at least one occasion because of being bullied.

About half the young people said they do not get bothered or upset about bullying that goes on; 29% said they get a bit upset about bullying that goes on; 23% said they get very upset about it. Forty-two per cent reported that they do something to stop bullying if they see it happening. In most cases, they tell a member of staff. Thirty-five per cent said they do nothing because it is none of their business. Several of these youngsters expressed the view that telling a member of staff would be 'grassing on a mate'. Fourteen per cent said they do nothing but think they ought to. One of these youngsters said she was afraid the bully might turn on her. Another youngster said that he was 'afraid of looking stupid'. Given encouragement and guidance on actions they might take, it is possible that the young people in this group would actively oppose bullying.

A few youngsters (9%) said they enjoy bullying and that they join in if they come across it.

Some youngsters put forward the view that they were generally opposed to bullying but thought it acceptable if the victim 'asked for it' or 'gets under everyone's nose'. In one of the homes a 'provocative victim' was being scapegoated to an extreme degree. The youngsters in effect vied with each other as to who had carried out the most extreme act of bullying. The youngsters expressed no concern that the target of the abuse might be harmed. One of the young people commented, 'He lets it happen so it's his fault.'

There were indications that the scapegoating was meeting the needs of the peer group. It was agreed that work would be carried out with the young people to help them face up to the tensions and frustrations that were fuelling the scapegoating process.

Action taken by the staff

The findings suggest that staff were taking action to stop bullying that was taking place but that in many cases the bullying did not stop. Seventy-three per cent of the young people and 76% of the staff reported that staff do try to stop bullying if they find out it is happening but that the bullying does not stop. It is encouraging that staff were attempting to sort out bullying problems, even if the attempts were not being successful.

About half the staff stated that action they took led to some improvement in the situation. About a third stated that action they took made no difference either way. Only one member of staff expressed the view that action taken by the staff made the situation worse. It seems that action taken by staff does not necessarily help but at least there is no suggestion that it makes matters worse.

One method staff sometimes adopt is to place a young person elsewhere because of involvement in bullying. This was said to happen, on average, once or twice a year. A surprising finding is that the victim of bullying was reported to be placed elsewhere as frequently as the perpetrator. Staff reported that the bullying problem was resolved in about half the cases where a youngster was placed elsewhere, whether it was the victim or the perpetrator who was moved.

There will sometimes be valid reasons for placing the victim of bullying elsewhere. It may, for example, be the only way of ensuring the victim's safety. There are, however, strong grounds for suggesting that it should normally be the bully rather than the victim who is moved. If the victim is moved, this doubly punishes the innocent party. It is a form of secondary abuse. One young man commented, 'I was moved because I couldn't cope with the girls. It made me feel I was nothing.'

Staff relationships

The majority of staff stated that staff helped and supported each other. Several members of staff expressed the view that they would not be able to manage the job otherwise. This finding is in contrast to the finding for the young people who stated that they do not generally help and support each other.

The findings suggest that the majority of staff value the support they receive from their line manager. All the staff reported that they had discussed behaviour difficulties presented by the young people with their line manager. Nearly all the staff reported that their line manager had listened to them and had made helpful suggestions.

Staff were also asked whether members of staff bullied each other. The questionnaire specified that this question was optional and 22% of the staff took the option of not answering. Fifty-eight per cent said that there was no bullying among the staff, 14% said that it did occur and 6% said they did not know. These findings suggest that staff-to-staff bullying was taking place in some of the homes. It is in fact likely that the findings under-estimate the prevalence of this bullying. It is possible that some members of staff who opted not to answer this question did so because they knew that bullying was taking place but did not wish to acknowledge this.

There were certainly indications that the issue of bullying among staff will need to be handled with sensitivity. Several members of staff only agreed to respond to the question when reassured that their responses would be genuinely anonymous. One person suggested that staff should complete the questionnaire using the same coloured ink so that responses would be less easily traced.

Bullying between staff and young people

The findings suggest that bullying does take place between young people and staff. Staff bullying young people was reported to be relatively less common, whereas young people bullying staff was reported to be relatively more common and sometimes of an extreme nature.

Twelve per cent of the staff reported that staff sometimes bullied the young people. No member of staff reported that staff often bullied the young people. Eighteen per cent of the young people stated that staff sometimes bullied them and 4% stated that staff often bullied them. All three children who reported that staff often bullied them were resident in the same children's home. Enquiries were made and it emerged that there was a genuine difficulty in this children's home which, shortly after, was resolved. In 9 of the 14 children's homes, every youngster reported that staff never bullied them.

Bullying by staff was said by the young people to be mainly verbal or psychological, e.g. 'They make you feel stupid', 'They hurt your feelings. They say your parents don't love you'. Reference is also made to staff 'getting other children to gang up on you' and to staff 'going over the top when restraining you'.

Forty-nine per cent of the staff stated that young people sometimes bullied them. Twenty-eight per cent said that the young people often bullied them. Fifty-four per cent of the young people reported that they sometimes bullied staff and 12% reported that they often bullied staff.

Bullying by the young people was reported to include verbal and physical abuse, threatening to make allegations against staff, stealing property belonging to staff, locking a member of staff in a room, spreading false rumours about staff and sexual harassment. One youngster commented that it was mainly staff who were weak or staff who were always nagging who were bullied. Another young person reported that it is 'when the children are boozed up or drugged up that they have it in for the staff'.

Generally speaking the young people do not live in fear of the staff. To a considerable extent, however, they do live in fear of each other. Young people bullying staff is an issue that needs to be addressed.

Summary

A number of the findings are encouraging. It is pleasing, for example, that most of the young people said they would tell a member of staff if they were being bullied. It is also pleasing that staff bullying young people was reported to be relatively uncommon.

Other findings suggest cause for concern. The overall level of bullying was high and many of the young people, and indeed staff, appeared to view bullying as an unavoidable aspect of life in a children's home. About a third of the young people said they had run away from the home on at least one occasion because of being bullied. Some young people reported that they were being bullied both at home and at school. One young person was being scapegoated in one of the homes to an extreme degree.

It is concerning that many of the young people who had used the complaints procedure expressed dissatisfaction with it. Another concern, in my view, is the finding that it was as likely to be the victim as the bully who was moved to a different establishment to resolve a bullying problem. A further issue is the extent to which young people bullied staff and the extreme form this sometimes took.

Following completion of the survey, training was implemented and guidelines produced on dealing with bullying problems in children's homes. Care was taken that the guidelines were consistent with and complemented guidelines produced by the Education Department.

Changes were made to policy and practice, for example relating to the reporting of bullying incidents, the implementation of complaints procedures and young people being placed in other establishments because of involvement in bullying.

It was also determined that each children's home would be required to produce a 'declaration' on bullying that would provide a framework for intervention and prevention. The survey had suggested that bullying in many of the children's homes was part and parcel of life in the home. It was considered that this would change only if the young people and staff examined their feelings and attitudes towards bullying. It was envisaged that the process of developing the declaration would require the staff and young people to examine their feelings and attitudes to bullying. The training sessions and guidelines provided guidance on developing a declaration on bullying.

References

Sinclair, I. and Gibbs, I. (1998) *Children's Homes. A study in Diversity.* Chichester: John Wiley.

The help provided by the staff and young people in the children's homes is gratefully acknowledged.

The help provided by members of a working group set up to have oversight of the initiative is also gratefully acknowledged. The group comprised: Pete Stephenson (Lead Officer), Specialist Psychologist; Sandra Robinson, Standards Development Officer; Alison Gard, Education Department; Sue Raynor, Children's Rights Officer; Stan Taylorson, Planning and Policy Officer; Maureen Howard, Development Officer (Child Protection); Trevor Myers, Resource Team Manager; Stephen Pearson, Unit Manager; Lynn Craddock, Unit Manager; Terri Brown, Unit Manager.

23

■ ■ ■

Bullying pays! A survey of young offenders

MICHELE ELLIOTT

- ▶ Unchecked school bullying can lead to youth crime
- ▶ Young offenders tell their stories
- ▶ 92% of young offenders in this study engaged in bullying behaviour while at school

Introduction

Kidscape, the children's safety charity, carried out a survey of young offenders in March and April 1994. The results indicate that unchecked school bullying tends to promote a climate of violence and aggression which can encourage crime.

Kidscape questioned 79 young offenders in two institutions, HMYOI Onley (Rugby) and HMYOI Glen Parva (Leicester), about their experiences of school bullying. Young offenders were asked whether bullying happened often in their school, whether they were involved in bullying, whether they thought unchecked school bullying led to a decrease in respect for authority, and what they thought schools should do to tackle bullying effectively.

Of the 79 young offenders we surveyed, 100% had been involved in bullying in some way. The majority (85%) were themselves bullies or were involved as gang members or bystanders, either encouraging the bullying or joining in from the sidelines. Fifteen per cent of the young offenders started out as victims of bullying – but some of these victims went on to become bullies themselves (0.7%). Some of these victims (0.5%) committed offences to emulate the bullies.

Kidscape found that 92% of the young offenders had engaged in bullying behaviour and went on to commit offences; 0.5% committed crimes under the influence of bullies; 0.3% of the total group of young offenders were and remain victims of bullying. It would seem from the survey that there is a direct correlation between unchecked bullying behaviour and juvenile crime.

Ninety-eight per cent of the young offenders thought that unchecked bullying did make pupils less respectful of authority and 95% of those who admitted to being bullies at school said that getting away with bullying for so long had made them more likely to commit offences. Only three inmates out of the total surveyed said that bullying happened rarely in their schools. All the other inmates indicated that bullying was a frequent and inescapable fact of school life. One inmate said that the 'pecking order in schools prepared you for real life'.

All the young offenders wanted bullying stopped in schools. The majority thought that the bully's parents should be involved and that more counselling should be available for bullies. Several favoured excluding persistent bullies altogether.

All those questioned, even victims of bullying, were against reporting bullying incidents to staff or naming particular bullies. 'Grassing' was seen as a far more heinous offence than even the most violent of bullying attacks.

The survey

Seventy-nine young offenders aged from 16 to 21 responded to Kidscape's initial questionnaire. The majority of respondents had attended schools in or near Rugby and Leicester. For ease of analysis and reference, Kidscape categorised respondents according to their answers as either 'bullies', 'victims' or 'witnesses' (i.e. those who had encouraged the bullying or joined in from the sidelines).

Respondents were also asked if they would be prepared to participate in an interview relating to the questionnaire. Those who did not wish to be interviewed remained anonymous. Kidscape then interviewed 33 respondents. In these interviews inmates were asked to expand on some of their answers to the questionnaire and were encouraged to describe their involvement in school bullying.

Bullying: who is involved?

The majority of the young offenders (62%) had themselves been bullies at school; 23% were involved as bystanders or witnesses and 15% had been the victims of bullying.

When Kidscape asked those who had admitted bullying others at school why they had become bullies, the answers were similar: 'To be number one in my year'; 'It made me feel big in front of my friends'; 'I did it to show off'; 'I wanted to show the girls who was best.' These were typical responses. One inmate said that he was a 'nobody' at home but that at school he was 'top dog and it was great'.

Generally the bullies belonged to a gang. Only six inmates said they had bullied on their own and one of these was unusual in that he fought other bullies when their victims asked him for help. Two of the bullies said they had joined their gang because if they hadn't they would have become gang victims. However, the majority of bullies were either gang leaders or had joined a gang because their friends belonged. 'I wanted to be with my mates,' was a frequent reason. Gangs often had a 'hard image' and belonging conferred high group status on members. 'It was really cool to belong to this tough gang.'

Most of the victims said they felt they had been bullied because of their small size or because they were quiet. The bullies admitted that they targeted weaknesses and what they perceived as differences. One victim said he had been picked on because of rumours that he was gay.

Only eight of the bullies had begun bullying in primary school; the rest had started bullying at 12 or 13. Most of the victims had only been bullied in secondary school, although a few had been bullied for the whole of their school careers. Witnesses confirmed that, although bullying happened only occasionally in their primary schools, it was very common in their secondary schools.

What sort of bullying?

The bullying ranged from name-calling and persistent taunting through theft, kicking, punching and beating to assault with weapons. Threats were usually backed up by violence. Obtaining money or possessions such as Walkmans or getting homework done were often motives. Weapons involved in bullying incidents included a decorating tack gun modified to fire darts and wooden clubs.

Violent and aggressive bullying was the rule. The bullies were very matter of fact about using violence to get what they wanted. One bully talked about giving a victim 'a couple of whacks' and another said, 'If they didn't pay up, I'd give them a good hiding and threaten to kill them next time.' Not surprisingly, he found this worked. The bullies had no compunction about using violence. For them it was merely an effective way of getting what they wanted. In fact, one bully told us that he never thought of the intimidation practised by his gang as bullying; for him it was nothing more than 'a bit of a laugh'.

Climate of violence

As the interviews progressed it became apparent that the violent bullying which seems to have been endemic in the majority of schools the young offenders had attended reflected the violence present in their lives outside school. Many said that fighting often took place around the estates and streets where they lived and these fights often involved different gangs. Two of the bullies were very specific about their involvement in these gang fights. One said he was always surprised when he saw other pupils giving in completed homework. He said he never had time for homework as he was out all evening fighting with rival street gangs.

When Kidscape asked one inmate why he had become a bully, he answered succinctly, 'Rough school, bad area.' He did not think he'd had a choice; as far as he was concerned, bullying and violence were an integral part of life inside and outside school. A victim said that when he'd told his mother he was being bullied, she had clouted him and told him that life was tough and he'd better learn to fight back if he was going to get on. Another victim said he had seen both his brothers beaten by his father when they had said they were being bullied so he hadn't dared tell when he was also bullied. His father expected all his sons to fight their way out of trouble. Another inmate told Kidscape that he had had to rescue his younger brother from bullies on several occasions and that he despised him because he couldn't stand up for himself.

It seems that the only way to win approval in a culture like this where violence is the norm is by being more violent than others. This is a fact recognised by all those Kidscape questioned. You could only be 'number one' if you were prepared to fight and use violence. Small, quiet or studious boys were held in contempt and a tough, 'hard' image was the ultimate goal. The endemic bullying these young offenders described in their schools reflects these beliefs. One inmate said, 'Violence is what bullies understand.' In fact, everyone at these schools understood violence: it was the touchstone of their lives.

A number of inmates commented that if victims had had the requisite physical strength, they would have been bullies. 'Everybody wants to be top' and it was accepted that the only way to be 'top' was to fight your way there. At the same time, a few witnesses recognised the hollowness of the successful bully's position. 'Bullies don't have friends,' one said. Nevertheless, being part of the top gang was important to many. One inmate said that he hadn't particularly enjoyed the bullying but he had gone along with the gang as they were his 'mates'. Belonging to the gang was essential for him.

Adult responses to school bullying

Two thirds of the victims said they had never told anyone about the bullying. They gave several reasons for their silence: 'I was too scared to tell'; 'If you tell, it will come back on you'; 'I just tried to keep my head down'; 'I was afraid it would get worse if I told.' The most common reason cited by the victims and witnesses for not telling anyone about the bullying was 'I'm not a grass'. Some of the witnesses explained that the bullies were their friends and they didn't 'grass' on mates.

This survey revealed very clearly that the taboo against 'grassing', 'sneaking' or 'ratting' is very strong. Victims would rather suffer continued bullying than face the opprobrium of being branded a 'grass'. It is apparent that if schools are to take effective action against bullying, the taboo against 'grassing' has to be broken. This means that the victims and bystanders who tell about bullying have to be protected from revenge attacks by bullies. The names of those who do pluck up the courage to tell should be kept secret so that the bully never learns who has reported him. Effective anti-bullying policies encourage pupils to report all incidents of bullying and the onus is on the adults to ensure that those who tell about bullying are safe.

Only a third of the victims said that they had ever told anyone about the bullying. Only one victim said that the adult he told had stopped the bullying. In all other cases, telling did not lead to effective action against the bullies. The actions taken by school staff usually consisted of no more than a general injunction not to do it again, although some imposed detentions. None of the bullies thought that this sort of punishment was effective. One bully said that he'd quite enjoyed detentions as they gave him 'a bit of peace'.

As a final resort, some schools excluded the bully, but the exclusion was rarely permanent and, on the bully's return, the problems started up again. One bully said that he'd been excluded and sent to a special boarding school but that on returning to his old school, no one, not even the staff, believed he could have changed and he said they all 'expected' him to go back to bullying. Another bully said that once he'd started bullying, everyone labelled him as a bully and that's how he was treated. One bully who took dinner money from other pupils said that even after he stopped threatening people or intimidating them, they'd still come and give him their money. By then his reputation as a bully was enough to frighten other students. It seems that after a while bullies get trapped in their role by other people's expectations and it is hard for them to change their behaviour without considerable support.

What respondants would do about school bullying

All the bullies said that punishment didn't work and wasn't the answer to bullying. Perhaps this was only to be expected! However, 52% of witnesses thought that punishment should be used. Witnesses also favoured excluding the bully. One bully said that he hated being excluded as he 'enjoyed school'. Some suggested that bullies should be sent to special schools where they would get a taste of their own medicine and one victim thought that 'quiet' pupils should be separated into different classes from 'noisy or rough' pupils.

The bullies all said that they thought counselling would have helped. One bully said he stopped bullying when he was 15 because a teacher he respected had taken the trouble to talk to him about his problems. Most of the young offenders thought that involving the bully's parents was important. One bully told us his mum had known about the bullying but she was 'soft' and hadn't wanted to tell his father. This bully said that if his dad had known what was going on he would have given him 'a right kicking'. Inmates thought that parents could punish bullies more effectively than school staff because they could stop privileges and 'ground' bullies. All the victims said that if they had children they wouldn't want them to suffer as they had done. They said they would certainly try to stop the bullying if their children told them they were victims.

There were two cases where schools had stopped bullying by threatening the bully with police action if he persisted.

Many of the bullies said that they hadn't realised the effect of bullying on a victim until they themselves were bullied in prison. One bully said that he had known that his victims suffered but he had 'blanked it out'.

In cases where victims had tried to stand up to the bullies they were usually forced into a fight. One bully said that if people stood up to him they had to be prepared to back it up with force. He said he respected them for taking a stand. One victim eventually turned on his tormentors and knifed one of the bullies. The gang 'avenged' this by beating the victim so badly he had to be hospitalised. In another case a victim waited until he grew bigger than those who had bullied him and then began to bully them in his turn. He said he then got into trouble for fighting.

Does unchecked school bullying lead to crime?

As school staff did not take effective action to check the bullying, it flourished and bullies concluded that bullying pays. In their experience, using intimidation, violence and blackmail to get what you wanted were successful strategies. They were told at school that bullying was wrong but, as nothing was ever done to stop their behaviour, they had never had to face the consequences of their actions. As far as they were concerned, bullying paid off and they were good at it.

Given this background, the progression from school bullying to crime was apparently inevitable. As one witness said, 'If they think they can get away with it, 'course they'll go nicking things.' Bullies who were never brought to task for their behaviour in school thought that they would continue to get away with theft, intimidation and violence outside school. They had got used to their power over weaker individuals and expected such 'easy pickings' to continue. They had not learned that they were accountable for their actions and they did not expect retribution.

The inmates Kidscape questioned had usually been convicted of stealing cars (*t*aking a *v*ehicle *w*ithout *o*wner's *c*onsent or 'twocking') or burglary. It appeared that twocking was generally the first criminal act committed by most of the inmates and some then 'progressed' to burglary. Some also had convictions for GBH. One bully told about a raid on a shop he and a friend had committed. Kidscape asked if they had used weapons. 'Not really,' he replied, 'I just had a baseball bat and my mate had an iron bar.' He seem surprised that anyone could take exception to this – after all, they hadn't used knives or guns and they had been using bats and bars for years at school. Another bully had sprayed CS gas at a security guard. He said the guard 'was this great big bloke. I thought he'd laugh if I punched him'.

A couple of inmates said that they had been bullied into twocking – they were told that they would be beaten up if they did not go along with the gang. One victim said he had started to take drugs to boost his confidence and then had become a thief to pay for the habit. Some commented on the fact that the bullies had built up a 'hard image' for themselves and that, once they had all left school, they could no longer intimidate their peers so easily. Crime was one way of maintaining their 'hard image'.

Kidscape asked all the young offenders whether they knew what had happened to the bullies in their schools. In every case where the inmate knew what had happened to the bullies once they had left school they said they were now in prison for a variety of offences. A few inmates told us that some of the bullies they knew had committed offences but hadn't been caught. In one case where the inmate had been one of a gang of eight bullies, he told us that the whole gang was now in prison and his own three-and-a-half year sentence was the shortest any of them had received.

Several of those Kidscape interviewed understood that what they had done had damaged their chances of finding jobs and making successful lives for themselves. A victim who had been convicted of twocking said he had done it to be 'like them' (i.e. the bullies) but he hadn't expected to end up in prison. Some of the bullies Kidscape interviewed said that they regretted the fact that they had wasted their school days and had left without qualifications. One bully of 20, who was serving his second sentence, said he had a wife and a baby and he wished he could get a job and settle down but no one wanted him with his record. Another said, 'It was stupid what I did – fighting and twocking, all that. I don't know what will happen when I get out or what I'll do.'

Summary

The results of this survey indicate that unchecked school bullying encourages bullies to believe that bullying gets them what they want and that, no matter how aggressive their behaviour, they can get away with it.

Although this Kidscape survey was qualitative rather than quantatitive, its findings are supported by other researchers. Professor Dan Olweus in his 30-year follow-up studies in Norway found that approximately 60% of boys who were characterised as bullies in grades 6–9 (11- to 14-year-olds) had at least one conviction by the age of 24. As many as 35–40% of these former bullies had three or more convictions by this age, compared with only 10% of the control group who had not been involved in bullying in grades 6–9 (Olweus, 1993).

If we ignore bullying in schools or if we tackle it half-heartedly, we are storing up trouble for the future. Bullies must learn as soon as they begin to bully others that such behaviour will not be tolerated and that sanctions will be imposed if they persist. The sooner bullies learn that their actions have consequences, the better it will be for them, for their victims and for society.

Many of the young offenders who took part in the Kidscape survey were intelligent and articulate. They were honest about their experiences and several of them had given considerable thought to the problem of bullying. However, they were all learning in prison a lesson they should have learned at school: society will not tolerate violent and criminal behaviour and will punish those who break its laws.

References

Olweus, D. (1993) *Bullying at School: What we know and what we can do.* Blackwell.

24

■ ■ ■

Bullying: recent research into the causes, diagnosis and treatment

DR L. F. LOWENSTEIN

▶ An analysis of research carried out between 1999 and 2000
▶ The assessment and treatment of victims of bullying

Introduction

Most research on bullying during the past two years has been carried out in the United Kingdom and the United States. Other nations that have contributed are Italy, Netherlands (Dutch & Flemish), Australia, Greece, Norway, Japan, Portugal and Ireland.

The research has been put into a number of general categories, despite the fact that there is considerable overlap in many cases. Most noteworthy is that where victims later became perpetrators of bullying. Therefore some researchers concentrate principally on the victims of bullying, others on the bullies themselves and still others on both groups, especially the interaction between them. There is now considerable research concerned with the procedures for ameliorating the condition or treating it. There is comparatively less which is concerned with what causes the phenomenon of bullying in the first instance. It may well be that this is too complex and applying diagnosis and treatment is more important.

While bullying occurs in a number of settings including the workplace, prisons, the military and families, the current research concentrates on bullying among children within and outside of school. The general headings into which the bullying phenomenon has been divided are:

1 the causes of bullying behaviour;
2 the incidence of bullying behaviour;

3 the victims of bullying;
4 bullies and types of bullying;
5 the diagnosis and treatment of bullying behaviour in victims and bullies.

A summary of recent research covering 19 countries was carried out by Smith *et al.* (1999a) and was similar to the one currently being carried out by the author, which hopes to bring up to date, through the most recent research, the five main areas.

The causes of bullying behaviour

In contrast to popular stereotype and research, the tradition of the 'oafish' bully lacking in social skills and understanding is wrong. The bully is a cold, manipulative expert in social situations, organising gangs and using subtle, indirect methods. 'Ringleader' bullies scored higher on social skills than 'followers' of bullies (those who helped or supported the bully) or victims and defenders of the victim (Sutton *et al.*, 1999). A study was carried out to differentiate between victims and their bullies (Boulton, *et al.*, 1999). It was found that if you were big and more socially preferred, you were less likely to be a victim and more likely to be a bully. If you spent time alone and were less socially preferred, you were more likely to be a victim. For girls, time in being alone was positively correlated with victim score. Network or socialisation was negatively correlated with bullying scores but positively correlated with social preference score and hence the ability to socialise effectively through social skills was likely to reduce the chance of being bullied.

Age factors also appeared to play a role in bullying behaviour. A school-based survey of bullying revealed a fairly steady downward trend through ages 8 to 16 years (Smith *et al.*, 1999b). Four hypotheses were examined which tried to explain the age-related decline: (1) younger children have more children older than them in school who are in a position to bully them; (2) younger children have not yet been socialised into understanding that you should not bully others; (3) younger children have not yet acquired the social skills to deal effectively with bullying incidents and try to discourage further bullying: and (4) younger children have a different definition of what bullying is, which changes as they get older.

A British study which examined the causes of bullying was carried out by O'Connell *et al.* (1999). Peers were coded for actively joining or passively reinforcing the bully and for actively intervening on behalf of the victim. Averaged across episodes, peers spent 54% of their time reinforcing bullies by passively watching, 21% actively modelling bullies, and only 25% intervening. Older boys were more likely to actively join in with the bully than were younger boys and older girls. Younger and older girls are more likely to intervene on behalf of the victims than were older boys. The results were interpreted as confirming peers' central roles in playground bullying processes. Implications for peer-led interventions and the need for whole-school interventions were noted.

The causes of bullying behaviour were studied also by Salmivalli *et al.* (1999). They considered that self and peer-evaluated self-esteem was significantly correlated with bullying, whereas defensive egotism was not connected. Adolescents' self-esteem profiles were associated with their behaviour in bullying situations; these connections were stronger among boys than among girls. Bullying others and assisting or reinforcing the bully were typical of adolescents with so-called 'defensive self-esteem'. Defending the victims of bullying was typical of adolescents with genuine high self-esteem. Being victimised by peers was most typical of adolescents with low self-esteem and, among girls, of those in the cluster, the authors named 'humble pride'. The social behaviour of the so-called self-belittlers did not clearly distinguish them from the other groups.

The causes of bullying were also studied by Sutton and Smith (1999). They considered bullying as a whole-group process. Four main factors were identified, indicating that the adapted scale role remained a reliable way of distinguishing the victim, defender of the victim, and outsider roles both from each other and from roles involved in bullying others. Progress in the measurement of bullying as a group process and the success of intervention strategies may depend on finding clearer distinctions between the ringleader, the bullied and the children who help them or reinforce their behaviour. To counteract bullying it is necessary to mobilise peer pressure and isolate ringleaders from their social group.

Salmon *et al.* (2000) revealed that depression was closely associated with adolescents who had been bullied in 70% of cases. In contrast, bullies, and bullies who were also victims, were most likely to present conduct disorders, which frequently combined with Attention Deficit Hyperactive Disorder (ADHD). The authors concluded that regardless of whether bully, victim, bully/victim or neither the most common psychiatric disorder of the emotionally behaviourally disturbed (EBD) school pupils was that of conduct disorder. This was sometimes combined with ADHD but was also seen alongside generalised anxiety disorder and major depressive disorder. A diagnosis of bullying by Sutton and Keogh (2000) showed that 'Machiavellianism' and 'Psychoticism' were closely related to bullying behaviour. Bullies scored significantly higher than controls in Machiavellianism and significantly lower in terms of pro-victim attitudes.

It was noted there was also a relationship between bullying and racism among Asian school children in Britain (Eslea and Mukhtar, 2000). Previous research on school bullying had largely rejected the issue of racism, and where it had been studied, the methods used had been unconvincing. The result was that little was known about bullying among ethnic minority children in British schools, and showed that bullying was widespread (57% of boys and 43% of girls had been bullied during a school term) and all ethnic groups suffered equally. However, bullying was at least as likely to be by other Asian children of a different ethnic group as it was by white children, and it was likely to relate to some religious or cultural difference. Bullying between members of the same ethnic group was comparatively rare, although a number of Hindu children reported insults related to the caste system.

A study of the use of weapons, especially guns in the United States, and bullying behaviour was carried out by Cunningham *et al.* (2000). They found reasons for gun ownership being strongly associated with rates of antisocial behaviour. Youths who owned guns for sporting reasons reported rates of anti-social behaviour that were only slightly higher than those reported by youths who did not own guns. Youths who owned guns to gain respect or to frighten others reported extremely high rates of antisocial behaviour. This included a tendency towards bullying.

A study of bullying in early adolescence by Espelage *et al.* (2000) suggested that family factors were responsible for bullying. This included physical discipline and adult contact and time with family. Negative peer influences, neighbourhood safety, access to guns, as previously mentioned, and feeling unsafe at school were assessed. Parental physical discipline, time spent without adult supervision, negative peer influences and neighbourhood safety concerns were all positively associated with bullying behaviour.

An interesting analysis of personality types using animal studies was carried out by Knauft (2000). He studied primate behaviour and most especially the alpha male or the male in authority and considered behaviour such as bullying to be a development of the past 2 million years in primates. Bernstein (2000) carried out similar studies and found that human morality began when several heads of households formed a coalition to limit the despotic bullying of an alpha male. The author admits that this is unlikely to be proved empirically. Finally, Schwartz and Proctor (2000) analysed violent victimisation associated with negative social outcomes through the mediation of emotion dysregulation. Witnessed violence was linked only to aggressive behaviour. There appeared also to be an association between community violence and peer group social maladjustment, including bullying behaviour towards victims.

The incidence of bullying behaviour

There are only three recent pieces of research associated with bullying behaviour. The previous section concerned itself with one of these regarding ethnic bullying behaviour. Glover *et al.* (2000) studied 25 secondary schools and considered the impact of antisocial behaviour in pupils and the effectiveness of intervention to secure improved behaviour patterns. Evidence showed that in any year, 75% of pupils were bullied, but that severe and repeated bullying was likely to be perpetrated and suffered by about 7% of pupils. Four behaviour patterns were identified in bullies: bullies, bullies who were also victims, victims and non-participants. The link between behaviour and factors in developing self-esteem included self, school, home and community factors. Successful intervention required a change of attitude on the part of both pupils and the community, a willingness to report events and an understanding of the bullying situation.

A Norwegian study by Roland (2000) of primary and secondary schools showed that approximately 5% of the pupils were bullied persistently and about the same percentage of pupils bullied regularly. Three national programmes to counteract bullying in schools were described and discussed.

Finally, an American study by Berthhold and Hoover (2000) examined the relationship between bullying and risk behaviours among 591 students, aged 9–13 years. More than one third of respondents reportedly experienced bullying and about one fifth reported bullying others. Victims tended to worry, dislike themselves, and desired to stay home from school (for the sake of physical safety). Bullies were more likely than other students to spend time at home without adult supervision, drink alcohol, smoke or chew tobacco, cheat on tests and bring weapons to school. In addition, bullies' peers pressured them to emit high-risk behaviour such as smoking and drinking.

The victims of bullying

The state of mind of the victims of bullying has already been described. The victims of bullying are relatively small in number in proportion to the population and yet their suffering is quite considerable. What has always been an interesting phenomenon is that victims of bullying often turn to bullying themselves, reversing their initial tendency to be victims. Schuster (1999) identified defensive as well as sensitive victims. A positive correlation existed between rejection and bullying, reflecting the fact that almost all bullied students were simultaneously rejected. In contrast, not all rejected students were victimised.

A Japanese study by Rios-Ellis *et al.* (2000) showed that there were multiple suicides among Japanese students due to bullying. This has been termed by the Japanese as *ijime* and has been identified as a serious problem of epidemic proportions. A Dutch study by Vermande *et al.* (2000) showed a 'combined central victim/aggressor model' to be the predominant pattern for both physical and general aggression. According to this model a minority of children were only victims and a minority of children were only aggressors.

Sharp *et al.* (2000) studied long-term as well as short-term bullying. Long-term bullying had not been investigated specifically and its consequences and susceptibility to change were very different from short-term bullying episodes.

A British study by Mahady-Wilton *et al.* (2000) suggested that victims of bullying lacked skills in emotional regulation, a process which facilitated coping with provocative situations to lessen the stress of negative emotions. Coping styles observed in victims of bullying were grouped into two distinct clusters:

1 problem-solving strategies that were associated with the de-escalation and resolution of bullying episodes; and
2 aggressive strategies that tended to perpetuate and escalate the bullying interaction.

Parallels were found between victims' and bullies' emotional displays.

Llewellyn (2000) found that handicapped children were more likely to be victims of bullying than non-physically handicapped children. It was also felt that schools failed to deal effectively with such problems and were simply unable to meet the psychological, social and clinical needs of pupils with physical disabilities.

It is of great interest to note that the effects of peer victimisation in school were likely to affect the capacity of the child to learn. Additionally, mental health suffered due to inadequate social support (Rigby, 2000). There have been examples, as already mentioned in a Japanese study, of bullies acting as killers of their victims, as noted by Carney (2000). Carney sought to explore the potential connections between being an adolescent victim of peer abuse and suicidal feelings and behaviours by examining the perception of adolescent victims and bystanders. The School Bullying Survey was used to collect general demographic information and specific items related to being a bully, a victim and an observer of peer abuse in the past two years. It was hypothesised that chronic peer abuse was an additional risk for adolescent suicidal behaviour. The results of the study upheld this contention and added a surprising component in that bystander perceptions supported victims' views.

Bullies and types of bullying

Bullies, on the whole, tend to select children who are likely victims, such as those who have special problems in communication (Hugh-Jones and Smith, 1999) or are physically handicapped or otherwise socially inadequate. They may even be children who are of high intelligence but who stand out as being 'very different'. A combination of envy or jealousy, inadequacy of a personal nature, insensitivity and even psychopathic tendencies such as sadistic behaviour may create the bully (Lowenstein, 1978a; 1978b; 1986; 1994; 1995; 1998). The behaviour of bullies tends to be to hit or kick or call names and use a number of more subtle methods to torment their victims (Boulton et al., 1999).

Males tended to outnumber females among bullies, bully/victims (children who both bully and are victims) and victims (Kumpulainen et al., 1999). Bullying tended to decline somewhat in time, and a substantial number of individuals changed status when this occurred. Nearly half of the individuals involved in bullying had been involved four years earlier. Hence there was a habitually forming pattern to being a bully. Individuals involved in bullying were found to have significantly more psychiatric symptoms than other children and to be psychologically disturbed. Males and children from low socio-economic backgrounds were more prone to continue to be involved in bullying over a four-year period.

The result of another study by Menesini et al. (2000) showed that when bullies and victims interacted, bullies showed a dominant style in the dyad, often regulating and opposing victims' initiatives. Victims, on the other hand, complied with the bullies' requests and presented a submissive style of interaction. However, interactions involving control patterns indicated that (a) bullies opposed those partners' initiatives less frequently and (b) victims tended to affirm themselves by asking for help and explanations. The study of pupil and parent attitudes towards bullying in primary schools, in a Portuguese study by Eslea and Smith (2000), found that most subjects held largely sympathetic attitudes towards victims, were supportive of intervention, but were less understanding towards bullies. There was little association between parental and children's attitudes, nor did parental attitudes predict children's behaviour. An association was noted between children's attitudes and their behaviour. Mothers were more sympathetic than fathers but there were no sex differences among children. Children with more siblings were more likely to bully than others with fewer siblings.

A study which analysed the personal characteristics and parental styles of bullies and delinquents found that bullying and delinquency were more common among boys than girls (Baldry and Farrington, 2000). Bullying did not vary significantly with age but delinquency increased with age. Bullying and delinquency were especially related for boys and for older students. Only bullies were younger, while only delinquents were older, which suggested that bullying might be an early stage on a developmental sequence leading to delinquency. Only bullies and only delinquents had different parenting correlates; only bullies had authoritarian parents and disagreed with their parents, whereas only delinquents had conflictual and low supportive parents. This suggested that bullying and delinquency are not merely different behavioural manifestations of the same underlying construct. It was felt by these authors that parent training interventions might prevent both bullying and delinquency.

An Australian study by Owens *et al.* (2000) studied teenage girls and their aggressiveness. Among such behaviour was talking aggressively about others or excluding peers from the group. Girls who bullied described the devastating effects of indirect aggression, particular on girls with certain characteristics that predisposed them to victimisation.

Teachers' attitudes to bullying were also studied in the UK in a study carried out by Craid *et al.* (2000a) and there appeared to be no sex differences between teachers and their attitudes to bullying. There was, however, some difference in what was to be labelled as bullying. Physical types of aggression were labelled more often as bullying, were viewed more seriously and were more likely to warrant intervention that verbal aggression.

A Greek study by Andreou (2000) used the bullying behavioural scale and the peer victimisation scale to study bullying in Greek schools. The children were aged 8–12 years. Machiavellianism was noted to be present in bullies who used this type of approach with victims. The results suggested that what sets bully/victims apart from bullies or victims is their low social acceptance and their high level of Machiavellianism and negative self-esteem. This led to implications for intervention against bullying.

A British study which observed behaviour in 185 school children in the playground and in their classroom was carried out by Craig *et al.* (2000b). Direct bullying was more prevalent in the playground while indirect bullying was more prevalent in the classroom. Non-aggressive children were more likely to bully in the playground, whereas aggressive children were more likely to bully in the classroom. In counteracting bullying, it was felt vital to consider not only the bullies and the victims but the peer group generally and the teachers. Mynard and Joseph (2000) considered types of bullying and identified four main factors:

- physical victimisation;
- verbal victimisation;
- social manipulation;
- attacks on property belonging to the victim.

Diagnosis and treatment of bullying behaviour in victims and bullies

A number of therapeutic approaches have been recommended, including an Australian study which emphasised the importance of the group setting with adolescents, to encourage them to recognise that bullying is wrong. The objective was to get bullies to work together in co-operation with others and to provide evidence of the negative behaviour of bullying. It recommended that the therapist adopt a flexible, focused approach to allow the group to determine the course of the therapy (Banks, 1999). Another approach combines school, individual approaches and parents to reduce victimisation in school (Noonan et al., 1999). The silent reinforcer such as the non-involved, non-participating individual is required to be involved and provide peer group pressure against the bully as recommended by Salmivalli (1999).

Peer support is also recommended by many other investigators, including Naylor and Cowie (1999) in a British study of 51 schools. The results suggested that, although the presence of a peer support system did not result in a decline in reported bullying, the peer support system was perceived to be effective in reducing negative effects for victims. Respondents perceived many benefits to users, supporters and the school, including helping to create a school climate of caring. Perceived problems included non-acceptance of those who bullied and the need to raise peer support to the status of a whole-school issue. Similar views were expressed by Peterson and Rigby (1999), who felt the counteracting of bullying must involve the peer group and the whole school as well as the staff of that school. After such a programme was initiated there was significant reduction in reported levels of victimisation. The anti-bullying activities throughout the school, it was felt, must be undertaken by students themselves.

An Italian study by Bacchini et al. (1999) indicated that verbal bullying was frequent, occurred several times a week and increased in frequency during the school year. The unfortunate noted view was that bullies tended to be popular but often were poor students. The emphasis in this study was to develop the social environment and direct teaching about relationships. The emphasis had to be on the intervention to protect the bullied and to reduce the acceptance of bullies (Berdondini and Fonzi, 1999).

Facts which influenced teachers' identification of peer bullies and victims were investigated by Leff *et al.* (1999). Factors that teachers took into consideration included the gender of the student, their socio-economic status and their ethnicity. A more important factor was likely to be adolescents with relationship difficulties, such as those studied by Smorti and Ciucci (1999) in an Italian study.

Stevens *et al.* (2000b) carried out an evaluation of an anti-bullying intervention in Flemish primary and secondary schools. They favoured a school-based anti-bullying approach. Three approaches were studied: treatment with support, treatment without support, and the last group involved students from schools that did not implement the anti-bullying programme and served as a control condition. Findings regarding the effects of the school-based anti-bullying intervention programme on the extent of bullying and victimisation showed a mixed pattern of positive changes in primary schools and zero outcomes in secondary schools. The findings regarding the effects of external support revealed limited outcomes. The outcomes of the evaluation study confirmed that a school-based anti-bullying intervention strategy was effective in reducing problems with bullying, especially within primary schools.

In the UK there has been an emphasis on using the talents or training of the educational psychologist to implement an anti-bullying policy in schools (Roffey, 2000). Tyson and Pedersen (2000) favour school counsellors to create a better atmosphere and the avoidance of bullying in schools. Of great importance in the first instance is to identify the victims of bullying – a combination of self-report and peer report have been used to identify such youngsters (Pellegrini and Bartini, 2000).

In an Italian study, Smorti and Ciucci (2000) encouraged the development of simultaneous strategies towards bullies and their victims. They used the diagnostic approach of stories to be completed by the students to identify bullies and victims of bullying. The bullies were more similar to the control group than the victims.

The effect of a support system on peer supporters, the whole school and teachers was discussed in an interview with 11–14-year-olds on the experience of being a peer supporter, and further analysis of the data collected in a survey on peer support from a range of perspectives. Overall, it was concluded that peer support had benefits for victims of bullying and for the school climate. The peer supports also benefited from the experience. Boys were noted to be significantly under-represented as peer supports, with a substantial number of male victims failing to report the bullying to anyone (Cowie, 2000).

A Dutch study by Limper (2000) stressed the importance of co-operation between parents, teachers and school boards to prevent bullying in the educational system. Some schools have been made aware of bullying as a real problem and the problems discussed regularly in schools and in the media.

An Irish study by O'Moore (2000) emphasised the importance of training teachers to identify victimisation through bullying – the need for training of teachers was crystallised in Ireland recently by the tragic death of a young student who had been bullied for five years at school. The results showed that children and adolescents who bullied shared with victims lower levels of self-esteem than peers who had never bullied or been bullied.

A Greek study by Kalliotis (2000) used the Life in School Questionnaire to study bullying, as well as using interviews with teachers in order to assess the degree and type of bullying. This was used as the first step towards curbing such behaviour. Bullying has long been recognised to have long-term negative consequences. Although physical bullying can be addressed, there are other types of indirect bullying which also need to be considered, as studied by Soutter and McKenzie (2000) in an Australian study. Again the peer group had been emphasised for support in serious problems of bullying among boys (Cowie and Olafsson, 2000).

An anti-bullying curriculum based on intervention programmes using peers and their attitudes towards bullying being changed were stressed as vital in a British study by Stevens *et al.* (2000a).

As far as the victims of bullying are concerned, there is a great need for social skills training, especially to help female students with emotional difficulties. One such therapy grouped used six sessions concerned with speaking and listening, friendships and how to make friends (Tierney and Dowd, 2000). This led to support for the girls who were the targets of bullying.

In the UK at least, many schools are now using a variety of anti-bullying treatment methods, especially to counteract the bully's view that victims deserve such handling. When there is a culture of silence, bullying will persist, and in one study, 30% of victims had told no one of the bullying (Smith and Shu, 2000). This is perhaps one of the reasons why disclosure training, assertiveness training and coercion management training have been used in one study in the United States to focus on enhancing self-esteem and promotion of peer support to counteract bullying and protect victims (MacIntyre *et al.*, 2000).

Summary of research results

Causes and associated aspects of children who become victims of bullying:

1 Inability to socialise.
2 Being ineffective, leading to rejection by others.
3 Inability to deal with provocative situations.
4 Being younger and smaller in size.
5 Low in self-esteem, i.e. dislike themselves.
6 Appearing to be different from others.
7 Suffering from depression.
8 Coming from lower socio-economic backgrounds.
9 Tending to adopt a submissive role.

Types of bullying:

1 Physical attacks through aggression.
2 Verbal attacks.
3 Social manipulation against victims.
4 Attacks on victims' property.
5 Various kinds of indirect bullying.

Characteristics of bullies and associated features:

1 Tend to be larger in size and dominant.
2 Often suffer from Attention Deficit Hyperactive Disorder(ADHD).
3 Often suffer from conduct disorders.
4 Tend to adopt a Machiavellian approach.
5 Often suffer from psychoticism tendencies.
6 Have themselves witnessed violence in the home.
7 Have noted community violence.
8 Tend to be more aggressive.
9 More likely to abuse substances (cigarettes, alcohol).
10 More likely to bring weapons to school.
11 Some practise insensitive behaviour, bordering on psychopathic demeanour.
12 Mostly males rather than females.
13 Suffer from psychological problems.
14 Come from large families, with a large number of siblings.
15 Tend to have authoritarian parents.
16 Suffer from negative self-esteem.
17 May well be popular with peer group.

Dealing with or treating the problem of bullying behaviour:

1 Identifying the victims of bullying and the bullies themselves.
2 Training teachers to identify victims of bullying as well as bullies.
3 Changing attitudes to victims of bullying and to bullies.
4 Developing problem-solving skills for victims of bullying.
5 Promoting social skills training for victims of bullies as well as bullies.
6 Training teachers to deal effectively with victims of bullying as well as the bullies.
7 Try to encourage the peer group not to adopt a neutralist stance against bullies and be mere observers but involve them in helping the victims of bullies and reducing the likelihood of the bully carrying out his actions.
8 Victims of bullying must be trained to become more assertive.
9 Group therapy involving the victims of bullying separately and also the bullies and the whole group or class.
10 Involving parents of victims as well as parents of bullies.
11 Getting peer support for victims.
12 Involving the whole school in a policy of dealing with bullies and protecting the victims of bullies.
13 Reacting firmly against bullies.
14 Individual therapy for victims of bullying as well as for the bully.
15 Promoting co-operation between parents and schools.
16 Dealing with the extremes of victimisation, including the possibility of suicide in victims of bullying.
17 In the extreme, if nothing else works, expel bullies from the school and send to special schools for treatment or to therapeutic communities.

Assessment and treatment of the victims of bullying in an outpatient clinic

It must be understood that in many instances the victims of bullying have been traumatised to various degrees by their unfortunate experiences. Many become what can only be termed 'social and emotional impaired', either temporarily or permanently. The educational progress or achievement that they might have achieved has often been affected. Many suffer from post-traumatic stress for years to come. Some unfortunately decide to reverse the victim state by bullying themselves.

This leads them into conflict at school and/or at home, with teachers and parents, as well as siblings, suffering from their behaviour. For any treatment to be effective, psychological treatment must involve the bullied client, the parents and the site where the bullying has taken place, i.e. the school normally, but also within the neighbourhood around the school. This is usually the only way of combating this condition. Hence, it is vital to involve also the school staff, these being essentially in *loco parentis* and hence responsible not merely for the education of children but for their care or welfare while they are in the school vicinity or in school.

It is only in recent times that this has been taken seriously by schools and local education authorities. Those which have failed in this respect increasingly have become the target for legal action by parents whose children have suffered from the prolonged torment of being victims of bullying. Many schools have been required to adopt a policy to counteract bullying and to implement that policy. It is unfortunate that numerous schools have failed to curb bullying or have merely paid lip-service to the need to do something about the problem or to pre-empt it in the first place.

The present investigator was at one time a Chief Educational Psychologist for a large authority and is currently employed as an Independent Forensic Educational Psychologist and Clinical Psychologist, investigating and treating the victims of bullying in schools. The present research shows how victims of bullying can be diagnosed and treated effectively.

Sketch of case history (female)

Mary (not her real name) came to me as a result of having suffered many years of bullying at the secondary school she attended. When she was in junior school there were no problems and she was a happy child, but at secondary school bullying began and got worse and worse.

Mary was an introverted child of 11 years when she arrived and due to her lack of social skills found herself being bullied by a group of girls as well as some boys. Even in the classroom things were thrown at her, and she was insulted and sometimes attacked physically in the street. Due to the fact that she was pretty, there was considerable jealousy from the girls and the fact that she refused to participate in some of the quasi sexual activities with the boys meant she was termed 'chicken'. She came from a home where high morals were expected and she intended to live up to these.

As a result of what she suffered, her education also became a difficult matter for her and she began to fail significantly, falling below her capacity for achievement.

Sketch of case history (male)

This illustration concerned a boy who eventually attempted suicide on two occasions, due to the bullying he suffered at school. He was physically hit and his clothes were stolen and his books thrown about. He eventually refused to go to school and the parents kept him at home. Again, he was an introverted boy, not very capable of mixing adeptly with the peer group. Unlike the previous example, a girl of considerably below-average intelligence, John was in fact above average in intelligence and before the bullying was an inquisitive and adventurous boy. However, after his experiences he decided to give up on his education at an early age, leaving secondary school early instead of following a promising career as a possible accountant.

His parents contemplated legal action to seek justice for what their son had suffered and the lack of protection he had received from the staff at the school.

Diagnosis of bullied children

The diagnosis of bullied children as practised by the present investigator consisted of an in-depth interview followed by cognitive and personality testing. The object was to ascertain the intellectual ability of the child and the symptoms resulting from the bullying through objective and projective personality testing. There then followed a period of intensive treatment which involved the psychologist, the parents and the child. Involvement of the schools was not possible as they had been rejected by the children in question who no longer attended the school where the bullying took place.

In most cases the children studied were more introverted than extroverted or ambivert personalities, i.e. neither introverted nor extroverted. They all suffered from the inability to mix with aggressive children effectively or to practise aggression themselves which would have saved them probably from being bullied in the first instance.

All the children suffered from a combination of anxiety and depression due to their experiences and additionally suffered from suicidal ideation. They tended to be very uncertain about their actions and their feelings were easily hurt through their suffering in the past and their natural personalities. They were nervous individuals on the whole, often extremely self-conscious, and had a tendency to worry about embarrassing experiences. They also tended to feel rather lonely.

Diagnosis and treatment of the victims of bullying

Diagnosis

The treatment of victims of bullying follows an intensive diagnosis of the individual. This involves:

1 an in-depth interview to obtain information that pre-dates the state of the person and concerns how he/she was prior to the bullying occurring. Much of this can be obtained from parents of the child himself/herself;

2 obtaining essential information as to an indication of the child's intelligence as measured by the Wechsler Intelligence Test for Children – Form R (UK) Version, UK Edition – the educational attainments as measured by reading, spelling and mathematics ages and the personality assessment using the Eysenck Personality Scales and the Thematic Apperception Test;

3 identifying the specific distressing symptoms from which the individual has suffered as a result of his experiences of bullying;

4 planning on the basis of this information a treatment strategy focusing on those areas principally requiring modification in order to reduce psychological stress.

The two cases mentioned earlier will now be illustrated presenting the results of but two diagnostic measures: the Wechsler Intelligence Test for Children and one for adults, followed by the results of the Eysenck Personality Scales. This test has norms for ages and sex of children and also adults. It can therefore readily provide information as to whether the individual is high or low on certain traits, as may be noted in the test result that follows, wherein both illustrations show a high neuroticism score.

The Eysenck Personality Scales, and most especially the neuroticism scale, tend to be appropriate for identifying pathological traits for the purpose of intervention. Bullied children appear to have high neuroticism scores or scores above the mean. Such traits as being easily upset, anxiety, worry, depression and feelings of guilt were noted in the two cases mentioned. Of particular concern was suicidal ideation, one of the areas measured in the test. Tables 24.1 to 24.6 that follow show the figures obtained in the psychological assessment of Mary and John.

Ten children were studied, some above and others below the age of 16. They were also treated using a combination of cognitive behaviour therapy. All the children had been victims of serious bullying for 4–5 years. None was currently attending the school where the bullying occurred.

The children studied could be placed into the eight categories shown in Table 24.7, with some overlap between them as to their particular problems. These categories represented the traits that distinguished bullied from non-bullied children. For purposes of comparison, ten children seen by the psychologist with non-bullying experiences were compared with ten children who had been bullied.

Table 24.1 Psychological assessment of Mary, aged 15 years

IQ measured	IQ index	%ile	95% confidence interval
Verbal	121	92	114–126
Performance	99	47	91–107
Full-scale	112	79	106–117
Verbal comprehension (VC)	127	96	119–132
Perceptual organization (PO)	98	45	90–106
Freedom from distractability (FD)	101	53	92–110
Processing speed (PS)	101	53	92–111

Table 24.2 Mary's subtests

Subtests	Scale scores	Mental age
Picture completion	11	15.1
Information	10	14.1
Coding	11	15.1
Similarities	16	16.1
Picture arrangement	6	9.6
Arithmetic	10	14.6
Block design	10	14.1
Vocabulary	15	16.1
Object assembly	12	16.1
Comprehension	16	16.1
Symbol search	9	13.1
Digit span	10	14.6

Table 24.3 Mary's traits

Trait	Score	Mean	Standard deviation
Psychoticism	4	7.06	4.11
Extro/introversion	3	15.47	4.99
Neuroticism	19	14.03	4.85
Lie score	11	5.45	3.25
Addictiveness	15	12.61	4.18
Criminality	16	9.01	4.54
Impulsiveness	0	9.73	4.64
Venturesomeness	0	9.55	3.38
Empathy	12	14.53	2.87

Table 24.4 Psychological assessment of John, aged 16

The Wechsler Adult Intelligence Test (WAIS) was administered and the results were as follows:

Full-scale IQ	108 (average)	75%ile
Verbal IQ	100 (average)	50%ile
Performance IQ	119 (high average)	91%ile

Table 24.5 John's subtests

Subtests – verbal

Information	5 (considerably below average)
Digit span	9 (average)
Vocabulary	8 (average)
Arithmetic	11 (average)
Comprehension	9 (average)
Similarities	9 (average)

Subtests – non-verbal

Picture completion	14 (considerably above average)
Picture arrangement	11 (average)
Block design	13 (somewhat above average)
Object assembly	12 (somewhat above average)
Digit symbol	8 (somewhat below average)

Table 24.6 John's traits

Trait	Score	Mean	Standard deviation
Psychoticism	3	9.57	5.26
Extro/introversion	4	15.97	5.64
Neuroticism	17	11.12	5.68
Lie score	8	5.37	4.18
Addictiveness	17	11.6	4.96
Criminality	14	9.01	4.54
Impulsiveness	1	9.84	4.13
Venturesomeness	3	11.51	3.34
Empathy	18	12.47	3.28

Table 24.7 Traits and categories measured in both groups

	Found in bullied group	Found in non-bullied group
1 Socially inadequate (unpopular)	10	1
2 Tendency towards introversion	6	2
3 Homes that had very high moral standards	4	1
4 Socially adequate (popular)	0	8
5 Tendency towards extroversion	0	6
6 Physically or mentally handicapped	3	1
7 Very bright children	1	4
8 High neuroticism scores	9	2

It may be noted that the children recorded in Table 24.7 more often than not fall into more than one category or trait. The table shows that bullied children tend, 'on the whole', to be more introverted, have a higher neuroticism score, are socially less adequate, come from homes with high moral standards, and are different in their capacity to learn effectively in school. They also differ as a result of physical and mental handicap.

Perhaps the most noteworthy difference between bullied and non-bullied children was being socially inadequate and unable or unwilling to interact positively and affectively with the peer group. Many were depressed, worried, anxious, felt guilty and had almost no expectations from adults, such as being protected. They frequently felt rejected.

It is almost certain that the individual is predisposed to such symptoms before bullying takes place. The bullying experience often merely exacerbates the tendencies of traits. It is unfortunate that one rarely has a pre-bullying, psychological assessment. This would give one the opportunity of comparing many of the neuroticism traits and ascertaining how much can be attributed to the bullying and how much was already present before this unfortunate experience began.

Treatment strategies and their results

The treatment commenced after the child had left the school where the bullying had taken place. The bullying had reached excessive proportions and the first priority was to safeguard the life of the child in question. The child or children had suffered considerably and now carried the scars of post-traumatic stress. They had suffered from one, but usually from many, of the following symptoms and attitudes as a victim of bullying. These were obtained not merely from the interview with the child but from the Eysenck Personality Questionnaire and Projective Testing. In order they were:

1 suicidal ideation;
2 general depression;

3 general worry about the future, health, etc.;
4 feeling easily hurt or upset;
5 loneliness;
6 over-sensitivity to many social interactions;
7 low frustration tolerance;
8 low self-esteem;
9 poor educational prospects and/or achievement.

Since the school where the bullying occurred was no longer in the picture, therapeutic intervention concentrated on the child and the parents. In some cases, it was possible to work with the school where the bullying took place to develop a truly active and effective anti-bullying policy. This, however, was not likely to be the case in a number of schools where bullying was rampant and where little was done to counteract it or to be effective in counteracting it. The victim's suffering incurred the impact of post-traumatic stress. In other words, the victim continued to suffer from the effects of cruel, intensive, long-term bullying.

Each session of treatment was based on a week or more of record keeping in the form of a detailed diary concerning relevant symptoms (see 1–9 above) and seeking to reduce these symptoms and the impact they had on the child's life. Relaxation therapy and breathing exercises were used together with other forms of treatment to encourage the child to relax and view himself in a more positive light. Each week the child was asked to rate on a 0–10 scale the severity of each symptom experienced each day. Although many symptoms were common among all bullied children, there were some that were relevant to a particular child. During the sessions, children were encouraged to emote or express their feelings openly, while at the same time being guided on their ability to control the impact of what they had experienced.

They were also encouraged and guided in how to develop 'assertiveness' (not aggressiveness) and to improve their social skills. Efforts were made to increase their self-esteem through praise of what they had achieved through the treatment received. Much as in the case of children who have been sexually abused, who blame themselves for what took place, physically and verbally abused children often blame themselves for the suffering and humiliation they have endured. In other words, the child asks himself/herself: 'What's wrong with me? Why should this happen to me? Why was this all done to me?'

At other times the child should lay blame, where at least in part the blame is due, i.e. the children who tormented him/her and the adults and other youngsters who stood by unwilling or unable to help in any way to prevent such behaviour by the bullies. The child has been, and still is, in a conflict situation. There is pressure on the child from parents and society to attend school, but there is the pain of being in an environment in which he/she dreads being, and even when they're not there, knowing what actually occurs.

Some children accept their victimisation in time as part of life. They and those who are meant to care for them have given in to the bullying, thereby perpetuating it. Other children crack up under the pressure, refusing to attend school or claiming to be too 'ill' to attend. If pressurised, such tragedies as self-harm and even suicide can be the outcome. It is this that the psychologist must treat.

It is for this reason, that for some years, the author ran a day centre where such children were able to receive an appropriate, individualised education and be protected in this environment from any further bullying.

There are a number of ways to redeem such children, but there is a need for a sensitive, positive and highly caring and protective approach in the first place, in order to both relax the child and gradually improve confidence. It is also necessary to improve their self-esteem and self-worth. The results of such treatment approaches are shown in Table 24.8.

Table 24.8 Results of treatment

Changes in behaviour	Treatment sessions required			
	1–6	7–12	13–18	19+
1 Very much improved and able to attend normal school	1	1	1	
2 Improved but needing a time of recuperative schooling		3	1	
3 Still receiving therapy			1	2

Summary

1 Experiences of long-term and intensive bullying were shown to lead to severe psychological problems, including a variety of post-traumatic stress disorders.

2 The chief symptoms and associated traits were depression, low frustration tolerance and fear of children, anxiety, a desire to avoid school, low self-esteem, poor social skills, loneliness and poor educational attitudes and achievement.

3 In the case where school failed effectively to implement the protection of victims of bullying and deal with the bullies, victims needed to be removed from such centres.

4 An intensive, sensitive and extensive treatment programme needs to be developed combining cognitive and behaviour therapy.

5 Some victims of bullying should be placed in a highly protective educational environment where both individualised teaching and therapeutic input exists.

6 Most of the children improved as a result of having received this type of therapeutic intervention but many suffered for some considerable time in recollecting their experiences of bullying. Often this affected them into adulthood.

References

Andreou, E. (2000) 'Bully/victim problems and their association with psychological constructs in 8–12 year old Greek school children', *Aggressive Behaviour*, Vol 26(1), pp 49–56.

Bacchini, D., Amodeo, A., Vitelli, R., Abbruzzese, R. and Ciardi, A. (1999) 'Evaluation of bullying by teachers', *Ricerche di Psicologia*, Vol 23(1), pp 75–103.

Baldry, A.C. and Farrington, D.P. (2000) 'Bullies and delinquents: Personal characteristics and parental styles', *Journal of Community and Applied Social Psychology*, Jan–Feb, Vol 10(1), pp 17–31.

Banks, Virginia (1999) 'A solution focused approach to adolescent groupwork', *Australian & New Zealand Journal of Family Therapy*, Jun, Vol 20(2), pp 78–82.

Berdondini, L. and Fonzi, A. (1999) 'Observational methods to evaluate an anti-bullying intervention', *Eta-evolutiva*, Oct, No 64, pp 14–23.

Berthhold, K.A. and Hoover, J.H. (2000) 'Correlates of bullying and victimisation among intermediate students in the Midwestern USA', *School Psychology International*, Feb, Vol 21(1) pp 65–78.

Bernstein, I.S. (1999) 'Logic and human morality: An attractive if untestable scenario', *Journal of Consciousness Studies*, Jan–Feb, Vol 7(1–2), pp 105–07.

Boulton, M. J. (1998) 'Concurrent and longitudinal relations between children's playground behaviour and social preference, victimisation and bullying', *Child Development*, Jul–Aug, Vol 70(4), pp 944–54.

Boulton, M. J., Trueman, M. Chau, C. Whitehand, C. and Amatya, K. (1999) 'Concurrent and longitudinal links between friendship and peer victimisation: Implications for befriending interventions', *Journal of Adolescence*, Aug, Vol 22(4), pp 462–66.

Carney, J.V. (2000) 'Bullied to death: Perceptions of peer abuse and suicidal behaviour during adolescence', *School Psychology International*, May, Vol 21(2), pp 213–23.

Cowie, H. (2000) 'Bystanding or standing by: Gender issues in coping with bullying in English schools', *Aggressive Behaviour*, Vol 26(1), pp 85–97.

Cowie, H. and Olafsson, R. (2000) 'The role of peer support in helping the victims of bullying in a school with high levels of aggression', *School Psychology International*, Feb, Vol 21(1), pp 79–95.

Craig, W. M., Henderson, K. and Murphy, J. G. (2000a) 'Prospective teachers' attitudes towards bullying and victimisation', *School Psychology International*, Feb, Vol 21(1), pp 5–21.

Craig, W. M., Pepler, D. and Atlas, R. (2000b) 'Observations of bullying in the playground and in the classroom', *School Psychology International*, Feb, Vol 21(1), pp 22–36.

Cunningham, P. B., Henggeler, S. W., Limber, S. P., Melton, G. B. and Nation, M. A. (2000) 'Pattern and correlates of gun ownership among non-metropolitan and rural middle school students', *Journal of Clinical Child Psychology*, Sep, Vol 29(3), pp 432–42.

Eslea, M. and Mukhtar, K. (2000) 'Bullying and racism among Asian school children in Britain', *Educational Research*, Summer, Vol 42(2), pp 207–17.

Eslea, M. and Smith, P. K. (2000) 'Pupil and parent attitudes towards bullying in primary schools', *European Journal of Psychology of Education*, Jun, Vol 15(2), pp 207–19.

Espelage, D. L., Bosworth, K. and Simon, T. R. (2000) 'Examining the social context of bullying behaviours in early adolescence', *Journal of Counselling and Development*, Summer, Vol 78(3), pp 326–33.

Glover, D., Gough, G., Johnson, M. and Cartwright, N. (2000) 'Bullying in 25 secondary schools: Incidence, impact and intervention', *Educational Research*, Summer, Vol 42(2), pp 141–56.

Hugh-Jones, S. and Smith, P. K. (1999) 'Self reports of short and long term effects of bullying on children who stammer', *British Journal of Educational Psychology*, Jun, Vol 69(2), pp 141–58.

Kalliotis, P. (2000) 'Bullying as a special case of aggression: Procedures for cross-cultural assessment', *School Psychology International*, Feb, Vol 21(1), pp 47–64.

Knauft, B. M. (2000) 'Symbols, sex and sociality in the evolution of human morality', *Journal of Consciousness Studies*, Jan–Feb, Vol 7(1–2), pp 130–39.

Kumpulainen, K., Raesaenen, E. and Henttonen, I. (1999) 'Children involved in bullying: Psychological disturbance and the persistence of the involvement', *Child Abuse and Neglect*, Dec, Vol 23(12), pp 1255–62.

Leff, S. S., Kupersmidt, J. B., Patterson, C. J. and Power, T. J, (1999) 'Factors influencing teacher identification of peer bullies and victims', *School Psychology Review*, Vol 28(3), pp 505–17.

Limper, R. (2000) 'Cooperation between parents, teachers, and school boards to prevent bullying in education: An overview of work done in the Netherlands', *Aggressive Behaviour*, Vol 26(1) pp 125–34.

Llewellyn, A. (2000) 'Perceptions of mainstreaming: A systems approach', *Developmental Medicine and Child Neurology*, Feb, Vol 42(2), pp 106–15.

Lowenstein, L. F. (1978a) 'Who is the bully?', *Bulletin of the British Psychological Society*, No 31, pp 147–49.

Lowenstein, L. F. (1978b) 'The bullied and the non-bullied child', *Bulletin of the British Psychological Society*, No 31, pp 306–18.

Lowenstein, L. F. (1986) 'The study, diagnosis and treatment of socially aggressive behaviour (bullying) of two boys in a therapeutic community', lecture given at the International School Psychology Ass. Conference held in Nyborg, Denmark, August.

Lowenstein, L. F. (1994) 'The intensive treatment of bullies and victims of bullying in a therapeutic community and school', *Education Today*, Vol 44, No 4. December, pp pp 62–68.

Lowenstein, L. F. (1995) 'Bullying – an intensive and multi-dimensional treatment approach in a therapeutic community', *Education Today*, Vol 45, No 1, March, pp 19–24.

Lowenstein, L. F. (1998) 'What makes for the bullies and the victims of bullying', *Counselling and Education Newsletter*, Feb, p 4.

MacIntyre, D., Carr, A., Lawlor, M. and Flattery, M. (2000) 'Development of the Stay Safe programme', *Child Abuse Review*, May–Jun, Vol 9(3), pp 200–16.

Mahady-Wilton, M. M., Craig, W. M. and Pepler, D. J. (2000) 'Emotional regulation and display in classroom victims of bullying: Characteristic expressions of affect, coping styles and relevant contextual factors', *Social Development*, Vol 9(2), pp 226–45.

Menesini, E., Melan, E. and Pignatti, B. (2000) 'Interactional styles of bullies and victims observed in a competitive and a cooperative setting', *Journal of Genetic Psychology*, Sep, Vol 161(3), pp 261–81.

Mynard, H. and Joesph, S. (2000) 'Development of the multi-dimensional peer victimisation scale', *Aggressive Behaviour*, Vol 26(2), pp 169–78.

Naylor, P. and Cowie, H. (1999) 'The effectiveness of peer support systems in challenging school bullying: The perspectives and experiences of teachers and pupils', *Journal of Adolescence*, Aug, Vol 22(4), pp 467–79.

Noonan, B., Tunney, K., Fogal, B. and Sarich, C. (1999) 'Developing student codes of conduct: A case for parent–principal partnership', *School Psychology International*, Aug, Vol 20(3), pp 289–99.

O'Connell, P., Pepler, D. and Craig, W. (1999) 'Peer involvement in bullying: Insights and challenges for intervention', *Journal of Adolescence*, Aug, Vol 22(4), pp 437–52.

O'Moore, M. (2000) 'Critical issues for teacher training to counter bullying and victimisation in Ireland', *Aggressive Behaviour*, Vol 26(1), pp 99–111.

Owens, L., Shute, R. and Slee, P. (2000) '"Guess what I just heard!": Indirect aggression among teenage girls in Australia', *Aggressive Behaviour*, Vol 26(1), pp 67–83.

Pellegrini, A. D. and Bartini, M. (2000) 'An empirical comparison of methods of sampling aggression and victimisation in school settings', *Journal of Educational Psychology*, Jun, Vol 92(2), pp 360–66.

Peterson, L. and Rigby, K. (1999) 'Countering bullying at an Australian secondary school with students as helpers', *Journal of Adolescence*, Aug, Vol 22(4), pp 481–92.

Rigby, K. (2000) 'Effects of peer victimisation in schools and perceived social support on adolescent well-being', *Journal of Adolescence*, Feb, Vol 23(1), pp 57–68.

Rios-Ellis, B., Bellamy, L. and Shoji, J. (2000) 'An examination of specific types of Ijime within Japanese schools', *School Psychology International*, Aug, Vol 21(3), pp 227–41.

Roffey, S. (2000) 'Addressing bullying in schools: Organisational factors from policy to practice', *Educational and Child Psychology*, Vol 17(1), pp 6–19.

Roland E. (2000) 'Bullying in school: Three national innovations in Norwegian schools in 15 years', *Aggressive behaviour*, Vol 26(1), pp 135–43.

Salmivalli, C. (1999) 'Participant role approach to school bullying: Implications for intervention', *Journal of Adolescence*, Aug, Vol 22(4), pp 453–59.

Salmivalli, C., Kaukiainen, A., Kaistaniemi, L. and Lagerspetz, K. M. J. (1999) 'Self-evaluated self-esteem, peer-evaluated self-esteem, and defensive egotism as predictors of adolescents' participation in bullying situations', *Personality and Social Psychology Bulletin*, Oct, Vol 25(10), pp 1268–78.

Salmon, G., James, A., Cassidy, E. and Javaloyes, M. (2000) 'Bullying, a review: Presentations to an adolescent psychiatric service and within a school for emotionally and behaviourally disturbed children', *Clinical Child Psychology and Psychiatry*, Oct, Vol 5(4), pp 563–79.

Schuster, B. (1999) 'Outsiders at school: The prevalence of bullying and its relation with social status', *Group Processes and Intergroup Relations*, Apr. Vol 2(2), pp 175–90.

Schwartz, D. and Proctor, L. J. (2000) 'Community violence exposure and children's social adjustment in the school peer group: The mediating roles of emotion regulation and social cognition', *Journal of Consulting & Clinical Psychology*, Aug, Vol 68(4), pp 670–83.

Sharp, S., Thompson, D. and Arora, T. (2000) 'How long before it hurts? An investigation into long-term bullying', *School Psychology International*, Feb, Vol 21(1), pp 37–46.

Smith, P. K. and Shu, S. (2000) 'What good schools can do about bullying: Findings from a survey in English schools after a decade of research and action', *Childhood: A Global Journal of Child Research*, May, Vol 7(2), pp 193–212.

Smith, P. K., Morita, Y., Jung, R. T., Olweus, D., Catalano, R. F. and Slee, P. (eds) (1999a) *The nature of school bullying: A cross national perspective*. Florence, KY, USA: Taylor and Francis/Routledge.

Smith, P. K., Madsen, K. C. and Moody, J. C. (1999b) 'What causes the age decline in reports of being bullied at school? Towards a developmental analysis of risks of being bullied', *Educational Research*, Winter, Vol 41(3), pp 267–85.

Smorti, A. and Ciucci, E. (1999) 'Narrative strategies in adolescents with relational difficulties', *Eta-evolutiva*, Oct, No 64, pp 90–100.

Smorti, A. and Ciucci, E. (2000) 'Narrative strategies in bullies and victims in Italian schools', *Aggressive Behaviour*, Vol 26(1), pp 33–48.

Soutter, A. and McKenzie, A. (2000) 'The use and effects of anti-bullying and anti-harassment policies in Australian schools', *School Psychology International*, Feb, Vol 21(1), pp 96–105.

Stevens, V., Van-Oost, P. and de-Bourdeaudhuij, I. (2000a) 'The effects of an anti-bullying intervention programme on peers' attitudes and behaviour', *Journal of Adolescence*, Feb, Vol 23(1), pp 21–34.

Stevens, V., De-Bourdeaudhuij, I. and Van-Oost, P. (2000b) 'Bullying in Flemish schools: An evaluation of anti-bullying intervention in primary and secondary schools', *British Journal of Educational Psychology*, Jun, Vol 70(2), pp 195–210.

Sutton, J., Smith, P. K. and Swettenham, J. (1999) 'Social cognition and bullying: Social inadequacy or skilled manipulation? ', *British Journal of Developmental Psychology*, Sep, Vol 17(3), pp 435–50.

Sutton, J. and Smith, P. K. (1999) 'Bullying as a group process: An adaptation of the participant role approach', *Aggressive Behaviour*, Vol 25(2), pp 97–111.

Sutton, J. and Keogh, E. (2000) 'Social competition in school: Relationships with bullying, Machiavellianism and personality', *British Journal of Educational Psychology*, Sep, Vol 70(3), pp 443–56.

Tierney, T. and Dowd, R. (2000) 'The use of social skills groups to support girls with emotional difficulties in secondary schools', *Support for Learning*, May, Vol 15(2), pp 82–85.

Tyson, L. E. and Pedersen, P. B. (eds) (2000) *Critical Incidents in School Counselling* (2nd edition), Alexandria, VA, USA: American Counselling Ass.

Vermande, M., van-den-Oord, E. J., Goudena, P. P. and Rispens, J. (2000) 'Structural characteristics of aggress-victim relationships in Dutch school classes of 4–5 year olds', *Aggressive Behaviour*, Vol 26(1), pp 11–31.

25

■ ■ ■

A whole-school approach to bullying

MICHELE ELLIOTT

- ▶ Finding out the extent of bullying from students
- ▶ Setting up an effective whole-school anti-bullying policy
- ▶ Suggestions for dealing with gangs of bullies
- ▶ Example questionnaire and contract
- ▶ 'What if' questions for students

Bullying makes life more difficult for teachers. Dealing with the aftermath of a bullying case means seeing the bully, the victim, perhaps the parents and then having to be on the alert for the revenge that will surely follow. In a day fraught with demands on the teacher's time, bullying is just one of a thousand things. No wonder it goes on. But life would be so much easier for everyone in the school if there were less bullying. With a little bit of effort, it is possible to substantially reduce bullying. In fact, by spending just a few hours dealing with the problem at the start of the school year, school staff could save hundreds of hours of aggravation later.

The most effective way to deal with bullying is to have a whole-school programme and policy (Besag, 1995; Elliott and Kilpatrick 2002; Olweus 1993). The law requires schools to have an anti-bullying policy, but it is the whole-school approach, including the policy, which makes the difference. The initiative for this can come from staff, parents or the children themselves. Once it is in place, it is difficult for bullying to go on as the combined force of the school and community will ensure that it simply is not tolerated – in any way, shape or form.

In setting up a whole-school policy, it is a good idea to find out the extent of the problem in the school. The following steps have been taken by many schools and are presented here as a possible model.

Steps

1 Survey

Ask students to fill out an anonymous questionnaire about bullying. Either make up your own or use the one at the end of this chapter (see Model 25.1 on pages 310–11). This will give you an indication of what is happening. Although some schools ask for the names of those who bully, this could affect the children's veracity and invites abuse. ('If I find out anyone's put down my name, I'll thump 'em'). What you are trying to find out in the survey is whether the students find bullying a problem. If the classroom teachers compile their own survey, it will not take long to put all the results together. Otherwise, ask a trusted parent-volunteer to compile the survey.

2 Staff meeting

Meet with staff to share results and discuss the implications of the survey. Decide on how to share the information with the students. A whole-school assembly takes less time, but a discussion brings out more information.

3 Class rules

Ask each class to put together five or ten 'rules' they would like everyone to live by in the school. You may wish to extend these beyond bullying. To protect those students who are shy or may be victimised, you could have the rules written and passed in. Ask a student to compile them.

4 School rules

With the students (perhaps the student council) put together a list of rules using the class rules as a guideline. Limit the number so that you don't end up with a manifesto which is impossible to live with. One group of teenagers compiled a list which would have done the Spanish Inquisition proud.

5 Staff approval

If you had a teacher meeting with the students in the previous step, then this stage may be eased through. Either ask the teachers who were involved to present the list to the staff or invite in the students or a combination of both. The problem, of course, with a combined meeting is time and sometimes the resistance of staff. However, a combined meeting helps to establish a more solid student/teacher response to bullying.

6 Student agreement

Either refer the school rules back to the students for a vote if there are dramatic changes to the original proposal or skip this stage if there are few changes. Make the ballot secret if you have a real problem with bullying. If not, a school assembly with a show of hands speeds up the process.

7 School contract

From the rules that are agreed, draw up a common contract which will be signed by each student. The contract works best if it is also signed by the parents so that no one can later say, 'I didn't know anything about the rules!' The contract should be run off on coloured paper, funds permitting, and kept in each student's file. Of course, you will need parental and governor support for this. (See Model 25.2 on page 312.)

8 School govenors

Depending upon your school, this stage may be the first. Most governors, however, will be able to make a more informed decision with the survey results and the proposed rules. Otherwise, you may spend time debating whether you have a problem and then having to have another meeting.

9 Parents

By now some of the parents will have heard something about bullying. You may want to send a letter home at an early stage to say you are looking into the problem. This could lead to 1,000 telephone calls from parents anxious to tell you about their child's problem or parents of bullies ringing to ask if you are starting a vendetta. If you want to send a preliminary letter home, there is an example (see Model 25.3 on page 313) at the end of this chapter.

Another approach would be a meeting of parents, perhaps as part of the normally called meeting. Have the students present the rules and ask for questions and concerns.

One school simply sent home a letter saying that the rules had been agreed and asked concerned parents to get in touch. They had only six calls in a school of 180 children, so this would seem to be the most time-efficient method, depending upon the verbosity of your parents. Parents are usually only too pleased that the school is taking this initiative and most parents sign the contract and agree the rules with no problem.

10 Local authority

Since the rules will be part of your policy, the local education authority should be informed. If you are part of an enlightened local authority, they may use your efforts as a model for other schools. Alternatively, the LEA may have suggestions from other schools or from its policy department that may be useful.

Reducing bullying

Once aware of the extent of bullying, and once the contracts have been signed by parents and students, there are, of course, many things teachers can do to reduce bullying on the playground and in the school building itself (see Chapters 2 and 16).

How do you continue to implement the policy once it has been agreed? The main strategies to employ follow.

School assemblies

During school assemblies, remind the students that yours is a 'telling' school and that everyone has the responsibility to tell if they see bullying happening. If the students are still worried about reporting, you can install a box so that they can put in notes anonymously. This rather defeats the purpose of open communication, but may be necessary in your school setting.

Rules

The agreed school contract should be posted on bulletin boards throughout the school.

Supervision

Although it may surprise some, teachers cannot be in all places at all times. Bullying tends to happen when there is no supervision or when the supervisors are untrained, but willing, volunteers. To decrease the possibility of bullying, invite these supervisors to the meetings on bullying, ensure that they know the rules and that they have a clear idea of what to do and who to tell if something happens. If you are unfortunate enough to occupy one of those buildings designed to enhance bullying, rotate student monitors, get in parent-volunteers, vary movement of classes by a few minutes if possible (see Chapter 2) and lobby your local authority for more funds for supervision. Structure the playground time with games or activities (see Chapter 16). Ask all the staff to keep a friendly eye on things as they pass by groups of students and places of known difficulty.

Posters

Have a poster contest and award prizes to those who best capture the ways to deal with bullies. Get a local business to give prizes and invite the local media to cover the story.

Curriculum

Sometimes children do what a bully tells them because they are frightened or just don't know what to do. We can help children with strategies by introducing programmes in school which deal with bullying. The Kidscape programmes for under fives, 5 to 11s and teenagers all have lessons on bullying based upon stories, role-plays and discussion (see the Resources section on page 320). On pages 313–15 are examples of 'What If?' questions for discussion (Model 25.4). For teenagers, try giving them a scenario and asking them to make up their own role-plays. The Teenscape programme has specific suggestions for teenagers.

Any work that it is possible to squeeze into the curriculum on self-esteem and assertiveness also helps. As Valerie Besag mentions in Chapter 16, the staff/pupil relationship is important in helping children to develop self-esteem, which helps prevent them from becoming both bullies and victims.

Transition

Ragging and initiation rites of passage have institutionalised bullying in many schools in the past. Hopefully, these practices have been stamped out, but children do still fear the transition period from primary to secondary. In a survey of 200 primary children (Elliott, 1996), 64% were worried that they might be bullied or picked on when they got to secondary school. Most good teachers are aware of children's concerns about this transition period. Children are invited to spend a morning in their new school and questions and worries are addressed.

Perhaps we can go one step further, as some schools have done, and assign the new students an older student to show them around and ease the way. Since much bullying comes from slightly older children, this might also help to change the attitude of the older children to one of protection instead of harassment.

Bystanders

If it is part of the school policy that there are no bystanders, it will be the responsibility of everyone to stop bullying (Elliott, 1994).

Intervention

The prevailing attitude, 'Let the kids sort it out themselves', plays right into the hands of the bully. It allows him or her unfettered power and this will be used to inflict misery. When bullying is identified, immediate intervention is crucial. This gives a clear message that bullying of any kind will not be tolerated and that action will be taken. After the initial action, it is important to consider help for the bully and victim (Chapters 6 and 7). If it is a serious bullying situation, the parents should be informed and the bully may face suspension (Chapter 4).

Consequences

As part of the school policy, there should be consequences or punishments meted out to those who break the rules. If these are clearly spelled out, perhaps as a letter home such as Linda Frost includes in Chapter 4, it lessens the hassle when teachers have to enforce the rules. These consequences can be posted, along with the rules, or explained to children in class or in assembly.

If there are no consequences to their actions, bullies will learn that bad behaviour is rewarded. One of the first consequences should be that the bully apologises and in some way makes up for his or her behaviour.

No blame

The no blame approach was originated in Sweden by Anatol Pikas and was called 'common concern'. The idea of this approach is to get the bullies and victims to work together to try to figure out a mutually agreeable way to deal with the bullying. It is based upon the assumption that the bullies actually want the bullying to stop. The adult who intervenes does not blame anyone for the problem. This approach may sometimes work in less serious cases of bullying when the bully and victim may have previously been friends but have fallen out. Kidscape surveys indicate that this method does not work if the bullies are picking on children they don't know or care about and if the patterns of bullying are so well established that the bullying itself has become a reward for the bullies. In addition, the children and young people who have been bullied find it unfair that the bully escapes blame.

Bully courts

In some schools, as part of the consequences for breaking rules, children are liable to come before a court of their peers. These courts can only work in schools which have established a caring atmosphere and in which the school contract is firmly in place (Chapter 15).

Bully gangs

The only effective way to break up bully gangs is to meet with them separately and break down the group identity and ethos which encourage bullying. The following suggestions for dealing with gangs come from various teachers and staff who have successfully dealt with the problem (Elliott, 2001).

1 Meet with victim or victims separately – have them write down what happened.
2 Meet with each member of the gang separately – have them write down what happened.
3 Agree with each member of the gang separately what you expect and discuss how she/he has broken the contract about guidelines for behaviour.
4 Meet with the gang as a group and have each state what happened in your individual meeting; ensure that everyone is clear about what everyone else said. This eliminates the later comment, 'I really fooled him', since everyone has admitted his/her part in front of the group.
5 Prepare them to face their peer group – 'What are you going to say when you leave here?'
6 Decide whether to involve the bully court – this will depend upon what you have agreed with the students.
7 Whatever is decided, reiterate to all students that they are all responsible if anyone is being bullied – there are no innocent bystanders.
8 Talk to parents of all involved – show them written statements.
9 Keep a file on bullying with all statements and penalties.
10 Teach victim strategies (as in Kidscape lessons).
11 Do not accept false excuses (see Chapter 3).
   - If the bullying was an accident, did the children act by helping the victim or getting help or giving sympathy?
   - If it was just for a laugh, was everyone laughing?
   - If it was a game, was everyone enjoying it?
12 If a child is injured, take photographs of the injury.
13 If gangs of bullies from outside your school appear, take photographs – they tend to run when they see the camera.
14 If there is serious injury, contact the police.

Summary

By setting up a whole-school approach to eliminating bullying, you are sending signals to the children that you do care about their welfare. This approach assumes good pupil–staff relations and creates an atmosphere which continues to foster those relationships. Involving parents and the community will help to change attitudes which encourage bullying.

The ultimate goal of all schools is to make bullying unthinkable.

MODEL 25.1 Kidscape bullying questionnaire

1 Do you consider that you have ever been bullied?

Yes ☐   No ☐

2 At what age?

under five ☐

5–11 ☐

11–14 ☐

over 14 ☐

3 When was the last time you were bullied?

today ☐

within the last month ☐

within the last six months ☐

a year or more ago ☐

4 Were you bullied:

once ☐

several times ☐

almost every day ☐

several times a day ☐

5 Where were you bullied?

at home ☐

going to or from school ☐

in the playground ☐

at lunch ☐

in the toilets ☐

in the classroom ☐

other ☐

6 Did/do you consider the bullying to have been:

no problem ☐

worrying ☐

frightening ☐

so bad that you didn't want to go out or to school ☐

7 Did the bullying:

have no effects ☐

some bad effects ☐

terrible effects ☐

make you change your life in some way (e.g.
change schools or move out of a neighbourhood) ☐

8 What do you think of bullies?

no feeling ☐

feel sorry for them ☐

hate them ☐

like them ☐

9 Who is responsible when bullying continues to go on?

the bully ☐

the bully's parents ☐

the teachers ☐

the head ☐

the victim ☐

children who are not being bullied,
but do not help the victim ☐

others ☐

10 Please tick if you are a:

girl ☐   boy ☐

11 Was the bully (bullies) a:

girl ☐   boy ☐

12 If you have ever been bullied, was the bullying:

physical ☐   emotional ☐   verbal ☐   (you may tick more than one)

13 What should be done about the problem of bullying?

_____

14 Have you ever bullied anyone?

Yes ☐   No ☐

(Elliott, 2002, *Teenscape*)

311

MODEL 25.2 Contract

1 We will not tolerate bullying or harassing of any kind.

2 We will be tolerant of others regardless of race, religion, culture or disabilities.

3 We will not pass by if we see anyone being bullied – we will either try to stop it or go for help.

4 We will not allow bullying or harassing going to or from school, either on the school bus or public transport or walking.

5 We will allow a quiet area in the playground for those who do not want to run around or be in games.

6 We will use our 'time out' room if we feel angry or under pressure or just need time to calm down or work out what is wrong.

7 We will not litter or draw on school property (walls, toilets, books, etc.).

8 We will be kind to others, even if they are not our friends, and will make new students feel welcome.

9 On school journeys we will act in a way which brings credit to our school.

10 We will have a discussion group once a week in class to talk about any problems that are bothering us.

11 We will be honest when asked about anything that we have done or are supposed to have done.

12 We will co-operate with and abide by the findings of the school court.

MODEL 25.3 Letter to parents

Dear

There has been much national media attention recently about the problem of bullying. As far as we are aware our school does not have a particular problem with bullying, but we would like to ensure that this is the case. We know that children learn better when they are happy and not worried.

Having talked with the children, we have decided that an anonymous survey about bullying might be helpful. We will be giving the children the enclosed questionnaire (Model 25.1) and thought that you would like to see a copy. We will obviously keep you informed of the results and value your support.

We are giving the children the survey on ...

If you have any questions, there will be a brief meeting for parents on ...

If you could keep any questions until this meeting, we would greatly appreciate it as we are so busy at the moment with the start of the school year.

Thank you for your support.

Yours sincerely,

MODEL 25.4 What ifs?

The suggested answers are for discussion only – the students may have ideas which will work just as well or better.

1   You are walking to school and a gang of older bullies demands your money. Do you

   a) fight them
   b) shout and run away
   c) give them the money?

   a) *Give them the money – your safety is more important than the money.*

2 You are on the school playground and someone accidentally trips you. Do you

   a) hit the person hard
   b) give him or her a chance to apologise
   c) sit down and cry?

   b) Give the person a chance. If it was an accident, then he or she should say 'sorry'.

3 You are in the school toilet and an older student comes in, punches you, then tells you not to do anything or 'you'll get worse'. You know who the person is and you have never done anything to him/her. Do you

   a) wait until the person leaves and then tell a teacher
   b) get in a fight with him/her
   c) accept what happened and don't tell?

   a) You didn't deserve to be punched and the bully was wrong to do it. If you don't tell, the bully will just keep on beating up other kids.

4 You are walking into the lunch room and someone yells out a negative comment directed at you. Do you

   a) ignore it
   b) yell back
   c) tell?

   a) You can either ignore it (if it is the first time and that's all that happens) or c) tell if it really bothers you. People should not yell out negative comments directed at you.

5 You are continually harassed by bullies calling you names, making rude comments about your mother and generally making you miserable. Do you

   a) tell them to bug off
   b) get a group together and make comments back
   c) if possible, get a witness and then tell
   d) it isn't really bullying so just live with it?

   c) Name-calling which makes you miserable is bullying and should not go on. Tell even if you don't have a witness.

6 You see someone you hardly know being picked on by a bully. Do you

   a) walk by and be thankful it isn't you
   b) immediately rush to the defence of the victim and push the bully away
   c) get help from other kids
   d) tell someone on the staff?

   c) *If possible solve the problem with other kids, but be careful not to fight the bully. Then tell what happened.*

7   You are walking in your neighbourhood on a Saturday morning. A kid you know from school comes by you, pushes you and grabs your money before running off. Do you

   a) tell your parents
   b) tell your teacher
   c) tell the police
   d) chase after him?

   c) *The person has committed a crime. You will also need to tell your parents. Be wary of chasing him – you could be hurt and possessions are not worth your safety. As for the school, this has nothing to do with it as it happened away from the school grounds. You may wish your teacher to know, but it is not his/her responsibility to do anything about it.*

8   Your sister (brother) bullies you all the time. Do you

   a) thump her
   b) sneak up behind her and dump a bucket of water over her head
   c) ask your parents for a family meeting to discuss ways to stop the bullying?

   c) *This is the sensible thing to do, even though you may wish to do a) and b). The problem is that acting like that might make the situation worse.*

9   Your teacher continually bullies you. Do you

   a) tell your parents
   b) talk to the teacher
   c) tell the head teacher
   d) put up with it?

   a) *It is best to start with your parents, though it will be necessary to tell the head teacher. Talk with the teacher if you think he/she doesn't realise it is bothering you, but whatever you do don't put up with it.*

10 Your father (mother) bullies you. Do you

   a) tell your teacher
   b) tell a favourite aunt (gran, uncle, etc.)
   c) do nothing as telling might make it worse?

   b) *If you have a relative to confide in, start there. Perhaps your other parent could help. Doing nothing is one way out, but it won't stop the bullying.*

References

Besag, V. (1995) *Bullies and Victims in Schools*. Open University Press.
Elliott, M. (2001) 'Stop Bullying', booklet, Kidscape.
Elliott, M. (1994) *Keeping Safe, A Practical Guide to Talking with Children*. Hodder Headline.
Elliott, M. (2002) *Teenscape*. Health Education Authority.
Elliott, M. (1996) 'Primary School Survey'. unpublished, Kidscape.
Elliott, M. and Kilpatrick, J. (2002) *How to Stop Bullying: A Kidscape Training Guide*.
Olweus, D. (1993) *Bullying at School: What we know and what we can do*. Blackwell.

Help organisations
■ ■ ■

Books

Mail order booksellers with up-to-date catalogues on bullying and disruptive behaviour:

Abbey Books
45 Bank View Road
Derby
DE22 1EL
Tel: 01332 290021

Advice and information

Kidscape
2 Grosvenor Gardens
London
SW1W 0DH
Tel: 0207 730 3300

Advice and information about prevention of bullying. The Kidscape website has free anti-bullying materials and information about training on www.kidscape.org.uk or send a large SAE for copies of the same materials.

The Anti-bullying Network
University of Edinburgh
InfoLine 0131 651 6100
Website includes a 'Bully Box' where messages can be posted: www.antibullying.net

ChildLine
Tel: 0800 1111
24-hour freephone helpline for children and young people.
Information about bullying and how to deal with it is available on ChildLine's website: www.childline.org.uk

Commission for Racial Equality
Tel: 0207 828 7022
Information and advice regarding racial bullying.

Samaritans
Tel: 08457 909090
24-hour helpline for anyone with problems.

Youth Access
1A Taylor's Yard
67 Alderbrook Road
London
SW12 8AD
Tel: 0208 772 9900
Gives information about local counsellors for young people.

Legal advice

Advisory Centre For Education (ACE)
1B Aberdeen Studios
22 Highbury Grove
London
N5 2EA
Helpline: 0808 800 5793, 2–5pm, Mon–Fri.
Exclusion Information Helpline: 0207 704 9822, 2–5pm, Mon–Fri.
Gives free advice for parents and publications for parents and professionals about education law.

Children's Legal Centre
Advice Line: 01206 873820 10am–12:30pm and 2–5pm, Mon–Fri.
Provides free legal advice regarding children and the law.

Education Law Association (ELAS)
37 Grimstone Avenue
Folkestone
CT20 2QD
Tel: 01303 211570
Gives names and addresses of solicitors throughout the country who deal with education law.

Scottish Child Law Centre
Tel: 0131 667 6333
Helpline for children under 18: 0800 328 8970
Provides free legal advice about children and Scottish law.

Advice on home education

Education Otherwise
Answerphone with a list of local contact numbers.
Tel: 0870 730 0074

Home Education Advisory Service
Send large SAE for comprehensive information pack to
PO Box 98
Welwyn Garden City
Herts
AL8 6AN

Advice on playground design

Learning Through Landscapes
Third Floor, Southside Offices
The Law Courts
Winchester
Hants
SO23 9DL
Tel: 01962 846258
Information, books and videos on improving playgrounds.

Advice on school phobia

No Panic
Helpline: 01952 590545 10am–4pm, Mon–Fri
Information and advice for all types of phobia.

Resources

■ ■ ■

Programmes for schools and training

Kidscape Under Fives Programme
52-page manual includes lessons for 3 to 5-year-olds and children with special needs about bullying, stranger danger and keeping safe.

Child Protection Programme
278-page manual and videos with lessons and follow-up activities about bullying, touching, stranger danger and other personal safety issues for 5 to 11-year-olds and children with special needs.

Teenscape
168-page guide for teaching teenagers about issues such as bullying, crime, abuse, saying no, gambling addiction and other safety topics.

How to Stop Bullying: A Kidscape Training Guide
262-page manual with over 90 practical anti-bullying exercises to use with students. It also has sections to use to train professionals about the issues involved in bullying, as well as a sample whole-school anti-bullying policy.

Bully-Free: Activities to Promote Confidence & Friendship
A manual for working with young people in various settings including youth clubs, PSHE courses and sixth form colleges.

The above materials are available from Kidscape (see address and telephone number on page 317).

Free information

See www.kidscape.org.uk for copies of:
Stop Bully!
20-page booklet including What If? questions and general information about bullying.

You Can Beat Bullying! A Guide for Young People
20-page booklet with information for teenagers about how to cope with bullying.

Preventing Bullying! A Parent's Guide
24-page booklet for parents includes advice about helping victims and bullies, as well as how to work with the school or make a complaint, if necessary.

Preventing Racist Bullying: What Schools Can Do
A4 leaflet with advice and suggestions for dealing with racist bullying.

Or send for free copies with a large SAE to Kidscape (address on page 317).

Materials for professionals

Aggression Replacement Training: A Comprehensive Intervention for Aggressive Youth
Author: Arnold Goldstein
Publisher: Research Press

Assertion Training: How to be who you really are
Author: S. Rees and R. Graham
Publisher: Routledge

Bully-Free: Activities to Promote Confidence & Friendship
Author: Michele Elliott
Publisher: Kidscape

Bullies and Victims in Schools
Author: Valerie Besag
Publisher: Open University Press

Bully No More! An Inter-Agency, Whole School, Non-Punitive Approach to Bullying (video/booklet package)
Author: Kevin Brown
Publisher: St Andrew's College of Education

Bully No More! Creating The New Climate
Author: Kevin Brown
Publisher: First and Best in Education

Bully Off! Towards a Whole New Ball Game of Relationships in Schools
Author: Kevin Brown
Publisher: First and Best in Education

Bullying: An Annotated Bibliography of Literature and Resources
Author: Alison Skinner
Publisher: Youth Work Press

Bullying: A Community Approach
Author: Brendan Byrne
Publisher: The Columbia Press

Bullying: A Practical Guide to Coping for Schools
Author: Edited by Michele Elliott
Publisher: Financial Times Prentice Hall (also available from Kidscape)

Bullying at School
Author: Dan Olweus
Publisher: Blackwell

Bullying: Don't Suffer in Silence
Publisher: Department for Education and Skills

Bullying – What *Can* Parents Do?
Author: Kevin Brown
Publisher: Monarch

Full Esteem Ahead: 100 Ways to Teach Values and Build Self-Esteem for All Ages
Author: Diane Loomans with Julia Loomans
Publisher: H J Kramer Inc

How to Stop Bullying: A Kidscape Training Guide
Author: Michele Elliott and Jane Kilpatrick
Publisher: Kidscape

Low Level Aggression: First steps on the ladder to violence
Author: Arnold Goldstein
Publisher: Research Press

Some Approaches to Bullying
Author: Des Mason
Available from Governors Support Unit, South Glamorgan Council

Tackling Truancy in Schools: A Practical Manual for Primary and Secondary Schools
Author: K. Reid
Publisher: Routledge

Teenscape
Author: Michele Elliott
Publisher: Department of Health (also available from Kidscape)

To Bully No More! – The Pupil Pack. Classroom Material to Overcome the Bullying Cycle (2-video/booklet/resource material package)
Author: Kevin Brown
Publisher: St Andrew's College of Education

Turn Your School Round
Author: Jenny Mosley
Publisher: LDA

We Don't Have Bullies Here
Author: Valerie Besag
Publisher: Calouste Gulbenkian Foundation

Reducing bullying in the playground

Can I Stay in Today Miss?
Author: Carol Ross and Amanda Ryan
Publisher: Trentham Books

Children's Games in Street & Playground
Author: Iona and Peter Opie
Publisher: Oxford University Press

The Outdoor Classroom
Author: Edited by Brian Keaney and Bill Lucas
Publisher: Scholastic

Using School Grounds as an Educational Resource
Author: Kirsty Young
Available from Learning Through Landscapes (details on page 319)

Theatre companies

Resources on issues of grief, bullying, self-esteem, sex education, multilingual theatre and using drama in the PSHE curriculum available from:

Neti-Neti Theatre Company
Quintin Kynaston School
Marlborough Hill
London NW8 0NL
Tel: minicom 020 7483 4239

Other theatre companies which have produced work on bullying include:

Foxtrot Theatre Company
326 Blackness Road
Dundee DD2 1SD
Scotland
Tel: 01382 666276
www.foxtrot.dircon.co.uk/HTML/Home.htm

Theatre Centre
Units 7 & 8 Toynbee Workshops
3 Gunthorpe Street
London E1 2RQ
Tel: 0207377 0349
www.theatre-centre.co.uk

TIE Tours
PO Box 25331,
London NW5 4ZG
Tel: 0207 619 9155
www.tietours.com/bullying.html

Videos

Bullies (The Wexford Series)
22 minutes 10–17-year-olds
A passive 15-year-old becomes more assertive with help from the gym teacher.
Educational Media Films & Video, Harrow, Middx. Tel: 0208 868 1908/1915

Bullies and How to Help Them
32 minutes 9–12-year-olds
Learning to be nice and help one another, with simple techniques to deal with bullying.
Educational Media Films & Video, Tel: 0208 868 1908/1915

McGruff's Bully Alert
15 minutes 5–10-year-olds
McGruff (the dog) helps two children who are bullied to figure out ways to stop the bullying. Children are real – McGruff is animated.
Educational Media Films & Video, Tel: 0208 868 1908/1915

My Life as a Bully
30 minutes 10–18-year-olds
Grange Hill-style drama set in a comprehensive school. Handbook included.
Educational Media Films & Video, Tel: 0208 868 1908/1915

Kicks and Insults
11 years and up
Monique sets up a bully council and sets out to help victims. Bullies and victims talk about their experiences and make suggestions about solutions.
Produced by Educational Media Film & Video, Tel: 0208 868 1908/1915

Only Playing Miss
56 minutes (playscript also available) 11 and up
Multicultural, multilingual video with Sign and a fully integrated cast of differently able actors. It deals with grief, bullying and challenges racist and ablist attitudes.
Produced by Neti-Neti Theatre Company, London, Tel: 0207 483 4239

Peer Pressure
22 minutes 10–17-year-olds
Learning to say no to 'friends' who pressure you to do things you don't want to do.
Educational Media Films & Video, Tel: 0208 868 1908/1915

Sticks and Stones
20 minutes 11–16-year-olds
Drama about bullies and victims, includes bully court set up by students.
Produced by Central Television in association with Kidscape.
Available from Kidscape, Tel: 0207 730 3300

Books for younger children

AGES

All About Bullying: Wise Guides
Author: Leslie Ely
Publisher: Hodder   7–9

The Anti Colouring Book
Author: Susan Striker/Edward Kimmel
Publisher: Hippo   4+

The Bad Tempered Ladybird
Author: Eric Carle
Publisher: Picture Puffin   3+

Bill's New Frock
Author: Anne Fine
Publisher: Mammoth   7–9

Billy the Conkerer
Author: Wendy Smith
Publisher: Puffin   6–8

The Bullies Meet the Willow St Kids
Author: Michele Elliott
Publisher: MacMillan (available from Kidscape)   7–11

Bully
Author: David Hughes
Publisher: Walker Books　　　　　　　　　　　　3–6

Cuckoos
Author: Roger Green
Publisher: Oxford University Press Childrens　　9+

Feeling Happy Feeling Safe
Author: Michele Elliott
Publisher: Hodder (available from KIDSCAPE)　2–6

Good and Bad: Bully
Author: Janine Amos
Publisher: Cherry Tree Books　　　　　　　　7–10

I Feel Bullied
Author: John Green
Publisher: Hodder Wayland　　　　　　　　4–8

I Won't Go There Again
Author: Susan Hill
Publisher: Walker　　　　　　　　　　　　3+

Picking on Percy
Author: Cathy MacPhail
Publisher: Barrington Stoke　　　　　　　　8–12

Ruby and the Noisy Hippo
Author: Helen Stephens
Publisher: Kingfisher　　　　　　　　　　2+

Run, Zan, Run
Author: Cathy McPhail
Publisher: Bloomsbury　　　　　　　　　　8–11
The Twits
Author: Roald Dahl
Publisher: Puffin　　　　　　　　　　　　6+

The Trouble With the Tucker Twins
Author: Rose Impey and Maureen Galvani
Publisher: Picture Puffins　　　　　　　　4–6

Who's a Big Bully, Then?
Author: Michael Morpurgo
Publisher: Barrington Stoke　　　　　　　6–10

Zartog's Remote
Authors: Herbie Brennan and Neal Layton
Publisher: Bloomsbury   7–11

Books for older children and teens

AGES

The Bailey Game
Author: Celia Rees
Publisher: Piper   12–teen

Bullies
Author: Ed Wick
Publisher: Kingsway   12–teen

Bully
Author: Yvonne Coppard
Publisher: Red Fox   10–teen

The Bullybusters Joke Book
Author: John Byrne
Publisher: Red Fox   9–teen

Bullying: Wise Guides
Author: Michele Elliott
Publisher: Hodder   10–teen

Chicken
Author: Alan Gibbons
Publisher: Orion Childrens Books   9–12

The Chocolate War
Author: Robert Cormier
Publisher: Lions, Tracks   9–13

Don't Pick on Me
Author: Rosemary Stones
Publisher: Piccadilly   11–teen

The Fish Fly Low
Author: Steve May
Publisher: Mammoth   10–teen

The Frighteners
Author: Pete Johnson
Publisher: Yearling Books   11–14

Lord of the Flies
Author: William Golding
Publisher: Faber and Faber   11–teen

The Present Takers
Author: A. Chambers
Publisher: Mammoth   12–teen

Tiger Without Teeth
Author: Bernard Ashley
Publisher: Orchard Books   12–teen

The Trial of Anna Cotman
Author: V. Alcock
Publisher: Mammoth/Octopus   10–teen

Whose Side Are You On?
Author: Alan Gibbons
Publisher: Orion Childrens Books   9–12

Index

■ ■ ■